Creative and Innovative Auditing

Bringing creativity and innovation into all professions and types of auditing today, this book meets the needs of auditing practices in the future. Recent criticisms of auditing practices by financial regulators, the traditional 'expectation gaps' between auditors and auditees and the continuing advances in technology make it even more important today to motivate creativity and innovation in the professions of auditors, be they internal, external, quality, environmental, social, clinical and so on.

In *Creative and Innovative Auditing*, Jeffrey Ridley studies all auditing practices, not just internal auditing, using an innovation model he has developed through research which is applicable to all auditing organisations and professions. He shows how motivating innovation in auditing practices will address the needs of today and tomorrow's auditing of governance, risk management and control.

Jeffrey Ridley was appointed a visiting professor of auditing at the London South Bank University, UK, in 1991, a visiting professor of corporate governance assurance at the University of Lincoln, UK, in 2013 and a visiting professor of corporate governance at the Birmingham City University, UK, in 2017. He is a Fellow of the Institute of Chartered Secretaries and Administrators and a Fellow of the Chartered Institute of Internal Auditors. His auditing experience spans both the public and private sectors. Before his academic career he was a senior auditor in General Motors Limited for three years and manager of internal auditing in Kodak Limited, England, for twenty-eight years. Prior to his industrial experiences he was a member of HM Government's Overseas Audit Service in Nigeria for ten years. During the past twenty-three years he has taught at undergraduate, postgraduate and now doctorate levels in London and has spoken at many conferences, nationally and internationally.

Creative and Innovative Auditing

Jeffrey Ridley

Routledge
Taylor & Francis Group

LONDON AND NEW YORK

First published 2018
by Routledge

2 Park Square, Milton Park, Abingdon, Oxfordshire OX14 4RN
52 Vanderbilt Avenue, New York, NY 10017

Routledge is an imprint of the Taylor & Francis Group, an informa business

First issued in paperback 2019

British Library Cataloguing-in-Publication Data
A catalogue record for this book is available from the British Library

Library of Congress Cataloging-in-Publication Data
Names: Ridley, Jeffrey, author.
Title: Creative and innovative auditing / Jeffrey Ridley.
Description: Abingdon, Oxon ; New York, NY : Routledge, 2018. |
    Includes bibliographical references and index.
Identifiers: LCCN 2017032209 | ISBN 9781472474629 (hardback) |
    ISBN 9781315574646 (ebook)
Subjects: LCSH: Auditing, Internal. | Auditing.
Classification: LCC HF5668.25. R5269 2018 | DDC 657/.458—dc23
LC record available at https://lccn.loc.gov/2017032209

ISBN: 978-1-4724-7462-9 (hbk)
ISBN: 978-0-367-88077-4 (pbk)

Typeset in Bembo
by Apex CoVantage, LLC

Dedicated to my mother and father
whose travels and adventures gave me imagination
and, to my brothers Tom and Alan
who always inspired me with their achievements.

Contents

PART III

Assurance   155

8 Auditors Are Sceptics   183   172

9 Auditors Are Lawyers   183

10 Auditors Are Quality Managers   197

13 Auditors Are Runners   275

Figures

Tables

Chronology of Author's Published Articles and Research in the Book

Notes

1 This paper was written and presented by me in 1975 as my presidential address, on the integration of the five separate United Kingdom Chapters of The Institute of Internal Auditors into the one United Kingdom Chapter. It was then published in the Chapter Audit Newsletter in the same year.

2 *Audit Opportunities in the TQM Environment Can Lead to World-Class Auditing* (1990), published in Internal Auditing (1990), IIA-UK and Ireland, London, England.

3 *Control Is Like a Well Lit Christmas Tree* (1994), published in Internal Control and Business Risk (1994), IIA-UK and Ireland, London, England.

4 *If You Have a Good Audit Recommendation – Look for a Better One*, published in Internal Auditing (April 1994 p. 6), IIA-UK and Ireland, London, England.

5 *Creativity and Inspiration are Essential for the Artist Auditor* (1995), published in Internal Auditing (March p. 12), IIA-UK and Ireland, London, England.

6 *You Are My Customer – You Are Also My Supplier*, published in Internal Auditing (October 1995), IIA-UK and Ireland, London, England.

7 *We Should Have a Vision to Be Innovators* (1998), published in Internal Auditing (March p. 12), IIA-UK and Ireland, London, England.

8 *Auditors Are Ambassadors in the Commonwealth, Across the European Union and Internationally* (2000), published in Internal Auditing and Business Risk, IIA-UK and Ireland, London, England.

9 *Risk, Change and Control – Challenges and Opportunities for All Auditors* (2000), published in Internal Control, Issue 28 (February 2000), ABG Professional Information, London, England.

10 *Weak Links in the Supply Chain* (2000), published in Internal Auditing (November 2000 pp. 8–9), IIA-UK and Ireland, London, England.

11 *A New Internal Auditor for a New Century* (2000), published in Internal Auditing and Business Risk January, IIA-UK and Ireland, London, England.

12 *Social Responsibility – A Challenge for Organisations and Internal Auditing* (2000), published in Internal Control, Issue 35 October, ABG Professional Information, London, England. Reproduced in Tottel's Corporate Governance Handbook (3rd Edition 2005 p. 1046), Tottel Publishing, Haywards Heath, England.

13 *How Effective Is Your Audit Committee* (2000), published in Internal Auditing and Business Risk (December p. 30), IIA-UK and Ireland, London, England.

14 *Quality Schemes and Best Value in the 21st Century – Challenges for Many Organizations and Internal Auditing*, Internal Control, Issue 38 (February 2001), ABG professional information, part of the CCH group, Institute of Chartered Accountants in England and Wales, London, England.

15 *Shout How Best You Are in All Your Internal Auditing Market Places*, Internal Control Journal (September 2001), Accountancy Books, London, England.

16 *What Was the Point of Cadbury – Today and Tomorrow?*, published in Internal Auditing and Business Risk (March 2002), IIA-UK and Ireland, London, England.

17 *Walk Faster This Year* (2002), published in Internal Auditing and Business Risk, IIA-UK and Ireland, London, England.

18 *Celebrate Internal Audit Professionalism* (2004), Jeffrey Ridley, published in Internal Auditor, The Institute of Internal Auditors, Orlando, US.

19 *The Road to Quality and Excellence Takes You to the Cutting Edge* (2008), published in Audit Viewpoint Issue 85, Chartered Institute of Public Finance and Accountancy, London, England.

20 *When Asking Questions, Be Modern and Confident* (2008), Cutting Edge Internal Auditing (p. 295), John Wiley and Sons Ltd., Chichester, England.

21 *Value of Objectivity* (2009 p. 72), Jeffrey Ridley, Internal Auditor – October, The Institute of Internal Auditors Inc., Orlando, US.

22 *Assurance of Sustainability Reports: Insights and Evidence from UK Companies* (2011), Professor Jeffrey Ridley, Professor Kenneth D'Silva and Anuj Saush, Paper presented at an international conference at Ashridge Management School, England.

About the Author

Professor Jeffrey Ridley FCIS FIIA CIA

I started my auditing career in 1953 as a colonial officer in the Colonial Audit Service, later to become Her Majesty's Overseas Civil Service. I served in Nigeria, West Africa, until 1963 auditing government and local authority accounts. My auditing career now spans some sixty-three years over a time of considerable change in the regulation of board stewardship and the independent assurances all organisations need to be excellent in their objectives and relations with their stakeholders. During all these years I have researched and published on the many changes that have taken place in the auditing professions and corporate governance to date and forecasted for the future. I have seen myself in all the creative and innovative auditor roles discussed in the chapters in this book – often all in the same audit engagement.

On returning to England, I joined Vauxhall Motors Ltd., a subsidiary of General Motors Corporation, as a senior internal auditor, auditing manufacturing operations and supporting services. In 1965 I joined Kodak Ltd.'s subsidiary of Eastman Kodak Inc. as a senior internal auditor. In 1971 I became its audit manager and remained in that position until 1993, auditing manufacturing, distribution and marketing operations, and their supporting administrative, financial and human resource services. During this time in Kodak I also managed its graduate accountant training scheme and later joined its Quality Council.

I joined The Institute of Internal Auditors in the United States in 1965 and was the first president of its United Kingdom Chapter in 1975 – now the Chartered Institute of Internal Auditors. From 1975 and into the 1980s I served on a number of its committees and committees in the United States: I am an Honorary Fellow of that institute, in 2010 being presented with its Distinguished Service Award for outstanding service to the profession of internal auditing. In 1967 I graduated as a member of the Institute of Chartered Secretaries and Administrators and am a Fellow of that institute, which now sees itself as The Governance Institute across the world.

In 1991 I was offered a visiting chair at the now London South Bank University and still hold that appointment. During my academic career I have taught auditing and corporate governance and researched quality, innovation and sustainability assurance, publishing papers on these themes and speaking at many conferences. I have also supervised research by students at postgraduate and doctorate levels, and for a period held a visiting chair at Birmingham City University, which has recently been renewed. I now also hold a visiting chair at the University of Lincoln. In 1998 I co-authored *Leading Edge Internal Auditing* with Professor Andrew Chambers, and in 2008 I authored *Cutting Edge Internal Auditing*. I have also published chapters on internal auditing and corporate governance themes in a number of edited books.

Throughout my auditing and academic careers I have promoted quality, continuous improvement and excellence in auditing and its valuable contribution to good governance. I have always learnt from the many travellers I have met during time across all levels in the organisations in which I have worked. I owe much to many for this learning. Today I hope my imagination, creativity and innovation in auditing also contributed to their learning. My hope now is this book and its creative thinking audit activities will contribute to the learning of many others in auditing and the travellers they meet in their assurance services.

Foreword

I was privileged to write the foreword to the author's 2008 trailblazing book, *Cutting Edge Internal Auditing*. Now again I have been given a similar opportunity for what is in many ways a sequel to that earlier work. While the lineage of this latest book is immediately apparent, the author breaks new ground here in many significant ways. His ideas have matured and expanded.

This is an inspirational book – especially if the reader is prepared to become immersed with an open mind. Undoubtedly it is a strongly integrated whole, yet each chapter stands on its own and can be read as such. Indeed it will be much better to regard each chapter as a rich entity in its own right rather than skim through this book from start to finish: to do the latter is likely to mean that the many challenging nuggets become blurred in the reader's mind.

This is not a heavy, technical read. It is shot through with humour. The novel concepts and challenges are clearly and attractively expressed and are straightforward to understand. But each merits being pondered over before moving on. Each has the potential to impact positively on the scope and conduct of the auditor's work.

The author shows how auditors need to learn from other professions. While this is a humble starting point, it does at the same time result in the articulation of a mission for all auditors that is rightly very ambitious. The history of the profession of auditing has been characterised by its members 'reaching for the stars' – crafting an ever more valuable, more demanding and more highly respected role. If each reader takes to heart just some of the author's stimulating guidance, then significant progress will continue to be made.

I believe the author is the profession's leading futurologist, as well as its most highly respected philosopher. Here we see both at play, woven through the tapestry of all the pages within this book. As with his *Cutting Edge Internal Auditing* (2008), this is an unusual book. Therein lies its attractiveness. It breaks the mould of auditing texts, being far removed from the ubiquitous 'cookbook'. Within these pages the author reveals himself as a genuine, profound exponent of the innovation he espouses.

Professor Andrew Chambers

Acknowledgements

F.R.M. De Paula, for his principles of auditing. These were the basis of my audit training for the Colonial Audit Service in 1953. Though auditing is much more complex today, in ever changing accounting and auditing standards and the speed of thought and change, they are still basic guidance for the science and quality of all auditing.

I am very grateful to Eur Ing Professor Andrew D. Chambers for his inspiring foreword and permission to use the cartoons at the beginning of some chapters – these are his copyright. The cartoons were drawn by Rev. Hugh Pruen: the captions are my choice.

The director of audit and audit staff in Kaduna, Nigeria, who started and guided me on my first explorations, adventures, challenges and opportunities in auditing.

The audit staff at General Motors, whose well-researched and cutting edge internal audit programmes and questionnaires started me on the path to being a modern internal auditor.

The finance directors at Kodak Limited, who supported my approach to modern internal auditing and its development into a professional assurance, consulting and teaching service.

The General Auditors of Eastman Kodak Company, who over many years encouraged me to have a vision to be at the cutting edge of internal auditing,

The directors at Kodak Limited, who encouraged me to contribute in their quality initiatives, which eventually led to the registration of my internal audit activity to the international quality standard ISO 9000.

All I have worked with and learnt from over many years in The Institute of Internal Auditors Inc. in the United States. I am grateful to The IIA and its Research Foundation for permission to reproduce their copyrighted material in my book. All this material is strictly reserved. No parts may be reproduced in any form without their written permission or reproduced, stored in any retrieval system, or transmitted in any form, or by any means electronic, mechanical, photocopying, recording or otherwise without their prior written permission.

The Chartered Institute of Internal Auditors in the United Kingdom, today's National Institute of The IIA. As a member since the 1960s and the first president in 1975 of its United Kingdom Chapter, I have met many of its members and staff, learning the challenges and opportunities facing all internal auditors everywhere in all nations. I am also grateful for the permission it has given me to reproduce some of my contributions to its journal over many years and quotations from its published material.

The Institute of Chartered Accountants in England and Wales for their futurist scenarios on auditing in the 21st century and permission to reference into their published material.

All the academic staff I have had the good fortune to meet and work with since 1991. I learnt my teaching and research skills from them all and continue to do so. In particular Professors Bruce Lloyd and Ted Fuller for their contributions to Chapter 7 and Professors Kenneth D'Silva and Paul Moxey for their contributions to Chapter 11.

All my students since 1961 and today. Too many to be mentioned. I have had the privilege to teach and supervise their studies, and at the same time I have learnt, and am still learning, from them.

I am grateful to the Financial Reporting Council (FRC) and Organisation for Economic Co-operation and Development (OECD) for permission to reference into their excellent published material and guidance on corporate governance today.

Lincs Rural Housing Association: recently I have had the privilege to work with its governors, senior management and staff in the achievement of its vision and mission in the provision of rural housing in Lincolnshire, England, a provision requiring Excellence in all of the components in my corporate governance framework: Stewardship, Change and Assurance.

The Scouting Association in the United Kingdom for permission to reproduce its scouting values, promise, law and motto. Each of these has inspired me through my life, from my early scouting days, leading a scout troop in the 1950s and to today. Each will continue to do so into my future.

Susan Rogers and Tudor Richards of Manchester Business School for Copyright permission to use Figure 2.3 – Attributes for Leadership in the Future.

All the staff at Routledge who have guided me in the preparation of the manuscript for this book. You have been very patient and helpful.

I apologise if I have missed anyone or organisation from the foregoing who should have been mentioned, or whose permission I have inadvertently not sought for material reproduced in my book. I am indebted to so many for the knowledge they have given me during my careers as an external auditor, internal auditor and academic over many years and adventures, including the writing of this book.

Preface

We should have a Vision to be Innovators[1]

Creativity and innovation are at the heart of all progressive and developing organisations. They are also at the heart of every profession. In 1998, I wrote and had published the following letter to the then Institute of Internal Auditors–UK and Ireland (now the Chartered Institute of Internal Auditors) on the occasion of its 50th year celebration: congratulating the institute on its progress in the development of professional internal auditing. The messages in that letter are still as important as they were then for the future of all auditing in the 21st century:

We should have a Vision to be Innovators

After 50 years as a profession we should now have a vision to be innovators! With the formation of The Institute of Internal Auditors (The IIA) in North America in 1941, internal auditors in the 1940s promoted the development of professional internal auditing. The IIA introduced in 1942 a worldwide image for internal auditing . . . as an 'added value' professional service, using the challenging statement:

Today's happenings pose new and perhaps perplexing problems to internal audi-tors. The requests and regulations of the several branches and agencies of Government demand a complete knowledge by internal auditors of their effect on the normal units of the companies they represent. The scope of internal audit requirements has increased tremendously.

Shortly after this, chapters of The IIA were established across North America and worldwide, including the UK. In 1978, growing membership in the UK resulted in a merger of the five chapters, into the first IIA affiliated national institute. I was proud and honoured to be elected its first president. The IIA-UK is now one of the foremost leaders in the development of internal auditing at national and inter-national levels. No small achievement for a young professional body, its members and staff.

The vision we set ourselves in 1975 was ' . . . to be a profession for the future.' Since then, many IIA developments have contributed to our claim to international status: international standards and a code of ethics, professional examinations based on an international common body of knowledge, global research into control and auditing, international quality assurance reviews, all have played their parts in our growth. However, our vision for tomorrow must be even higher than just being a profession. We also need to be seen as innovators in the world of regulation, control and auditing.

Creativity, innovation and experimentation are now key to our professional success. They must be the vision of all internal auditing functions. This means improving old and developing new products and services for delighting our customers, with a focus on their objectives. This means being at the leading edge in all the markets in which we sell our internal auditing services. This means beating our competitors and knowing who these are. This means having the imagination, and foresight of what our organisations will require from us, not just in 2000, but also beyond.

In this 50th year celebration of our national institute's past and present teamwork, all IIA-UK members should continue to set their sights on being inventors of an improved and new internal auditing, to delight all their customers . . . and increase its status as a profession.

Creativity and innovation are not just at the heart of progressive and developing professions – they are at the heart of all progressive and developing nations. In 2013 Xi Jinping, general secretary of the National Congress of the Communist Party of China, expressed his views on creativity and innovation to the Chinese people:[2]

I hope you will be more innovative and creative. Innovation is the soul of a nation's progress, the inexhaustible force driving a country's prosperity, and indeed the profound endowment of the Chinese nation.

In his speech on 28 September 2015 to the United Nations Annual General Assembly in New York, US President Obama linked creativity and innovation to individual rights and governance, introducing the concept of personal cultures and values into the progress of nations and people to better standards of living, lives and security:

The strength of nations depends on the success of their people – their knowledge, their innovation, their imagination, their creativity, their drive, their opportunity – and that, in turn, depends upon individual rights and good governance and personal security.

The spirit in which these words are spoken are in similar statements by many nation leaders and governments across the world; that spirit is what will always be needed in all auditing and assurance services. It will be the key to the success of all those who follow an auditing career.

What I have written about creativity and innovation is not about nations but for auditors and their contributions to the organisations in which they provide their services and the nations in which they work; all auditors who provide an independent and objective auditing service in organisations of whatever size, shape or sector; and for those who receive and monitor the effectiveness of those services. Audit societies of today and tomorrow are continuing to grow and change. Auditing standards, practices and the way auditors communicate with their stakeholders are demanding more transparency in audit planning and reporting. How auditors observe, question, listen, sample and verify the evidence of their audits will be influenced by more and faster technology, access to more data, better education and confidence from their creative thinking. Their contribution to society, wherever they work and travel, will always be a significant contribution to that nation's progress, standard of living, life and security.

All auditing services should understand what is meant by creative thinking and innovation, not just in the services they provide but also in the operations they audit. Their professions are built on creativity and innovation and so must be the services they provide. In 1975, I described[3] the environment in which all internal auditors, if not all auditors, worked as follows:

> We live in times of high economic risk and important social and business decisions. Every day we are reminded at work, in newspapers and by television of the opportunities that can be taken to develop ourselves and the profession we have chosen. The apparent insoluble problems of the present economic situation; the controversial discussions caused by exposure drafts and new accounting practices; involvement in the European Community; a new awareness of social responsibilities; higher health and safety standards; the now clearly recognised need for more efficient manpower planning and training; the urgency of energy saving; the complexity of advanced computer technology are all changes that management cannot ignore, and neither can we as internal auditors. To be successful we must be sensitive to the problems of each day. All can have an impact on our professional activities far beyond the changes we may foresee at the present time.

Little has changed. Today, more than forty years later, all auditors work in the same environment. The challenges I saw then have driven creative thinking and innovation by many auditors in all types of auditing practices across the globe: this creativity and thinking will and must continue through this century.

Also in 1975, I organised an exhibition of myself and internal auditing – not just me, but fourteen other internal auditor members of the newly created United Kingdom Chapter of the profession The Institute of Internal Auditors Inc.,[4] formed by the amalgamation of five existing chapters of the profession of internal auditing in the United Kingdom. These chapters had been operating for the previous thirty years in regions across the nation. We developed and took part in a public exhibition of professional internal auditing in our organisations, held in the Greater London Council County Hall, London. We were creatively thinking and innovating in the art of promoting internal auditing as a professional service to management and at board level. Our pioneering and innovative exhibition at that time was a first of its style on a national or international scale.

Each of the contributors to the exhibition created a professional marketing stand demonstrating their internal auditing services. Many visitors attended the exhibition, including representatives from government, local authorities and professional bodies. A series of discussion seminars was held during the day to present professional internal auditing in more detail. What we were exhibiting was not just internal auditing but its contribution to the governance of so many varieties of organisations at that time. This is a contribution which has continued to grow worldwide, not just in its professional internal auditing knowledge and skills, but also in its contribution to all the assurance services boards and their stakeholders needs in the 'direction and control' of their operations and interests.

Today, exhibition halls at conferences on auditing at the national and international levels are an important part of their programmes. In 1975, this was not so. Making an exhibition of auditing was unique. My book is about that uniqueness and its associated innovations that make auditing so appealing. In my book, *Cutting Edge Internal Auditing*,[5] I compared internal auditors to the first astronauts landing on the moon, and I still believe this exploration is what all auditing is about:

> Key to space exploration is the political and strategic commitment, imagination and teamwork of those who worked to enter space, and who eventually stood on the Moon's surface. In many ways I have always seen internal auditors, individually and as teams, following a similar strategic path of commitment, imagination and teamwork in the exploration of each audit engagement. They start with organisation and auditing strategies and step along a path that is not familiar, with an achievement in mind. They do this with teamwork. They are trained to do this. They are taught to be good auditors: but they cannot be taught to be the best auditor. That depends on their commitment and imagination: how they can coordinate their work with others: how quickly they can react to the situations they find themselves in; how innovative they can be in their practices: how sensitive they are to their environment. They may not be aiming for the Moon, but at the beginning of every engagement they are looking into the unknown.

My book is not a book about auditing standards. It is about auditing explorations. Auditing standards are very important, if not essential, in today's government and regulatory auditing and reporting. Nor is it about the contributions so many have made in professional institutions across the world to develop qualifications and codes of conduct for auditing: these contributions have created a world today of best practice auditing for many stakeholders, best practices which have grown over the past century and this one, continuously improving by the use of technology and the skills of many auditors. My book is about imagination and continuous improvement in auditing practices and services. It is the instinct of most of us, if not all of us, to continuously improve: to be better, if not best, in whatever we do, whether in our communities of living, play, sport or work. It can lead to better and best quality in what we achieve: it can lead to changes in what we do. It can be motivated by satisfaction, enjoyment and inspiration, but more often just using common sense and imagination.

All auditors have a significant role to play in the organisations in which they practice their services. From the viewpoints of those they audit and their interested stakeholder groups, all auditors are lines of defence in governance practices in today and tomorrow's organisations – be they business, government or charity. Traditional '*expectation gaps*' between auditors and those they audit; different stakeholder group assurance needs; continuing advances in technology – all make it essential to approach all auditing with a creative mind and innovation in its practices.

Professor Michael Power[6] in his 1997 book, *The Audit Society*, writes on the 'explosion of auditing activity in the United Kingdom and North America' in the early 1980s. He saw this growth of auditing at that time as having 'its roots in political demands for accountability and control'. This growth and investment in auditing has continued at national and international levels, fuelled by many financial scandals; laws and regulations at national and international levels; best practice visions and excellent performance models; and more recently, corporate governance code requirements and guidance – growth of all types of financial and operational auditing, inspection, compliance and control, all influenced by many different stakeholders, across all sectors of society.

My book uses an interactive governance framework of the components **STEWARDSHIP**, **CHANGE**, **ASSURANCE** and **EXCELLENCE**, which I have grown and developed since the 1980s from my research into the creative thinking needs for auditors. The components of this framework all have underlying theories explored over many years, if not centuries, by many philosophers, scientists, academics, researchers and students – theories which have influenced improvements and created innovations in organisations worldwide. The chapters are arranged around these components. Each chapter includes creative audit thinking activities to start readers on a path of innovations in the auditing services they provide, innovations which will be an essential part of auditing in the future and throughout this century.

Whatever my readers' interests in auditing, I feel confident they will find in this book at least one, if not many, inspirations and imaginative suggestions, which will change for the better and best the auditing services they provide or receive today and in the future. There are also those who do not see themselves as auditors but who could find the contents of interest, if not inspiration. Everybody is an auditor, whether at work, home or at play. We all observe, question, assess, evaluate and have rules and apply values we obey in whatever we do. We all creatively think and innovate from birth. Nurturing that creativity is what life, play, sport and work is all about. I am often inspired about the spirit of the game of golf and how this patterns the codes of best practice in governments and businesses we see being developed today in nations across the world. That spirit was illustrated for me again in a visit I made to a local golf club just recently. On display to all its members, staff and visitors was the following notice:

Spirit of the game of golf

Honesty, integrity, courtesy: three words that have come to represent the spirit in which the game of golf is played. Part of that spirit sits beneath the term, 'etiquette' and part of it relates to the Rules of Golf. But the Spirit of the game owes much deeper than those two tangible terms. It is something that every golfer should develop, an innate sense of something that is born of golf's unparalleled history, and something which lifts golf, one could argue, above other sports. Whether it is through divot and pitch-mark repair, or simply through silence on the tee, the Spirit of the Game dictates that players make sure they give others on the course, often opponents, a fair chance to play the best shot they can. For most of us, the game of golf is self-regulating, there is seldom a referee present, and so we are reliant upon our own honest adherence to the Rules in order to enjoy the game. As a result we are all occasionally forced to call a penalty on ourselves for infringements which, often, will go unnoticed by everyone else. Honesty, integrity, courtesy, three words that have come to represent *the Game of Golf*. It is this dependence upon honesty and courtesy that has elevated 'integrity' to sacrosanct status. Without them, we may as well hang up our clubs.

Do all golfers understand all the game's etiquette and rules? Given a test on the first tee, how many would pass with distinction? What is relied upon is the collective knowledge and understanding of the group, team and club, and sometimes referee and caddy, to ensure the rules are applied in every match, whether friendly or in competition. That Spirit of the Game of Golf is the culture of the game and always will be. It creates the friendships, collaborations and partnerships seen in every golf club in every nation and throughout the world in every international tournament. That same spirit should be seen in the **STEWARDSHIP**, **CHANGE**, **ASSURANCE** and **EXCELLENCE** in every organisation, in every nation. Yet, is this always so? If the same suggested test on etiquette and rules for golfers at the first tee be applied to every board member, politician and those in power, how many would pass with distinction? It is that spirit which underlies all the chapters in my book and the creative audit thinking activities it contains.

Surprisingly, in a world of governments, trading and charity, where creative thinking and innovation is seen as the pinnacle of achievement in economics, competition and success, it is rarely, if ever, seen as an attribute in notices advertising audit employment vacancies. I can only assume this also applies today in job descriptions for auditors – only the reader can confirm this in their own job description. Yet, continuously improving all auditing through creative thinking and innovation is what good professional auditing is all about. The future for auditing and all assurance activities depends on this.

As I write this, I am indebted to Lawrence Sawyer, a pioneer of creativity in auditing, both in his advice and writings over many years in the last part of the 20th century. His contribution to the development of professional internal auditing was significant across the world and still is today. His wisdom[7] on creativity in internal auditing still applies today in all types of auditing and across all sectors:

> Creativity is not reserved for the arts and sciences. It is needed in our profession as well. But it will never be tapped if we do not develop a divine discontent with what we see and if we fail to search for new ways of solving the problems which we identify or which management presents to us. We can offer a new presence to the business community – as creative problem-solving partners to managers at all levels.

As a final thought, I quote advice from a recent book on marketing remarkable ideas I acquired called the *Purple Cow: Transform your Business by Being Remarkable*, published in 2002.[8] Directed at those who market products and services, it has many messages and experiences for those who market creative and innovative auditing. The book is introduced by the following:

> I don't think there is a shortage of remarkable ideas. I think your business has plenty of great opportunities to do great things. Nope, what's missing isn't the ideas. It's the will to execute them.

Enjoy being creative and innovative with your ideas for better auditing. I have for over sixty years.

Jeffrey Ridley
16 June 2017

Notes

1 *We Should Have a Vision to Be Innovators*, published in Internal Auditing (March 1998 p. 12) on the celebration of the IIA-UK and Ireland 50th year celebration.
2 *The Governance of China – Right Time to Innovate and Make Dreams Come True* (2014 p. 63), Xi Jinping, Foreign Languages Press Co Ltd, Beijing, China.
3 This message was written and presented by me in 1975 at my presidential address, on the integration of the five separate United Kingdom Chapters of The Institute of Internal

Auditors into the one United Kingdom Chapter. It was then published in the Chapter Audit Newsletter in the same year.

4 The Institute of Internal Auditors Inc. in New York, United States, at that time consisted of chapters in 50 countries around the world, founded in 1941 to develop the profession of internal auditing and to provide a medium for the interchange of ideas and information among those engaged in its practice, now providing 'dynamic leadership for the global profession of internal auditing' in 190+ countries and with 180,000+ members.

5 *Cutting Edge Internal Auditing* (2008 p. xxvi), Jeffrey Ridley, John Wiley and Sons Ltd, Chichester, England.

6 *The Audit Society – Rituals of Verification* (1997), Michael Power, Oxford University Press, Oxford, England.

7 *The Creative Side of Internal Auditing* (1992 pp. 57–62), Internal Auditor December Issue, The Institute of Internal Auditors Inc., Orlando, US.

8 *Purple Cow: Transform Your Business by Being Remarkable* (2002 p. 24), Seth Godin, Penguin Group, New York, US.

1 Creativity and Innovation in Management and Auditing

Theories and Practices

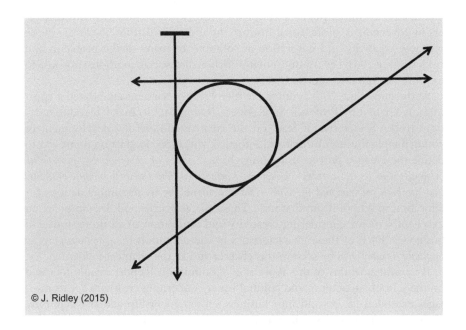

Take a triangle and a circle add arrows and you have a Corporate Governance Framework.

In this chapter, I introduce the reader to the theories of creativity and innovation and discuss how they are part of the steps in all auditing processes. Creativity and innovation always start with a vision, preferably a shared vision by a team and the organisation. Visions that are exciting statements, motivating changes in behaviour and creative impact. I discuss how achieving innovations in auditing requires addressing four themes in governance – STEWARDSHIP, CHANGE, ASSURANCE and EXCELLENCE across all the supply chains in an organisation. Understanding the importance of these themes in all organisations can inspire creativity and innovation in all auditing services and the assurances they provide to all levels in an organisation.

1.1 Creativity and Innovation Theories

Science of knowledge and its understanding owes all to creative thinking and innovation: it is the evolution of mankind, if not before. We all create and innovate, for survival, for security and gain – not just gain in the financial sense, but also for excitement, comfort and even just satisfaction. All these motives drive change: creative thoughts, behaviours and impacts in everything we do and everything around us. All managers must innovate to continuously improve their outputs and the resulting outcomes. Creativity and innovation are key to successful entrepreneurship. In today's global economic market place, we all enjoy products and services created over centuries of imagination and the drive to improve, not only in the provision of products and services in the private sector, but also in the public and not-for-profit sectors. Politicians and managers in government, professional institutions and organisations across the globe promote creativity and innovation as solutions to many of the problems and risks we face today: economic, environmental and social; solutions; not just to improve but often to survive.

At the end of the 20th century, the then UK government established a commission, chaired by Professor Sir Kenneth Robinson,[1] to make 'recommendations to the Secretaries of State on the creative and cultural development of young people through formal and informal education.' Its starting point was to define the creative process using four characteristics of *imaginatively: purposeful: original: value*. Its definition – *Imaginative activity fashioned so as to produce outcomes that are both original and of value* – set the scene for its recommendations for education in schools from that time. These characteristics and definition are an excellent start for considering creativity and innovation in all professions and businesses. Each of these characteristics in the definition (*imagination: purpose: originality: value*) will be seen in this chapter and all the chapters following.

Recommendations of the 'Robinson' Commission Report mainly focussed on the school curriculum and cultural issues concerning creativity. Yet its messages extended far beyond into business, entrepreneurship and the economy, even social life and play. Since its publication, many government and professional institutions and other associations have progressed their creative and innovative policies and practices: examples of this can be seen in most organisation websites across the globe. One association example is the Districts of Creativity Network (www.districtsofcreativity.org) and its projects, an association founded in 2004 which today unites thirteen regional members across the globe 'that puts creativity and innovation high on the agenda'. Its annual Creativity World Forum schedule of speakers contains many creative thinking messages for all auditors.

Later in 2006, the 'Roberts' Report[2] on nurturing creativity in young people produced a response[3] from government referencing into and reinforcing the Robinson definition of creativity: 'Creativity can be a powerful contributing factor to achieving each of five outcomes for every child Health: Safety: Enjoyment: Achievement: Contribution'. Note the similarity at the beginning of this chapter to 'We all create and innovate, for survival, for security and gain: not just gain in the financial sense, but also for excitement, comfort and even just satisfaction.' This report highlights the importance of teachers being 'supported through Continuing Professional Development (CPD) and peer mentoring to adapt their teaching styles to improve teaching and learning and to encourage and reward creative responses from their pupils'. This is an important message for all professionals and their professional institutions, and certainly for all auditors.

All governments are promoting and motivating creativity and innovation as a technique to solve today's financial crisis, improve economic and sustainable performances and meet global competition. This is not new. Innovation across the globe in all sectors has been encouraged over many centuries, driving continuous improvement in the quality and length of our lives. Organisations in competitive market places across the world sell creativity and innovation of their products and services, investing in research and development to create new businesses to delight existing and new customers. For evidence, see the content of many advertisements and packaging of products and services promoting the words 'creative' and 'innovative'.

Study of creativity by economists, psychologists, humanists and sociologists has been a science over many centuries and still is today. Many have researched what motivates all of us to do what we do, to create what we create, to change what we change. Theories for creativity have been published by many. It is not the intention of this book to re-study the science of creativity. This has been, is and will be a task for others. However, a few words on their contributions to the theories of creativity are still appropriate and need to be understood by all auditors.

For readers who wish to explore the psychology of change in behaviours, there is much to study across many centuries. One of the more recent and famous is Abraham Maslow,[4] an American psychologist, known for creating his 'hierarchy of needs' through motivation steps. His theory of psychology, published as a pyramid hierarchy in 1943, consisted of five levels, rising to a peak – starting with psychological needs through *safety, love/belonging, esteem* to *self-actualisation*. Later, in further publications, he added *curiosity* – an essential attribute for all auditors. Each one is a motivation for creating change in behaviour: each one motivates creativity in all of us today and will do tomorrow.

Other theories on creative thinking bring in scientific studies of the brain's left and right hemispheres, to explain our creative processes. These studies are not covered in this book. It is acknowledged by these theories that creative thinking skills vary across us all. Pink (2005)[5] goes further and introduces the reader to a new *conceptual age* of creators and emphasisers directed by the right hemisphere of the brain: an age which is now following the *information age*. However, this is not to say that creative thinking can or cannot be improved by motivation, learning and experience. I leave this aspect of creativity for others to explain and the reader to study and understand.

Torr (2008)[6] writes on 'understanding how, when and where to get the best out of that most precious of resources – the imagination of the talented individual'. His background as creative director at one of the world's largest advertising agencies and in consultancy places him in a unique position to write on managing creativity in individuals and organisations. His book cites many philosophers and writers on creativity as examples of how ideas should be motivated, managed and led to successful change in products and services. One cited writer (Osborne) in particular caught my imagination with his following *'Seven-Step Model for Creative Thinking'*:[7]

1   orientation: pointing up the **problem**
2   preparation: gathering pertinent **data**
3   analysis: breaking down the **relevant** material
4   ideation: piling up alternatives by way of **ideas**
5   incubation: letting up to invite **illumination**
6   synthesis: putting the pieces **together**
7   evaluation: **judging** the resulting ideas.

In Step 5, Torr writes of Osborne's invitation to his readers 'to go for a walk, keep a pencil handy while you're in the bath, or go to church, Cold showers are optional'. Activities I have practiced over many audits and research in all the steps – and still do!

Torr also cites Annabile et al.'s[8] *Three Component Model of Creativity*. This model is represented by three overlapping circles representing the three components of creativity in the individual and domain – Expertise; Skills; Task Motivation. The area where the circles overlap is called Creativity. Each of the three components can and does have an influence on the level of creativity in both individuals and the organisations in which they work and for whom they work. Each of Annabile's components is a necessary part of all best practice auditing.

We recognise innovation today as creating something that is different in processes, products and services – by being different to be better and best, rather than doing the same. Theories on innovation have many followers and publications. A recent new concept on the DNA of disruptive innovators researched by three professors from different schools discusses five discovery skills for all innovators:

Association – linking ideas together not obviously related
Questioning – penetrating the 'status quo'
Observing – looking with intensity beyond the ordinary
Networking – communicating across the world with diversity
Experimenting – researching at the centre of all activities.

Most if not all auditors and assurers will recognise these five discovery skills as very important in the delivery of their services using their own DNA. These skills are all important if not essential in the services they provide. They can be seen in many forms in the standards and practices of all the best auditors and assurers. All textbooks on auditing and assurance say so. Therefore, we can deduce all innovators have the DNA of the best auditor. If so, do all auditors have the DNA of the best innovator? Readers must judge this for themselves.

1.2 Creativity and Innovation Starts With a Vision

I have on my bookshelf a guide to 33 management gurus across the world, written by Carol Kennedy,[9] published in 1991. Most of the gurus were born in the 20th century, and one in the 19th: Henri Fayol. I have often in my teaching quoted Fayol's five foundation stones of modern management – *to forecast and plan, to organise, to command, to co-ordinate and to control* – together with his fourteen principles of management as the basis of good corporate governance codes as we know them today. Kennedy writes:

> Fayol believed that a manager obtained the best performance from his workforce by leadership qualities, by his knowledge of the business and his workers, and by the ability to instil a sense of mission.

Kennedy's *Glossary of Management Terms* defines the mission statement as 'The distillation of a company's philosophy and corporate goals and values. It can range in length from a sentence to a book.' Vision statement is not defined, but motivational theories are. Today Bain and Company (2015)[10] define the mission and vision statement as follows:

> A Mission Statement defines the company's business, its objectives and its approach to reach those objectives. A Vision Statement describes the desired future position of the company. Elements of Mission and Vision Statements are often combined to provide a statement of the company's purposes, goals and values. However, sometimes the two terms are used interchangeably.

The importance of a vision in creative thinking and innovation was seen by Senge (1990)[11] as one of the vital disciplines for learning. His innovative thinking on the learning organisation at that time drew 'on science, spiritual values, psychology, the cutting edge of management thought and his work with leading companies'. Senge describes extensively his role of mental models, which he says are integral in order to 'focus on the openness needed to unearth shortcomings' in perceptions. His book also focuses on team learning, with the goal of developing 'the skills of groups of people to look for the larger picture beyond individual perspectives'. His following thoughts on visions as inspirations for 'people to excel and learn' live on, being as true today as they were when first written:

> If any one idea about leadership has inspired organisations for thousands of years, it's the capacity to hold a shared picture of the future we seek to create.

Mastering the discipline of a shared vision stimulates the process of inventing through seeing shared pictures of the future in every profession and walk of life.

My own thoughts on the use of visions for continuous improvement were written in an article on achieving success which I published in 1997:[12]

> A vision is a forecast of a future desired state at a point in time, which is attractive to the beholder. All people have visions. Visions change: they need to be appropriate to their time. Not all people use their visions to select, educate and develop themselves or others. Good managers create visions for organisations and, through the cycle of selection, education and development establish commitment for the future state: commitment, not just by people, but also by teams of people. Once the vision is agreed, key strategies and tactics must follow, linked and measured to the required future state. A wish for success is part of everyone's vision, though the measure may be different for each person. Personal visions need to be built into team and group visions. All visions should stretch people and teams to improve. All visions should demand change for the better. All visions should aim for success. The art of good management is to establish and achieve visions by the cycles of selection, education and development of people and teams.

Use of visions by organisations is now seen by management to be an important part of the creative thinking and innovation processes. The United Kingdom Institute of Chartered Accountants in England and Wales (2010)[13] summed this up well with a series of articles on developing a vision, which included the word 'create' 34 times in its various forms – create, creative, creativity, creation:

> Creativity and inventiveness play a role in vision creation, but it is also the product of the synthesis of disparate information. Knowledge of one's industry's recent developments and future trends is important. In addition, it is useful to learn about new developments and emerging trends occurring outside of one's immediate business domain. Courage and audacity are important to not only stretch the range of possibilities, but commit to turning such possibilities into a new reality.

Good advice not just for the creation of a vision, but also the knowledge needed to achieve the vision and the qualities needed to create an innovative product or service and to make it happen. Consider the visions in organisations in my life at present – see Figure 1.1 – and then consider the visions in your life at present. Do these and your visions motivate creative thinking and innovation? Note how each vary in their construction. Each in its own way encourages, if not inspires, creativity and innovation.

London South Bank University, London, England

MISSION: *To be recognised as an enterprising civic university that addresses real world challenges.*

University of Lincoln, Lincoln, England

VISION: *By 2021 be a global 'thought leader' for the 21st Century higher educa-tion. We will be known for addressing the opportunities and challenges presented by the changing world by developing a new approach to education and knowledge development.*

MISSION: *'A university looking to the future' where we serve and develop our local, national and international communities by creating purposeful knowledge and research, confident and creative graduates and a dynamic and engaged staff team.*

Lincolnshire Rural Housing Association, Spilsby, England

VISION: *Sustainable Rural Communities*
MISSION: *Providing Homes for Rural People in Need*

Institute of Chartered Secretaries and Administrators

VISION: *Our aim is to promote the highest standard of governance and reporting positioning ICSA as the professional centre of excellence and thought leadership in governance and compliance.*

Chartered Institute of Internal Auditors, London, England

VISION: *Internal audit will be universally recognised as essential to the success of organizations; and that the Institute will be acknowledged as an essential enabler of the success of internal audit professionals.*

MISSION: *To support and develop internal audit professionals throughout their careers, and to promote the role and value of the profession. We aspire to be recog-nised as the authoritative professional body for the internal audit profession, and as widely influential amongst our stakeholders.*

The Institute of Internal Auditors, Orlando, Florida, US

MISSION: *To serve our members and to advance the internal audit profession around the world.*

Figure 1.1 My work and professional institute visions and missions in 2016
Sources from Websites September 2016

1.3 Creativity and Innovation in Management

In 1991 Jane Henry wrote on creative management:[14]

> We live in remarkable times. The planet is faced with the spectre of cata-
> strophic climate change. Information not industry rules our lives. New
> patterns emerge to meet the needs of our new order. We are one world,
> with a global economy, climate and increasingly similar cultural milieu,
> inextricably intertwined in interdependence. The world needs a different
> form of perception, one that accepts change as part of everyday life, that
> enables us to build on the opportunities change thrusts upon us, that coop-
> erates with others, valuing the part we all play, and recognises personal and
> organisational development, as a way of life.

This was part of the introduction to her book, a Course Reader for The Open
Business School's postgraduate MBA course B882 *Creative Management* in 1991.
This course developed into a learning programme *Creativity, Innovation and Change*
in *2007* (cited as a case study in my book *Cutting Edge Internal Auditing*[15]). At that
time it was introduced on the Open University website as follows:

> How do perception, style and culture affect thought and action? How can
> you develop a more creative approach in yourself and a more creative cli-
> mate in your organisation? This interdisciplinary course for managers will
> give you an excellent grasp of the principles underlying creative thinking
> and problem-solving and help you to promote imaginative, flexible and
> practical thought and action. You'll learn about organisational restructuring
> and renewal strategies; how to develop partnerships across organisational
> boundaries, and how to involve people and share knowledge. You'll also
> discover how to use various processes and systems to develop ideas and
> manage innovation, leading to organisational transformation.

Excellent advice also for all today and tomorrow's auditors.

Henry,[16] in later books, discusses the use of metaphors underpinning creative
management thinking and how these can influence creativity, knowledge and innovation. Such metaphors can influence the way management acts and is perceived.
She asks her readers to try to pick five metaphors for the process of management:

> Did you see management in terms of keeping your head down, of getting
> a fresh view of the situation, of battling through the waves, of keeping peo-
> ple happy or holding them off? A person who perceives management as a
> business will probably behave differently from someone who sees it as an
> art. Similarly, people who believe that the skill of managing lies in bringing
> out the best in others will probably adopt a style at variance with people
> thinking in terms of fighting their corner.

In her book, she considers changes to management style in many organisations over the 20th century, based round metaphors of team sports and spiritual

sources, with the use of vision and mission statements to inspire and seek commitments, recognising metaphors we use to reveal our values and beliefs can be different across the globe. Metaphors change perceptions both in whom they apply and those who perceive their actions. They also change over time.

Every day we are reminded of the importance of innovation from news in the media and in promotions of products and services in all the competitive market places we enjoy. I was reminded of this recently, travelling through Kings Cross Railway Station in London seeing '*The STORY of Hotel Chocolat*' explaining – INNOVATION – as one of its secret ingredients. 'A spirit of innovation and creativity permeates the company', headlined in the leaflet outside its Concourse shop. I need say no more about the imagination of my selection!

Creativity and innovation have always been seen to be key to successful entrepreneurship. In today's global economic market place, we all enjoy products and services created over centuries of imagination and the drive to invent, not only in the provision of products and services in the private sector, but also in the public and not-for-profit sectors. Creativity is the thought process, encouraged by imagination, which generates ideas for change to 'make things happen': making ideas happen is the process of innovation. Global, national and professional governments and institutions promote creativity and innovation as solutions to many of the problems and the risks we face today, financial, environmental and social: solutions, not just to improve but survive.

Innovation in the private sector has been encouraged over many centuries. Encouragement for innovation as a strategy in the public sector is relatively new, but this has not stopped it from happening – evidence many laws, regulations and changes in social and environmental practices at global and national levels. The UK government and its National Audit Office have been promoting and encouraging research and its associated innovations across the business and government departments for many years – with a catalogue of publications on the importance of this for the economy, environment and society.

Success and growth in any organisation depends on continuous improvement through a cycle of imagination, experimentation and innovation: continuous improvement creates efficiency, effectiveness, economy and continuous customer satisfaction, if not delight. Innovation is at the heart of all value for money reviews, customer relationship management and supply chain management. Best practice and quality in all products and services are achieved through creative and innovative ideas.

Most uses of the term 'innovation' – and there are many by politicians, management and professions – define it as 'the successful exploitation of new ideas'. At the beginning of the current financial crisis, the UK coalition government saw innovation as one of the keys to the nation's recovery. In its White Paper (2008),[17] it set out to motivate everyone into innovating for success:

> Government creates the conditions for innovation by ensuring macroeconomic stability and open and competitive markets. In many sectors of the economy maintaining this framework and investing in people and knowledge are sufficient for innovation to flourish. In some specific areas, government can provide more direct support using regulation, public

procurement and public services to shape the market for innovation solutions. Innovation is essential to meeting some of the biggest challenges facing our society like global warming and sustainable development.

This was not the first time this century the UK government recognised the challenge of innovation for success in today's global market place. The early 2000s saw similar statements, recognising the importance of government influencing 'innovation through policies which shape innovation systems (e.g. regulation, competition policy, education) or via the provision of subsidies to encourage innovation or knowledge transfer'.[18] If you analyse this sentence and interpret its meanings, it covers all the ingredients for successful innovation in processes, products and services at organisation and operations levels:

Policies – Strategies and Structures
Shape – Change and Continuous Improvement
Systems – Processes
Regulation – Measurement
Competition – Quality and Excellence
Education – Academic Knowledge and Qualifications
Subsidies – Motivation.

One good international example of this focus on innovation comes from the US Council on Competitiveness (USCC). In its website[19] assessment of today's business environment, it sees innovation as the way you play the game of globalisation in the 21st century, recognising 'The ability to rapidly translate knowledge and insights into new high-value products and services is imperative to addressing many of the grand challenges facing the United States, and the world.' This recognition is seen even more so when you consider the USCC five key drivers of competitiveness:

1   drive innovation and entrepreneurship
2   engage the global economy
3   manage risk and active resilience
4   secure energy and create sustainability
5   win the skills race.

Interpret each of these into your organisation and its objectives, at strategic and operations levels. Look for them in its policies and procedures as well as its auditing, all of which should be seen in the scope of every audit engagement, whether it be assurance or consulting. This benchmarking applies also in the public and not-for-profit sectors. Profit and growth are not the only motivations for organisations; excellent public service and charitable activities are equally important, and on many occasions more so. The Council[20] drives exploration into innovation and its importance as key to commercial success, customer satisfaction and society achievements in the rapid and significant changes taking place in the United States and across the world – explorations all auditors will need to do now and in their future professional roles to satisfy their customers and civil societies at large.

The Organisation for Economic Co-operation and Development (OECD) (2010)[21] promoted the need for a global innovation strategy in every organisation in every country using its five policy principles for innovation. Later, OECD (2015)[22] updated its 2010 innovation strategy recommendation 'to strengthen innovation performance and put it to use for stronger, greener and more inclusive growth', reflecting the growing importance of today's 'growth and job creation and efficient delivery of public services, but also to address specific social and global challenges, including green growth, health, food, security and the fight against poverty'. The OECD in its statement of priorities also sees importance 'for the public sector . . . extending the methodology to public sector innovation and innovation for social goals'.

1.4 Creativity and Innovation in Auditing

Both the OECD principles and priorities make excellent advisory statements for every auditor in every audit process, and can be seen in publications on innovation by the UK National Audit Office (NAO) and International Organisation of Supreme Audit Institutions (INTOSAI),[23] whose core values include innovation. The NAO (2006)[24] recognises one of the factors helping innovation to be successful as 'regular internal review or audit'. In its 2009 report[25] on innovation across government departments, it listed the factors most significantly helping innovation as follows (independent and objective audit activities are bold):

> The number of innovative or creative individuals in the organisation
> Efficiency of savings targets
> **External review by the National Audit Office**
> **Internal reviews, for example by internal audit**
> The organisation's approach to researching, developing, testing and piloting programmes that may not be rolled out more widely
> PSA targets/departmental strategic objectives
> Three-year budgets
> The organisation's attitude to risk
> The capability of the organisation's main suppliers to provide innovative solutions
> Departmental capability reviews.

If auditing is to be a significant contributor to innovation across all sectors, it is not sufficient for it to establish measures for reviews of its performance, however efficient and effective; auditing needs to continuously improve and innovate as part of its quality management. Such improvement requires appropriate metrics and benchmarks. These are clearly seen in professional standards, practice papers, advisories and guides. However, continuous improvement and innovation is more than training of staff, correction of weak methods or rectification of mistakes: it is about paradigm shifts to increase the value of the service to all, from the top of an organisation to operations level change, across all its supply chains – suppliers and customers, and relationships with its regulators.

In all its engagements, auditing should also assess creativity and innovation in the functions it reviews. Its experience of paradigm change in its own function fits it well for adding the same value to all other operations. Observations and recommendations it makes on governance, risk management and control can all be considered as potential opportunities for inventing new ways and practices through design and skills. Meetings with clients and their staff are occasions when brainstorming and benchmarking can encourage paradigm shifts to improve efficiency, effectiveness and economy.

A good start for any audit activity implementing an innovation policy is to review the ingredients of innovation mentioned in its POLICIES, SHAPE, SYSTEMS, REGULATION, COMPETITION, EDUCATION and SUBSIDIES. In each of these areas, audit has a role to play to encourage 'the successful exploitation of new ideas'.

The first step in an audit innovation policy is to include in all audit engagement planning a review of the implementation of innovation policies in the operations being audited. This may not be as new as it seems. The National Audit Office 2009 inclusion of internal audit in central government as a helper of innovation supports Sawyer's[26] views:

> Creativity is not reserved for the arts and sciences. It is needed in our profession as well. But it will never be tapped [in internal auditing] if we do not develop a divine discontent with what we see and if we fail to search for new ways of solving the problems which we identify or which management present to us. We can offer a new presence to the business community – as creative problem-solving partners to managers at all levels.

That attribute is never more evident than in the inclusion of the value for money objectives of economy, efficiency and effectiveness in an audit programme. Such objectives are not new in central government and other public authorities, but possibly less so in the private and charity sectors, yet they are just as important in those sectors.

In the 1970s and 1980s, as manager of an internal auditing department in a large company, manufacturing, marketing and distributing across thirty sites in the United Kingdom, my challenge and opportunity was to recruit and train auditors for their and the company's future. To do this, I developed the slide presentations at Figure 1.2 as an introduction to the future of internal auditing and their careers. In hindsight I now realise I was forecasting what has since been seen as now essential for all auditing today and will continue to be in the future. I used the four slides in this training for both my internal auditors and the promotion of internal auditing as an innovative professional service to management and the board of my company. Consider these today as you read one or more of the chapters in this book.

My slide presentations for the recruitment of internal auditors

CHARACTERISTICS OF INTERNAL AUDITING OBJECTIVE/INDEPENDENT ACCOUNTABLE INTEGRITY/COMPETENT VALUE/JUDGEMENT PROACTIVE CLEAR COMMUNICATOR	**INTERNAL AUDIT BEST ATTRIBUTES** RIGOROUS ASTUTE SELF STARTER INNOVATIVE OUTSTANDING LEADER
INTERNAL AUDIT MOST VALUABLE ASSETS OBJECTIVITY INDEPENDENCE	**A BIGGER ROLE** CUSTOMER FOCUS PARTNERS PROFESSIONAL RISK & CONTROL EXPERT CONSULTANT SUCCESSFUL CAREER

Figure 1.2 My slide presentations for the recruitment of internal auditors

Source: J. Ridley (1970)

Chambers,[27] in his *Corporate Governance Handbook*, discusses the future for auditing:

> At the outset, we mentioned that, today, shareholders are more inquisitive and better informed. Rational markets require reliable and complete information. Companies already place their annual reports on their websites, and it will not be long before companies that report in real-time are rewarded with a premium on their P/E ratios. Real-time reporting will require real-time auditing – a continuous, very automated audit approach with a recharged emphasis upon confirming the reliability of the system of internal financial control.

This statement applies, today, to all an organisation's stakeholders, not just shareholders – all those having an interest in an organisation's operations and financial stability. Real-time reporting already exists in today's speed of collecting, analysing and publishing data in many organisations: how auditors react to this reporting with creative thinking and innovative approaches to the services they provide is what my book is about.

In 1998,[28] I wrote of the importance of imagination for internal auditors at the 'leading edge' of their profession as key to its success: 'It [imagination] uses vision to create innovative auditing products and services. It continuously improves these to meet anticipated new and increasing expectations by both internal auditors and all its customers.' This message was also a forerunner to my book, *Cutting Edge Internal Auditing*, in 2008, and still applies to all auditors and their objectives. Auditing today must be seen imaginatively more and more by many, as a service to the government, stakeholders of the organisations in which they audit and the public at large. It is a service to be trusted. To win that trust, all auditors face the challenge of continuously re-inventing their services; creating new standards, practices and processes; using their imaginations to create new visions, products and services; and using their independent and objective roles to scrutinise economic, environmental and social issues. This is what all auditing should be about today and will need to be in the future.

Creativity and innovation has not been neglected by the auditing professions. Their research and professional standards, statements and codes of ethics at national and international levels have included both over many years: creative thinking through their qualifications, learning and development strategies; innovation in research, benchmarking and conference/training projects. Hindsight, insight and foresight have been the foundation of growth in the pattern of auditing since its conception. Flint (1988)[29] summarised this pattern as follows:

> In no case can an auditor express an opinion or make a report without making an investigation and obtaining evidence. In all audits the pattern of the process is the same and consists in:
>
> (a) identifying the objective of the audit;
> (b) planning the investigation and specifying the evidence to be obtained;
> (c) carrying out the investigation and collecting the evidence;
> (d) evaluating the evidence – pertinent, competent, sufficient; persuasive;
> (e) proceeding to conclusions from the evidence – rational deduction, calculation, comparison;
> (f) exercising judgement on the information obtained;
> (g) formulating the report or opinion.

These elements make up the three distinct stages of the audit process:

1   obtaining, evaluating and drawing conclusions from the evidence
2   exercising judgement
3   reporting.

One can argue that today there are five stages to every audit process. There is one at the beginning, which is the assessment of risks and planning the scope of the audit, and the other at the end, which is a follow up on previous audit recommendations. Either of these can be the weakest part of every audit process.

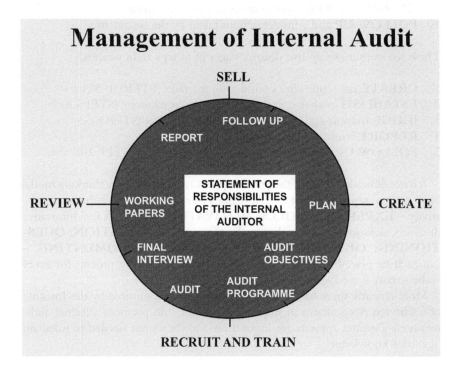

Management of Internal Audit

Figure 1.3 Management of internal audit
Source: J. Ridley (1970)

In the 1970s I saw four stages – CREATE:RECRUIT & TRAIN:REVIEW: SELL – in the management of an eight-step audit process – see Figure 1.3.

Since then, creating a vision and strategies for the audit function linked to professional auditing standards, seeking insight into the area being audited and assessing its risks have all taken a much higher profile: each is now seen as a separate step in the audit process. Consider my following ten.step non-linear process, which can be seen in the processes used by most auditors:

1 **CREATE** the audit **VISION** and **STRATEGY** to motivate excellence, quality and add value and improvement in all auditing processes.
2 **PLAN** each audit engagement over a period of time.
3 seek **INSIGHT** into operations being audited – theory and best practices.
4 assess **RISKS** involved by the operations being audited and the audit.
5 establish **SCOPE** and **OBJECTIVES** for the audit engagement.
6 develop a risk-based audit **PROGRAMME** and identify **CONTROLS**.
7 select **TECHNIQUES/METHODOLOGY** to search for appropriate **EVIDENCE**.
8 objectively evaluate audit **OUTPUTS**, consider **OUTCOMES** and agree **FINDINGS**.

9   **COMMUNICATE** audit findings to those accountable.
10   **FOLLOW-UP** and consider actions taken by the organisation.

These ten steps make up five distinct stages of today's audit process:

1   **CREATE** the scope after considering the risks (STEPS 1–5).
2   **ESTABLISH** evidence, evaluate and draw conclusions (STEPS 6–7).
3   **JUDGE** outputs and outcomes, and agree findings (STEP 8).
4   **REPORT** results of the audit (STEP 9).
5   **FOLLOW-UP** on actions taken by the organisation (STEP 10).

It is not difficult to also see the seven steps of Osborne's creative thinking model in all the ten steps and five stages. Annabile's three components influencing creativity – **EXPERTISE: SKILLS: MOTIVATION** and Torr's five innovative discovery skills mentioned earlier in the chapter – **ASSOCIATION: QUESTIONING: OBSERVING: NETWORKING: EXPERIMENTING** – can each be placed in the ten steps to create the following process for every audit activity – see Figure 1.4.

More recently there has been activity by a group sponsored by the Institute of Chartered Accountants in England and Wales,[30] to promote external auditors with 'a greater appetite for innovation' and the rigour needed to maintain 'specialist knowledge':

> Auditors with a wider vision, a deeper sense of personal accountability and a greater appetite for innovation need support to become professional learners.

---

1   Create the audit vision and strategy to **MOTIVATE** excellence, quality and add value and improvement in the **EXPERTISE** and **SKILLS** needed in all auditing processes.
2   Plan each audit engagement over a period of time.
3   Seek insight into operations being audited – their theory and best practices, through **ASSOCIATION: QUESTIONING: OBSERVING: NETWORKING**.
4   Assess risks involved by the operations being audited and the audit.
5   Establish scope and objectives for the audit engagement.
6   Develop a risk-based audit programme and identify controls.
7   Select techniques/methodology and **EXPERIMENT** to search for appropriate evidence.
8   Objectively evaluate audit outputs, consider outcomes and agree findings.
9   Communicate audit findings to those accountable.
10   Follow-up and consider actions taken by the organisation.

Figure 1.4 Creative thinking and innovation in the Ten Step Audit Process

Source: J. Ridley (2016)

Rigour of course needs to be maintained in terms of specialist knowledge, but, in the long term, it is the learning skills of tomorrow's doctors, architects and accountants that will be critical. We believe that education and training for audit should become much broader. To deliver a more enlightened profession, new skills, capabilities and attitudes will be essential, some of which may feel alien to professionals schooled in harder-edged disciplines.

As part of their learning programmes, all auditors need to continuously improve. Continuous improvement is more than qualification and training of staff, correction of weak methods or rectification of mistakes: it is about paradigm shifts to increase the value of the service to all, from the board down to operations level, across all supply chains, including suppliers and customers and other stakeholders. Continuous improvement is part of all quality management programmes; so is creative thinking and innovation.

In 2001,[31] I wrote on the 'variety and depth of knowledge and expertise required' to be an internal auditor, ending with the following, which applies to all auditors:

> Knowledge management will always be key to creativity and innovation in all sciences. Whether you view internal auditing as a profession, science or art, or none of these, there is no doubt that it requires wisdom and well-managed knowledge to add value in all the services it provides. Knowledge not just of the organisation, but also knowledge that is available outside the organisation. There are many roles for internal auditors to occupy in knowledge management, as a user, as a communicator and a provider of assurance. Roles that now require wise internal auditors to have the knowledge to be not only good auditors, but also to be good teachers and consultants.

Using metaphors to explore and name the behavioural relations and actions of auditors is not new. In the famous legal case *Kingston Cotton Mills Co.* (1896), Lord Justice Lopes defined an auditor as a watchdog and not a detective or bloodhound, and duty of care as follows:

> It is the duty of an auditor to bring to bear on the work he has to perform that skill, care and caution which a reasonably careful, cautious auditor would use. What is reasonable skill, care and caution must depend on the particular circumstances of each case. An auditor is not bound to be a detective, or, as was said to approach his work with suspicion, or with a foregone conclusion that there is something wrong. He is a watchdog, not a bloodhound. He is justified in believing tried servants of the company in whom confidence is placed by the company. He is entitled to assume that they are honest and rely upon their representations, provided he takes reasonable care.

Metaphors defining the role and standards of the company external auditor role during the 20th century caused considerable debate and still do today, although many legal cases of fraud have followed in the English courts, and today an auditor is expected to have an enquiring sceptical mind – not suspicious of dishonesty, but suspecting that there can be mistakes or even fraud. Following the global financial crisis in 2008, the UK Financial Reporting Council (FRC)[32] debated a proposition that all company external auditors should apply 'an appropriate degree of professional scepticism when auditing financial institutions and other sectors' – 'sceptics' is another name for all auditors; see Chapter 8.

- **The Good Guys** – Good guys, guys/gals in white hats, positive asset, considerate, honest fair, integrity, auditor's first name.
- **Helpers** – Advisor, helper, here to help people and the organisation, independent assistant, independent in-house consultant, trainer, management trainer, human resource developer, counsellor, mentor, listener, friend.
- **Team Players** – Co-worker, associate, partner, cooperative, management team member, team player.
- **Idea People and Change Agents** – Imaginative, the good idea people, the better idea people, creative, innovator, change catalyst, change agent, initiator, leader.
- **Management Resources** – Management representative, management tool, valuable tool, management resource, management's right hand, management's eyes and ears, management consultant, consultant to senior management, audit committee arms, management facilitator, ombudsman.
- **Guardians** – Safety net, watchdog, back stop, guard dog, fiscal guardian angel, corporate guardian, security blanket, deterrent, troubleshooter, conscience of the organisation, corporate monitor.
- **Control and Efficiency Experts** – Cost saver, efficiency expert, internal control consultant, compliance clerk, compliance officer, control expert, expeditor, operation reviewer, reviewer, system reviewer, quality control, professional reviewer, evaluator, checker of financial systems.
- **Information Specialists** – Truth seeker, super sleuth, fact finder, accurate information gatherer, objective reviewer, objective, factual, reporter, communicator, info provider, the company library, our expert, politics/procedures expert, expertise, operations expert, financial systems expert, analyst, problem solver, knowledgeable, competent, thorough, specialist, jack of all trades.
- **Business Professionals** – Businessman, professional, real world, hard worker, aggressive, balanced, respected, auditor.

Figure 1.5 Names internal auditors found pleasing for their service in 1989

Source: Roles and Relationships of Internal Auditing (1989 p. 75), Donna J. Wood and James A. Wilson, The Institute of Internal Auditors Research Foundation, Orlando, US.

Research by Wood and Wilson (1989)[33] into the roles and behaviours of internal auditors strongly influenced my own approach to auditing, both practice and academic. Metaphors at that time for the internal auditor showed how varied the perceptions internal auditors had of their roles, not dissimilar to today, to the perceptions all auditors have of their roles – see Figure 1.5, which shows the names chosen in 1989 by internal auditors for their services. Although not used by me in the metaphors I have chosen for my book, there are not surprisingly many links between the nine themes for the metaphors listed and mine. I am sure readers will see these links in the auditing services they provide today. Note the theme 'Idea People and Change Agents' and its associated metaphors!

1.5 Framework for Creative Thinking and Innovation in Governance

Take a triangle and a circle, add arrows and you have a Corporate Governance Framework. Creating a framework for innovation in governance must be around the main themes that underlie the governance of every organisation. In the 1970s I experimented with this as an internal audit manager. At that time I created an Audit Quality Framework with an interlocking triangle of lines surrounding a circle representing the principles in total quality management – each line touching the circle – see Figure 1.6. This framework represented my management of internal auditing as a professional service, with a wide scope of responsibilities.

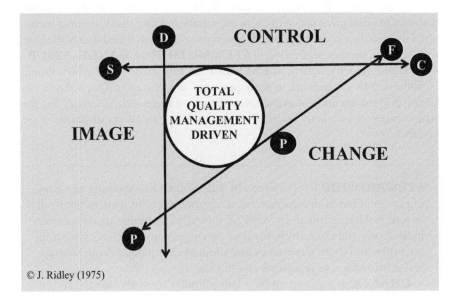

Figure 1.6 Audit quality framework 1975

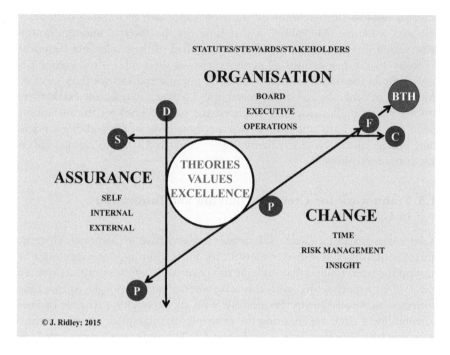

Figure 1.7 Creative thinking and innovation governance framework

Over the years I developed the same framework structure to represent the maturity of good governance in every organisation. These needs are now recognised today in law and every code of governance now published. Today the lines represent the themes underlying – **STEWARDSHIP: CHANGE: ASSURANCE** and the achievement of **EXCELLENCE** in each – all of which should be addressed by all auditors in their practices and processes. This today is my Creative Thinking and Innovation Governance Framework, necessary for the achievement of excellent governance and auditing in all organisations – see Figure 1.7.

STEWARDSHIP is represented by a horizontal line showing the 'duty of care' required in all organisations: a care, not just to its owners, but to all its stakeholders, across all its SUPPLY CHAINS. Stewards are responsible individually and collectively for how an organisation operates within its own rules and those imposed by any adopted external standards, contractual relationships, its regulators and the law.

CHANGE is represented by a line pointing upwards into the future. This represents the importance of recognising time in the assessment and management of risk in organisation – PAST: PRESENT: FUTURE – in all decision-making at all levels and reporting of performances against key indicators. It also represents the importance of a continuous research into what lies in the future and BEYOND THE HORIZON.

ASSURANCE is represented by a vertical line pointing downwards showing the importance of depth in assurances covering all operations in an organisation at all levels. Important in all decision making in an organisation, whether from self-assurance, self-assessment, supervision, management, independent internal auditors, external auditors, regulators, inspectors and so forth. How these assurances are provided by structures, skills, delegation, employment, appraisal and control creates an assurance map every organisation should understand and keep up to date.

EXCELLENCE is represented by a circle touching each of the other components. This circle represents the team(s) in every organisation, within and across all functions and all levels, not just starting with the board but including engagements with all the organisation's stakeholders. These teams are responsible for the seven components of excellence[34] from which the added values an organisation makes can be created – Strategy, Structure, Systems, Staff, Skills and Style – all interlinked and focused on Shared Values.

EFMD (2005 p. 19)[35] and the UN Global Compact report on globally responsible leadership in governance recognise the importance of creativity as a purpose in every business:

> The core of corporate action is creativity. Observe successful companies over the medium or longer term, and you will notice one thing that they share: pulled by daring leadership, many have adapted, renewed and/or transformed themselves, proving their capacity to act creatively. Creativity is a concrete blend of human commitments and qualitative realities. These can include a clearly stated and widely shared vision; the willingness to take risks and face up to uncertainty; listening and learning; the weaving of strong relationship networks; the patient build-up of diversified approaches; the productive management of tensions and efforts; the recruitment and shaping of competent teams and leadership at all levels. Instruction or training may enhance creativity, but only in a highly supportive environment that encourages individual initiative, trial and error, risk taking and learning from both positive and negative experiences. Given that many of the most creative impulses arise from distress, ambiguity and uncertainty, the challenge of enabling such thresholds in a learning and development environment is not to be underestimated.

This statement carries so many messages for the management of creativity in organisations and all auditors. Its themes will be seen in many of the following chapters.

1.6 Chapter Review

In this chapter I have touched on what science believes makes creativity and innovation happen and how this is seen to occur in management and auditing. Today there are bookshelves of writings and books on this science. I have introduced the reader to a small sample of these. Creativity and innovation are covered in many, if not most, academic and training programmes across the world. Each will continue to be researched, taught and practiced by scientists, academics, consultants and others. They are both an essential part of all auditing and have been since it began and developed as a profession. Auditing today and tomorrow at all levels of an organisation, across all supply chains and including all stakeholders. I have approached each through my own imaginative and interactive governance Framework of **STEWARDSHIP, CHANGE, ASSURANCE** and **EXCELLENCE**, encouraging the reader to do the same. I end this chapter with three Creative Audit Thinking Activities for every auditor to consider as a step to developing their creative audit thinking in the auditing services they provide.

1.7 Introduction to the Following Chapters

The following chapters take the theories and exciting practices and creative thinking in this chapter to where and how creative thinking and innovation can lead all auditors to the cutting edge of their professions and practices. They are structured around the four interacting themes – **STEWARDSHIP: CHANGE: ASSURANCE** and **EXCELLENCE** – already discussed, which need to be addressed by all auditors in their practices and processes.

To start the reader's and my creative thinking process, each chapter focuses on a metaphor for the auditor of significant importance for all auditing. I have chosen each metaphor as being relevant to today and tomorrow's auditing: these are how all auditors should creatively think of themselves in all their audit engagements. Throughout my book I include articles I have written and published during the past forty years – articles which at the time they were published forecast many creative thinking and innovative thoughts for the future of all auditing, and still are relevant for today and tomorrow. At the end of each chapter there are more Creative Audit Thinking Activities relating to the theme of the chapter.

PART I STEWARDSHIP

I discuss the importance of stewardship in every organisation and its responsibility to be 'good' and fight 'evil' in today and tomorrow's economic, environmental and social world of laws, regulations and values at national and international levels across the globe.

PART II CHANGE

I discuss the importance of time in an organisation for every audit and auditor, be it the past, present, future or beyond the horizon. The auditor in every audit engagement travels through time during each audit question and evaluation of evidence.

PART III ASSURANCE

I discuss the added value of independent and objective assurance by auditors at board, executive and operations levels, and how this is achieved for the satisfaction of all an organisation's stakeholders.

PART IV EXCELLENCE

I discuss how excellence is achievable through passion and a commitment to best practices in an organisation by the creation of shared values in its vision, mission, policies, procedures, decision-making and actions.

Epilogue

I conclude with a signpost of directions for every auditor in the 21st century.

1.8 Creative Audit Thinking Activities

Activity 1   Study Creativity and Innovation

In my book *Cutting Edge Internal Auditing*, I included a case study titled *Why Study Creativity? – Here Are Twelve Solid Reasons*, written by Professor Gerard J. Puccio PhD,[36] Chair, International Centre for Studies in

Creativity, Buffalo State University of New York. The case was prefaced by the following:

> The scientific study of creativity has enjoyed a more than fifty-year history. The list below provides a summary of some of the main reasons why this field of study has drawn the attention of researchers, practitioners and teachers.

All twelve of the professor's 'reasons' are fundamental for the creative thinking in this book and the creative thinking all auditors must possess. They relate to all aspects of auditing from the creation of knowledge and understanding through leadership and learning, to the solving of problems, using resources effectively and discovering better ways of efficiently achieving objectives. They provide a summary of the main reasons why this field of study has drawn the attention of researchers, practitioners and teachers: has it drawn the attention of all auditors?

List your solid reasons for studying Creativity and Innovation in Auditing

Consider the following letter I recently wrote to the *Financial Times* in the United Kingdom in response to an opinion article on the poor value of external financial auditing to organisations and their stakeholders. How does your study of creativity and innovation in auditing contribute to the quality of external financial auditing in the context of today and tomorrow's corporate governance needs in all developing economies?

> Dear Sir,
>   Ewan Brown's (Loosen the straightjacket of a compulsory audit – 24th April 2017) raises many governance issues, not just concerning independent external and internal audit, but also the role of audit committees in monitoring all aspects of governance – nationally and internationally across their organisations' supply chains. Audit committees with independent board members, and in some outside consultants, exist today at board level in all sizes of organisations across all sectors. They are important monitors of auditors and assurances from executive teams and many other compliance functions. Some regulators now see audit committees as extensions of their regulatory arms and place significant importance on their role, reporting and effectiveness. In this century audit committees at board level are becoming 'the self-regulators' of organisations and as such fit well into Mr. Ewan's proposal for loosening the straightjacket of compulsory audit, but only if their effectiveness improves.

Too many audit committees today are not required to monitor and challenge all aspects of governance in their terms of reference – many still do not report directly to their organisation's stakeholders on their performance. Many internal audit functions do not report directly to their audit committees and/or boards to increase their independence as recommended by the Chartered Institute of Internal Auditors. How many audit committees question and challenge the quality practices of all their assurance providers? There are still many improvements to be made to the role of audit committees in the United Kingdom, if not internationally.

This year the Institute of Chartered Secretaries and Administrators (The Governance Institute)[37] published recommended revised model Terms of Reference guidance for audit committees. All audit committee members and their boards would do well to benchmark their own TOR against this. For many there will be gaps. All audit committees should have one or more independent members who are not board members; all audit committees should monitor and challenge the governance practices in their organisations at all levels and across all their supply chains. All internal auditors should independently report directly to their organisation's audit committee and/or board on their evaluation of governance, risk management and control. All audit committees should report their performance and results throughout the financial year direct to their organisation's stakeholders. Only then should we consider loosening the straightjacket of compulsory audit.

Jeffrey Ridley FCIA FIIA
Visiting Professor of Corporate Governance Assurance
University of Lincoln
Published in *Financial Times* 5th May 2017

Activity 2 Enlightening Professions Are Creative and Innovative

Read the following executive summary from *Enlightening Professions? A Vision for Audit and a Better Society* (2014), a joint research project by the RSA's Action Research Centre and AuditFutures, a thought leadership programme of ICAEW, run in partnership with Finance Innovation Lab (co-convened by ICAEW and WWF-UK). Regardless of your auditing or assurance profession, consider how many new metaphors for auditing are mentioned in or related to the views expressed in this research and forward thinking. List at least five. Reflect creatively on these as you read the following chapters and innovate in your practices and processes.

Executive summary

A future characterised by unprecedented organisational and informational complexity across business and public services, and where the public will demand more transparency, will need a body of people skilled at removing opacity in the service of the public interest. Yet the profession that could provide this service – the audit profession – is caught in controversies, and labouring within technical and defensive debates.

Following the financial crisis, and a series of scandals, the audit profession finds itself in the dock alongside a financial sector whose reckless self-interest plunged much of the world into deep and long recession. Many in the profession feel wounded or irritated by what they regard as guilt through association and misunderstanding. Nevertheless, at precisely the point in its history when the profession needs to be conducting a searching and candid conversation with itself and wider society that could redefine its value in preparation for, and in service of tomorrow's world, it lacks the confidence and voice needed to reach out and move forward.

As currently constituted, audit assesses and reports on a system of business and finance that no longer enjoys broad social confidence, and reports on it in a variety of ways that miss the big picture. Political and social demands have changed, and so too have the demands of modern business. Audit's foundation stone – the statutory financial statement audit – risks being swept aside by events. The retrospective assurance of a clean audit report on historic and dated information in the annual report buys relatively little confidence in a business world where fortunes can fluctuate overnight on the basis of a tweet or a negative news story, and shareholding periods are measured in days, not months or years.

Audit is a service that can provide form and structure to the trust that business and society need to operate. That trust is bruised, as is trust in numerous established professions whose claims on knowledge and authority are fraying as a result of massive changes to information technology and social attitudes. Audit has been particularly disadvantaged by the fact that the benefits it generates for business owners or the wider public have often been hard to pin down. As a preventative service – a health check conducted with quiet diligence outside of public view – it has too often been known through its failures, or the failures of its client organisations.

To win back the public trust, audit faces the challenge of re-envisaging its service through its primary purpose. Audit is largely a publicly mandated service, designed by government to support a public good; and this is the case whether audit is being performed on a private corporate or a public authority. It is a public service, and the auditor should recognise him or herself as a public servant working in the public interest.

An elusive and messy concept, the public interest cannot be seized simply through regulations and tests. It can only be realised in ongoing dialogue. Audit can become exemplary in this regard. Instead of an audit report being a trust-producing *product*, the audit process should become a trust-producing *practice* in which the auditor uses his or her position as a trusted intermediary to broker evidence based learning across all dimensions of the organisation and its stakeholders, and bring into consideration all aspects of the organisation's value – economic, social and environmental. From being a service consisting almost exclusively of external investigation by a warranted professional, modern technology will allow auditing to become more co-productive, with the auditor's role expanding to include that of an expert convenor willing to share the tools of enquiry.

The auditor as convenor will need new skills, and will need to work in a more agile and interdisciplinary environment. Technical rigour will need to be maintained through training and professional support, but qualities like empathy, imagination and moral reasoning should be an increasingly important part of the training and support package. The auditor of the future will be a multidisciplinary team member, operating within and between companies as the market takes on the form of flexible platforms and innovative start-ups.

Activity 3　Audit Artists Are Creative and Innovative

The same skills used by artists, such as line, tone, colour, perspective, scale and composition, can be used by auditors to create the final results from their audit engagements. Encouraging creative auditing using the artist's rules improves the performance of audit work. It develops a divine discontent with what is seen and opens new paths for problem solving. Consider these skills and how they can be interpreted into your next audit.

Creativity and Inspiration Are Essential for the Artist Auditor[38]

Consider how I have interpreted the artist's creative skills into the ten steps of the audit process. Improve on my interpretation and try each in your next audit engagement:

Line

Line starts with the audit survey. A time when the internal auditor can be fluent and expressive; a time of high imagination. Background information about the activities to be audited starts the drawing process and links loose lines into a pattern of audit objectives to achieve the audit scope. Lines establish plans.

Tone

All objects are intrinsically light and dark. There are many tones between white and black. Knowledge is the internal auditor's tone. Once the survey lines of the audit are planned, the levels of knowledge required for the audit must be set. Knowledge provides atmosphere and interest. Like tone the right levels of knowledge in the audit team will attract those being served by the audit.

Colour

There is no colour without light. Colour is closely linked to tone. The internal auditor's choice of audit tests establishes the colour palette for the picture audit. Creative skill is needed in mixing the tests so that they focus light into all of the audit objectives and complement each other. Just as it is very easy to end up with a muddy colour palette, it is also very easy to end an audit with 'muddy' objectives if the mix of tests is not right.

Scale

Objects in themselves have no scale – they can only be small or large scale in relation to something else. Audit scale is size in relation to the risks for the organization as a whole and not just for the activities being audited. Risk assessment provides scale for the audit. To be creative during risk assessment requires the process to continue from the organization level through the audit objectives to the selection of audit tests and review of the results.

Perspective

Perspective is the three-dimensional reality of the world created by leading lines to viewing points. Each line in the audit must lead to a viewing point. Not all viewing points are within the activities being audited. The creative internal auditor looks for viewing points in other parts of the organization and frequently leads lines to viewing points outside the organization.

Composition

The arrangement of an audit has to attract those it is serving. A picture with poor composition will fail to find a buyer. The composition of the audit report must [like a painting] lead the customer's eyes into its subject matter and keep interest throughout the viewing.

For further reinforcement on the power of the artist to be creative and innovative, see the 12 March 2016 article in the *Financial Times*: 'Japan's Executives swap pens for pastels' (p. 12), referring to www.whiteship.net and its corporate programmes – *Unlocking the capacities of individuals – the power to create answers.*

Notes

1 *All Our Futures: Creativity and Cultural Education* (1997 p. 30), Report of National Advisory Committee on Creative and Cultural Education, UK Government.
2 *Nurturing Creativity in Young People* (2006), Paul Roberts, Department for Culture, Media and Sport, UK Government.
3 *Government Response to Paul Roberts' Report on Nurturing Creativity in Young People* (2006), Department for Education and Skills, UK Government.
4 *A Theory of Human Motivation* (2013), Abraham H. Maslow, Black Curtain Press, United Kingdom.
5 *A Whole New Mind* (2005), Daniel H. Pink, Penguin Group, New York, US.
6 *Managing Creative People* (2008 pp. 108–109 and 216–225), Gordon Torr, John Wiley and Sons, Ltd, Chichester, England.
7 *Applied Imagination* (2001), Alex F. Osborne, Creative Education Foundation Press, New York, US.
8 *Creativity in Context* (1996), Teresa M. Annabile, Mary Ann Collins and Conti Regina, Westview Press, New York, US.
9 *Guide to the Management Gurus – Shortcuts to the Ideas of Leading Management Thinkers* (1991), Carol Kennedy, Century Business, Random House UK Ltd, London, England.
10 *Management Tools – An Executive's Guide* (2015 p. 40), Darrell K. Rigby, Bain and Company Inc., Boston, US.
11 *The Fifth Discipline – The Art & Practice of the Learning Organisation* (1990 p. 9), Peter M. Senge, Bantam Dell Doubleday Publishing Group Inc., US.
12 *What Is Success* (1997), published in Internal Auditing (April 1997 pp. 22–23), IIA-UK and Ireland and as a case study in *Leading Edge Internal Auditing* (1998 pp. 172–176), Jeffrey Ridley and Andrew Chambers, ICSA Publishing, London, England.
13 *Launching Your Organisation into an Actionable Future* (2010), Ira Levin, Institute of Chartered Accountants England and Wales – included in Finance and Management Faculty Special Report *Developing a Vision for Your Business* containing a series of articles by different authors, London, England.
14 *Creative Management* (1991 p. XI). Edited by Jane Henry, Published in association with The Open University, Sage Publications, London, England.
15 *Cutting Edge Internal Auditing* (2008), Jeffrey Ridley, John Wiley and Sons Ltd., Chichester, England.

16 *Creativity and Perception in Management* (2001 pp. 71–86), Jane Henry, Open University Business School, Sage Publications, London, England.
17 *Innovation Nation* (2008), White Paper presented to UK Parliament by Department of Innovation, Universities and Skills, London, England.
18 *Competing in the Global Economy – The Innovation Challenge* (2003) The Department of Trade and Industry, London, England.
19 www.compete.org/explore/drieve-innovation-entreprer, accessed 10 October 2012.
20 *Making Impact – Annual Report 2014–2015* (2015 p. 14), Council on Competitiveness, Washington, US.
21 *Innovation Strategy* (2010 p. 4), Organisation for Economic and Co-operation Development, Paris, France. www.oecd.org.
22 *Innovation Strategy – An Agenda for Policy Action* (2015) Organisation for Economic Co-operation and Development, Paris, France. www.oecd.org.
23 *Strategic Plan 2011–16* (2011), Supreme International Organisation of Supreme Audit Institutions, Vienna, Austria.
24 *Achieving Innovation in Central Government Departments* (2006 p. 26), National Audit Office, London, England.
25 *Innovation Across Central Government* (2009 p. 47), National Audit Office, London, England.
26 *The Creative Side of Internal Auditing* (1992 pp. 57–62), Lawrence B. Sawyer, Internal Auditor, December, The Institute of Internal Auditors Inc., Orlando, US.
27 *Chambers' Corporate Governance Handbook* (2014 6th Edition), Professor Andrew Chambers, Bloomsbury Professional Ltd., Haywards Heath, England.
28 *Leading Edge Internal Auditing* (1998), Jeffrey Ridley and Andrew Chambers, ICSA Publishing, London, England.
29 *Philosophy and Principles of Auditing* (1988 p. 102), David Flint, McMillan Education Ltd., Basingstoke, England.
30 *Enlightening Professions?* (2014), Institute of Chartered Accountants in England and Wales, London, England.
31 *Wise Internal Auditors Manage Knowledge Well* (2001) Internal Control Issue 47, ABG Professional Information, London, England.
32 *Auditor Scepticism: Raising the Bar – Feedback Paper* (2011 p. 1), Financial Reporting Council, London, England.
33 *Roles and Relationships in Internal Auditing* (1989 pp. 73–75), The Institute of Internal Auditors Research Foundation, Orlando, US.
34 *In Search of Excellence* (1982), Thomas J. Peters and Robert H. Waterman Jr., Harper and Row Publishers New York, US.
35 *Globally Responsible Leadership – A Call for Engagement* (2005 p. 19), European Foundation for Management Development and The UN Global Compact, Brussels, Belgium.
36 *Why Study Creativity?* (1995), Professor G.J. Puccio (1995 pp. 49–56), Copley Publishers, Acton, MA, US.
37 *Guidance Note: Terms of Reference for the Audit Committee* (2017), Institute of Chartered Secretaries and Administrators, London, England.
38 *Creativity and Inspiration Are Essential for the Artist Auditor* (1995 p. 12), published in the Internal Auditing Journal (March 1995), Chartered Institute of Internal Auditors, London, England.

Part I

Stewardship

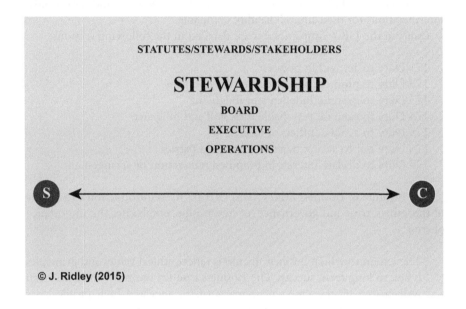

STATUTES/STEWARDS/STAKEHOLDERS

STEWARDSHIP

BOARD

EXECUTIVE

OPERATIONS

© J. Ridley (2015)

Trust and integrity play an essential role in economic life.[1]

In Part I I address the importance of the duty of care associated with good **STEWARDSHIP** in an organisation at **BOARD:EXECUTIVE:OPERATIONS** levels across all its **SUPPLY CHAINS**. Today's corporate governance is based on the **RULE OF LAW** and its regulation, engaging with all an organisation's **STAKEHOLDERS**. I discuss the values of life in good stewardship, which we all take for granted and too often find missing from what we observe in the cultures and behaviours of all within organisations. These values are at the heart of all corporate governance codes and charters in nations across the globe.

Stewardship Is All About Ethics, Trust and Compliance

Corporate governance is all about ethics, trust and compliance. How ethics, trust and compliance are led and perceived in any organisation by its stakeholders is of paramount importance for its reputation. In the United Kingdom, the Companies Act 2006 does not use the term 'stewardship' for the responsibilities of directors in the companies in which they are appointed. It uses the term 'duties' based 'on certain common law rules and equitable principles as they apply in relation to directors and have effect in place of those rules and principles as regards the duties owed to a company by a director': *duties* echoing the 'ethics, trust and compliance' of stewardship and how these should be reported to a company's stakeholders. Most governments across the world have similar interpretations for their limited liability companies.

Duties in the UK Companies Act are detailed in the following sections:

171 Duty to act within powers
172 Duty to promote the success of the company
173 Duty to exercise independent judgment
174 Duty to exercise reasonable care, skill and diligence
175 Duty to avoid conflicts of interest
176 Duty not to accept benefits from third parties
177 Duty to declare interest in proposed transaction or arrangement.

The Institute of Business Ethics (IBE) (2013),[2] in its introduction to a review of the 'ethics, trust and governance' of stewardship, emphasises the importance of trust:

> The extent to which business decisions reflect ethical values and principles is key to long term success. The Business case for business ethics has been well proven by the costs and impacts of the repeated high profile cases of corporate greed and misconduct, often by senior individuals crossing ethical boundaries as well as ignoring or circumventing the rules set out in law. Trust is essential in establishing an organisation's licence to operate. Maintaining successful business relationships and operations requires businesses to manage their risks, including their integrity risks, and guard their reputations. Trustworthiness is a valuable asset and guarding that trust asset is a core remit for those running a company; it is a core remit of good governance.

In its concluding remarks to this review, The IBE recognises 'business ethics, sustainability and social responsibility, and also tomorrow's ethics as characterising the right way to run a business as well as being essential for long-term success'. Such recognition is also included in the recently required strategic reporting by quoted companies registered in Great Britain:[3]

(7) In the case of a quoted company the strategic report must, to the extent necessary for an understanding of the development, performance or position of the company's business, include –

    (a) the main trends and factors likely to affect the future development, performance and position of the company's business, and

    (b) information about –

        (i) environmental matters (including the impact of the company's business on the environment),

        (ii) the company's employees, and

        (iii) social, community and human rights issues, including information about any policies of the company in relation to those matters and the effectiveness of those policies.

Embedding sustainability issues in an organisation is now seen at both national and international levels as an essential part of 'ethics, trust and compliance' in every organisation. In the United Kingdom, His Royal Highness Prince Charles recognised this in the establishment of his Accounting for Sustainability Project established in 2006.[4] Later, in reporting on this project, His Highness promoted recognition of the role at board and senior management levels for urgency in this action and the contribution possible by audit:

> **Board and senior management commitment**. Senior management needs to be committed to the process of embedding sustainability. In particular the Chief Executive needs to show urgency in both action and message. Only when the enthusiasm and motivation comes from the top will sustainability become an essential and unquestioned part of an organisation's procedures. Larger organisations often establish a Board committee to identify and address environmental and social issues, which might otherwise be marginalised during a full Board meeting. Another option is to broaden the scope of more traditional standing committees to include sustainability, for example the audit committee.

Over recent years, at international levels, this same commitment to the process of embedding sustainability and audit is included in a number of reports by the UN Global Reporting Initiative over recent years. At an internal audit conference in 2013, I a ran a workshop comparing internal auditors to butterflies, using the tiger, peacock, gamekeeper, copper and skipper butterflies as metaphors, emphasising the importance of butterflies (and internal auditors) to sustainability of the planet. Delegates were asked to vote as to which butterfly they thought they were; not surprisingly, all were chosen from the group – a mix of interesting and challenging metaphors!

    The United Nations Global Compact[5] defines 'sustainability' as encompassing 'environmental, social and corporate governance issues, as embodied' in its

Ten Principles (see Appendix A), covering 'areas of human rights, labour, the environment and anti-corruption', derived from its Universal Declaration of Human Rights and:

• the International Labour Organisation's Declaration on Fundamental Principles and Rights at Work
• the Rio Declaration on Environment and Development
• the United Nations Convention Against Corruption.

This definition and principles should influence 'ethics, trust and compliance' in governance, risk and control practices in every organisation, at board, management and operational levels. To be at the cutting edge of their profession every auditor should address sustainability of their organisation and the planet in every audit engagement. In 2015, I wrote the following on measuring sustainability and the need for internal auditors to contribute to its achievement. The following is an extract from that article, which applies to all auditors:

Measuring Sustainability[6]

Maintaining a socially responsible approach to business plays an integral part in the operations of many of today's most successful organizations. In fact, whereas sustainable business practices may have once been viewed largely as an obligation, they are now central to organizational success.

The United Nations Global Compact defines sustainability as encompassing "environmental, social, and corporate governance issues" as embodied in its Ten Principles, which covers human rights, labour, the environment, and anti-corruption. With each passing year, it becomes more and more important for internal auditors to be involved in sustainability and to help ensure effectiveness in this critical area. Stewardship and safeguarding assets have long been key to assessing risk and helping manage an organization's resources. To be at the cutting edge of our profession requires addressing sustainability strategies in every internal audit engagement.

This level of commitment to sustainability requires pioneering and developing new paths in professional internal audit services. Sustainability is key to the economy, effectiveness, and efficiency of an organization achieving its objectives and to the communication relationships with all its stakeholders. In this century, more than ever before, the integration of sustainability into financial and management reporting has become a requirement in law and a priority in performance management dashboards – and sustainability assurance is essential for an organization's reputation.

Sustainability is also an essential part of an organization's governance, risk management, and control, across all its supply chains – internal and external, national, and global. It should be guided by an organization's social and environmental policies, and it should satisfy the U.N.'s 10 Principles, which aims to help organizations adopt socially responsible practices. Each policy should have a direct bearing on the organization's entire decision making at board, management, and operational levels.

Over the past decade, corporate focus on sustainability has increased in almost every country in the world, driven not only by international organizations, institutes, and governments, but also many professions and standard makers. The Committee of Sponsoring Organizations of the Treadway Commission (COSO) (www.coso.org), for example, linked sustainability to the components of its enterprise risk management framework in the 2013 COSO thought paper, Demystifying Sustainability Risk.

Sustainability is also an essential part of an organisation's governance, risk management and control, across all its supply chains, internal and external, national and global. It should be guided by an organisation's social and environmental policies, which satisfy the UN ten principles: each policy should have a direct bearing on its entire decision-making at board, management and operational levels. Sustainability is key to the economy, effectiveness and efficiency of an organisation achieving its objectives and communication relationships with all its stakeholders. In this century, more than ever before, its integration into financial and management reporting has become a requirement in law and priority in all performance management dashboards. Sustainability assurance is now essential for an organisation's reputation.

Today, sustainability of the planet and its assurance is well-recognised, still developing, increasingly being integrated into the risks associated with economic, efficient and effective results. COSO[7] has now linked sustainability into the components in its ERM framework with a thought-provoking paper, providing tips on how to integrate both and the competitive advantages of doing so.

Since 2005 the focus on sustainability has increased in almost every country in the world, driven not only by international organisations, institutes and governments, but also many professions and standard makers.

How creative thinking and innovation is encouraged and contributes through auditing to 'ethics, trust and compliance' is of paramount importance to stewardship in every organisation. Today the values of corporate governance are taking on a new profile through the focus of attention on conduct, behaviour and culture in organisations. In my inaugural lecture[8] at the University of Lincoln in 2014, I talked of the values of life and how these are seen in 'ethics, trust and compliance' in today's economic and government cultures. What follows is a summary of that lecture:

Values of Life

It will never be sufficient just to have a code of conduct representing the values of life in an organisation. These values must be seen as an essential part of its performance. Seen by 'all', both in and outside the organisation. A governing body must also have assurance that its values are being complied with at all times and in all decision-making. In the UK Corporate Governance Code (2014),[9] the Preface emphasises importance of the 'tone at the top' and its link to performance – 'The directors should lead by example and ensure that good standards of behaviour permeate throughout all levels of the organisation. This will help prevent misconduct, unethical practices and support the delivery of long-term success.'

Much has been written of late on the importance of beliefs and values in the cultures governing bodies create in their organisations and in some cases the lack of these. Corporate governance is all about conduct and establishing trust in and between organisations. Strengthening trust in the corporate system was at the heart of Sir Adrian Cadbury's (1992)[10] corporate governance report for listed companies. Reflected in his committee's definition of governance – to direct and control – and the principles of Accountability, Integrity and Transparency on which his Code of Best Practice is based. His views on the importance of codes of conduct in business practices and their communication internally and externally also underpin all his recommendations and subsequent codes of governance worldwide.

In November last year the importance of code of conducts in governance of organisations was re-emphasised in published draft recommended changes by the Organisation for Economic and Co-operative Development to its 2004[11] international corporate governance principles and guide. These changes include advice on ensuring an effective ethics and compliance programme is established and an involvement of the audit committee in this assurance. Such ethics and compliance to include measures **'covering securities, competition, taxation, human rights, and work and safety conditions.'**

Lord Bew, in his capacity as chairman of the Committee on Standards in Public Life, recently reinforced awareness of the ethical responsibilities of everyone in public life and their need to act as **'ethical leaders'**: *a reminder of Lord Nolan's[12] seven principles of public life first published in 1995. These principles of –* **Selflessness, Integrity, Objectivity, Accountability, Openness, Honesty and Leadership** *– pattern well those of Cadbury in 1992. There can be little argument against their choice as a requirement at all levels in every governed body. One focus of his committee's 2014 report[13] to the Prime Minister was to highlight the need for induction programmes for all those in public life* **'whether employed, appointed or elected'** *to include an understanding of ethical awareness. This wide embrace of 'all' reflects many of the culture concerns today in governed bodies at all levels and worldwide.*

There is research evidence today of established codes of conduct based on life's ethics and values in many organisations across all sectors today. This is more prevalent than twenty years ago. Such codes are promoted and seen by many through organisation communications and the internet. Yet, the same research provides evidence codes of conduct and communications are still not in all governed bodies.

Beliefs and values are becoming of increased importance in governance and reporting as organisations worldwide move into a new style of communicating integrated reports of ethical behaviours in their financial, social and environmental capitals, strategies and practices. This is clearly evident in the following statement, published by the International Integrated Reporting Council (IIRC) (2013)[14] as part of the development of its Integrated (IR) Framework:

Accountability is closely associated with the concept of stewardship and the responsibility of an organisation to care for, or use responsibly, the capitals that its activities and outputs affect. When the capitals are owned by the organisation, a stewardship responsibility is imposed on management and those charged with governance via their legal responsibilities to the organisation. When the capitals are owned by others or not owned at all, stewardship

responsibilities may be imposed by law or regulation (e.g., through a contract with the owners, or through labour laws or environmental protection regulations). When there is no legal stewardship responsibility, the organisation may have an ethical responsibility to accept, or choose to accept stewardship responsibilities and be guided in doing so by stakeholder expectations.

Table A.1 supports the choice of my references and text to describe stewardship and explain its importance in governance and auditing. Using 21 key stewardship word/terms from the preceding text (shown in alphabetical order), I have content analysed recently published United Kingdom Annual Reports from five organisations: one from manufacturing, one from finance, one from charity, one from health and one from an auditing profession. In each case, all of the words (or word/terms of a similar meaning) are used in their text to describe their good stewardship, though the number of times varies for each. I have highlighted the top six word/terms: CARE, COMPLIANCE, CUSTOMERS, GOVERNANCE, LEADERSHIP and TRUST. Commitment to each of these 21 word/terms is key to the success of every organisation and all auditing.

Interestingly, the term 'stewardship' is rarely used, though its meaning is represented by many of the other terms. Try the same exercise in organisation and auditing statements in your own organisation and country. What will it tell you about attitudes to and perceptions of good stewardship? Study all these terms

Table A.1 Stewardship content analysis of five annual reports (2015)

	Industry	Finance	Charity	Health	Profess
Part I					
Stewardship					
Accountability	Y	Y	Y	Y	Y
Behaviour	Y	Y	Y	Y	Y
Beliefs	Y	Y	Y	Y	Y
Care	Y	Y	Y	Y	Y
Compliance	Y	Y	Y	Y	Y
Culture	Y	Y	Y	Y	Y
Customer	Y	Y	Y	Y	Y
Duty	Y	Y	Y	Y	Y
Ethics	Y	Y	Y	Y	Y
Governance	Y	Y	Y	Y	Y
Law	Y	Y	Y	Y	Y
Leadership	Y	Y	Y	Y	Y
Principles	Y	Y	Y	Y	Y
Responsibilities	Y	Y	Y	Y	Y
Stakeholder	Y	Y	Y	Y	Y
Stewardship	Y	Y	Y	Y	Y
Supplier	Y	Y	Y	Y	Y
Sustainability	Y	Y	Y	Y	Y
Transparent	Y	Y	Y	Y	Y
Trust	Y	Y	Y	Y	Y
Values	Y	Y	Y	Y	Y

and use them in your auditing and assurance reporting. They all appear again and again in the parts and chapters in my book, demonstrating their importance in creativity and innovation in auditing. All are now seen by regulators and stakeholders as important in the culture of every organisation. The meanings of these terms are now part of excellent corporate governance in every organisation at every level – board, executive and operations.

In recent years, some countries have begun to consider adoption of so-called stewardship codes. Institutional investors are invited to sign up to these codes on a voluntary basis. The UK Stewardship Code (2012), published by the UK Financial Reporting Council (FRC)[15] recognises effective stewardship as benefiting 'companies, investors and the economy as a whole'. It traces its 'nine stewardship principles' to 2002, though the principles of stewardship go back much further than this:

> The UK Stewardship Code traces its origins to 'The Responsibilities of Institutional Shareholders and Agents: Statement of Principles,' first published in 2002 by the Institutional Shareholders Committee (ISC), and which the ISC converted to a code in 2009.

Sir Adrian Cadbury (1992)[16] reported, 'The responsibilities of the board include setting the company's strategic aims, providing the leadership to put them into effect, supervising the management of the business and reporting to shareholders on their stewardship.' (Cadbury uses the term 'stewardship' frequently as a responsibility of the board.) All issues that should start creative thinking on stewardship for innovative auditors and in keeping with my Creative Thinking and Innovation Framework in Governance described in Chapter 1. In its Annual Report 2014 on developments in corporate governance and stewardship, the UK Financial Reporting Council (FRC)[17] reminds investors and companies of its work 'in the areas of . . . governance and stewardship' and the issues facing companies and investors in 2015 in the importance of 'good corporate culture and embedding sound governance behaviours'. This report is worth studying for its *insight* into governance practices. It can be downloaded from the FRC website (www.frc.com).

Today, the final word on stewardship in organisations must go to Tomorrow's Company[18] and its definition of stewardship by investors: 'The active and responsible management of entrusted resources now and in the longer term, so as to hand them on in a better condition,' and in its statement on tomorrow's stewardship:

> An efficient investment system is one where pension fund trustees and other clients of fund managers start to exercise choice about stewardship, and where fund managers who show that they are serious about stewardship gain more business as a result. Institutional investors acting as stewards on our behalf play their part in two ways. First they ensure that individual companies which happen to be their portfolio at a particular point in time are well stewarded. They become more involved in the appointment of the right directors to act as stewards on their behalf and they make sure that their own people have the skills to challenge the strategy and intervene

where necessary. Secondly they influence investment performance more generally by the actions that they take across the system to promote the better stewardship of companies.

What Tomorrow's Company are describing and promoting for companies applies to all organisations at all levels across all their supply chains, and all their auditors.

Creative Audit Thinking Activities

Activity 4   Create Good Conduct

Consider the following comments by Sir Adrian Cadbury in 1998 on the importance of ethics in business. Think how this importance is reflected in stewardship theory and practice. How can this importance be reflected through innovation in your audit process?

The Role of Business Ethics in Economic Performance[19]

Ethical standards matter to companies. If unethical practices are ignored or condoned in a business, there is no means of knowing where the line between unacceptable and acceptable behaviour is to be drawn. The danger is that this uncertainty will result in a downward slide in standards, which may in turn become cumulative through time and lead to disaster. A further consideration for a business is its need to attract able recruits to its ranks. A company whose ethical standards are seen to be uncertain has to be at a disadvantage in recruitment, against those with higher reputations and against other occupations which are ranked further up the ethical scale than business. Thus business standards matter to individual companies and to the company sector in aggregate. The development of company codes is, therefore, to be encouraged with the objects of contributing to debate on the place of ethics in business and of raising standards of business conduct. In the end, business morality is personal morality.

Activity 5   The 'Concept of Stewardship' Is in All Creative Auditing

Tomorrow's leaders must always be disciples of the 'concept of stewardship'; so should all auditors in the independent and objective assurance services they provide. That concept is also an essential part of the principles of corporate governance and its practices through requirements in the law, regulations and many standards for conduct and behaviour. Consider Tomorrow's Company's views on tomorrow's leaders and how these can be applied to all auditing:

A Changing Perspective on Tomorrow's Leaders[20]

Against a similar backdrop of change at different times over the past 15 years, Tomorrow's Company has asked the question: what would tomorrow's leader look like? Looking across this body of work, there are many similarities, at the heart of which is the ability to build strong and lasting relationships and inspire people inside and outside the organisation. In 1999, shortly after the original Tomorrow's Company inquiry, the leadership style and approach identified as being a 'good fit' with the 'inclusive approach' were:

- the inspirational and visionary qualities of transformational leadership
- the willingness to learn, and to facilitate the learning of others
- the concept of stewardship – of acting as a custodian of the organisation's reputation and resources
- the perception of leadership as service.

To achieve an inspiring and achievable vision requires a deep understanding of the nature of the interdependence which exists between the organisation and its dynamic environment.

Nearly a decade later, **in 2007**, the response from the team of business leaders that worked on the Tomorrow's Global Company programme of inquiry was captured in this imaginary advert:

Tomorrow's CEO Wanted:

> *Our company is operating on a global scale, facing great opportunities but also major challenges. Our top executive team already comprises five men and six women of different nationalities. We want to break away from the pack, become an industry leader and make a lasting contribution to society as well as providing top rank shareholder returns. We are seeking a CEO who can take the company to new heights in innovation, teamwork, performance and influence at the same time as reconciling the differing demands of investors, customers, governments, regulators, partners, NGOs and the public.* ***We're looking for a person with clear vision; strong values; courage; empathy; accessibility; high level negotiating and interpersonal skills; a passion for teamwork; humility and a commitment to future leaders.***

Activity 6   Create Trust and Care across All Supply Chains

Study the label at Figure A.1 on milk cartons prepared and sold by Waitrose Ltd. Consider all the strong stewardship messages it contains on the management of its supply chains and the product it is supplying. Are these messages seen in the supply chains you audit in your Ten Step Audit Process? If not, build these aspects of stewardship into your audit objectives, evaluations and reporting.

Supply chain stewardship values

essential Waitrose

Our fundamental belief is that few things in life are more important than the food you buy. Good quality is essential.

From a carefully selected group of British dairy farmers who share our values and commitment to:
- delivering high animal welfare standards
- consistently ensuring high quality milk
- working together to protect our environment, encouraging wildlife to flourish and promote sustainable farming

for further information on Waitrose milk and recipes go to waitrose.com

By choosing LOVE life products you are improving the nutritional balance of your daily diet. A varied balanced diet together with frequent activity supports a healthy lifestyle.
waitrose.com/lovelife for more information

UK
(See Code Panel)
EC

Waitrose has donated £150,000 to The Prince's Countryside Fund (reg. charity no. 1136077) this year through Countryside Fund Trading Ltd.

Waitrose Limited Bracknell Berkshire RG12 8YA UK waitrose.com

Plastic widely recycled

Plastic check local recycling

Figure A.1 Few things are more important than the food we buy

Source: Reproduced with permission from Waitrose Ltd 2016

Notes

1 *Principles of Corporate Governance* (2004 p. 4) (Revised 2015), Organisation for Economic Co-operation and Development (OECD), Paris, France. www.oecd.org.
2 *A Review of the Ethical Aspects of Corporate Governance Regulation and Guidance in the EU* (2013 p. 6), Institute of Business Ethics and EcoDa, Occasional Paper authored by Julia Casson, London, England.
3 *Companies Act 2006 (Strategic Report and Director's Report) Regulations* (2013), House of Parliament, Great Britain.
4 *Accounting for Sustainability* (2008), Sustainability at Work, London, England. www.accountingforsustainability.org.
5 *A New Era of Sustainability* (2010), United Nations Global Compact, New York, US.
6 *Measuring Sustainability* (2015), Internal Auditor Online January 30, The Institute of Internal Auditors Inc., Orlando, US.
7 *Demystifying Sustainability Risk- Thought Leadership in ERM* (2013), Committee of Sponsoring Organisations.
8 *Values: Take Your Life Principles to Work* (2015), Audit and Risk (January 2015) – *View from the Top*, Journal of the Chartered Institute of Internal Auditors, London, England.
9 *The UK Corporate Governance Code* (2014), Financial Reporting Council, London, England.
10 *The Financial Aspects of Corporate Governance* (1992), Sir Adrian Cadbury, Gee Professional Publishing Ltd. London, England.
11 *Principles of Corporate Governance – Draft for Public Comment* (2014), Organisation for Economic and Co-operative Development, Paris, France. www.oecd.org.
12 *First Report of the Committee on Standards in Public Life* (1995), Lord Nolan Presented to Parliament by the Prime Minister by Command of Her Majesty. England.
13 *Ethics in Practice: Promoting Ethical Conduct in Public Life*, Lord Bew's Foreword addressed to the Prime Minister, Committee on Standards in Public life, July 2014. www.gov.uk/government/organisation/thcommittee-on-standards-in-public-life.
14 *The International (IR) Framework* (2013 p. 18), The International Integrated Reporting Council (IIRC), London, England.
15 *The UK Stewardship Code* (2012 pp. 1–2), Financial Reporting Council, London, England.
16 *Financial Aspects of Corporate Governance* (1982 section 2.5), Sir Adrian Cadbury, Gee (a division of Professional Publishing Ltd), London, England.
17 *Developments in Corporate Governance and Stewardship – Annual Report 2014* (2015 p. 25), Financial Reporting Council. London, England.
18 *Tomorrow's Stewardship – Why Stewardship Matters* (2011 pp. 2 and 20), Tomorrow's Company, London, England.
19 *The Role of Business Ethics in Economic Performance* (1998 p. 83), edited by Ian Jones and Michael Pollitt, Macmillan Press Ltd., Basingstoke, England.
20 *Tomorrow's Global Leaders How to Build a Culture That Ensures Women Reach the Top* (2014 p. 58), Tomorrow's Company, London, England.

2 Auditors Are Responsible Leaders

Today, the most frequently used superlatives describing internal auditors in job vacancy notices are rigorous, self-starter, innovative, outstanding and LEADER.

Walk Faster This Year (2002), Jeffrey Ridley
re-published in
Cutting Edge Internal Auditing (2008), Jeffrey Ridley

The leadership required now and in the future can be described as globally responsible leadership.[1]

In this chapter I discuss the importance of all auditors (not just internal auditors) being seen as responsible leaders with the skills and experiences they have in all aspects of governance in organisations, including compliance to continuing professional development and code of ethics of their professions. Responsible leaders, not just as auditors, but also understanding the needs of responsible leaders and managers at all levels in an organisation: particularly the importance of values in the stewardship of resources for which organisation leaders and managers are responsible to all their stakeholders and civil societies in which they operate. Resources that will always include the sustainability of today and tomorrow's planet.

2.1 Importance of Responsible Leadership Today and Tomorrow

As a Patrol Leader and Scoutmaster in the boy scout movement in the 1940/50s I was taught and taught the following promise and law created by Lord Baden Powell in 1910 – 'On *my honour I promise that I will do my best – To do my duty to God and the Queen – To help other people at all times and – To keep the Scout*

Law'. The first Scout Law is '*A scout is to be trusted'* [www.scout.org}. I was also taught to Be Prepared Little did I realise at the time I was being taught and teaching the fundamentals of responsible leadership for all auditing in the context of today's good corporate governance principles for governments and organisations across the world – Honour: Promise: Best: Duty: Help: Always: Law: Trusted and the management of risk

Globally responsible leadership is an essential contributor for good corporate governance across our growing world of economic, environmental and social performance and protection. The European Foundation for Management Development (2006) research, from which the preceding quote is taken, supported by the United Nations Global Compact recognised this in its definition of responsible leadership and the difficulties to achieve this status by those involved in its promotion:

> Globally responsible leaders openly communicate values related to corporate global responsibility. They reinforce them through each and every action. This requires introspection, courage, humility, openness to learning, deep thought and careful planning, as well as a conviction to face and engage while being willing to acknowledge both intended and unintended consequences of their decisions and actions. We believe that globally responsible leaders in the business world share a number of broad characteristics and values:
>
> • They embrace the global view and global ethics – such as those reflected in the principles of the UN Global Compact and the Millennium Development Goals.
> • They value human development and natural resources as much as financial and structural capital.
> • They trust in people and process as much as systems and structure.
> • They have a global consistency in their general principles and standards, yet are sensitive and flexible to each local context.
> • They accept that international policies are failing to keep up with the pace of globalisation and that there are additional responsibilities above and beyond the law, since legal requirements often trail technological innovation and global development.
> • They recognise that business has the creativity and resources to address, and make a big contribution to, many of the most important social and environmental challenges before us.
> • They recognise that, beyond their responsibility for creating value at company level they also have responsibility to contribute to a broader, common good locally and globally.
> • They seek to balance business, family and community obligations.
> • They balance and contextualise paradoxes and manage contradictions.
> • They actively engage stakeholders not only to communicate how a business is demonstrating its globally responsible leadership, but also to

understand their expectations and concerns and to identify solutions to problems and opportunities.
* They commit to life-long learning.

What needs to happen for this cadre of globally responsible leaders to be developed? It would be wrong to understate the changes now necessary. They must involve a re-definition of the very purpose of business and a new configuration for how we organise, manage and reward corporations. This profound change in corporate culture must be accompanied by the adoption of ethics and guiding principles for globally responsible behaviour. This requires significant individual and cultural development, dialogue and engagement with others and other organisations – including non-governmental organisations (NGOs), governments and business schools – in developing globally responsible leaders.

This research created a Globally Responsible Leadership Initiative (www.grli.org) and its subsequent growth in a global movement into responsible leadership learning today. The United Nations Millennium Goals mentioned now should be read as the United Nations Sustainability Goals (2014)[2] and its recognition of good governance and law in responsible leadership at the national and international levels as 'essential for sustained, inclusive and equitable economic growth, sustainable development and the eradication of poverty and hunger'.

Globally responsible leadership is not just a theory and hope. Practices are coming now annually from many national and global organisations. Each one of these published sustainable targets has legal, regulatory, governance, standards, compliance and behaviour implications, as well as independent audit and assurance needs at all levels in an organisation – board, executive and operations. Cleverley and Manwaring (2014)[3] define the importance of great leadership in today and tomorrow's organisations as essential for their success and good governance:

> Leadership is no longer the preserve of top-down command and control hierarchies. Great leadership demands drawing on qualities that would typically be identified as masculine and feminine, but which men and women individually and together must develop and demonstrate at all levels up and down and across the networks that make up today's complex organisations.

Earlier comments by Drake and Turnbull (2013)[4] on leadership apply to all leaders of auditing activities:

> The new breed of leaders are reinventing the way things are done. From the general to the specific, they create a new culture, expect business decisions to fit with agreed values, communicate and engage about difficult issues with clarity and confidence: collaborate with others and develop leaders at every level.

Leadership is not just an art, skill or quality you are born with. It can and is an ability that can be learnt at home, at school, at university, in sport and all aspects of business, political and social life. It usually requires practice to be good and develops from experiences and confidence. It requires a commitment to be a leader and understanding of what is good leadership. It also requires followers, not just as followers but also as competitors. Good leaders learn from those that are 'treading on their tails'. Good leaders are also good in the way they conduct 'direction and control' of their visions and missions and leading others in their own conduct.

Globally responsible leadership is not a new concept – it's the basis of good stewardship. Management gurus through centuries have examined, analysed and defined what leadership is and how it differs from management. Understanding the difference between leadership and management is a start in understanding how and why every auditor is a leader. Management is defined in a general way as 'getting things done'; leadership is defined as 'getting things done right by everyone'. By 'right' is meant being responsible and by using the values of life already discussed in Chapter 1 and Part I. Writings and books have created a wealth of knowledge on leadership skills and values: skills and values now in training programmes, workshops and professional examination syllabi across the world: skills and values taught in theories and practices in colleges and universities across the world; skills and values in all governance codes. Culture and governance are today and tomorrow's key components in the promotion of stewardship, governance, risk management and control. Evidence of excellence in both is now part of the everyday life and reporting of most organisations and public services. Table A.1 in Part I supports this evidence. Yet, for many organisations and public services this excellence is difficult to achieve.

Globally responsible leadership is now seen as key to the success of every organisation in today's market places The United Nations Global Compact organisation was established in 2000 to promote good citizenship in public-private sector organisations across the world through a mission to encourage ten principles of good leadership, based on the principles in the United Nations Declaration of Human Rights signed into by its membership of nations across the world. These ten principles – see Appendix A, discussed in Part I – are now seen in many organisations in many countries as the basis of responsible leadership and management, In 2010[5] these principles were celebrated by one major international auditing firm and introduced by 'The Global Compact's ten principles resonate highly with the KPMG Values, which define our member firms' culture and our commitment to the highest standards of personal and professional conduct.'

Crane and Matten (2010)[6] discuss the difference between management and leadership. They cite Kotter (1990),[7] who sees management as 'imposing order' and leadership as

> coping with change – setting direction and vision, motivating and inspiring people, and facilitating learning. For many writers then leadership is an intrinsically moral terrain, for it is fundamentally entwined with a particular set of values or beliefs about what is the right thing to do.

In 2012, the then UK central government Department for Business Innovation & Skills (BIS)[8] researched and promoted good leadership in business, though its recommendations could be applied to all sectors and professional services, and are almost certainly promoted by governments in many other countries. At that time it saw good leadership as the 'key factor in fostering innovation, unlocking the potential of the workforce and ensuring organisations have the right strategies to drive productivity and growth', emphasising:

> All managers need to be effective leaders. While a command and control culture will ensure that employees comply with organisational procedures and the terms of their employment contract, it does not create the enthusiasm, innovation and engagement that modern organisations need to compete effectively in a global marketplace. By developing their leadership capability, managers can achieve outstanding results from ordinary people and businesses, getting the best out of their employees and benefiting from the knowledge and skills that often they are not even aware that they possess. Above all, leaders need to inspire trust in their capability to take the organisation in the right direction.

This guidance applies also to all auditors, in monitoring of leadership skills in the management they audit; leadership in their own professional work; and how their leadership skills motivate changes in others. The BIS paper recommends:

> The third key players in this triumvirate are business intermediaries and support organisations. Those of you who work closely with businesses, offering trusted advice and support, have a vital role to play in providing the help and encouragement businesses will need to enable them to take the first steps along the path *[of achieving outstanding results]*. I hope you will use the evidence presented in this report to convince employers that improving their leadership and management skills is a key to building productivity, securing profitability and ensuring competitiveness.

BIS goes on to list ten top tips for improving leadership skills – see Appendix B. Look particularly at Tip 8, which states 'Make sure you are aware of the support available. There are a number of organisations that provide free, independent advice and guidance and that have developed tools to assess and support management capability, such as the EFQM Excellence Model'[9] – see Figure 2.1.

Self-assessing practices in organisations and achieving the requirements of each of the nine Criteria of this Model has been the strategy of many organisations across all sectors and will continue to be so. Its underlying Concepts of Excellence – see Figure 2.2 – will continue to be the essential foundation for achieving excellence in any organisation. Note how many of its concepts promote and drive learning, creativity and innovation and are reflected in themes in the previous chapters. Others will be in future chapters.

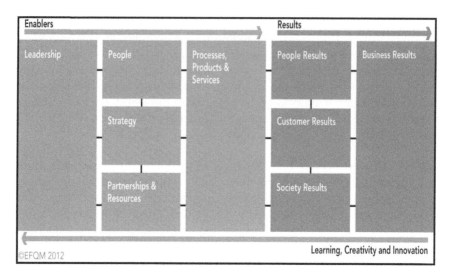

Figure 2.1 EFQM Excellence Model 2012

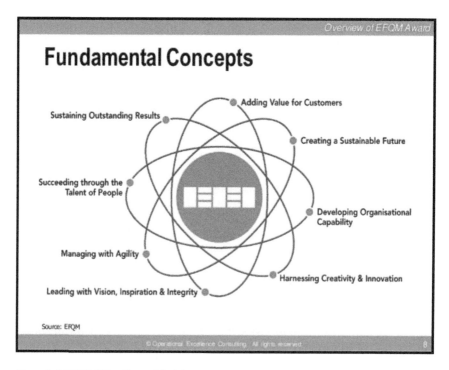

Figure 2.2 EFQM Excellence Model

The UK Corporate Governance Code 2014[10] Leadership Principles require leadership 'within a framework of prudent and effective controls which enables risk to be assessed and managed'. The principles go on to require the board to 'set the company's strategic aims, ensure that the necessary financial and human resources are in place for the company to meet its objectives and review management performance'. But, the final word on leadership must go to Manchester Square Partners[11] in its 2015 insight into leadership challenges for the future, following interviews with a sample of chief executive officers: 'There are many attributes that have always been important for leadership. There are also skills and behaviour that must be acquired, or further developed, specifically to deal with the challenges ahead.' These skills and behaviour must also be acquired by all auditors – see Figure 2.3.

There are many attributes that have always been important for leadership. There are also skills and behaviour that must be acquired, or further developed, specifically to deal with the challenges ahead. We conclude by summarising both types of leadership traits:

ENDURING LEADERSHIP SKILLS

Being authentic
Demonstrating integrity
Being rational
Being emotionally intelligent
Being adaptable
Seeing the big picture
Creating and building strong teams
Being resilient
Making an impact

LEADERSHIP SKILLS FOR THE CHALLENGES AHEAD

Being open to difference
Demonstrating value and purpose
Exercising soft power
Digital fluency
Interacting more closely with employees and customers
Handling intense scrutiny
Making time for reflection

Figure 2.3 Attributes for leadership in the future

Source: Preparing Leaders for the Challenges Ahead a guide for companies and individuals (2015 p. 26) Manchester Square Partners, London, England.

2.2 Auditors Are Responsible Leaders Today and Tomorrow

We all recognise auditors as managers of their own performance, whether as senior partners in firms, executives in organisations and the public sector, or just auditors carrying out an audit. My metaphor in this chapter suggests we should think more of auditors at all levels as responsible leaders and, in that creative way of thinking, consider paradigm shifts we can make in the ten steps of the audit process discussed in Chapter 1.

Today, and certainly tomorrow, many auditors will be products of university education, either through full- or part-time attendance or the qualifications they pursue for the skills they need to audit. Following the BIS report, research by the Association of Business Schools (ABS)[12] 'showed that business schools play an important part in driving innovation and growth in the UK'. This is almost certainly a statement that applies to business schools across the globe. Further research by the Chartered Management Institute,[13] together with ABS and the Quality Assurance Agency for Higher Education, recently 'explored how business schools, professional bodies and employers can work together to develop leaders fit for the 21st century'. One part of this research was a survey, which resulted in the following ten qualities being recognised as essential for good leadership today and tomorrow:

Can-do-approach
Honest and ethical
Work ethic
Resilience, grit and determination
Collaborative
Curiosity and willingness to learn
Creativity
Entrepreneurial
Global mind-set
Risk-taking

All these qualities are seen in the training and professional learning of auditors and in their visions and practices. Consider how they are seen in the professions of accounting and auditing as they promote themselves through websites. One example is the Institute of Chartered Accountants in England and Wales (ICAEW):[14]

> Our members provide financial knowledge and guidance based on the highest technical and ethical standards. They are trained to challenge people and organisations to think and act differently, to provide clarity and rigour, and so help create and sustain prosperity. ICAEW ensures these skills are constantly developed, recognised and valued. Because of us, people can do business with confidence.

All the attributes of a responsible leader should be seen in every auditor in each step of the audit process.

2.3 Auditors Are Responsible Leaders of Governance

Good governance is the encouragement, if not requirement, for good and the deterrence, if not rejection, of evil. Governance is more than just risk management, control and auditing, though these are important in every organisation, whether the auditing is independent or by management, or both. Governance is about responsible leadership and direction, how it is implemented across an organisation, from top to bottom and across all its structures, operations and supply chains. It offers many choices in how it is imposed, from tightly to loosely. It is applied at all levels in an organisation and by many means, strategies, policies, procedures, systems, instructions, visually, verbally, even sometimes by intuition. It requires trust to be implemented successfully. It requires respect from those who direct and those who are directed.

In my book, *Cutting Edge Internal Auditing*, in 2008 I started the chapter on internal auditors know how to govern well with the quote from William Gladstone (1809–1898):[15] 'The proper function of a government is to make it easy for people to do good, and difficult for them to do evil.' This sums up well the output of good governance by responsible leaders: the outcome is trust between the organisation and all its stakeholders. For 'a government' in the quote, read 'governance'. It is important that governance does not stifle innovation but encourages it to happen for the good of the organisation, its performance, and the performance of those who are committed to its vision, mission and objectives. It is also important governance makes it difficult for evil to happen. It is unlikely to stop evil but it can assess the risks associated with it: control to try to prevent it, detect it when it happens and take appropriate action to investigate it, then start the cycle of risk assessment and prevention again. This cycle of activities fighting evil takes place in every organisation every day.

Evil covers a wide variety of causes and effects. It can be minor: it can have a strong influence on performance – sometimes the wrong way: it can be disastrous, having significant impact on all stakeholders, communities, nations and internationally: it can mean failure, even death, of the organisation and individuals associated with it. It is not nice! There are many leadership roles for auditing in the prevention, detection and investigation of 'evil', but the primary responsibility for this lies with management.

Good in an organisation should be seen in its vision and mission statements as well as its ethics and performance. There has to be a direction and commitment at the top of an organisation, and at all other levels, for its resources, practices, ethics and performance 'good'. That goodness has to be managed well. There are many responsible leadership opportunities for auditing in an organisation in the development, promotion and monitoring of goodness, but the primary responsibility for this lies with management.

There have been many books, articles and research papers published on corporate governance principles and practices, and there will be in the future. Many revisions have been made to existing codes of corporate governance and its regulatory requirements in almost every nation. Yet, few laws, national or international, define what is meant by corporate governance, though many of its components are often covered, particularly concerning board, governing body leadership, management duties, responsibilities, auditing and regulation. Corporate governance as a term is used in every sector of society as a benchmark for good, if not sometimes excellent, practices. Cadbury (1992) defined it as 'direction and control':

> **2.5** Corporate governance is the system by which companies are directed and controlled. Boards of directors are responsible for the governance of their companies. The shareholders' role in governance is to appoint the directors and the auditors and to satisfy themselves that an appropriate governance structure is in place. The responsibilities of the board include setting the company's strategic aims, providing the leadership to put them into effect, supervising the management of the business and reporting to shareholders on their stewardship. The board's actions are subject to laws, regulations and the shareholders in general meeting.

This statement has been interpreted across civil societies in most nations in many different ways, linked to different organisational visions, strategies, structures, systems and laws. Today, it is also now linked to the need for appropriate staff, skills, styles and the importance of shared values in an organisation and across all its stakeholders and supply chains.

Today, many organisations are influenced by external stakeholder pressures to reinforce existing governance practices or adopt new ones. Tricker (1994)[16] saw governance not as a separate theory but as a development of both 'stewardship theory' and 'agency theory', emphasising 'research in this area has hardly begun'. He saw governance then at present mainly based on two bodies of knowledge 'the legal and the operational perspectives'. Looking to the future, he added another theoretical focus 'essentially ideological and political', deriving 'insights from the worlds of political science, sociology and philosophy', and leading 'to insights into the importance of values, beliefs and culture'. How true today was his prediction! In the third edition of his book, published in 2014, he comments in the preface: 'Creating the company's ethical culture, determining its corporate social responsibility and integrating economic, social and environmental performance are increasingly recognised as part of the board's corporate governance responsibilities.' I would add also part of responsible leadership for all auditors.

Tricker (2014)[17] discusses the development, role and influence of the audit committee as it is seen today in many organisations across the globe as a standing committee of the board with a charter to assist the board in its financial accounting, reporting and audit responsibilities: 'Today all codes of governance in corporate governance and stock exchange listing requirements require listed companies to have audit committees.' In practice many regulators now recommend and review the activities of audit committees in the organisations they regulate. Audit committees can and should be leaders in the quality and understanding of the practices of all assurance activities in an organisation, not just financial, but all assurances provided to the board on all matters concerning its performance, including in all aspects of corporate governance. This is not yet so. An examination of many audit committee charters will find 'corporate governance' or 'governance' not mentioned in its responsibilities, even though its monitoring responsibilities will cover many aspects of corporate governance and its assurances.

Many auditors have reporting lines to an audit committee and in many cases to the chairman of the audit committee outside of its meetings. In many ways auditors can and do influence and lead audit committee discussions, monitoring activities and reports to the board. This access to the audit committee and board can provide auditors with many opportunities to responsibly lead in the pursuit of 'good' in an organisation and deterrence of 'evil'.

There are strong arguments that all organisations have accountability to society in the way they operate and the resources they use, whether this is at national or international levels. How all types of organisations govern themselves can have good and evil impacts and influences on their owners, stakeholders, governments and society at large. How that governance is established and monitored to provide benefits to society is important for everyone. Board and shareholder expectations from the audit committee have changed very little since they first were established as monitors of financial reporting and auditing, with the exception that for some committees the role has been increased to review risk management and internal control throughout their organisations. This has been influenced in the United Kingdom not only by corporate guidance and codes published by the Financial Reporting Council (FRC), but also guidance from many of the professional accounting and audit firms in this country, the European Commission and internationally.

Chambers (2014)[18] describes well the role of audit committees today in the United Kingdom with examples of their terms of reference and governance leadership from different sectors. He references audit committee guidance published by the FRC,[19] which recognises the audit committee in carrying out its role in listed companies as 'wide-ranging, time consuming and sometimes intensive work to do': requiring appropriate resources, independence of its members with the right skills, led by a committed and able chairman, guided by independent audit. Today audit committees are a key part of corporate governance in both the private and public sectors and increasingly being involved in all aspects of its principles and practices at board level and throughout the organisation structure.

The role of the audit committee will see changes in the future led by regulators, audit committee chairmen and auditors. Current demands by governments and society for sustainability and integrated reporting of an organisation's financial performance and values, including addressing compliance with the United

Nations Global Compact Ten Principles, covering areas of human rights, labour, environment and anti-corruption, will also add more responsibilities to the audit committee role. How audit committees report internally and externally to their organisation's stakeholders and society is also under scrutiny today and will change in the future. All these changes will require responsible leadership from all auditors demonstrating their skills and knowledge of governance, risk management and control. All auditors are experts in controls, or should be.

Control is based on its own theories of formality and informality; law and regulation; direction, prevention and detection; monitoring, feedback and correction; punishment and reward. Control has always been seen as an essential management activity. Yet, it applies and is applied across all levels of an organisation and integrates many objectives. The US Treadway Commission (1987)[20] researched 'environments in which fraudulent (financial) reporting occurs'. This research established a demand for control guidance in the USA, which resulted in its Committee of Sponsoring Organisations (COSO) (1992)[21] developing nine interrelated components for control theory, which subsequently evolved into six now internationally recognised control elements – 'control environment, risk assessment, control activities and monitoring; all linked by accurate and timely information systems and communications'. These elements and their underlying theory are now in worldwide use by auditors, boards, executives and managers to guide their assessments of reasonableness of control. They are there also for all auditors to be creative and innovative in a responsible leadership role.

2.4 Auditors Are Responsible Leaders of Culture

Good behaviour is an essential part of the service provided by all auditors. Behaviour is also in the culture of an organisation and is key to its reputation and performance. What auditors seek is evidence of good behaviour. By good behaviour I mean evidence of efficiency, effectiveness and economy in all that they observe and examine. These are not new concepts; they have been fundamental to best behaviour for a long time and the three principles underlying any value for money assessment, particularly in the public sector but also in all sectors. By efficiency is meant doing things right the first time: this principle also underlies all aspects of total quality management and achievement of quality to meet the needs of customers. By effectiveness is meant doing the right things: this principle underlies the achievement of visions, missions and objectives in an organisation. By economy is meant achieving efficiency and effectiveness at the best cost, which may not always be the lowest cost but one that takes in not just immediate best results, but best results that are sustainable for both the organisation and the geographic and social environments in which it operates. Sustainability is never just about an organisation, but about all the organisations across its supply chains and their supply chains. It is also about the planet.

A true story, which was told to me at the beginning of my operational auditing career, is that of the auditor forming a first opinion on the behaviour of management in any organisation. First, visit the toilets. The state of these in terms of cleanliness and tidiness represents the focus management place on the disposal of waste in an organisation. That disposal extends far beyond the toilets but to the disposal and reuse or recycling of all waste materials across every organisation. How waste is created, reduced and disposed is critical to how we treat all the resources we use. This observation can be extended to waste time and energy and lead into all three measures of behaviour – efficiency, effectiveness and economy and the values associated with each.

Much has been written of the 'tone at the top' concerning governance, risk management and control' but less about how that tone is led in all the three levels of every organisation – BOARD:EXECUTIVE:OPERATIONS – and across all its stakeholders throughout its many supply chains: in particular its suppliers and customers. Auditors were reminded of the importance of the 'tone at the top' as early as the 1980s by COSO,[22] from which many of the guidelines on audit committees, risk management and control have been developed:

The Tone at the Top

The tone set by top management that influences the corporate environment within which financial reporting occurs. To set the right tone, top management must identify and assess the factors that could lead to fraudulent financial reporting; all public companies should maintain internal controls that provide reasonable assurance that fraudulent financial reporting will be prevented or subject to early detection – this is a broader concept than internal accounting controls – and all public companies should develop and enforce effective, written codes of corporate conduct. As a part of its ongoing assessment of the effectiveness of internal controls, a company's audit committee should annually review the program that management establishes to monitor compliance with the code. The Commission also recommends that its sponsoring organisations cooperate in developing additional, integrated guidance on internal controls.

The Institute of Business Ethics (2005)[23] explains 'tone' in this context and recognises how leading the 'tone at the top' is applied across and assisted by all levels in an organisation:

Leadership in an organisation is often viewed as emanating from one person: the chairman or the CEO. But it is usually the collective tone set from the top that is of primary importance to employees. The board exists to set the strategic direction of an organisation, and under the UK unitary board structure, the board is collectively responsible for that strategy. The way that the board members work together reinforces leadership – particularly in the area of business ethics. It is also important to recognise that there are 'leaders' at every level in an organisation; for instance divisional leaders, team leaders, project leaders and so on. Each leader will, by example, have an effect on the performance of the team being led. So the tone set from the top will almost certainly cascade down the organisation and be played out at many different levels and in many different situations.

There is a message in this statement for all auditors. In the assurance and consultancy services they provide when they travel and monitor all levels in an organisation. They have the opportunity to responsibly lead on culture and governance principals with all they meet and with whom they communicate. List the questions you should be asking concerning how good is the culture in the organisations in which you audit. In Appendix C, look at the questions I ask: questions every auditor should lead on in their assessments of culture in an organisation; questions to be asked at every level in an organisation – BOARD:EXECUTIVE:OPERATIONS.

2.5 Auditors Are Responsible Leaders of Sustainability

In a new venture into leadership, the UN Global Compact Lead[24] programme is registering organisations to lead sustainability practices and reporting. In its promotion of this programme, former UN Secretary-General H.E. Ban Ki-moon writes:

> HUMANITY IS FACING A CRITICAL MOMENT IN ITS EXIST-ENCE. The game-changing consequences of the multiple crises we currently face – market disturbances, social unrest, ecological devastation and economic inequality – have sent a clear message: we must build a new era of sustainability. To achieve this, we need to foster a new kind of corporation; one that responds to the real needs of people and societies, takes a long-term and holistic approach to value creation, and fully accounts for externalities and the company's impacts. Leading companies recognise that this transformation of business is not only good for societies and the planet, but that building sustainability into business strategies and practices is the only recipe for long-term profitability and success. To guide the transformation of business everywhere, we need innovation, experimentation and genuine leadership. By bringing companies together with relevant experts and stakeholders, Global Compact LEAD provides a collaborative space to generate and implement advanced corporate sustainability practice. As an integral part of the United Nations and the UN Global Compact, LEAD is uniquely positioned to inspire the widespread uptake of sustainability solutions among businesses around the world.

In 2011 I contributed to research[25] on sustainability assurance with the following conclusions on policy considerations and recommendations, each of which has responsible leadership roles for all auditors:

Assurance of Sustainability Reports: Insights and Evidence from UK Companies

Our research paper addresses today's theory of sustainability assurance in some detail but is limited in its evidence of what is happening in practice in UK companies and globally. We believe the sustainability reports we examined represent current best practice today in UK companies, and there are probably many more similar reports not declared to GRI. If our research net had been more widely cast with a sample of organisations across all sectors and of different sizes we would have seen many sustainability reports (and the absence of them) not meeting current global guidance, or even legal requirements, with weaker assurance processes for stakeholders. The main policy considerations resulting from our research and recommendations are:

1   Sustainability reporting and assurance of its content has evolved over the past ten years as an important, but seen too often as separate, part of good corporate governance theory and practices. This evolution has generated many changes in strategies and structures in organisations, from direction at Board level through sustainability strategy. policy statements and processes, to the creation of new co-operative teams in the form of committees at Board level (audit and risk) and working groups of interested internal parties (health, safety and environmental), including as members in some cases internal and external stakeholders. These organisational changes will continue. They are already taking place in the United Kingdom with the increased focus on risk management in corporate governance across other sectors. There was evidence in the some of the reports we examined of assurance involvement by Audit and Risk committees.

Recommendation:

In future, sustainability assurance should be seen to involve all Board committees, e.g. Audit (through assurance); Risk (through assessment and management); Remuneration (through reward systems); and. Nomination (through appointment and training of directors).

2   The links between assurance, stakeholder and governance in all organisations, through the principles of good governance [accountability, integrity and openness] are strong and evident in all sustainability guidance in the European Union and globally. The European Commission (2011 p. 2) proposed corporate governance framework starts with the following paragraph and continues with:

It is of paramount importance that European businesses demonstrate the utmost responsibility not only towards their employees and shareholders but also towards society at large. Corporate governance and corporate social responsibility are key elements in building people's trust in the single market. They also contribute to the competitiveness of European business, because well run, sustainable companies are best placed to contribute to the ambitious growth targets set by 'Agenda 2020'. In the field of corporate social responsibility the Commission has already issued a public consultation on non-financial disclosure by companies3 and will put forward a new framework initiative later this year to tackle issues related to the societal challenges that enterprises are facing.

This message was also repeated in the EcoDa (2010 p. 50) developed corporate governance principles for unlisted companies in Europe.

Principle 14: The Board should present a balanced and understandable assessment of the company's position and prospects for external stakeholders, and establish a suitable programme of stakeholder engagement.

Merger of agency and stakeholder theory in corporate governance practices is driving change and has become the global force for what is happening today in sustainability reporting and assurance. This force will continue to influence the future of sustainability assurance and grow in importance, as more organisations invest in sustainability processes and reporting of these, either through altruism or probably more by legal requirement. And, more stakeholders demand accountability, integrity and openness in the organisations in which they have interests.

There is also evidence of this by the implementation of the Integrated Reporting Committee, established following the King III (2009): with its global membership and terms of reference. IRC (2011 p. 3) in the Introduction to its Discussion Paper on integrated reporting sets the objective of integrated reporting in the future as:

The overarching objective of an integrated report is to enable stakeholders to assess the ability of an organisation to create and sustain value over the short-, medium- and long-term. The users of the report should be able to determine whether the organisation's governing structure has applied its collective mind in identifying the environmental, social, economic and financial issues that impact on the organisation, and to assess the extent to which these issues have been incorporated into the organisation's strategy. An integrated report is the organisation's primary report.

Its recommendations already see the integrated report in the future as the main published report, addressed and reviewed by a board's audit and risk committee:

Recommendation

Development of an integrated reporting strategy, and how its reporting content will be assured, should be the main driver for all future sustainability legal, programme and reporting requirements, both nationally and globally.

3   The motivation and empowerment of an organisation's quality management culture, including its quality auditing, should form an important part of management of sustainable policies and processes. Continuous improvement, measurement and assurance of key quality and sustainability performance indicators (covering all of an organisation's objectives) will become the norm for all organisations in competitive market places. Such motivation and empowerment will lead to more organisations seeking registration to sustainability standards and achievement of sustainability awards. Evidence of this and its related assurance and certifications will increase in sustainability reporting – this is already happening in the eight reports we examined.

Recommendation

The contribution to sustainability assurance made by registration/certification to sustainability and quality standards, models of excellence and awards should be given more prominence in sustainability strategies and processes. Assessment and verification processes (internal and external) are an integral part of such registrations and certifications. A sustainability report without demonstrating achievement to external standards, models of excellence and awards should always be the exception.

4   Both the professions of internal auditing and external auditing are focusing more attention on providing assurance over sustainability reporting. Both, have current published statements and guidance on their contribution to an organisations 'going concern' in the short and long-term. An internal auditing contribution to verification and assurance is evident in four of the company reports we examined. We believe this contribution will grow in companies where there is an internal audit function. External audit already offer assurance services for sustainability reports and will be drawn more into developing and providing this service as the integration of corporate governance and sustainability reporting develops.

> ### Recommendation
>
> Internal and external auditing professions and related standard development bodies should continue to develop their assurance role and methods to meet the sustainability challenges of today and tomorrow. These roles and methods should be given a continuous high profile in both their research and standards.

Linked to responsible leadership and management, though not directly, is a parallel leadership initiative by the International Integration Reporting Council (IIRC).[26] In this, its first publication, it sees auditing as a mechanism to enhance the reliability of information as an integral part of internal control: its focus on integrated reporting starts with strategy and leads the responsible leader and management through what has happened, is happening and will happen today and tomorrow and the influence of each on an organisation's direction. This includes the status of its governance, risk management and control practices in its economic, social and environmental issues and impacts. It opens up a new world of creative thinking and innovation, requiring effective leadership skills to achieve:

a world in which integrated thinking is embedded within mainstream business practice in the public and private sectors, facilitated by Integrated Reporting (<IR>) as the corporate reporting norm. The cycle of integrated thinking and reporting, resulting in efficient and productive capital allocation, will act as a force for financial stability and sustainability. <IR> aims to:

- improve the quality of information available to providers of financial capital to enable a more efficient and productive allocation of capital
- promote a more cohesive and efficient approach to corporate reporting that draws on different reporting strands and communicates the full range of factors that materially affect the ability of an organisation to create value over time
- enhance accountability and stewardship for the broad base of capitals (financial, manufactured, intellectual, human, social and relationship, and natural) and promote understanding of their interdependencies
- support integrated thinking, decision-making and actions that focus on the creation of value over the short, medium and long term.

These developments in leadership and reporting are opening up a new world of integrated principles leading to new governance, risk management and control integrated practices: with new goals to be achieved by organisations and new integrated monitoring and assurance practices. Responsible leadership in all of these new practices will be critical to their success. All auditors across the globe should be important contributors to the effective leadership of these and the aims of the United Nations Global Compact LEAD programme.

There is a world of sustainability opening up many opportunities for creative thinking and innovative auditors to provide new recommendations and assurances at board level. Assurances, from which integrated auditing can bring better observations and recommendations at all levels in an organisation and across all its supply chains.

Stewardship

Stewardship is based on trust between a principal and agent. That trust emanates from a demonstration of good governance practices. Trust is fundamental to good governance. The culture of an organisation should be one of trust between everyone within its structure and all external stakeholders. Building stewardship theory into an integrated audit opens up new objectives for assurance and new clients interested in the results. It takes the internal auditor into the boardroom. The scope becomes external as well as internal; it includes all suppliers and customers; it requires new audit techniques; it focuses on what motivates the board and managers to be successful in the short, medium and long term.

Collaboration

Auditors have always recognised the term 'cooperation', specifically in the relationships between internal auditors and external auditors. Other 'co' words are associated with auditing – *coordination, cooperation and corroboration* are three of these but there are others. The one that gets the least publicity is *collaboration*, yet, it underpins one of the most important relationships today between auditors and their clients – *the act of working together in order to achieve objectives*. Imagine the possibilities of leading collaboration with your clients. The increased knowledge, experience and resources that can be brought into the audit planning and engagement are considerable. In many of my audits in the past I have recruited staff from the audit client to work alongside the auditors to increase the knowledge and experience available to the audit team. This really does work well if managed and led well. Today there is more than ever a need for collaboration in leadership across all organisations. In its drive for sustainable strategies and practices, UN Global Compact (2014)[27] recognises this in its promotion of a new level of collaboration corporate leadership in the new era, 'working with others on an entirely new scale':

> The pieces are in place for such coordinated action on a level never before seen. Over the past decade, all major stakeholder groups – including business, investors, Governments, UN entities, civil society, and labour – have

developed orientations, strategies and capacities in relation to sustainable development in the broadest sense of the term. With respect to business, a very important development has been the creation of a large variety of global sustainability initiatives and platforms as well as local initiatives and capacities, which means that the opportunities and resources now exist to truly scale up efforts. In order to fully realize the benefits and outcomes – and contribute to sustainable development in the most meaningful ways – companies will need to move beyond first-mover approaches and embrace partnerships and collective action initiatives that unite business peers, often for the first time, as well as other stakeholders.

A content analysis of the stewardship terms in the European Foundation for Management Development (2006) research referred to at the beginning of this chapter provides an interesting comparison with Table A.1 in the previous chapter – see Table 2.1.

Note how the stewardship word/terms are used in the EFMD report and the terms 'Collaboration', 'Partnership' and 'Manage' appear in the text in all six of the reports. How are 'Collaboration', 'Partnership' and 'Manage' used in your

Table 2.1 EFMD (2005) compared with Table A.1

	Industry	*Finance*	*Charity*	*Health*	*Profess*	*EFMD*
Part I Stewardship						
Accountability	Y	Y	Y	Y	Y	Y
Behaviour	Y	Y	Y	Y	Y	Y
Beliefs	Y	Y	Y	Y	Y	Y
Care	Y	Y	Y	Y	Y	Y
Compliance	Y	Y	Y	Y	Y	Y
Culture	Y	Y	Y	Y	Y	Y
Customer	Y	Y	Y	Y	Y	Y
Duty	Y	Y	Y	Y	Y	Y
Ethics	Y	Y	Y	Y	Y	Y
Governance	Y	Y	Y	Y	Y	Y
Law	Y	Y	Y	Y	Y	Y
Leadership	Y	Y	Y	Y	Y	Y
Principles	Y	Y	Y	Y	Y	Y
Responsibilities	Y	Y	Y	Y	Y	Y
Stakeholder	Y	Y	Y	Y	Y	Y
Stewardship	Y	Y	Y	Y	Y	Y
Supplier	Y	Y	Y	Y	Y	Y
Sustainability	Y	Y	Y	Y	Y	Y
Transparent	Y	Y	Y	Y	Y	Y
Trust	Y	Y	Y	Y	Y	Y
Values	Y	Y	Y	Y	Y	Y
Chapter 2 Responsible Leadership						
Collaboration	Y	Y	Y	Y	Y	Y
Partnership	Y	Y	Y	Y	Y	Y
Manage	Y	Y	Y	Y	Y	Y

organisation statements and in your auditing and assurance reporting? Do you see auditors as leaders of collaboration, partnerships and management in good corporate governance, risk management and control? Are you promoting these leadership roles in your organisation and auditing? There are many creative and innovative ways of doing this in every step of your audit process.

2.6 Chapter Review

In this chapter I have discussed the opportunities and challenges every auditor has to lead responsibly at all levels in an organisation in all corporate governance practices, by developing a full understanding of its principles and the concept of stewardship underlying those practices. These same leadership skills are required by all auditors in the performance of their assurance services. Finally, on the auditor as a leader, Blowfield (2013 p. 90)[28] cites Senge in his study of business and sustainability, recognising the individual leader as a guide leading change 'from one state to another more appropriate one. The sustainability leader's role, therefore, is to steer the company through a transformation n process, Typically, in large companies at least, it is not the leader's vision of sustainability that matters, but his[/her] organisational intelligence: the knack of connecting with what matters most to others in the company so as to unleash their latent collective imagination and energy.' All auditors develop 'organisational intelligence'. They are responsible leaders in the services they perform.

2.7 Creative Audit Thinking Activities

Activity 7 The Creative and Innovative Audit Leadership Process

Creatively think about how each step in the Ten Step Audit Process developed and discussed in Chapter 1 needs to be led by a globally responsible auditor. Consider the first step: planning and promoting an audit strategy is the first step to globally responsible leadership by an auditor. It demonstrates both professionalism and communication skills. It is key to establishing respect from those being audited: establishing and communicating that professionalism is not just about qualifying as an auditor, holding a certificate of competency and evidence of continued professional development. It requires a passion for the profession of auditing: representing this as a globally responsible leader of that passion at the preparation interviews when the audit strategy and its plans are being discussed at board, audit committee, executive and operational levels. Not just for long-term plans but also short-term and engagement planning when an audit is being promoted. At board/audit committee levels this can be achieved by recognition of compliance with auditing standards and codes of ethics being included in the audit terms of reference, charter or contract. At executive and operational levels this can be through independence and objectivity of the services being provided. It is an excellent opportunity to demonstrate an auditor's professional code of conduct.

Now consider the other steps and how an auditor's globally responsible leadership can lead to innovations in the audit process.

Ten Step Audit Process

1 Create the audit vision and strategy to **MOTIVATE** excellence, quality and add value and improvement in the **EXPERTISE** and **SKILLS** needed in all auditing processes.
2 Plan each audit engagement over a period of time.
3 Seek insight into operations being audited – their theory and best practices, through **ASSOCIATION: QUESTIONING: OBSERVING: NETWORKING**.
4 Assess risks involved by the operations being audited and the audit.
5 Establish scope and objectives for the audit engagement.
6 Develop a risk-based audit programme and identify controls.
7 Select techniques/methodology and **EXPERIMENT** to search for appropriate evidence.
8 Objectively evaluate audit outputs, consider outcomes and agree findings.
9 Communicate audit findings to those accountable.
10 Follow-up and consider actions taken by the organisation.

Activity 8   Create a Stakeholder Engagement Map

In today's organisations engaging with all stakeholders is key to the leading of good governance practices. This is recognised in most corporate governance principles and codes. How this key is turned by auditors leading auditors can change their role and responsibilities as well as the perception the organisation has at board, executive and operations levels on auditing and its reporting. Consider the following guidance on stakeholder engagement and compare this with your audit reporting and relationship with all your organisation's stakeholders. Create a stakeholder map and use this to introduce innovations in your audit reporting.

Stakeholder Engagement in Governance Practices[29]

Relevant stakeholders are those individuals, groups of individuals or organisations that affect and/or could be affected by an organisation's activities, products or services and associated performance with regard to the issues to be addressed by the engagement. An organisation may have many stakeholders, each with distinct attributes and often with diverse and sometimes conflicting interests and concerns. Establishing a methodology for systematically identifying groups and individuals that can contribute to achieving the purpose of the engagement and/or could be affected by its outcome is fundamental to the engagement process. A method for systematically identifying stakeholder groups should consider the scope of the engagement and may be guided by attributes of stakeholders such as the following:

- **Dependency** – groups or individuals who are directly or indirectly dependent on the organisation's activities, products or services and associated performance, or on whom the organisation is dependent in order to operate.
- **Responsibility** – groups or individuals to whom the organisation has, or in the future may have, legal, commercial, operational or ethical/moral responsibilities.
- **Tension** – groups or individuals who need immediate attention from the organisation with regard to financial, wider economic, social or environmental issues.
- **Influence** – groups and individuals who can have impact on the organisation's or a stakeholder's strategic or operational decision-making.
- **Diverse perspectives** – groups and individuals whose different views can lead to a new understanding of the situation and the identification of opportunities for action that may not otherwise occur.

Stakeholders may also include those who, through regulation, custom, culture or reputation, can legitimately claim to represent any of these interests as well the interests of the voiceless such as future generations and the environment.

Activity 9   Sustainability Auditing Is Creative and Innovative

Today and tomorrow, there is a world of sustainability opening up many opportunities for auditors to provide new recommendations and assurances at board level. Assurances, from which globally responsible leading auditing can bring stronger convictions and confidence. STEWARDSHIP and COLLABORATION are just two of many scenarios focused on sustainability that can benefit from an audit. Such scenarios can be created to meet the needs of all an organisation's stakeholders. Read again the European Foundation for Management Development (2006) research discussed at the beginning of this chapter and the selection of three values and characteristics repeated below. Consider these statements in your next audit and use these to innovate new audit techniques to seek assurance that each of the statements is being addressed by globally responsible leaders at board and executive levels.

Globally Responsible Leadership Auditing

Globally responsible leaders openly communicate values related to corporate global responsibility. They reinforce them through each and every action. This requires introspection, courage, humility, openness to learning, deep thought and careful planning, as well as a conviction to face and engage while being willing to acknowledge both intended and unintended consequences of their decisions and actions. We believe that globally responsible leaders in the business world share a number of broad characteristics and values:

1   They embrace the global view and global ethics – such as those reflected in the principles of the UN Global Compact and the Millennium Development Goals.
2   They recognise that business has the creativity and resources to address, and make a big contribution to, many of the most important social and environmental challenges before us.
3   They actively engage stakeholders not only to communicate how a business is demonstrating its globally responsible leadership, but also to understand their expectations and concerns and to identify solutions to problems and opportunities.

Notes

1 *Globally Responsible Leadership – A Call for Engagement* (2005 pp. 2 and 18), European Foundation for Management Development, Brussels, Belgium.
2 *Sustainable Development Goals* (2014 Introduction p. 12), United Nations Global Compact, New York, US.
3 *Tomorrow's Global Leaders – How to Build a Culture That Ensures Women Reach the Top* (2014 p. 2), Pat Cleverly, Tony Manwaring, Tomorrow's Company, London, England.
4 *Developing a New Breed of Leaders*, Dr. Jacquie Drake and Professor Kim Turnbull James, Management Focus Issue 35 (Autumn 2013 p. 16), Cranfield University School of Management.
5 *UN Global Compact Communication on Progress* (August 2010 p. 5), KPMG International, Switzerland.
6 *Business Ethics: Managing Corporate Citizenship and Sustainability in the Age of Globalisation* (3rd Edition 2010 p. 223), Crane Andrew, Matten Dirk, Oxford University Press, Oxford, England.

7 *What Leaders Really Do* (1990), Harvard Business Review Issue 68 (May–June pp. 103–111).

8 *Leadership & Management in the UK: The Key to Sustainable Growth* (2012 pp. 4, 24 and 37), Department for Business Innovation and Skills, London, England.

9 *EFQM Excellence Model* (2013), European Foundation for Quality Management, Brussels, Belgium.

10 *The UK Corporate Governance Code* (2014), Financial Reporting Council, London, England.

11 *Preparing Leaders for the Challenges Ahead: A Guide for Companies and Individuals* (2015 p. 22), Manchester Square Partners, London, England.

12 *The Role of UK Business Schools in Driving Innovation and Growth in the Domestic Economy* (2013 p. 1), Richard Thorpe, Leeds University Business School, and Richard Rawlinson, Booz and Company, The Association of Business Schools, London, England.

13 *21st Century Leaders: Building Practice into the Curriculum to Boost the Economy* (2014), Chartered Institute of Management, England.

14 *Developing a Vision for Your Business* (2010), ICAEW Finance and Management Faculty, Chartered Accountants' Hall Moorgate Place, London, England.

15 Cited in *Wisdom of the Ages* (1948 p. 149), The St. Catherine Press Ltd., London, England.

16 *International Corporate Governance* (1994), Tricker R.I., Prentice Hall, Singapore.

17 *Corporate Governance – Principles, Policies and Practices* (3rd Edition 2014), Oxford University Press, Oxford, England.

18 *Chambers' Corporate Governance Handbook* (6th Edition 2014), Bloomsbury Professional, Haywards Heath, England.

19 *Guidance on Audit Committees* (December 2012), Financial Reporting Council, London, England.

20 *Report of the National Commission on Fraudulent Financial Reporting* (1987), New York, US.

21 *Integrated Control Framework* (1992), Committee of Sponsoring Organisations of the Treadway Commission (COSO), New York.

22 *Report of the National Commission on Fraudulent Financial Reporting* (1987), a private-sector initiative, jointly sponsored and funded by the American Institute of Certified Public Accountants (AICPA), the American Accounting Association (AAA), the Financial Executives Institute (FEI), the Institute of Internal Auditors (IIA), and the National Association of Accountants (NAA), US.

23 *Setting the Tone – Ethical Business Leadership: Executive Summary* (2005 p. 1), Institute of Business Ethics, London, England.

24 *Global Compact LEAD Advancing Sustainability Leadership Through Innovation and Action* (2015 cover), United Nations Global Compact, New York, US.

25 *Assurance of Sustainability Reports: Insights and Evidence from UK Companies* (2011), Professor Jeffrey Ridley, Professor Kenneth D'Silva and Anuj Saush, Paper presented at an international conference at Ashridge Management School, England.

26 *The International IR Framework* (2013), International Integrated Reporting Council, London, England. www.theiirc.org.

27 *Architects of a Better World Building the Post-2015 Business Engagement Architecture* (2014 p. 3), United Nations Global Compact, New York, US.

28 *Business and Sustainability* (2013 p. 90), Michael Blowfield, Oxford University Press, Oxford, England.

29 *AA1000 Stakeholder Engagement Standard* (p. 19).

3   Auditors Are Ambassadors

We must find ways to use our bridges to communicate, share and help our customers.[1]

In this chapter I stress the importance of auditors never being seen as isolated from those they audit. Auditing is always about building bridges across organisations and their supply chains and communicating well at all levels. I compare auditors to ambassadors and the importance of diplomacy in the audit process. Ambassadors operate in a foreign country and culture. As representatives of their own country and culture, they need to have a full understanding of diplomacy at their meetings and in their communications. Auditors are ambassadors of good governance best practices and represent these at all their meetings and in their communications. An understanding of the role of ambassadors and diplomacy will always open the mind to creative thinking and innovation in the audit process.

3.1 Ambassadors Are Envoys Who Represent a State

Most dictionaries will define ambassadors as diplomats of the highest rank and diplomacy, tactful at dealing with people, representing the government and culture of a state. Although diplomacy may be seen as an art, it requires skills which can and are taught practically and conceptually as academic subjects at most universities and in training programmes. Today, one such university, the London Academy of Diplomacy,[2] has partnered with the University of Stirling to offer such academic programmes at postgraduate and doctoral levels. These programmes aim to develop 'the essential skills for the practice of diplomacy, with an emphasis on assessment of situations, negotiating skills, communication and persuasion'. Today these programmes see the style of diplomacy as changed but still the essential risks of diplomacy remain – the management of external relations and contribution to international order and stability, and 'the ability to critically analyse and evaluate events, situations and policies'.

University education in diplomacy and the training of diplomats is not new: the 21st century, with its globalisation, economic and technological developments, has seen a significant growth in a search for better diplomats. Crawford (2015)[3] writes on how to train your diplomat following a visit to the seventeenth Dubrovnik Diplomatic Forum. See Appendix D. At this same forum, Professor Joseph Mifsud, of the London Academy of Diplomacy, reminded everyone of the content of *The Ambassadors*, the splendid Hans Holbein painting featuring Jean de Dinteville, 29, French ambassador to England in 1533, and his even younger friend Georges de Selve, variously ambassador to the Holy Roman Emperor and Venetian Republic, describing this as follows:

> The portrait includes intricately painted objects used by these youthful ambassadors, also denoting their distinguished learning. Celestial and terrestrial globes. A portable sundial and other clever instruments for understanding the heavens and measuring time. A lute and flutes. A hymn book. A book of arithmetic. These items ooze symbolism. The lute has a broken string: discord in Christendom? Plus, of course, the painting has the famous distorted skull. The macabre transience of diplomacy.

Today's governments depend on the skills of ambassadors to understand the political and commercial chains needed to establish the relationships needed between nations for the benefit of society. These skills will always be needed in the future and as the world grows smaller, through the speed of travel, will continuously have to be improved.

Does the description of Holbein's painting create in your mind anything about auditing practices in today's governance, risk and control in all economic, environmental and social issues, in every nation and internationally? It should: presentation, learning, understanding, space and time travel, harmony, regulation, tragedy – you may see other similarities. Ambassadors represent their state brand of 'political, economic and strategic relations'. They manage that brand in the countries they are placed and visit. They are brand ambassadors.

Brand ambassadors are recognised today as a marketing management process for not just products and services but also 'personal brand management'. Wikipedia includes the following quote:

> The brand ambassador is meant to embody the *corporate identity* in appearance, demeanor, values and ethics. The key element of brand ambassadors is their ability to use promotional strategies that will strengthen the customer-product-service relationship and influence a large audience to buy and consume more.[4]

'Audit brand ambassadors' can be those to whom auditors report – their boards, executive teams, managers, suppliers, customers; their professions; and even the auditors themselves in the ways they promote their products and services, both the quality and importance. There are many opportunities for creativity and innovation in the ways auditors market and sell their brand of services. Too often these ways are not always developed to their advantage. Such brand ambassadorial roles apply also to all those who are marketing good stewardship and corporate governance within organisations and across their supply chains, whether national or global.

3.2 Auditors Are Ambassadors for the State of Good Stewardship

Earlier in my academic career, following a visit to the National Gallery in London in 1998, I wrote about and published a paper on Holbein's *The Ambassadors*, linking it to the role of internal auditors in their global travels. I have now adapted this article to apply to all auditors. In its discussion I describe the painting's contents, relating these to the tools and practices of every auditor as ambassadors.

Auditors are Ambassadors in the Commonwealth, across the European Union and Internationally[5]

Those auditors familiar with paintings on exhibition at the National Gallery will probably be aware of, and have seen, Holbein's 'The Ambassadors'.[6] This painting is considered to be his finest work. On public view for over a century it was recently restored to all its original splendour. I first became aware of its background, and the 'auditing' story it tells, during an afternoon visit to the Gallery, with a friend, in early 1998. At that time the painting was on exhibition in the 'Making and Meaning' series: a series of complex paintings, researched and analysed, to explain their technical, scientific and historical context.

My interest lay in the exhibition's promotion of 'The Ambassadors',[7] as a mystery '. . . most intriguing, with its array of objects, many of them unfamiliar today, and its famous distortion of a skull, which has long puzzled observers . . .' The painting contains two portraits, one of Jean de Dinteville, French ambassador to England in 1533, and the other, Georges de Selve, Bishop of Lavaur, a close friend, who visited him in the same year. The story told is that, at the time, Jean de Dinteville had been sent by the French King to the English court to safeguard relations with Henry VIII. Probably a difficult and politically complex task – not unlike auditing! "It was hardly a plum posting, and in this dispiriting process he contrived to grow tired both of London and life." The visit of his friend was an important event to be commemorated. Dinteville commissioned Holbein to paint both their portraits.

The painting contains shelves full of apparently unrelated objects, shown in great detail, providing much of the painting's mystery. These include globes, quadrants, a sundial, a torquetum, an arithmetic book, set-square, dividers, a hymnbook and musical instruments. (Perhaps no different to many a travelling auditor's briefcase!). Over the centuries there has been much research and speculation into why these objects, some related to time and space, were chosen, and their relationship to each other.

In the foreground is a concealed skull '. . . using the distortion known as anamorphosis'. This is a representation of an object, unrecognisable except when seen from a particular viewpoint. Because of its prominence and distortion, the skull creates much of the painting's interest. Requiring the viewer to see clearly what it is, only from a side view.

During our viewing of the painting I commented to my friend, who is also an auditor, that the painting is an example of auditing at its best: a political environment, measurement of time and space, technical skills, considerable detail, apparently unrelated objects with unusual relationships, mystery, some distortion and the importance of a right point of view: all part of modern auditing. To add to this is the appropriateness of the painting's title.

I have always strongly believed that auditors are 'ambassadors' of good governance conduct and best practices, at all levels in their organisations, and in all their travels. I hope I can be forgiven the 'ambassador' analogy because of my early auditing ambassadorial experience. As a member of the Overseas Audit Service (OAS) in the 1950s, I served in Nigeria. OAS was established as Colonial Audit, a branch of the Colonial Office, in 1910: responsible for the audit of accounts of all British Colonies and Dependencies. During the last century, it established and maintained auditing standards in government and local authorities across the 'Empire', in both developed and undeveloped territories. Although only a small group – around 150 British staff during my time, it managed significant indigenous audit resources across the globe. Much of its influence on the standards of auditing, control and accounting in many governments during the 20th century continues in Commonwealth countries today through many Auditor-General Departments.

Like all audit work at the time I was trained using the principles of auditing written by De Paula (1914).[8] The role of the Colonial Auditor was mostly routine, yet sometimes exciting and very much ambassadorial. A central administrative office in London and a global office – on which the sun never set – established the organisational framework. At any one time Colonial Auditors and local audit staff were examining, verifying and signing accounts across the world, frequently in remote places. We were trained as envoys of good accounting, auditing and conduct. Much like the role of the present day UK National Audit Office and Audit Commission, merged into one!

My own experiences took me on many travels to remote areas in Nigeria. The audits covered all the services provided by government departments and local authorities, in both rural and urban environments, often spanning many years. (It was not uncommon to be auditing three to five years of financial statements during an audit visit.) A typical tour of audits in the 1950s could last up to six months, living in many isolated locations. Some in difficult and extreme geographical, political and climatic conditions. A portable typewriter, mental arithmetic, 'green' pencil and a local language dictionary, being the only office technology; government manuals of accounting, financial instructions and circulars being the standards of conduct; a copy of De Paula's Principles and Practices of Auditing, the standards; a camp bed and bath, kerosene lamp, battery radio and 'some refreshments', the only comforts. Faith and a belief in one's invincibility being the only security. Even today, these situations are probably not too uncommon for some auditors, in both developed and underdeveloped countries!

I was reminded of Holbein's painting and my 'wild' Colonial Audit days when I read the recently issued (November 1999) Commonwealth Association for Corporate Governance (CACG) principles for corporate governance.[9] CACG, is a new organisation: established in 1998, in response to the Edinburgh Declaration of the Commonwealth Heads of Government meeting in 1997, to promote excellence in corporate governance in all Commonwealth countries. Its guidelines are intended to promote and facilitate best business practice and behaviour. What an excellent 'flag' for all auditors, working and travelling in Commonwealth countries, including the UK!

CACG has developed 15 principles of corporate governance; each aimed at boards of directors of all business enterprises, whether private or state-owned. They represent the good business practice and corporate governance codes already developed by many of the Commonwealth countries (again including the UK). They are seen as a 'living document' applicable to all forms of enterprise. They emphasise the importance of leadership for efficiency and probity. They require responsibilities that are transparent and accountable. Any auditor who travels and audits in Commonwealth countries should be aware of their content and use their guidance. All professional auditing institutes should use the development and use of these principles to fly the flag of their auditing statements of responsibilities, behaviours, training programmes and standards, across the world.

CACG also prevails on professional bodies to focus on corporate governance issues and become involved in these in Commonwealth countries. Its list of professions includes accountants, auditors, corporate secretaries, lawyers, directors, etc. 'The fact is that good corporate governance practices are now becoming a necessity for every country and business enterprise, and are no longer restricted to the activities of public-listed corporations in advanced industrial economies.'

Since I wrote this article, the Charter of the Commonwealth with its core set of values was signed by Her Majesty Queen Elizabeth II, in March 2013,[10] following its signing by His Excellency Kamalesh Sharma, Commonwealth secretary-general, on 14 December 2012, on which day Commonwealth heads of government adopted the Charter of the Commonwealth. The core values in this charter represent the values all auditors should represent in their auditing, creative thinking and innovations in their audit processes. See Appendix E for the full charter. There can be few audits that should not reflect some if not all of the values it contains – in the objectives and reporting.

In Chapter 1 I discussed the value of vision and mission statements in motivating creativity and innovation in auditing. Figure 1.1 listed some of the vision statements and mission statements in organisations in which I am currently associated. Global auditing also has some exciting statements demonstrating ambassadorial ambitions in today and tomorrow's market places and governments. One good example is the International Organization of Supreme Audit Institutions (INTOSAI),[11] with its Strategic Plan and vision and mission statements to promote good government, public trust and continuous improvements – see www.intosai.org – its following core values give significant importance to its recognition of the importance of innovation in the services supreme audit institutions (SAIs) provide:

CORE VALUES – Inclusiveness: Cooperation: Innovation: Interdependence: Professionalism: Credibility: Integrity

INTOSAI is the organisation of SAIs with now more than 190 country members, founded in 1953 to promote the role of auditor-generals in 'auditing government accounts and operations and in promoting sound financial management and overall accountability in their governments'. It promotes auditing best practices, international standards and guidance for good governance. In 2011[12] the United Nations adopted a resolution promoting the 'efficiency, accountability, effectiveness and transparency of public administration by strengthening supreme audit institutions'. Recognising the important role independent SAIs play in 'promoting efficiency, accountability, effectiveness and transparency of public administration, which is conducive to the achievement of national development objectives and priorities'.

All of the word/terms in Table 2.1 and many in the logo at the beginning of Chapter 2 are seen in the INTOSAI Strategic Plan – see Table 3.1. Note how the word/terms 'Represent', 'State', 'Brand' all appear in the text in all six of the reports. How are 'Collaboration', 'Partnership' and 'Manage' used in your organisation and its statements? How are they and in your auditing and assurance reporting? Do you see auditors as ambassadors of good corporate governance, risk management and control? Are you promoting your ambassadorial role in your auditing and assurance reporting? There are many creative and innovative ways of doing this in every step of your audit process.

Table 3.1 INTOSAI (2010) compared with Table 2.1

	Industry	Finance	Charity	Health	Profess	EFMD	INTOSAI
Part I							
Stewardship							
Accountability	Y	Y	Y	Y	Y	Y	Y
Behaviour	Y	Y	Y	Y	Y	Y	Y
Beliefs	Y	Y	Y	Y	Y	Y	Y
Care	Y	Y	Y	Y	Y	Y	Y
Compliance	Y	Y	Y	Y	Y	Y	Y
Culture	Y	Y	Y	Y	Y	Y	Y
Customer	Y	Y	Y	Y	Y	Y	Y
Duty	Y	Y	Y	Y	Y	Y	Y
Ethics	Y	Y	Y	Y	Y	Y	Y
Governance	Y	Y	Y	Y	Y	Y	Y
Law	Y	Y	Y	Y	Y	Y	Y
Leadership	Y	Y	Y	Y	Y	Y	Y
Principles	Y	Y	Y	Y	Y	Y	Y
Responsibilities	Y	Y	Y	Y	Y	Y	Y
Stakeholder	Y	Y	Y	Y	Y	Y	Y
Stewardship	Y	Y	Y	Y	Y	Y	Y
Supplier	Y	Y	Y	Y	Y	Y	Y
Sustainability	Y	Y	Y	Y	Y	Y	Y
Transparent	Y	Y	Y	Y	Y	Y	Y
Trust	Y	Y	Y	Y	Y	Y	Y
Values	Y	Y	Y	Y	Y	Y	Y
Chapter 2							
Leadership							
Collaboration	Y	Y	Y	Y	Y	Y	Y
Partnership	Y	Y	Y	Y	Y	Y	Y
Manage	Y	Y	Y	Y	Y	Y	Y
Chapter 3							
Ambassadors							
Represent	Y	Y	Y	Y	Y	Y	Y
State	Y	Y	Y	Y	Y	Y	Y
Brand	Y	Y	Y	Y	Y	Y	Y

3.3 Professional Associations Are Brand Ambassadors for Auditors

If any further evidence is needed by the reader for seeing the role of auditors as ambassadors of good stewardship and governance, consider and analyse the following strategies, missions and values of five international professional associations for auditors, which teach and train auditors to practice across the world.

Institute of Chartered Accountants in England and Wales (ICAEW)[13]

STRATEGY: World leader of the global accountancy and financial profession.

OUR BUSINESS VALUES AND STANDARDS OF BEHAVIOUR:
Integrity: Competence and Due Care: Fraud: Bribery and Corruption: Corporate Responsibility: Objectivity: Respect for Others: Confidentiality

Association of Chartered and Certified Accountants (ACCA)[14]

MISSION: ACCA's mission is to be a global leader in the profession by:

- providing opportunity and open access to people of ability wherever they are in the world
- supporting our members throughout their careers
- achieving and promoting the highest ethical, governance and professional standards
- advancing the public interest.

CORE VALUES: Opportunity: Diversity: Innovation: Accountability: Integrity

American Institute of Certified Public Accountants (AICPA)[15]

VISION: The world leader in driving vitality, relevance and quality across the accounting profession, furthering trust and influence.
VALUES: Integrity: Passion: Innovation: Collaboration

Association of International Accountants[16]

OUR PURPOSE: AIA remains focused on the mission and core values on which we were founded:

- provide access to the accountancy profession on a global scale;
- provide member support and resources;
- maintain the highest standards in education, professionalism and ethics;
- promote the accountancy profession;
- further the recognition of AIA and its members.

OUR VALUES: Regulation: Ethics: Opportunity: Integrity and Transparency

The Institute of Internal Auditors (IIA)[17]

VISION: Internal Audit Professionals will be universally recognised as indispensable to effective governance, risk management, and control.
CORE VALUES: Collaboration: Courage: Unity in Diversity: Global Mindset: Innovation: Integrity: Service Excellence: Respect: Professional

Note the use of many of the word/terms in Table 3.1, also, in particular the values 'Innovation' and 'Passion' (a motivation not often associated with auditing and corporate governance but essential for creative thinking and innovation).

3.4 Chapter Review

In this chapter auditors are seen as ambassadors throughout the Ten Step Audit Process: an ambassador of the state of professional auditing and all the theories, principles and elements that make up good stewardship and corporate governance. As such, knowledge of diplomacy is an important attribute for all auditors, whether in the development of a brand image for the products and services they provide, in the management of all the practices they use to carry out their audit engagements, in the hats they wear during these engagements, or in their analysis of the feedback they receive from their clients or customers at the end of their audit. This ambassadorial role can be seen in the visions and missions of all the auditing professional institutions worldwide. Creatively thinking of this role as an ambassador should open up new, innovative ideas for the auditor in the audit process.

3.5 Creative Audit Thinking Activities

Activity 10   Create Innovation through Due Diligence Auditing

Consider the due diligence role of the auditor in mergers and acquisitions. Read the following description of mergers and acquisitions (M&As) and rewrite this in the context of the auditor ambassador representing the state of good stewardship and corporate governance, in not just the M&A processes, but in any restructuring in an organisation and its supply chains. What innovative auditing processes can you imagine for the auditor in a brand ambassador role in such changes?

Mergers and Acquisitions[18]

Over the past decade, Mergers and Acquisitions (M&As) have reached unprecedented levels as companies use corporate financing strategies to maximise shareholder value and create a competitive advantage. Acquisitions occur when a larger company takes over a smaller one; a merger typically involves two relative equals joining forces and creating a new company. Most Mergers and Acquisitions are friendly, but a hostile takeover occurs when the acquirer bypasses the board of the targeted company and purchases a majority of the company's stock on the open market. A merger is considered a success if it increases shareholder value faster than if the companies had remained separate. Because corporate takeovers and mergers can reduce competition, they are heavily regulated, often requiring government approval. To increase the chances of a deal's success, acquirers need to perform rigorous due diligence – a review of the targeted company's assets and performance history – before the purchase to verify the company's standalone value and unmask problems that could jeopardise the outcome.

Activity 11   Good Stewardship Creates Good Governance

Consider the following introduction to the UK Stewardship Code published by the UK Financial Reporting Council (FRC)[19] published to motivate investors and sets the tone for their stewardship:

> In publicly listed companies responsibility for stewardship is shared. The primary responsibility rests with the board of the company, which oversees the actions of its management. Investors in the company also play an important role in holding the board to account for the fulfilment of its responsibilities.

How can auditors as brand ambassadors of good stewardship and corporate governance innovate in their audit processes to support the stewardship role and responsibilities of their boards and customers?

Stewardship Word/Terms

Study Table 3.1 and select ten of the word/terms you consider to be most important in the stewardship responsibilities at board level. In your next audit, study how many of these appear and are used to direct and control the functions you are monitoring. The results should influence your choice of questions, selection of evidence, discussions with your customers and recommendations.

Activity 12   Create Responsible Business Conduct by Diplomacy

Benchmark your skills with Appendix D. Score yourself against each of those for a diplomat selected below. Use your score to creatively think and innovate how your skills and the audit processes can be changed/improved in your next engagement so you are seen not just as an auditor but as an ambassador of good corporate governance, risk management and control.

Appendixe skills

Selection of key points

> CONDUCTING MEETINGS BOTH FORMALLY AND
> INFORMALLY
> NEGOTIATING AUDIT ISSUES AT ALL LEVELS
> BE GOOD AT LISTENING
> BE FLEXIBLE BUT FIRM
> KEEP EVERYTHING IN THE RIGHT PERSPECTIVE

Notes

1 *Building Bridges* (1998), Internal Auditor (Augus), Jean-Pierre Garitte, chairman of The Institute of Internal Auditors, Orlando, US.
2 *Pathways to Diplomacy* (2013 p. 4), London Academy of Diplomacy and University of Stirling, London, England.
3 Accessed from *The Ambassador Partnership LLP* in July 2015. www.ambassadordllp.com.
4 Staff Writer (February 10, 2013). *'Brand Ambassadors' Give Your Business a Boost*, Business Courier (April 15, 2002). Accessed from Wikipedia. www.en-wikipedia.org/wiki/Brand Ambassador, accessed on May 2016.
5 *Internal Auditors Are Ambassadors in the Commonwealth . . . Across the European Union and Internationally* (2000), Internal Auditing and Business Risk, Chartered Institute of Internal Auditors, London, England.
6 The painting can be seen on the website www.en.wikipedia.org/The_Ambassadors_ (Holbein).
7 *Making & Meaning – Holbein's Ambassadors* (1997), Susan Foister, Ashok Roy and Martin Wyld, National Gallery Publications, London.
8 *The Principles of Auditing – A Practical Manual for Students and Practitioners* (1914), F.R.M. De Paula, first published by Sir Isaac Pitman and Sons Ltd., London, England early in the 20th century and later through that century, into its thirteenth Edition.
9 *CACG Guidelines – Principles for Corporate Governance in the Commonwealth, Commonwealth Association for Corporate Governance* (1999). www.,cbc.to.
10 *The Commonwealth Charter* (2013), Her Majesty's Government, Her Majesty's Stationery Office Ltd., London, England.
11 *Mutual Experience Benefits All – Strategic Plan 2011–2016* (2010), International Organisation of Supreme Audit Institutions (INTOSAI), General Secretariat, Vienna, Austria.
12 *Citizen Engagement Practices by Supreme Audit Institutions* (2013), Division for Public Administration and Development Management Department of Economic and Social Affairs United Nations, New York, US.
13 *Building the Accountancy Profession of the Future* (2015 p. 10), Annual Review 2015, Institute of Chartered Accountants in England and Wales (ICAEW), London, England. www.icaew.com.
14 *Think Ahead – Annual Report and Accounts* 2014–15, Association of Chartered and Certifies Accountants (ACCA), London, England.
15 *American Institute of CPAs, Values & Vision Statement* (2015), accessed www.aicpa.org/About/MissionandHistory accessed on 7 August 2015.

16 *Annual Report and Accounts* (2014), The Association of International Accountants, New-castle-upon-Tyne, England.
17 *IIA Global Strategic Plan 2015–20* (2014), The Institute of Internal Auditors Inc., Orlando, US.
18 *Management Tools – An Executive's Guide* (2015 p. 38), Darrell K. Rigby, Bain and Company Inc., Boston, MA, US.
19 *The UK Stewardship Code* (2012), Financial Reporting Council, London, England.

4   Auditors Are Gatekeepers

In both economic and moral terms, we are all affected by fraud and must accept a part of the total responsibility to deal with it effectively.[1]

In this chapter I see auditors as gatekeepers in the lines of defence boards establish in their organisations to be assured the control and controls they implement through policies, procedures and actions are appropriate and operate properly to safeguard their assets and reputations. Auditors detect and correct adverse situations which could lead to fraud, error, bad practices, criminal acts or disaster, whether by accident or design. Understanding how control and controls integrate and operate in an organisation is an essential competency for all auditors, if not all boards and everyone they relate to, whether in their organisations or across their supply chains – in fact, all their stakeholders.

4.1 Stewardship Is About Care and Protection

Good stewardship is always about care and trust; stewardship is also about performance and protection, not just physical security but about positive defences in all policies and practices against all the known likelihoods of dangers and disasters around and within every organisation, every day. These dangers and disasters can arise from a variety of internal and external sources and actions, some with an immediate effect and others where the effect may not be known for some time. Knowing the possibilities of such dangers and disasters is a responsibility at all levels in an organisation. They can occur at any time in the cycle of daily events, especially those linked into other organisations, either within the same organisation group structures or with external organisations. They can impact all of an organisation's assets and liabilities; its income and expenditure; its information and people; its suppliers and customers; those with whom it is in partnership, association and collaboration; its stakeholders, communities, environment and planet. They can happen in every organisation, whatever the size or location.

Coffee (2006)[2] discusses a new metaphor for those professionals who 'protect' organisations – *Gamekeeper* – defining this as a 'form of outside or independent watchdog or monitor – someone who screens out flaws or defects or who verifies compliance with standards or procedures'. His discussion centres around different professions and their roles. In particular he debates the 'Rise, Fall and Redefinition of Auditing' and sees the auditor as one of the gatekeepers an organisation and its board, owners and stakeholders rely upon for protection. He also sees the audit committee as key to monitoring the effectiveness of all the gatekeepers. Since his recognition of this audit committee role, guidance in how such committees should operate has developed more to see the audit committee as a monitor of all gatekeepers and their practices in their organisations.

One of the dangers and disasters in organisations is fraud. It can be small in loss; it can be great in loss; its loss can sometimes be recovered, but not always; but it can be the end of the organisation. Auditors do not always see themselves as fraud detectors, but their clients do! Thinking creatively of how an organisation is protected against and affected by fraud can lead sceptic auditors to innovate in the audit process with new and innovative suggestions for control. Other significant risks auditors should protect organisations from are health and safety and more worldly all those that endanger the survival of the planet, whether caused by the organisation or its supply chains. The board has a significant role to play in its prevention: audit also has a significant role to play in its prevention. Tickner (2010)[3] created his own definition for fraud in 2010:

> Fraud is an offence, resulting from dishonest behaviour that intentionally allows the fraudster or a third party to gain, or cause a loss to another. This can occur through false representation, failure to disclose information or abuse of position.

The UK Fraud Advisory Panel definition in 2015[4] is not too dissimilar:

> Fraud is deliberate use of deception or dishonesty to deprive, disadvantage or cause loss (usually financially) to another person or party, Definitions of fraud vary from country to country and between legal systems.

Compare these with your own country/legal system definition.

All organisations build defences to protect themselves against possible dangers and disasters. These defences take many different forms depending on their visions and missions, how they structure their organisations, their policies, systems, staff and style of management – most importantly, their values. One action every board should take is to publish an anti-fraud policy within its organisation and externally. Such a policy is a formal statement indicating a board's attitude to fraud and the actions taken to prevent it:

> An anti-fraud policy (sometimes called a 'fraud policy statement') outlines an organisation's attitude to, and position on, fraud and sets out responsibilities for its prevention and detection. It also communicates important deterrence messages to staff and third parties that fraudulent conduct will not be tolerated by the organisation and that the fight against fraud is endorsed and supported at the most senior level. A good anti-fraud policy should aim to outline an organisation's commitment to:
>
> - take appropriate measures to prevent and deter fraud
> - introduce and maintain necessary procedures to detect fraud
> - encourage employees to report any suspicions of fraud
> - investigate all instances of suspected fraud
> - take appropriate disciplinary, civil or criminal proceedings
> - report all suspected fraud to the appropriate authorities.
>
> Some organisations may be subject to obligations to report fraud to law enforcement and/or regulatory authorities.[5]

Many examples of anti-fraud policy statements can be found on the website. Their issue is now commonplace in organisations. Commitment to the measures and controls they contain is not always practiced. Good stewardship and corporate governance can deter, prevent and detect fraud if it happens. Its latest cost estimate in the United Kingdom was £52 billion per annum.[6] What is it in your country?

4.2 Prevention and Detection of Fraud

In the famous legal case in the United Kingdom, *Re: Kingston Cotton Mills Co.* (1896), Lord Justice Lopes defined an auditor's duty:

> to bring to bear on the work he has to perform that skill, care and caution which a reasonably careful, cautious auditor would use. What is reasonable skill, care and caution must depend on the particular circumstances of each case. An auditor is not bound to be a detective, or, as was said to approach his work with suspicion, or with a foregone conclusion that there is something wrong. He is a watchdog, not a bloodhound. He is justified in believing tried servants of the company in whom confidence is placed by the company. He is entitled to assume that they are honest and rely upon their representations, provided he takes reasonable care.

In a later case, *Fomento (Sterling Area) Ltd. v Selsdon Fountain Pen Co. Ltd.* (1958), Lord Denning put it this way:

> To perform his task properly he must come to it with an enquiring mind – not suspicious of dishonesty – but suspecting that someone may have made a mistake somewhere and that a check must be made to ensure that there has been none.

Since then there have been more changes of attitudes to dishonesty, almost to the point that auditors should be bloodhounds, not just watchdogs, approaching their audits and searches for evidence with suspicion. To some extent, assurance that controls are in place in an organisation to deter fraud is now required across the world in many countries by legislation, regulation and professional auditing standards.

Over the past twenty years there have been a number of discussion papers and consultations on the external auditor's responsibilities for the detection of fraud and misstatements in financial accounts. These have produced changes to laws, guidance, requirements and regulatory standards at both national and international levels. Much of this focuses on the competency of the auditors, their independence, objectivity, professionalism and scepticism when conducting their audit processes. The growing introduction of audit committees at board level has also improved the profile of audit contracts and the quality of audit work, both with external and internal auditors. That profile also includes a greater awareness at board level of the possibilities of fraud and misstatements at all levels in an organisation.

Current international auditing standards[7] require an external auditor to be professionally sceptical throughout an audit and to consider 'the potential for management override of controls and recognising the fact that audit procedures that are effective for detecting error may not be effective in detecting fraud'. A similar statement applies to internal auditors in their international professional standards. Any compliance inspection or regulatory standard reviews also expect similar scepticism.

Cadbury (1992)[8] in the United Kingdom recognised the existence of the expectation gap between auditors and their clients at that time. An expectation which included disclosure of all fraud or irregularities existing during and at the end of an audit:

> A further problem is the lack of understanding of the nature and extent of the auditors' role. This is the so-called 'expectations gap' – the difference between what audits do achieve, and what it is thought they achieve, or should achieve. The expectations gap is damaging not only because it reflects unrealistic expectations of audits but also because it has led to disenchantment with their value.

Cadbury also recommended in his Code of Best Practice for companies that listed companies should establish audit committees at board level to overview the roles of both internal and external audit, providing additional scrutiny to the likelihood of fraud and other irregularities occurring. Such committees now are commonplace in many organisations across all sectors, providing a review of the quality of planning and reporting for all auditing and other related scrutiny activities in their remit: reducing the expectation gap at committee and board level. Guidance now exists both nationally and internationally for the terms of reference for such committees and their practices to be externally visible to all stakeholders, though this is still varied and developing across organisations and sectors.

Much earlier, Russell (1977) cited an article by William E. Hanson in the *US Financial Executive* (1975), which aptly sets the scene for this chapter:

> The containment of fraud is founded on three closely related functions: (1) a strong, involved investigative Board of Directors; (2) a sound, comprehensive system of internal controls; and (3) alert, capable independent auditors . . . In all my years in the profession I have not seen any case of sizeable management fraud where all three functions were pursued with full diligence and professionalism. Working hand in hand with the Audit Committee (of the Board of Directors) are the financial officers of the company and the entire internal audit team. Needless to say, this team must be competent and conscientious. But it also must be dedicated, aggressive and creative.

As an internal auditor I worked with and for Harold Russell over a number of years. His belief in the role of all three of the functions mentioned as protectors against fraud was emphatic, taught and practiced. Not surprisingly considering the history of fraud across previous centuries and more recently in the 20th century, and even more closely in the 1970s. The absence of 'diligence and professionalism' in any or all of the three functions has also been too evident in many discovered frauds since the 1970s. The same 'diligence and professionalism' in the three functions is still essential today in the fight against fraud – fraud not just by management but by anyone in and outside an organisation.

In the introduction to Russell's book, Professor Victor Brink of Columbia University prophesied accurately on an inevitable increase in fraud:

> In this modern world, it is almost inevitable that the impact of fraud will become increasingly significant. There are a number of reasons why this is so. Some of these are as follows:
>
> - The scope of human interrelationships is continuously expanding in both a national and international sense. The resulting complexities provide greater opportunities for all kinds of fraudulent actions, including many new types.
> - The growth in population and the rising standard of living will result in an increased volume of all types of transactions and activities, providing more opportunities for fraud.
> - Increasing world resources are an increasingly attractive target for those who generate fraudulent activities.
> - Advances in technology and other types of knowledge give us better means of dealing with fraud. But, at the same time, they provide new tools which can be used by the perpetrator of fraud.
> - There have been major threats to the maintenance of high moral standards. The forces here include evidence of wrongdoing in government, excessive affluence in certain sectors of our society, and the depersonalisation of human relationships through automation and electronic data processing. Under these conditions we tend more to accept the existence and expansion of fraud.
>
> In total, various forces have combined to induce more fraud, to extend its range, and to neutralise the forces which could otherwise oppose its expansion.

Sadly most, if not all, of Brink's predictions have occurred and are still true today in governments and all sectors of business and trading activities. Fraud will always be with us as one of the risks in society across every nation and internationally. Russell studied fraud cases across the world and drew the following conclusions for the auditor:

> Fraud in the marketplace, embezzlement in positions of trust, bribery in public life, theft of securities, check kiting, illegal political donations, mail frauds, overloaded expense accounts, manipulation of payrolls, issuance of false financial statements, credit-card swindles, illegal competition, kickbacks and payoffs, bankruptcy frauds, and arson are a few of today's challenges. The outside criminal – the burglar or robber – usually visits his victim but once and leaves telltale evidence of his entry. But the inside criminal is a different story. How is he tracked down? The inside criminal

may be the owner, the manager, or the lowest employee. All are in a position to steal on a continuing basis. Here are four ways by which fraudulent activities are uncovered:

- reduction of the resource to a noticeable level of depletion
- accidental discovery of the fraud
- revelation by an informer
- diligence of an inquisitive. member of the accounting or audit staff.

Tickner's study into the investigation of fraud and its deterrence, based on personal experience, highlights the importance of auditors carrying out fraud risk analysis in an organisation using measures including the organisation's board-level anti-fraud policies and adequacies of control (note the similarity to the Hanson three functions mentioned earlier). Have all auditors been creative enough to protect organisations against this risk? Should they have been or should they be more protective? What of the auditor's creative and innovative role in the other two functions recognised by Hanson: '(1) a strong, involved investigative Board of Directors; (2) a sound, comprehensive system of internal controls'? Both are well covered in national and international legal duties and codes of corporate governance, with specific references to the avoidance and detection of fraud, as well as its diligent investigation if detected.

4.3 Auditors Are Gatekeepers at Board Level

How boards approach the prevention and detection of fraud depends on their effectiveness: their individual and group experiences, skills and competency. Corporate governance codes today focus well on these attributes at board level, how they are achieved and continuously improved. But do all boards? Inductions for directors at board level, their training and appraisals, including a board and its committees' self and independent appraisals into effectiveness vary and may not always be well conducted. Research in 2010 by the Chairman's Research Group[9] resulted in the following:

> We interviewed 30 Chairmen of FTSE 350 companies about how they undertake reviews of board effectiveness. Our study revealed that the practice of reviewing board effectiveness remains in its infancy, partly because effectiveness as a term is undefined. Many of the reviews we discussed still seemed to evaluate governance rather than the broader issue of effectiveness. Nonetheless the trend is clear: an initial focus on process and governance has been expanded to include the group dynamics of the board, and now is shifting to encompass a focus on how the board is contributing to the underlying business. Chairmen agreed unanimously that there is substantive value in undertaking an annual board review, but were less consistent about how to involve an external third party, and about the value to be gained from doing so.

In 2011 the UK Financial Reporting Council[10] published its views on board effectiveness and the importance for this to be measured:

> Boards continually need to monitor and improve their performance. This can be achieved through board evaluation, which provides a powerful and valuable feedback mechanism for improving board effectiveness, maximising strengths and highlighting areas for further development. The evaluation process should aim to be objective and rigorous.

Board evaluation is now an industry by both professional institutions and consultants. Its formulation and delivery at board, director/trustee and committee level varies. Whatever the process, it should be transparent, resulting in a measured improvement of performance. This may not always be so. Auditors have a protection role to play in this to see that it takes place as part of their review of an organisation's governance. It is not sufficient to just review board minutes, strategies, policies, conflicts of interest, codes of conduct and decision-making at board level. Auditors should form an opinion on board effectiveness processes and how they are carried out, results reviewed, and plan for continuous improvement implemented by the board.

4.4 Auditors Are Gatekeepers of the Control Environment

Control environments today are more complex than ever before. Control is now not just within an organisation but across its whole structure of levels and relationships and its supply chains, including all its stakeholders. Speed of change has added significant risks and challenges; organisations do not stand still to succeed or survive – there is constant change; the world is smaller – governments and organisations operate in global market places; technology has introduced new opportunities and threats. Fraud is a major threat for every organisation. The board and its 'tone at the top' is key to establishing the most appropriate control environment to achieve its objectives.

Control is a protector of an organisation's formation and assets and the directions in which it chooses to go. Control of an organisation's strategic thinking, decision-making and performance will always be essential for its success and survival. Control takes many forms in and around an organisation, laws to regulations; standards and codes to best practices; self-control and assessment to control by others; formal to informal; explicit to implicit; discipline to freedom; written to verbal; key and lock to open; password to easy access; memory to records; performance feedback to scorecards; evaluations to independent and objective audits and other compliance inspections. It is essential in every organisation that the board create the culture of how an organisation is governed. One aspect of control must always be protection against fraud – its prevention and detection.

There are many books written on how organisations should be controlled. Child (1977)[11] wrote a chapter on control in his book, *Organisation – A Guide to Problems and Practices*, a book that guided me often in my auditing career. He starts this chapter with:

> 'Everything is under control'. Managers say this with thinly disguised desperation as often as they say it with conviction. Controlling was only one of the five basic managerial functions which Henri Fayol identified back in 1916. Yet, it generally received a lion's share of attention in discussion in organisation structure. Many writers have seen the main contribution of organisation structure to be it provides for controlling behaviour. In fact, organisation is often taken to be synonymous with the organisation chart, which in its conventional form lays down official channels of control. Control is essentially concerned with regulating the activities in an organisation so that they are in accord with the expectations established in policies, plans, and targets.

Fayol's five basic functions, 'Planning: Organising: Leading: Controlling: Coordinating', can be seen throughout the Ten Step Audit Process mentioned earlier in Chapter 1 – Figure 1.4. Look for these in each step. Child[12] ended his chapter on control as follows:

> Control is an element of management which has received considerable attention in writing and debate. On the whole, control has been regarded as a process flowing down from the apex of hierarchies, and it is the directive element concerned with giving of instructions which has been singled out. Today, there is somewhat more appreciation that effective control requires a positive commitment from employees if instructions are to be followed and accurate feedback secured on results. The main organisational design decisions concerned with control are, first, how far to delegate decision making, second, how much to formalise procedures and working practices and third, how much emphasis to place on direct supervision.

This guidance in organisational behaviour underlies much of the framework of corporate governance principles and national codes for corporate governance practices and regulation. It also highlights many of the weaknesses that can occur in corporate governance when the components are not effective or efficient in an organisation.

The history and development of corporate governance codes has in the main over the past twenty-five years focused more on internal accounting control and its derivative 'internal control': Treadway (1977) used this word/term throughout its report (on 126 occasions), and even today the UK Corporate Governance Code (2014) uses the term 'internal control'. In its Provision C.2.3, it states:

> The board should monitor the company's risk management and internal control systems and, at least annually, carry out a review of their effectiveness, and report on that review in the annual report. The monitoring and review should cover all material controls, including financial, operational and compliance controls.

Today control is not just about internal control or even just 'financial, operational and compliance controls' within an organisation. Responsibility at board level for control is about risk and control within all an organisation's structures and across all its supply chains – good customer relationships and supply chain management requires this, and if not effective can seriously affect an organisation's performance, protection and reputation. Bain and Company (2015)[13] describe these as:

Customer Relationship Management (CRM) is a process companies use to understand their customer groups and respond quickly – and at times, instantly – to shifting customer desires. CRM technology allows firms to collect and manage large amounts of customer data and then carry out strategies based on that information. Data collected through focused CRM initiatives helps firms solve specific problems throughout their customer relationship cycle the chain of activities from the initial targeting of customers to efforts to win them back for more. CRM data also provides companies with important new insights into customers' needs and behaviours, allowing them to tailor products to targeted customer segments. Information gathered through CRM programs often generates solutions to problems outside a company's marketing functions, such as Supply Chain Management and new product development.

Supply Chain Management synchronises the efforts of all parties – suppliers, manufacturers, distributors, dealers, customers and so on – involved in meeting a customer's needs. The approach often relies on technology to enable seamless exchanges of information, goods and services across organisational boundaries. It forges much closer relationships among all links in the value chain in order to deliver the right products to the right places at the right times for the right costs. The goal is to establish such strong bonds of communication and trust among all parties that they can effectively function as one unit, fully aligned to streamline business processes and achieve total customer satisfaction.

Key to the governance and success of control in customer relations and supply chains is management of quality in all its processes. This applies whatever the product or service – even in audit. Protection by auditors of control at all levels in an organisation requires total quality management of efficiency and effectiveness throughout the Ten Step Audit Process.

In 1994 I wrote and had published the following article on control, which will always apply to all auditors:

Control Is Like a Well Lit Christmas Tree[14]

December is the time of year when all internal auditors and managers can remind themselves of the important characteristics of control when they prepare and admire their traditional Christmas tree. The Institute of Internal Auditors Standards[15] set out the environment for adequate control in an organisation is present ' . . . if the management has planned and organised (designed) in a manner which provides reasonable assurance that the organisation's objectives and goals will be achieved efficiently and economically. These objectives are four important qualities for the festive Christmas tree. It must be:

ATTRACTIVE IN SHAPE
DECORATED COLOURFULLY
POSITIONED SO THAT IT CAN BE RECOGNISED
USED AS A FOCUS FOR CELEBRATION

The tree that achieves these qualities – whether large or small – in home, street or workplace – creates an environment that will influence the actions of those who are in its presence.

SHAPE, COLOUR, RECOGNITION and CELEBRATION are also very important characteristics of internal control. Each plays an important part in establishing the 'adequate' and 'reasonable' levels of control essential if 'expected results' are to be achieved.

SHAPE is the result of good design. In control, this design is in the planning and direction of all management and work practices. The required shapes of control must be thought out carefully with the purpose clearly in mind. There needs to be a vision of the shape that the organisation requires if it is to achieve its objectives. Attractive shapes promote effectiveness, efficiency and economy. Unattractive shapes create weaknesses in control.

COLOUR brightens the shape. It arouses emotions. In the same way colourful controls encourage compliance. The relationships and connections between all the visions, strategies, policies and operational rules in an organisation need to be carefully coloured if reasonable control is to exist. Motivation is the brightest colour in control. It makes relations and links work well in the many supply chains in and across organisations. It sets the tones in the control environments. An understanding of how motivation influences control is an important part of control planning.

RECOGNITION is like the placing of control so that its shape and colour can be seen and recognised by all in the environment in which it is placed.

CELEBRATION around a well positioned tree is a highlight of the festive season. It is also important good control generates celebration for those participating in its success. When control contributes to success and achievement. Awards and positive reinforcements is an important part of management at all levels in the organisation. Linking control to success and celebration should be a part of the reporting of all audit results.

SHAPE, COLOUR, RECOGNITION and **CELEBRATION** are still key today and will always be tomorrow for the implementation of control and controls in every organisation: assessing controls will always require an evaluation of how each is seen by everyone in an organisation and across all its supply chains.

The Committee of Sponsoring Organisations of the Treadway Commission (COSO), in collaboration with The IIA (2015)[16] recently published guidance to help organisations enhance their overall governance structures: promoting an innovative *Three Lines of Defence Model* to demonstrate how organisations manage their risks and controls to achieve their objectives. See Figure 4.1.

The first two lines of defence are the controls established by management at the direction of the governing body/board with support from the audit committee, recognising it owns the risks and controls to mitigate these. The second line lists management assurances needed to ensure controls are operating efficiently and effectively. The third line provides independent and objective assurance by internal audit activities over both the first two lines and importantly its reporting to both management and the governing body/board/audit committee. The third line of defence also will, or should, include other internal independent assurance providers working in collaboration with internal audit. The three lines of defence are reviewed by external audit and today by an organisation's stakeholders including its regulators. The aim of the model is to demonstrate how organisations protect their enterprise value through an effective governance structure while achieving their objectives:

> The goal for any organisation is to achieve its objectives. Pursuit of these objectives involves embracing opportunities, pursuing growth, taking risks, and managing those risks – all to advance the organisation. Failure to take the appropriate risks, and failure to properly manage and control risks taken, can prevent an organisation from accomplishing its objectives.

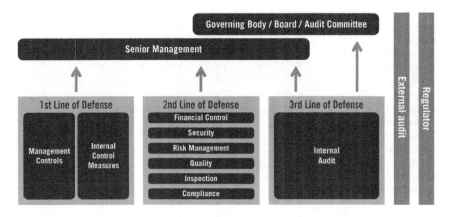

Figure 4.1 Internal audit as the third line of defence

There is, and always will be, tension between activities to create enterprise value and activities to protect enterprise value. The *Framework* provides a structure to consider risk and control to ensure they are appropriate and properly managed. The Model provides guidance as to an organisational structure to be implemented, assigning roles and responsibilities to parties that will increase the success of effective management of risk and control.

Many of the word/terms in Table 3.1 are seen in the COSO/The IIA *Three Lines of Defence Model* reflecting the importance of these word/terms in any audit and promotion of the role of the auditor as a gatekeeper of good stewardship and governance – see Table 4.1.

Table 4.1 COSO (2015) compared with Table 3.1

	Industry	Finance	Charity	Health	Profess	EFMD	INTOSAI	COSO
Part I								
Stewardship								
Accountability	Y	Y	Y	Y	Y	Y	Y	Y
Behaviour	Y	Y	Y	Y	Y	Y	Y	Y
Beliefs	Y	Y	Y	Y	Y	Y	Y	Y
Care	Y	Y	Y	Y	Y	Y	Y	Y
Compliance	Y	Y	Y	Y	Y	Y	Y	Y
Culture	Y	Y	Y	Y	Y	Y	Y	Y
Customer	Y	Y	Y	Y	Y	Y	Y	Y
Duty	Y	Y	Y	Y	Y	Y	Y	Y
Ethics	Y	Y	Y	Y	Y	Y	Y	Y
Governance	Y	Y	Y	Y	Y	Y	Y	Y
Law	Y	Y	Y	Y	Y	Y	Y	Y
Leadership	Y	Y	Y	Y	Y	Y	Y	Y
Principles	Y	Y	Y	Y	Y	Y	Y	Y
Responsibilities	Y	Y	Y	Y	Y	Y	Y	Y
Stakeholder	Y	Y	Y	Y	Y	Y	Y	Y
Stewardship	Y	Y	Y	Y	Y	Y	Y	Y
Supplier	Y	Y	Y	Y	Y	Y	Y	Y
Sustainability	Y	Y	Y	Y	Y	Y	Y	Y
Transparent	Y	Y	Y	Y	Y	Y	Y	Y
Trust	Y	Y	Y	Y	Y	Y	Y	Y
Values	Y	Y	Y	Y	Y	Y	Y	Y
Chapter 2								
Leadership								
Collaboration	Y	Y	Y	Y	Y	Y	Y	Y
Partnership	Y	Y	Y	Y	Y	Y	Y	Y
Manage	Y	Y	Y	Y	Y	Y	Y	Y
Chapter 3								
Ambassadors								
Represent	Y	Y	Y	Y	Y	Y	Y	Y
State	Y	Y	Y	Y	Y	Y	Y	Y
Brand	Y	Y	Y	Y	Y	Y	Y	Y
Chapter 4								
Gatekeepers								
Defend	Y	Y	Y	Y	Y	Y	Y	Y
Protect	Y	Y	Y	Y	Y	Y	Y	Y
Monitor	Y	Y	Y	Y	Y	Y	Y	Y

4.5 Chapter Review

In this chapter I see the auditor as a gatekeeper in the protection of an organisation and the achievement of its objectives and compliance with its policies and procedures – protection not just to prevent or detect malpractices and errors, but also to continuously improve efficiency and effectiveness of that protection at board, executive and operations levels. All auditors have an important role to play as gatekeepers in their evaluation of control and controls during their engagements.

4.6 Creative Audit Thinking Activities

Activity 13   Understand the Creative Thinking Fraudster

The legal definition of fraud varies across countries and legal systems. Understand the definition in the countries and sectors in which you audit. In an article I had published in 1994[17] I wrote:

> Preventing fraud is management's responsibility in any organisation. Using an integrated control framework to prevent and detect fraud can be an important part of the internal auditor and manager's activities. Understanding what fraud is and how it can be carried out in any organisation, at all levels, and from both inside and outside, is key to its prevention and detection. Control and governance as fraud deterrents are essential for the success of all organisations. The risk of fraud is always present. Approaches to its investigation and disclosure vary. Almost without exception it can impact all of society and an organisation's stakeholders. It can cause considerable damage, far beyond the value of its loss, leading sometimes to significant performance failures and even closure of operations, and whole businesses. In the public sector it can lead to political unrest and loss of power.

Consider the implications of this quote and the following statement on fraud today. How are you creatively thinking about fraud and its prevention and detection in your audit processes? What creative and innovative *'close alliances'* can you establish in your auditing to 'prevent, prepare and detect' fraud?

A National Strategy to Combat Fraud[18]

In an era of declining crime rates, fraud and, in particular, cyber-fraud stands out as one of the country's fastest growing crime types. As more and more criminals – both individual operators and organised gangs – move online to commit economic crime, many of the established rules of policing and techniques to catch law breakers have become obsolete. The technology that has revolutionised our lives in the past 20 years has been harnessed to commit economic crime on an unprecedented scale. In the past year the force ran several complex and high profile investigations, leading to successful prosecutions at court. But, with fraud at unprecedented levels, to simply pursue is no longer enough. There has to be a much greater emphasis on prevent, prepare and protect, with police forces and the counter fraud community working in close alliance to ensure *people* and businesses have the information they need to keep the threat of online crime out of their homes and workplaces.

Activity 14   Build Creativity and Innovation Into Your Fraud Checklist

Consider the following checklist developed by Harold Russell and included in his 1977 book *Foozles and Frauds*. Add your own interpretations for each advice. What would you change and/or add today to create a forward-looking checklist for the complex fraud risk and control environments of the 21st century?

A Fraud Checklist for the 1970s[19] [and 21st Century]

1 When something does not look right, be persistent in running it down.
2 To obtain the best results, establish proper relationships with the people you audit.
3 Recognise improper actions, entries and figures when you see them.
4 Develop your ability to remember bits of information and, by association, place them in an overall pattern.
5 Dishonest people are poor liars – listen for their double-talk.
6 Learn to ask open-ended questions – but only the right kind.
7 Do not trust an informer's allegations, but never ignore them.
8 Be alert to the possibility of false documentation.
9 Do not rely on evidence that cannot be fully supported.
10 Make sure that audit sampling is not only scientific but also sensible.
11 Do not be misled by appearances.
12 Do not be satisfied with unreasonable answers to audit questions.
13 Do not ignore unrecorded funds for which the organisation has a legal or moral responsibility.
14 Learn as much about the auditees as you possibly can.
15 Keep audit programmes from becoming too limited or stereotyped.

Activity 15   Create Your Own Innovative Fraud Risk Assessment Process

Every organisation has the likelihood of fraudulent activities, whether low or high risks, whether low value or high value. Every organisation should have an anti-fraud policy published for all levels to see and communicated externally to its stakeholders. Risk-based audits should address the possibility of fraud in every audit engagement audit. Consider the following statement on fraud risk assessment as both an internal and external auditor. Develop this type of assessment for your audit process.

Internal Audit Services Should Be a Defence against the Threat of Fraud[20]

The fraud risk assessment process is a structured method to identify possible fraud schemes, identify internal controls that help to prevent or detect identified fraud schemes, document the results of testing the controls, and implement corrective action plans where needed. The objective of this process is to identify the existence of controls and how they operate, not necessarily to seek out fraud. Adequate controls reduce the opportunities for fraud to be committed. The assessment considers the various ways to which a company can be subjected to fraud and misconduct, along with its vulnerability to management override and other potential schemes to circumvent existing controls. Fraud risk assessment is a continuous process. **Always remember fraud can be perpetrated both within an organisation and from external sources.**

Notes

1 *Foozles & Frauds* (1977 p. XII) Introduction by Professor Brink, Harold F. Russell, Institute of Internal Auditors Inc., Orlando, US.
2 *Gatekeepers – The Professions and Corporate Governance* (2006 p. 2), John C. Coffee Jr., Oxford University Press, Oxford, England.
3 *How to Be a Successful Frauditor – A Practical Guide to Investigating Fraud in the Workplace for Internal Auditors and Managers* (2010), Peter Tickner, John Wiley and Sons, Chichester, England.
4 Fraud Advisory Panel website www.fraudadvisorypanel.org/prevention accessed 29 August 2015.
5 *Fact Sheet – Anti-fraud Policy Statements* (2010), Fraud Advisory Panel, London, England.
6 *UK National Fraud Authority Annual Report 2013–14*, London, England.
7 *The Auditor's Responsibilities Relating to Fraud in an Audit of Financial Statements* (2010), International Standard on Auditing (UK and Ireland) 240, Financial Reporting Council, London England.
8 *Report of the Committee on Corporate Governance* (1992 section 5.4), Sir Adrian Cadbury, Gee and Co. Ltd., London, England.

9 *Reviewing Board Effectiveness – A Study of Current Practice* (2010 p. 6), The Chairman's Research Group, The Board Advisory Partnership LLP, London, England.
10 *Guidance on Board Effectiveness* (2011 p. 11), Financial Reporting Council, London, England.
11 *Organisation – A Guide to Problems and Practices* (1977 p. 117), John Child, Harper and Row Publishers, London, England.
12 *Organisation – A Guide to Problems and Practices* (1977 pp. 134–135), John Child, Harper and Row Publishers, London, England.
13 *Management Tools – An Executive's Guide* (2015 pp. 26–56), Darrel K. Rigby, Bain and Company Inc., Boston, US.
14 *Leading Edge Internal Auditing* (1998 p. 82), Jeffrey Ridley and Andrew Chambers, ICSA Publishing Ltd., London, England. (First published in 1994 in Internal Control and Business Risk, Chartered Institute of Internal Auditors, London, England).
15 *Standards for the Professional Practice of Internal Auditing* (1994), The Institute of Internal Auditors, Altamonte Springs, Orlando, Florida, US. (Today this standard is incorporated in The IIA *Professional Practices Framework* – Practice Advisory 2100–1: *Nature of Work*.)
16 *Leveraging COSO Across the Three Lines of Defense* (2015 p. 3), Authors Douglas J. Anderson and Gina Eubanks, Committee of Sponsoring Organisations of the Treadway Commission, New York, US.
17 *Think Like a Criminal* (1994 p. 7), Internal Auditing, Chartered Institute of Internal Auditors, London, England.
18 *City of London Police – Annual Report* (2014–15 p. 12). www.cityoflonfon.police.uk, accessed 31 August 2015.
19 *Foozles & Frauds* (1977 pp. 244–249), Harold F. Russell, Institute of Internal Auditors Inc., Orlando, US.
20 *How Internal Audit Can Help Against a Company's Fraud Issues* (2011 p. 150), Gail Harden, contributor in Internal Auditing Best Practices Approaches to Internal Auditing, Bloomsbury Information Ltd., London, England.

Part II

Change

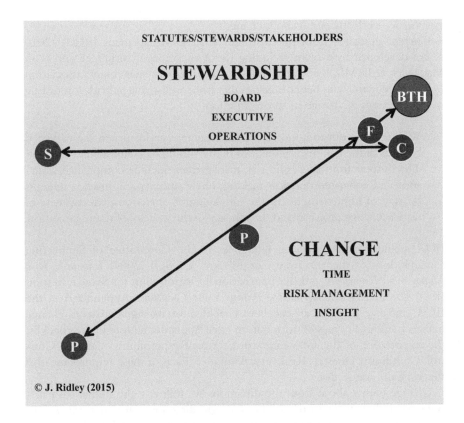

STATUTES/STEWARDS/STAKEHOLDERS

STEWARDSHIP

BOARD

EXECUTIVE

OPERATIONS

BTH

F

C

S

P

CHANGE

TIME

RISK MANAGEMENT

INSIGHT

P

© J. Ridley (2015)

Corporate sustainability is a significant part of the solution to poverty, risk of catastrophic climate change and other global challenges that the world currently faces.[1]

Change is not a new concept. It has been with us since the world began. It is not always about improvement, but more often this is its goal. It surrounds us all every minute of the day, in every part of our social lives, work and play. Today we are much more aware of change in our own lives in our own worlds and the lives of others in their worlds, partly because of the speed in which it now takes place, but also because of the many new ways in which it is communicated. The concept of change comes in many different forms; its impact can be immediate or delayed. It can be transitional and transformational. It can have little impact, or be dramatic and epic. It can impact culture and the organisations which we rely on for our enterprise, products, services, health and safety. Change is always about time. It is constantly with us – has been in the past, is in the present and will be in the future and beyond the horizon (BTH). It is always part of the risks we face and mitigate in our lives. Risks exist everywhere in all our worlds and even in the sustainability of the planet we occupy and the universe in which it exists. Most importantly, change should be forecast, well-led and managed; this is not always so. In too many instances its effect is not fully considered, and as a result we and often others suffer pain or loss. Social, environmental and governance performance is about change.

Current guidance from the Institute of Risk Management (IRM) (2010 p. 2),[2] developed by a team including the Association of Insurance and Risk Managers (AIRMIC) and the public sector risk management association (Alarm) recognises the benefits achievable from well-managed risk forecasting in the processes of change in an organisation:

> When setting out to improve risk management performance, the expected benefits of the risk management initiative should be established in advance. The outputs from successful risk management include compliance, assurance and enhanced decision-making. These outputs will provide benefits by way of improvements in the efficiency of operations, effectiveness of tactics (change projects) and the efficacy of the strategy of the organisation.

IRM includes in its guidance references to the Committee of Supporting Organisations of the Treadway Commission (COSO) (2004) *Enterprise Risk Management Framework* and the International Organization for Standardization (ISO) (2009) *Risk Management – Principles and Guidelines*. Appendix A in the IRM guidance provides an excellent checklist for managing risks in change management in all types of organisation – see Appendix F. Note in the checklist the importance of the following word/terms: Responsibility; Culture; Control; Continuity; Disaster; Recovery; Assurance. Each of these requires creative thinking and innovation.

Change comes about from the directions we follow – the individual pathways we follow from birth, to the strategic directions created from visions and missions of the governments and organisations surrounding the way we live, work and play. It affects the way we evaluate and judge those around us. It is part of every audit in the past, present and future; the way the audit is conducted – each of the ten steps of the audit process; the persons who are responsible for the audit; the persons being audited; and the operations being audited. An assessment of the risks of change is an essential part of all audit programmes. That assessment can change the scope of the audit, its methods and how the results are communicated and to whom.

The scope of assurance in every audit should evaluate changes in economics, efficiency, effectiveness, ethics and the environment. Each of these five issues interacts with the others; each is an important element in the strategies, structures and systems of all organisations and their operations; each is essential in good stewardship, compliance with corporate governance principles and codes, and the achievement of excellence by individuals, organisations and governments. Evaluation of accountability, integrity and transparency and an assessment of the risks of future change should be documented in the working papers of every audit.

Risks and change underlie all aspects of corporate governance and sustainability, in its establishment, practices and regulation. Most organisations will refer to both in reports to their stakeholders; the organisation communications analysed in Table 3.1 are no exception to this rule. Each, in its own way, addresses its responsibilities for sustainability in itself and market place. In a 2014 publication, *Building the Post-2015 Business Engagement Architecture* (from which the part epigraph is taken) recognised the growth of sustainability movements across the world with responsible management and business practices at their heart discussing the 'building blocks' needed for this to happen – *The Post-2015 Business Engagement Architecture illustrates the main building blocks necessary to enhance corporate sustainability as an effective contribution to sustainable development, creating value for both business and society*. In its introduction it recognises the actions by many of today's organisations:

> Companies are increasingly helping to tackle the world's most pressing problems through their core businesses, and realising benefits and opportunities from doing so. There is a growing recognition that, in a globalised world, general prosperity can only be built on the foundations of collaboration between public and private sectors.

That collaboration will be a significant driver for change in the future across organisations of all sizes in all sectors and countries across the world. All auditors are going to have to recognise this change in their audit engagements today and in the future. It will not only motivate innovations in all organisations but also require innovations in all auditing. In Table B.1 I have compared Table 3.1 with the content of the UN Global Compact architecture for the future. This shows how each of the previous word/terms is reflected in it, and by adding CHANGE, RISK and FUTURE, how these important messages are reflected in each of the previous statements. All will build innovations. Are 'Change', 'Risk' and 'Future' used in your organisation and its statements? How are they used in your auditing and assurance reporting? Do you see auditors as change agents, risk managers, focused on the future as well as the past and present? Are you promoting these roles in your auditing and assurance reporting? There are many creative and innovative ways of doing this in every step of your audit process.

Table B.1 UN Global Compact (2015) compared with Table 3.1

	Industry	Finance	Charity	Health	Profess	EFMD	INTOSAI	COSO	Global
Part I									
Stewardship									
Accountability	Y	Y	Y	Y	Y	Y	Y	Y	Y
Behaviour	Y	Y	Y	Y	Y	Y	Y	Y	Y
Beliefs	Y	Y	Y	Y	Y	Y	Y	Y	Y
Care	Y	Y	Y	Y	Y	Y	Y	Y	Y
Compliance	Y	Y	Y	Y	Y	Y	Y	Y	Y
Culture	Y	Y	Y	Y	Y	Y	Y	Y	Y
Customer	Y	Y	Y	Y	Y	Y	Y	Y	Y
Duty	Y	Y	Y	Y	Y	Y	Y	Y	Y
Ethics	Y	Y	Y	Y	Y	Y	Y	Y	Y
Governance	Y	Y	Y	Y	Y	Y	Y	Y	Y
Law	Y	Y	Y	Y	Y	Y	Y	Y	Y
Leadership	Y	Y	Y	Y	Y	Y	Y	Y	Y
Principles	Y	Y	Y	Y	Y	Y	Y	Y	Y
Responsibilities	Y	Y	Y	Y	Y	Y	Y	Y	Y
Stakeholder	Y	Y	Y	Y	Y	Y	Y	Y	Y
Stewardship	Y	Y	Y	Y	Y	Y	Y	Y	Y
Supplier	Y	Y	Y	Y	Y	Y	Y	Y	Y
Sustainability	Y	Y	Y	Y	Y	Y	Y	Y	Y
Transparent	Y	Y	Y	Y	Y	Y	Y	Y	Y
Trust	Y	Y	Y	Y	Y	Y	Y	Y	Y
Values	Y	Y	Y	Y	Y	Y	Y	Y	Y
Chapter 2									
Leadership									
Collaboration	Y	Y	Y	Y	Y	Y	Y	Y	Y
Partnership	Y	Y	Y	Y	Y	Y	Y	Y	Y
Manage	Y	Y	Y	Y	Y	Y	Y	Y	Y
Chapter 3									
Ambassadors									
Represent	Y	Y	Y	Y	Y	Y	Y	Y	Y
State	Y	Y	Y	Y	Y	Y	Y	Y	Y
Brand	Y	Y	Y	Y	Y	Y	Y	Y	Y
Chapter 4									
Gatekeepers									
Defend	Y	Y	Y	Y	Y	Y	Y	Y	Y
Protect	Y	Y	Y	Y	Y	Y	Y	Y	Y
Monitor	Y	Y	Y	Y	Y	Y	Y	Y	Y
Part II Change									
Change	Y	Y	Y	Y	Y	Y	Y	Y	Y
Risk	Y	Y	Y	Y	Y	Y	Y	Y	Y
Future	Y	Y	Y	Y	Y	Y	Y	Y	Y

In 2000 I wrote and published an article on internal audit, risk management and control in insurance companies and how these word/terms were changing the role of internal auditors for the 21st century. The following is this article adapted to today and to apply to all auditing in every organisation for tomorrow.

Risk, Change and Control: Challenges and Opportunities for All Auditors[3]

All auditing professional strategies recognise the importance of risk and change in their promotion of auditing standards and practices. Authoritative statements on risk management and change by boards exist in most organisations and in both auditing research and guidance. The feet of all auditors are now firmly placed in the boardrooms of most organisations. A place some auditors are still not familiar with, either in their audit work or in their advisory roles. The future of professional auditing will always depend on how creative and innovative auditors are in the tone at the top of every organisation.

The Institute of Directors and Chartered Institute of Internal Auditors 2013 p. 3) published Guidance on what all directors should know about internal auditors:

> Internal audit is the eyes and ears of the board and its committees, above all its audit committee. Working independently within the organisation, internal audit provides assurance to the board that, in the pursuit of the company's objectives, risks are being managed effectively, financial and other controls are in place, and the organisation is being properly governed.

They followed this with ten essential actions for boards to ensure their organisations were maximising the value of internal audit to gain maximum protection from its audit activities, recommending these also for '... boards in the public sector and third sector ...' – see Figure B.1.

I have taken these recommended ten actions and changed them to apply to all auditing and assurance functions in an organisation, whether provided internally or externally:

1   Evaluate the need for all audit and assurance activities.
2   Assess and approve terms of reference for all audit and assurance activities and review regularly.
3   Ensure close working relationships with all audit and assurance activities at board level or through an audit or risk committee.
4   Assess the resourcing of all audit and assurance functions.
5   Monitor the quality of all audit and assurance, both in-house and external.
6   Evaluate, approve and regularly review the risk-based annual audit and assurance plans.
7   Oversee the relationship between audit and assurance with centralised risk monitoring.
8   Ensure the collective audit and assurance roles are coordinated.

9   Assess all audit and assurance findings and the breadth and depth of audit reports.
10 Monitor management implementation of all audit and assurance recommendations.

Any review of annual reports will refer to audit, risk and change and how each is being addressed to achieve an organisation's vision and mission statements in the short, medium and long terms, often through audit and risk committees at board level. This profile is now required by not just the organisation but many of its stakeholders, including its regulators. Audit and risk committees are seen by most financial regulators as essential monitors of an organisation's audit, risk and change. Treadway (1987) reflected on their importance in its report using the word/term audit on 1,287 occasions, risk on 110 occasions, and change on 91 occasions. Treadway's audit committee guidelines for public companies set a seed for these to grow throughout the globe and can be seen in guidelines for audit and risk committees at board level across the world in all sectors.

All auditors in their audit planning processes will use risk management techniques to review key controls. Risk assessment is crucial to the development of effective audit work schedules. The risk assessment process includes identification of auditable activities, identification of relevant risk factors, and an assessment of their relative significance. This requirement

---

1   Evaluate the need for internal audit where it does not exist.
2   Assess and approve the internal audit charter (terms of reference) and review regularly.
3   Ensure a close working relationship with the Head of Internal Audit, promoting effective formal and informal communication.
4   Assess the resourcing of the internal audit function.
5   Monitor the quality of internal audit work, both in-house and external.
6   Evaluate, approve and regularly review the risk-based annual internal audit plan.
7   Oversee the relationship between internal audit and centralised risk monitoring.
8   Ensure the collective assurance roles of internal audit, other internal assurance providers and external audit, are coordinated and optimised.
9   Assess internal audit findings and the breadth and depth of internal audit reports.
10 Monitor management implementation of internal audit recommendations.

Figure B.1 Ten essential actions for boards to ensure that their organisation maximises the value of its internal audit and gains maximum protection

Source: *What Every Director Should Know About Internal Audit* (2013 p. 3), Chartered Institute of Internal Auditors and Institute of Directors, London, England.

received a public profile in North America with the publication of an integrated model for control in organisations, recommended by a committee of professional institutions – COSO (1992),[4] established following publication of the Treadway Report. Since that time this integrated model has grown in its importance across governance and regulatory codes across the globe. It revolutionised the way organisations, regulators and auditors looked at the control environment. It identified six key inter-related factors for control – control environment, risk assessment, control activities, monitoring, information systems and communication. Its control environment is described as a:

- Commitment by directors, management and employees to competence and integrity and the development of an appropriate culture to support these principles.
- Communication of appropriate agreed standards of business behaviour and control consciousness to managers and employees (e.g. through written codes of conduct, formal standards of discipline, performance appraisal).
- Structure within which business can be planned, executed, controlled and monitored to achieve the company's objectives.
- Time and resources by the board, senior management and the company to internal control and risk management issues.
- Creation of an environment that promotes learning within the company on risk and control issues, including the provision of relevant training.
- Delegation of authority, with accountability, which has regard to acceptable levels of risk.

Across the world there are now many codes of practice to encourage and require regulation of good stewardship and corporate governance in the management and leadership of change and risk. All are based on the same principles of accountability, integrity and transparency, promoted by the Cadbury (1992) committee's focus on the 'control and reporting functions of boards, and on the role of auditors'. Cadbury studied the financial aspects of corporate governance and recommended a code of best practice for directors, audit committees for all listed companies and board reports on control, which is still relevant today and will be tomorrow. Subsequent commissions and studies have refined these and added new principles to cover more than just financial issues – environmental, social and economic issues embrace more than just shareholders. They include stakeholders and civil societies across the world.

Underlying the recommended reviews of a widely defined 'control: delegation: reporting' in an organisation is a need for all organisations to continually review and monitor change and risk across their supply chains. Surprisingly, the implications of control over supply chains external to an organisation have received little attention in the corporate governance codes. Yet there can be few organisations now that are not dependent on external supply chains with links to customers, suppliers, contractors, alliances, associates, joint ventures and so forth. Change and risk across external supply chains is as important as control in an organisation, and should receive board, management and audit attention.

It is also important to review the quality of established audit functions annually as to review the need to have such services. In my experience, and that of current researchers, too few organisations have a continuous quality assurance review of their existing audit functions, both internal and external. True, the new role of audit committees in organisations now provides a continuous monitoring of audit plans and activities. But quality assurance goes much deeper than this. Designing quality into audit structures and processes requires auditors to be committed to formal processes and a new culture of professionalism and continuous improvement. That new culture must embrace the principles of quality management. In my book with Chambers[5] (1998), I quote these principles as follows:

> Many audit providers use the quality principles of customer focus, management leadership, teamwork, analytical approach and continuous improvement – to market their auditing products and services. Some link these principles into other consultancy products and services associated with control, risk and governance.

Boards and management have always assessed change and risk in their decision-making processes. Risk managers and assessors, both internal and external, have developed and provide professional services to organisations in these decision-making processes. What is now new is the focus on risk in the corporate governance debate. The new integration of risk management, control and governance will change the risk management process in many organisations. New processes are already being created with a new 'risk' language, for boards, management and auditors. It is important that all in the same organisation speak a common risk language and use similar risk management processes.

There is now ample evidence to show that many organisations have implemented management control self-assessment programmes as part of their reviews of control. An industry of consultants now provides such services to many organisations. Auditors will have to take the power of risk assessment to their elbows, if they are to meet the needs of their organisations. Not all internal auditors have addressed this issue in their service strategies. They will have to do so in the future.

Kubitscheck[6] (1999) provides an excellent guide to the links between control and risk assessment in an insurance company: 'In my approach,

I have sold the "concept of control" as "best management practice" while stressing that controls are not obstacles but ways in which we manage "business risks" to ensure the achievement of "business objectives".' Her perception is that financial service organisations have, by and large, been playing the catch-up game in the corporate governance arena. She identifies four main driving forces of change over the last two decades, which are still with us today:

- new consumer behaviour
- technology
- competition and globalisation
- regulatory and statutory requirements.

In her latest book (2014)[7] Kubitscheck ends her first chapter with the following key points, all of which have change and risk implications for every board in every sector. Look for these as you read the points:

1   A modern approach to corporate governance is values based, holistic and integrated across all aspect of enterprise strategy, economic, social and environmental that is underpinned by sound principles of risk management that take a longer term view.
2   Aoards should re-examine the questions they ask to gain better quality assurance that is joined up to provide one truth – that is, a consistent view and understanding of the risks and state of control.
3   Failure to be alert to or act on red flags can render corporate governance ineffective, as found in the downfall of major organisations.
4   Assurance that is based on defective information – that is, incomplete or invalidated – cannot inspire confidence.
5   Assurance can be provided against three truths – expected, alleged and actual.
6   Assurance in the boardroom cannot be taken for granted as regulation is heightened to strengthen standards of governance.
7   A more conscious approach to corporate governance is necessary to help restore trust and confidence in the boardroom.

In one of my early audit engagements, I reviewed the impact of a change programme, with its aim to improve processes by changing labour, materials and processes – resulting in improving economics, efficiencies and effectiveness. The evaluation and evidence sought for the audit started at the proposal stage through to the approval and final implementation of the changes. The audit found what started as good intentions in too many cases ended sometimes in increased costs, inefficiencies and ineffectiveness, often without the risks being clearly assessed at the beginning and results seen by any formal feedback. I was reminded of this audit on a management development programme I attended in Geneva in the early 1990s, when one of the case study workshops was titled 'The Road to Hell is Paved with Good Intentions' – an English proverb, which probably has many translations in other languages; a proverb probably seen in too many organisations in their decision-making processes at all levels and across all their supply chains.

I was reminded again of this audit when I saw the results of research by both Cass Business School, City University London (2011)[8] and Cranfield School of Management (2014)[9] on behalf of the Association of Insurance and Risk Managers in Industry and Commerce (AIRMIC), titled *Road to Ruin* and followed by *Roads to Resilience*. As to be expected, both executive summaries of this research use the word/terms 'change' and 'risk' frequently. Cass sees a drive for change in boardroom thinking (2011 p. 19):

> This report should be the impetus for a change in boardroom thinking, transforming risk from a tedious Cinderella 'hygiene' subject into one that is, with risk appetite, as comprehensively a part of the currency of strategy discussion as its siblings, Opportunity and Reward. NEDs and executive directors may need to obtain specialist education to increase their understanding of risk and boost their confidence in discussing it.

Cranfield (2014) introduces us to five Rs for resilience in organisations:

> the research found five capabilities or principles in common. This report refers to them as the five Rs. It is not sufficient to have just one or even most of them; an organisation must seek to have all five to achieve resilience. These are:

- **Risk radar**: the ability to anticipate problems and see things in a different way will help an organisation develop an early warning system and be able to seize new opportunities.
- **Resources and assets**: well-diversified *resources and assets* provide the flexibility to respond to opportunities as well as adverse or changing circumstances.
- **Relationships and networks**: risk information flows freely throughout the organisation up to directors to prevent the 'risk blindness' that afflicts many boards.
- **Rapid response**: capability that prevents an incident escalating into a crisis or disaster because people and processes are in place to quickly restore things to normal.
- **Review and adapt**: learn from experience, including near misses and make the necessary changes and improvements to strategy, tactics, processes and capabilities.

These common principles apply to all change and risk management programmes and form a good summary for this part and introduction for creative thinking and innovation by auditors to the next three chapters.

Creative Audit Thinking Activities

Activity 16   Manage Creativity and Innovation in Change

Consider the process of change management below and its part in creativity and innovation in your future auditing. Test out this process in changes you identify taking place or recommend in your next audit engagement. Look for evidence that the actions recommended to be taken by managers have taken place and review the results.

Control the Installation of New Processes

Bain and Company (2015)[10] define change management as a process 'that enables companies;

. . .to control the installation of new processes to improve the realisation of business benefits. These programs involve devising change initiatives, generating organisational buy-in, implementing the initiatives as seamlessly as possible and generating a repeatable model for ensuring continued success in future change efforts. A change management program allows leaders to help people succeed, showing where and when trouble is likely to occur, and laying out a strategy for mitigating risks and monitoring progress. Change management programs require managers to:

- ***Focus on results****. Maintain a goal-oriented mind-set by establishing clear, non-negotiable goals and designing incentives to ensure these goals are met.*
- ***Overcome barriers to change****. Identify employees who are most affected and also work to predict, measure and manage the risk of change.*
- ***Repeatedly communicate simple, powerful messages to employees****. In times of change, alter communication frequency and the methods to manage how a shaken workforce perceives and reacts to information:*
- ***Ensure sponsorship throughout the organisation****. To allow sponsorship to reach all levels of the organisation, enlist multiple sponsors to provide all individuals with access to and the influence of a sponsor.*
- ***Reorganize around decision-making****. Develop a system for identifying, making and executing the most important decisions.*
- ***Continuously monitor progress****. Follow through and monitor the progress of each change initiative to tell if it is following the intended path or veering off course.'*

Activity 17   Corporate Governance Principles Inspire Creativity and Innovation in Change

In today's corporate governance debate on the transparency of information provided by company boards to their stakeholders, auditors should have a full understanding of the Cadbury (1992) principles on which his committee's Code of Best Practice was based. Worldwide adoption of accountability, integrity and openness[11] as fundamental principles for corporate best practice has stood the test of time well. Yet, these are little mentioned or referenced into as a separate integrated trilogy of underlying principles, essential in the practice of risk assessment and change management. Over the past twenty-five years, each of these three principles has influenced the development of laws, corporate governance codes, policies and practices in all company operations. The US Sarbanes-Oxley Act 2002, UK Companies Act 2006 and its Corporate Governance Code 2014 require compliance with these principles in their sections. And not just companies: organisations in the public, professional and education sectors have all been impacted by corporate governance codes requiring accountability, integrity and openness criteria in their operations and regulatory activities. Consider the following definitions of these principles by Sir Adrian Cadbury in 1992 and how they can be used in your creative and innovative changes today and tomorrow.

Definitions of Accountability, Integrity and Openness

Boards of directors are **accountable** to their shareholders and both have to play their part in making that accountability effective. Boards of directors need to do so through the quality of the information which they provide to shareholders, and shareholders through their willingness to exercise their responsibilities as owners.

Integrity means both straightforward dealing and competencies. What is required of financial reporting is that it should be honest and that it should present a balanced picture of the state of the company's affairs. The integrity of reports depends on the integrity of those who prepare and present them.

Openness on the part of companies, within the limits set by their competitive position, is the basis for the confidence which needs to exist between business and all those who have a stake in its success. An open approach to the disclosure of information contributes to the efficient working of the market economy, prompts boards to take effective action and allows shareholders and others to scrutinise companies more thoroughly.

Activity 18   Inspire Creativity and Innovation in Change

Consider the following views on the role of internal auditors inspiring change and relate this to your own auditing activities. What changes have you inspired to create innovation in your audit processes, methodology and recommendations to your clients?

Become an Agent for Change[12]

> Internal audit agency is a rare phenomenon, and internal auditors who challenge the status quo are the exception than the rule. Inspiring others to change may be the best avenue to success.

Becoming agents of change is one of the IIA Global's latest mottos. 'To be effective, internal auditors must possess not only sound judgment and critical thinking, they must compel others to an appropriate and sometimes urgent response.' I suggest that effective internal auditors can go further than compelling others to change, as IIA Global suggests in its most recent annual report; they can inspire that change. The notion of internal auditors as change agents is, for the most part, aspirational. In practice, internal audit agency is currently a rare phenomenon. However, internal auditors may become change agents on a much greater scale. In doing so, the stereotypical model may transform from being reactive, responsive and seeking to meet others' expectations, to being an agent who drives change at the very heart of a business.

A change agent breaks with institutionalised practices and contributes to establishing new patterns. That requires particular personal characteristics and competencies including, but not limited to, liaising successfully with auditees, senior management and the board or audit committee; business acumen; leadership and communication skills; listening and influencing skills; and the ability to develop relationships. When seeking to make a difference, and create a unique and sustainable identity, inspiring others to change may become the best avenue to success.

In seeking to heighten the efficacy of the audit, it is worth acknowledging that some of an internal audit function's shortcomings and limitations can be self-inflicted. The self-perception IAs can distance them from key stakeholders and cause avoidable problems. An overly modest self-perception (the IA acting as the servant) and the use of self-evident and empty, jargonistic language (the IA as consultant) display a lack of identity and may lead to marginalisation in the eyes of the stakeholder. Overly ambitious claims and pretending to be the expert of everything can pave the way to disappointment in the eyes of stakeholders, as internal audit over-promises and then under-delivers.

Inspiring others to change may be the more promising path. This requires a focus on strengthening existing controls and processes, thus acknowledging that there is already something good in place; bolstering the overarching organisational culture; looking for the root cause of risks: as well as asking questions rather than claiming to know it all. A healthy dose of modesty also helps. Change agents do not alter processes or people by themselves, rather they sow the seeds that inspire change in others.

Notes

1 *Architects of a Better World Building the Post-2015 Business Engagement Architecture* (2014 pp. 1–2 and 9), United Nations Global Compact, New York, US.
2 *A Structured Approach to Enterprise Risk Management and the Requirements of ISO 31000* (2010), The Institute of Risk Management (IRM), London, England.
3 *Risk Changes and Control Challenges and Opportunities for Internal Auditors* (2000), Internal Control Issue 28 (February 2000), ABG Professional Information, London, England.
4 *Internal Control- Integrated Framework* (1992), Committee of Sponsoring Organisations of the Treadway Commission, USA. www.coso.org.
5 *Leading Edge Internal Auditing* (1998), Ridley J. and Chambers A.D., ICSA Publishing Ltd., London, England.
6 *Control Self-Assessment* (1999), Wade K. and Wynne A. (Chapter by V. Kubitscheck – *CSA in Financial Services Organisations*), Wiley and Sons, London, England.
7 *Integrated Assurance – Risk Governance Beyond Boundaries* (2014), Vicky Kubitscheck, Gower Publishing Ltd., Farnham, England.
8 *Road to Ruin: A Study of Major Risk Events – Their Origins, Impact and Implications* (2011 p. 19), Cass Business School on behalf of AIRMIC, London, England.
9 *Roads to Resilience: Building Dynamic Approaches to Risk to Achieve Future Success* (2014 Executive Summary), Cranfield School of Management on behalf of AIRMIC, London, England.
10 *Management Tools* (2015), Bain and Company Inc., Boston, US.
11 *Cadbury Report of the Committee on the Financial Aspects of Corporate Governance* (1992 Sections 3.2, 3.3, 3.4), the principles on which the Code is based are those of openness, integrity and accountability. They go together.
12 Source: *Effective Audit – Inspiring Change, Audit and Risk* (2015 p. 7), Lenz R. (2016), Journal of Chartered Institute of Internal Auditors, London, England.

5   Auditors Are Time Travellers

Only time (whatever that may be) will tell.[1]

In this chapter I consider the importance of time throughout the Ten Step Audit Process. At the start of an audit, each step has some predictable and unknown consequences; each step is a journey into the past, an evaluation of the present and a forecasting of the future. The importance of time for all auditors is critical to the success of every audit and its outcomes, critical as the audit process is travelled and managed using many different measures and layers of information and knowledge. Every audit process is a de-layering of time, often uncovering many fossils in the process.

5.1 Time Travel – Past, Present and Future

H.G. Wells's concept of a time machine and time travel caught the imagination of its readers and the public when *The Time Machine* (1895) was published, and has been the focus of many imaginations since. It will go on being in the imaginations of many in the future. Will it become a reality? As Professor Stephen Hawking states in his book, *A Brief History of Time*, 'only time will tell'. Without exception, all management gurus over past centuries have considered, spoken and prophesied on the importance of managing time, timing and the management of change and innovation to achieve objectives. These include early philosophers and the 19th- and 20th-centuries, gurus – Taylor, Fayol, Drucker, Humble, Deming and many others recognised today as successful management leaders across the world. Time, time management and timing have always been travelled through learning spaces, creating change and innovations in products and services through the recognition of risks, challenges and taking of opportunities. Auditing is no exception.

Drucker wrote on the three learning spaces that relate to innovation and entrepreneurism in management: the leader's learning space, the manager's learning space and the customer's learning space. Interpret this in the time travelled by auditors as the auditors' learning space, the manager of the audit team's learning space, and the audit client's learning space. Strong links and an understanding of these spaces are important in the audit process and improve both the findings and their implementation. Recognising and measuring time, time management, time travel and good timing across these same strong links also improves creative thinking and innovations in the audit process.

Consider and reflect on what Drucker (1993)[2] wrote on innovation, his principles and opportunities – see these on the Drucker Institute website. Consider how they are there in your innovations in auditing. Although change is mentioned only once, almost without exception change is there in all the five principles and seven opportunities. So is the need for time travel through learning spaces. Think creatively about this and see in each your time travelling leading to innovations.

5.2 Time Travel and Change in the Audit Process

Nobody, no organisation, no system remains the same through time. All are subject to change, sometimes by their own decision-making, sometimes by the decision-making of others, sometimes unexpectedly by accident or disaster. Change is constant and this must be reflected and travelled in every audit boundary and space. Understanding this is essential in the timing and time management throughout the audit process, starting with the planning through to the outputs and outcomes.

In auditing, time and time management is an essential part of the process. Time travel receives less attention, yet all auditors in their audit processes travel time into the past, through the present and into the future. From audit planning to results and follow-up, time has a significant impact on an audit. Too often that travel is in the present into the past but not into the future. Yet, the future and its impact on the present can be more important in an audit than travel into the past.

Audit planning takes place at a macro and micro level: macro over a period of time, usually a year or years, taking into consideration scope, available resources and change; micro at the audit engagement level with known resources, when timing, period of time to be covered and length of time to achieve its objectives, report and follow-up are estimated and decided. During these planning and audit processes the auditor is travelling into the past, observing the present and travelling into the future, searching for the impact of change and possible change. As these travels take place, the auditor has to form opinions on the boundaries for the audit engagement's scope, objectives and learning spaces needed by the audit team to achieve the engagement objectives.

Consider the 'times' travelled and managed throughout my Ten Step Audit Process:

1 Create the audit vision and strategy to **MOTIVATE** excellence, quality and add value and improvement in the **EXPERTISE** and **SKILLS** needed in all auditing processes.
2 Plan each audit engagement over a period of time.
3 Seek insight into operations being audited – their theory and best practices, through **ASSOCIATION: QUESTIONING: OBSERVING: NETWORKING**.
4 Assess risks involved by the operations being audited and the audit.
5 Establish scope and objectives for the audit engagement.
6 Develop a risk-based audit programme and identify controls.
7 Select techniques/methodology and **EXPERIMENT** to search for appropriate evidence.
8 Objectively evaluate audit outputs, consider outcomes and agree findings.
9 Communicate audit findings to those accountable.
10 Follow-up and consider actions taken by the organisation.

During each of these steps, every auditor is a time traveller in a learning space of gathering knowledge, experience and feedback from their auditing skills to continuously improve their time-travelling performance.

Consider the time messages for auditing in the following article I wrote in 2000, and how they are managed and controlled in your own audit process. How important is time in your own products and services as seen by your stakeholders? Can it be managed better by creative thinking and innovation?

Weak Links in the Supply Chain[3]

There can be few in the UK, in or outside auditing, that were not impacted by the petrol flow crisis during September this year. There will be many who were not aware of the high risk of such just-in-time (JIT) supply chains in a civilised and highly developed society – politicians, directors, managers, auditors and customers. JIT in supply chains can bring significant economic and quality benefits to organisations and stakeholders. It can also be complex, not easy to control and can be the weakest link.

In October 1999, I wrote on my concerns that the Turnbull[4] report of that year did not comment on the importance of management's control across supply chains. Turnbull uses the accounting term internal control with a focus on the control environment within the organisation. There is little or no reference to management's responsibility for ensuring reasonable control across those parts of supply chains external to the organisation.

Control across supply chains is not a new concept. Establishing control over contractors and suppliers has always been fundamental to the direction and management of procurement. Over the years the extent of that control has increased significantly with cost, ownership, quality, technology, environmental, health and safety and conduct requirements. These are familiar control issues for many auditors involved in contract audit. There has also been a significant growth of JIT, outsourcing and use of joint venture partnerships for procurement of services and manufacturing. This has increased the importance in risk assessment and control of all external supply chains – primary and secondary.

The OECD (2000)[5] in published guidelines for multinationals includes as one of its general policies 'Encourage where practicable, business partners, including suppliers and sub-contractors, to apply principles of corporate conduct compatible with the Guidelines.' This policy clearly recognises responsibility for the application of corporate governance principles across external supply chains and the importance of using organisation rules to improve relationships in supply chains. In some organisations this is already part of the procurement and control agenda. Is it in yours?

Chambers and Rand (1997)[6] addressed the implications of JIT for auditors. 'Auditors will need to coordinate their approach to operational reviews of JIT systems so as to take into account such diverse aspects as product planning, cost accounting, process design, related information flows, quality issues and relationships with suppliers.' They list useful actions, from understanding the cultural change to broader control implications and relationships with suppliers.

If nothing else, the petrol crisis this year should have brought home to all auditors the importance of addressing JIT and supply chain theory in their risk assessment and auditing processes. Hopefully, gone are the days when internal auditors only matched invoices to purchase orders and receipt notes – though this is still important!

5.3 Time Travel in the Audit Learning Space

Recognition of risk and change requires appropriate and relevant learning spaces for the audit team and management of those being audited. In too many audits this requirement is overlooked by both at their peril. Creative thinking by the auditors during travelling through the audit planning and audit process should always evaluate and critique the learning spaces of the audit team and those being audited. Absence of the right learning spaces can weaken significantly the audit process and the operations being audited.

Like ambassadors, auditors learn and travel with baggage and other travellers, each of which can make a significant difference to creative thinking and innovation in their audit process and results. Reflecting on my own learning space over many years I see this containing *values, principles, practice, standards, study, examinations, certificates, reading, experiences, observing, questioning, networking, collaborating, cooperating, coordinating, teamwork, supervising, managing, auditing, analysing, evaluating, judging, insighting, forecasting, lecturing, research, writing, thinking critically* and even *dreaming.* Reflect on your own learning space and that of others involved in your audits – how do they compare? Each learning space around an audit can have an influence on its results. Can mine and yours be improved? In today's digital age and tomorrow's innovations, almost certainly yes. Can the others involved be improved? Evidence of continuous learning is an essential part of time travel in every profession and audit. That evidence can influence each of the ten steps in the audit process, either through its absence or through its existence.

5.4 Risk, Control and Change Management in Time Travelling

Everyone is travelling and controlling risk and change at all times every day. Management of risk and change is with all of us every moment of each day and in every organisation at all its levels of board, executive and operations in the seeking to achieve objectives – personal, functional and for the organisation. We do not think of risk all the time, but intuitively we recognise it as we play, work and enjoy our social life. We learn from it, often by mistake and accident, but also from learning and experience. Formal management of risk is an essential part of the governance of every organisation, with responsibilities for this clearly seen at board, executive and operation levels. Sometimes our risk management is by choice, but more and more it is now part of compliance with laws, regulations, standards, policies, procedures and job descriptions, all to achieve objectives related to strategic directions and controls. We ignore some risks at our peril, both in our lives and in our organisations, not just because of the adverse effects of the consequences, but also because of the failure to take opportunities, which if lost can have a significant impact on our future.

All auditors as they travel through time in their planning and audit engagements need to recognise and react to the risk, control and change management involved to achieve their vision and objectives and the vision and objectives of the operations being audited. How well management assesses and manages risk, control and change, both within the audit team and in the operations being audited, is critical to the success of every audit. For many audit engagements this is not an easy task and even overlooked.

The use of risk-based auditing techniques today has changed many audit processes for the better. Audit planning, macro and micro, has improved considerably since the use of this technique. So has the agreement, establishment and achievement of audit objectives in the audit engagement. The right risk assessments are essential for this technique – not just management assessment but also assessment by the auditor, benchmarked to assessments by other assurance providers and the relevant sector(s). Such comparisons are key to successful risk, control and change management in time travelling in every audit.

The past, present and future times are very important when managing risk and assessing their importance in the audit process. Risk-based auditing has been born and developed because of this. Risk-based auditing is a relatively new concept for many auditors. It has been adopted widely across all auditing practices and takes many different approaches in its implementation. Do management and the board receive timely, relevant and reliable reports on progress against business objectives and the related risks? Does management receive timely information from inside and outside the company for decision-making and management review purposes? This includes performance reports and indicators of change, together with qualitative information such as on customer satisfaction, employee attitudes and so forth.

Risk assessment and control is not just about personal, function and organisation risks and opportunities. Risk is now much broader, taking into account the impact/influence an organisation has on all its stakeholders and the sustainability of the planet, including all its civic societies and people – and the impact all its stakeholders and sustainability of the planet, all its civic societies and people can have on the achievement of its objectives. This takes the auditor travelling outside of the organisation into new past, present and future time explorations, sometimes revealing significant new risks and opportunities for both the auditor and the organisation being audited.

King (2009 p. 12)[7] covers extensively and very well the concept that governance in an organisation is not just within the boundaries of the organisation's strategies and operations but much wider, with accountability, integrity and openness responsibilities to all its stakeholders, including not least sustainability of the planet: all integrated in its governance, risk management, control functions and reporting. 'A key challenge for leadership is to make sustainability issues mainstream. Strategy, risk, performance and sustainability have become inseparable; hence the phrase "integrated reporting" which is used throughout this Report.' King's integrated reporting guidance and recommendations recognise the need for and an improved 'combined assurance model' to cover the risks and opportunities associated with its strategies, all its stakeholders and including sustainability of the planet. Kubitscheck (2014)[8] discusses the need for 'integrated assurance' in all organisations, defining this as a framework 'with the aim of supporting effective corporate governance':

> Integrated assurance refers to a structured approach for gaining a holistic picture of the principal risks and the level of residual exposure an organisation is required to manage. It involves aligning and optimising the organisation's assurance over the management of those risks and the core business activities in line with the board's risk appetite and exists to support the board's risk oversight and risk taking. It promotes shared risk intelligence and accountability with a common goal to strengthen the organisation's risk management and oversight.

Today there are moves by some nations and internationally to develop better holistic financial, governance, risk management and control reporting to satisfy the needs of an organisation's stakeholders, using 'integrated thinking' and 'integrated reporting'. The International Integrated Reporting Council (IIRC) (2013)[9] recommends such thinking:

> Integrated thinking takes into account the connectivity and interdependencies between the range of factors that affect an organization's ability to create value over time, including:
>
> * the capitals that the organization uses or affects, and the critical interdependencies, including tradeoffs, between them
> * the capacity of the organization to respond to key stakeholders' legitimate needs and interests
> * how the organization tailors its business model and strategy to respond to its external environment and the risks and opportunities it faces
> * the organization's activities, performance (financial and other) and outcomes in terms of the capitals – past, present and future.

IIRC currently promote Guiding Principles and Content Elements for 'integrated reporting' – see Appendix G. These principles and elements open many new doors for the auditor to travel through time – past, present and future – leading to 'connectivity of information flow into management reporting, analysis and decision-making ... better integration of the information systems that support internal and external reporting and communication, including preparation of the integrated report', and most importantly leading to creativity and innovation in the Ten Step Audit Process for the time traveller auditor.

The more that integrated thinking is embedded into an organisation's activities, the more naturally will the connectivity of information flow into management reporting, analysis and decision-making. It also leads to better integration of the information systems that support internal and external reporting and communication, including preparation of the integrated report.

5.5 Chapter Review

In this chapter I discuss the importance of auditors travelling through time in every audit engagement and the timing for each of the steps in the Ten Step Audit Process. Searching the past, examining the present and forecasting the future are essential at board, executive and operations levels in every organisation. This also applies in every audit engagement, not just as an evaluation of operations in an organisation but also across all its supply chains. Today the need for organisations to address sustainability issues and goals is more important than ever it has been. Today every auditor must time travel in every audit.

5.6 Creative Audit Thinking Activities

Activity 19   Create Sea-Changes in Your Audit Time Travelling

Study the following extract from *Enlightening Professions*[10] and consider how the IIRC (2013) Guiding Principles and Contents Elements can create a 'sea-change' in time travelling through your next Ten Step Audit Process.

Experience the New Ecosystem in Every Audit

The audit profession has been accustomed to incremental change and consistent methodologies. It now has the chance to create a sea-change in practice through understanding and embracing open and social auditing, new technology, real-time auditing, co-creation with social enterprises, and crowdsourcing. These developments all provide opportunities for more direct contact with the wider stakeholders of the organisation being audited, opening up dialogue and access to information. In many areas – and particularly when it comes to public services – the driver of change is a focus on what is produced with stakeholders. In many cases, a clearer focus on outcomes means 'going back to the drawing board' and redesigning how things are administered and delivered. This process needs to be expansive: exploring the whole ecosystem the service is delivered in, including technological and social developments.

Activity 20   Transforming Our World Through Creative Auditing

The outcome document from the United Nations Summit in 2015[11] for the adoption of its post-2015 development agenda established the United

Nations 2030 Agenda for Sustainable Development, including its new Sustainability Goals and Targets for up to 2030 – see Appendix H for these Goals. For each of these goals there is a time to be travelled in every audit – from past history in the world and in the organisation and its environment, through today's key performance indicators and values in every organisation travelling into the future to 2030 and beyond. Consider how your creativity and innovation in auditing can contribute to this journey.

Stimulate Action in the UN Sustainability Goals through Your Auditing

This Agenda is a plan of action for people, planet and prosperity. It also seeks to strengthen universal peace in larger freedom. We recognise that eradicating poverty in all its forms and dimensions, including extreme poverty, is the greatest global challenge and an indispensable requirement for sustainable development. All countries and all stakeholders, acting in collaborative partnership, will implement this plan. We are resolved to free the human race from the tyranny of poverty and want and to heal and secure our planet. We are determined to take the bold and transformative steps which are urgently needed to shift the world onto a sustainable and resilient path. As we embark on this collective journey, we pledge that no one will be left behind. The 17 Sustainable Development Goals and 169 targets which we are announcing today demonstrate the scale and ambition of this new universal Agenda. They seek to build on the Millennium Development Goals and complete what these did not achieve. They seek to realize the human rights of all and to achieve gender equality and the empowerment of all women and girls. They are integrated and indivisible and balance the three dimensions of sustainable development: the economic, social and environmental. The Goals and targets will stimulate action over the next fifteen years in areas of critical importance for humanity and the planet:

Activity 21   There Is a Time for Everything in Creative Auditing

In 935 BC and late in his life, King Solomon in his wisdom wrote the Hebrew book of Ecclesiastes, largely as an autobiographical story containing proverbs, maxims, sayings collected during his life, and mainly as advice for future generations. In his chapter 3 he writes on times for everything. There are also wise words in this chapter, verses 1–8, for the imaginative time travelling auditor to consider. Do you see any of the following times in creativity and innovation in your time travelling as an auditor?

Words of Wisdom for the Time Traveller Creative Auditor

For everything there is a season, a time for every purpose under heaven:

A time to plant and a time to uproot,
A time to tear down and a time to build,
A time to weep and a time to laugh,
A time to mourn and a time to dance,
A time to scatter stones and a time to gather them,
A time to search and a time to give up,
A time to tear and a time to mend,
A time to keep and a time to throw away,
A time to be silent and a time to speak,

Notes

1 *A Brief History of Time: From the Big Bang to Black Holes* (1988 Revised 2011), Stephen Hawking, Transworld Publishers, London, England.
2 *Innovation and Entrepreneurship* (1993), Peter F. Drucker, Harper Publishing, New York, US. (for *Drucker's Five Principles of Innovation and Seven Opportunities for Innovation*, visit www.druckerinstitute.com, accessed May 2016.)
3 *Weak Chains in the Supply Chain* (2000 pp. 8–9), Published in Internal Auditing November, IIA-UK and Ireland, London, England.
4 *Internal Control – Guidance for Directors on the Combined Code* (1999), Institute of Chartered Accountants in England and Wales (ICAEW), London, England.
5 *Guidelines for Multinational Companies* (2000 p. 10), Organisation for Economic Co-operation and Development, Paris, France. www.oecd.org.
6 *The Operational Auditing Handbook* (1997 pp. 450–453, 2nd Edition 2010), Andrew Chambers and Graham Rand, John Wiley and Sons Ltd., Chichester, England.
7 *King Report on Governance for South Africa and the 'King Code of Governance Principles'* (King III) (2009 p. 12), Institute of Directors South Africa, Cape Town, South Africa.
8 *Integrated Assurance – Risk Governance Beyond Boundaries* (2014 p. 119), Vicky Kubitscheck, Gower Publishing Limited, Farnham, England.
9 *The International <IR> Framework* (2013 p. 2), International Integrated Reporting Council, London, England.
10 *Enlightening Professions?* (2014 p. 23), Institute of Chartered Accountants in England and Wales (ICAEW), London, England.
11 *Transforming Our World – The 2030 Agenda for Sustainable Development* (2015), Outcome Document from the United Nations Summit 2015, United Nations, New York, US.

6 Auditors Are Scientists

The science of auditing can be traced back over many centuries.[1]

In this chapter I consider auditing as a researching, experimenting science from
the 19th century to today. It is a science in its arts and pursuits by every auditor,
in every audit investigation and engagement; a science in its creative thinking,
innovation, research, pursuit of knowledge, development of skills, ethical behaviour, quality and professionalism; a science in its own developed and continuously improved auditing principles and practices; excellent in its own conduct
of accountability, integrity and transparency, responsibility, commitment, caring
and quality.

6.1 Scientists Are Auditors

One of the overriding concepts in my book, demonstrated by my use of many metaphors, is that everybody is an auditor in whatever capacity they are in or whatever activity they undertake. In the same concept, everything we do is an audit. Scientists have always audited in their continuous pursuit, research and creation of new knowledge. They have been auditing through most of evolution, brilliant brains always challenging, questioning, analysing, judging, creating and continuously changing the world we live in. Change through increased knowledge and the tensions of challenging what is seen and practiced; change by creation of wisdom and development of concepts, principles, laws and predictions; change through improved understandings of time, space, behaviours and practices; change in the future often beyond our imagination. Scientists are auditors and science the ultimate audit.

Aristotle, like all philosophers of his time, was a scientist creating and pursuing knowledge in an independent, objective, systematic and disciplined process to advance understanding of his ideals and ideas. He sought Good and prophesised how this could and should be achieved. 'Every art and every investigation, and likewise every practical pursuit or undertaking, seems to aim at some good, hence it has been well said that the Good is that at which all things aim.'[2] Aristotle was an auditor. His investigations covered a range of sciences from logic, philosophy, physics, biology, psychology and politics, and is perhaps best known for his writings and teachings on ethics. Few would recognise Aristotle and the many scientists that have followed him as auditors. Yet all science is a continuous investigation into the unknown. This is not too dissimilar from auditing and the pursuit by every auditor in the audit process.

The many values of ethics have been at the forefront and influence of what has developed as the Good we see today in the world. There is much evidence in all nations and across all cultures to evidence this, in the form of charters, codes, standards, religions, concepts, laws and regulations. Today's philosophy of the values in people, cultures, organisations and governments owes much to the thoughts and proclamations of Aristotle and other philosophers, followed across the world by the thoughts and principles of management gurus and introduction and development of professions and other associations of Good and Best practices – and they are many: every nation has philosophers, management gurus, professions and associations with Good aims.

Today, we all live in a world of constant and continuous change, moving faster and faster every year. Change all scientists audit and create, not always resulting in the achievement only of Good. The by-products of changes for Good can sometimes result in Evil. How we manage and control the risks of change is as important as change itself. There are many examples of Good and Bad management of change in the world, throughout previous centuries and into today, and there will be more tomorrow. Overriding all change by scientists must be the commitment of people, cultures, organisations and governments to a set of values for Good.

6.2 All Auditors Are Scientists

Every audit is a continuous pursuit and research into knowledge. Not just knowledge for the auditor, but also knowledge for those being audited. It should always be seen as a science – a systematic and disciplined process of examination seeking evidence of past and present facts and forecasting future events. I hope the previous chapters have demonstrated this. Auditing has its own developed independent and objective processes of examination in the tensions of how organisations of all sizes, structures and objectives govern, take risks and control their operations. It is a science with its own pursuit of knowledge to advance development of its own concepts, principles, laws and predictions; a science to improve organisations and their methods through theory and practice; a science to seek Good and improve, not just for those in an organisation, but for all those stakeholders who have an interest in its performance.

Barnes-Swarney (1995),[3] in the introduction to her edited *Science Desk Reference*, convinced me that auditing is a dynamic science. It includes all the basics of a science – theories, principles, observations, verifications, measurements, analysis, ideas and new understandings of how people and methods can operate to achieve improved outputs and outcomes, for all types of organisations and their variety of stakeholders. It is dynamic because auditing changes constantly to meet ever-changing needs of those being audited and the organisations they direct and operate. In her introduction, she states:

> Science, at its very heart is never constant. The study of any science entails looking at things, measuring and defining them, analysing their properties, or figuring out how they work. Along with the observing and measuring are the ever-changing new technologies to accomplish these goals.

When auditors audit they are scientists in a constantly changing environment. Their questioning, analysing, judging, creativity and innovation is a science with its own concepts, standards, and laws. The science of auditing has developed since the beginning of the 20th century. First, by practice within and external to organisations; then by the development of its own principles and standards.

6.3 Principles and Standards of Auditing

My first introduction to the principles and standards of auditing was by learning from F.R.M. De Paula's[4] classic *Principles of Auditing*, first published in 1914 (with many revised editions and lately re-published in classic form). This has been followed by many published principles and standards of auditing across the world, both for commercial, charitable and government auditing.

De Paula's principles taught me my first understanding of auditing in 1953 as I prepared to become an auditor of financial accounts and statements in the then Colonial Audit Service. These were his thoughts and statements on auditing as a science:

> The science of auditing can be traced back over many centuries but it is only within recent years that the full benefits that are derived from a periodical audit have begun to be appreciated fully by the commercial world.
>
> A knowledge of accountancy is essential, but that alone will not make a competent auditor, for the science of auditing is quite apart and distinct from accountancy.
>
> An auditor requires a considerable legal knowledge and must be complete master of the principles of auditing in all its bearings. In addition to his scientific knowledge, he must be above all things a man of affairs, and possess tact and character; he must not be easily led and influenced by others, but knowing what his duty is, he must be able to do it in spite of direct or indirect pressure.

How many auditors see the work they perform, its preparation, its methods, judgements, and prophesies as a science? Yet, thinking of auditing as a philosophy can change not only its image but the pursuit of its discipline by those who audit, creating new methods and innovations in its processes. For those who think of auditing as a science, this has motivated and driven many of the concepts in auditing we use today. Though not all authors on auditing theory and practices since De Paula have seen it as a science, almost all have recognised it in their writings as a systematic and disciplined pursuit of knowledge. I prefer to call it a science. As auditing has become more difficult in today and tomorrow's complex world of laws, regulations, standards, codes of practice and technology, it must continue as a science to attract the best auditors.

Mautz and Sharaf (1960)[5] developed a theory of auditing starting with their interest in the nature of evidence. The result was a philosophy of auditing around a structure of its methodology, postulates and concepts. Like De Paula, they saw auditing as a separate discipline from accounting. They end their book with the following prediction on the future development and use of theory in the science of auditing:

> We hope we have indicated the close connection between the theory and practice of auditing, for we are convinced that the only sure solution to practical problems is through the development and use of theory. Auditing stands at the threshold of service opportunities we can yet scarcely foresee, even in dim outline. With a well developed theory it will not only be prepared to take advantage of such opportunities but will be able to escape confusion and misplaced effort in the desire for real service.

Mautz and Sharaf discuss in their philosophy of auditing primary concepts in auditing of evidence, due audit care, fair presentation independence and ethical conduct. Each of these concepts underpins auditing practices today. Examples of these theories in auditing can be seen published by all the professional institutes representing auditors, in their learning programmes, continuing professional development requirements and standards of conduct. Other examples of Mautz and Sharaf's auditing theories underpinning standards of auditing practices can be seen in most if not all auditing practices worldwide. Their philosophy of auditing also underpins codes of corporate governance, regulations and in some cases requirements in laws.

Creativity and innovation has not been neglected by the auditing professions. Their research and professional standards, statements and codes of ethics at national and international levels have included both over many years: creative thinking through their qualifications, learning and development strategies; innovation in research, benchmarking and conference/training projects. Hindsight, insight and foresight have been the foundation of growth in the pattern of auditing since its conception. Flint (1988)[6] summarised the audit process similar to my Ten Step Audit Process, emphasising the seeking of evidence. In his views on the concept of auditing, he also saw it as a science. He examined the theory, authority, process and standards of audit, mainly from a financial audit perspective, but recognised his views applied across many other types of audit. He references into the early work of Mautz and Sharaf to support theory in his text.

Other theories have been developed and used since the DePaula, Mautz, Sharaf and Flint concepts. One in particular stands out today in all auditing and governance in organisations as being to me the most significant evolution of creative thinking – the COSO (1992)[7] integrated internal control framework discussed in a previous chapter and its developed definition of internal control – see Figure 6.1.

This framework has stood the test of time well. Its scientific linear thinking and developed principles can be seen today in law, regulation and codes of governance across the world. It is as relevant today as when first researched and published for consultation: its pyramid base of CONTROL ENVIRONMENT, sometimes referred to as 'tone at the top', is still the start to effective internal control. It is that tone for Good control and its known presence that motivates commitment to and compliance with Good practices within an organisation and across all its supply chains and with all its stakeholders. RISK ASSESSMENT is now recognised clearly as a continuous board responsibility, to be managed at each of the three levels of every organisation – board, executive and operational. It is or should only be after risks have been assessed that CONTROL ACTIVITIES should be established to mitigate the risks being taken to achieve an organisation's objectives. These activities fall into three categories – preventive, detective and corrective – and can be active and/or passive. Overseeing the control environment, risk assessment and control activities is MONITORING, in the form of self-assessment, supervision, management, inspection or independent auditing and compliance.

Linking across the pyramid from top to bottom and bottom to top is COMMUNICATION and the reporting of INFORMATION relevant to the achievement of an organisation's objectives. Today this takes many forms in a

Figure 6.1 COSO Integrated Control Framework

Source: Internal Control – Integrated Framework (1992), Committee of Sponsoring Organisations of the Treadway Commission (COSO), New York, US

network of communication and information in and outside an organisation, of verbal to written, informal to formal, hard data to digital, instant to periodic. Each form is essential to all parts of the integrated control framework.

COSO[8] also researched and developed its integrated enterprise risk management framework and more recently used this framework as a lens to study how to evaluate sustainability risks across its four categories of Strategic, Operations, Reporting and Compliance, discussed in earlier chapters. Every auditor should recognise and use today's COSO integrated control framework in every audit they undertake: it can be used to think creatively in each step of the in my audit process discussed in earlier chapters.[9] When I was auditing, I always reminded those I audited of this framework, though in some of the audit process steps this was not always accepted at first by those being audited. By the end of the audit, it was important that the framework was understood and accepted by everyone associated with the audit. On some occasions it was not, and the consequences for the function were not Good for its governance, risk management, controls or success in the achievement of its objectives.

More recently COSO[10] has developed and introduced seventeen principles 'representing the fundamental concepts associated with each component' of the integrated framework. These principles underpin all controls in an organisation and should be understood and studied by all those who direct, manage and audit – see Appendix I. It is not difficult to recognise the concepts underpinning these principles are fundamental to the creative thinking required in auditing discussed throughout my book.

6.4 Rules of Conduct for Scientists and Auditors

All sciences create and promote codes of conduct to establish values in their philosophies and activities. De Paula addresses auditor conduct in his principles:

> He [the auditor] may find himself in positions when his duty to his client is opposed to his own interests, and in such circumstances he must have the courage to carry out his duty faithfully, regardless of the effects it may have upon himself. In the long run, the reputation he will thus gain for absolute integrity will prove of far greater value to him than any temporary loss in the first case.

Although the terms 'conduct' or 'behaviour' are not specifically mentioned, they are implied as Good in all De Paula's principles. Mautz and Sharaf consider an auditor's ethical conduct flowing 'directly from his professional status'. This conduct is described as a specific set of rules or ideals.

Auditing, like many if not all professions, has developed codes of conduct since the 20th century for its practices – though for some professions these existed before then. These are codes which members of a profession have to recognise, comply with and are regulated. Most of these codes are national, but latterly some are emerging as international codes. The United Kingdom Auditing Practices Board (APB) Ethical Standard requires the values of *Integrity, Objectivity* and *Independence* for external financial auditors. In most professional auditing firms these are expanded into wider codes of conduct to profile other values including the importance of quality and excellence in the services being provided.

All professional accounting firms have codes of conduct for their members. The Association of Chartered and Certified Accountants (ACCA)[11] has adopted the principles of *Integrity, Professional Competence and Due Care, Confidentiality* and *Professional Behaviour*. The International Organisation of Supreme Audit Institutes (INTOSAI)[12] represents public auditing of government accounts and operations across the world. Its values are expressed and promoted to its members in its standards as *Interdependence, Integrity, Professionalism, Credibility, Inclusiveness, Cooperation* and *Innovation*. These values are also promoted individually by Supreme National Institutes. The National Audit Office in the United Kingdom, for example, in its Code of Conduct[13] promotes its values of *Integrity Objectivity, Professional Competence, Due Care,*

Confidentiality and *Professional Behaviour.* Similarly, the code of conduct for the European Court of Auditors[14] promotes its values and code of conduct as *Independence, Integrity, Confidentiality, Professionalism, Adding Value, Excellence* and *Efficiency.*

The Institute of Internal Auditors Inc.,[15] based in the United States with international membership in countries around the world, introduced its own international code of ethics in 1968, which has since been developed into the code at Appendix J. Note its four principles of *Integrity, Objectivity, Confidentiality* and *Competency* with supporting rules of conduct. This is an excellent example of a code of ethics for all auditors. Its principles and values can be seen across the world in other auditing professions, if not all professions, and many organisations across the world. In the United Kingdom, the Chartered Institute of Internal Auditors[16] has added to The IIA Code of Ethics the following ethical 'public interest' and 'courtesy and respect' requirements for its membership, reflecting its chartered status:

Principle of Professionalism – acting in the public interest

Acting in the public interest involves having regard to the legitimate interests of those who rely upon the objectivity and integrity of the assurance about governance and the management of risk, including control, that the internal audit profession provides to support the orderly functioning and propriety of organisations. These include employers, employees, investors, the business and financial community, clients, regulators and government. This reliance imposes a public interest responsibility on the internal audit profession.

Professional internal auditors should take into consideration the public interest and reasonable and informed public perception in deciding the actions to take, bearing in mind that the level and nature of the public interest varies between organisations depending on their role, size, systemic importance or public prominence.

Therefore, a professional internal auditor's responsibility is not exclusively to satisfy the needs of an individual employer or client. In acting in the public interest a professional internal auditor should observe and comply with the ethical requirements of this Code.

Courtesy and respect

Professional internal auditors should treat all people fairly without prejudice on any grounds.

A recent example of these theories being seen and understood as the foundation for its auditing standard framework is the introduction by The Institute of Internal Auditors of its new core principles on which its standards of auditing have been and will be developed – see Figure 6.2.

- Demonstrates integrity.
- Demonstrates competence and due professional care.
- Is objective and free from undue influence (independent).
- Aligns with the strategies, objectives, and risks of the organisation.
- Is appropriately positioned and adequately resourced.
- Demonstrates quality and continuous improvement.
- Communicates effectively.
- Provides risk-based assurance.
- Is insightful, proactive, and future-focused.
- Promotes organisational improvement.

Figure 6.2 Core principles for the professional practice of internal auditing

Source: The Institute of Internal Auditors Inc., website accessed 1 November 2015

In all these requirements of values and codes of conduct, and many for other auditors, there is a message of trust underpinning the independence and objectivity of the science of their auditing processes – a trust essential for the services they provide to their customers and civic society at large; a trust that has been promoted and developed over the past century. This trust will go on being developed and seen throughout this century. It is a trust that should be the start for creative thinking and innovation in all auditing.

6.5 Science of Data Mining, Analysis and Diagnosis

When I first started auditing financial statements in the early 1950s in Africa, I was given a green pencil and portable typewriter as my auditing tools. I had no calculator – manual or electronic – both did not exist in the environment in which I was auditing. I relied on mental arithmetic for my calculations. The data I was auditing often spread over a number of years, and choices of data to examine were by random and judgemental sampling. Evidence was recorded in manual working papers. The past sixty plus years have seen significant strides in the use of technology in the audit of financial statements and operation systems. In the 1970s and onwards, great strides were made in developing computer-aided auditing techniques (CAATs), and these have continued to develop and still are used today. But have these been creative enough for today and tomorrow's data? Does auditing lag behind the strides taken by other professions in the use of technology to mine, analyse and diagnose data?

Since auditing first developed into its science and principles, the mining, analysis and diagnosis of data to seek evidence has been at the core of every audit. In the last forty years, the volume of that data has grown exponentially in the amount stored, its growth and complexity. In my auditing in the late 1960s and 1970s I experimented with continuous auditing of operational financial data with some successes, by the use of secured audit checks embedded in accounting system computer programmes. It was clear to me then, and still is, that the use of computers and technology would change the process of auditing forever. That change has been dramatic with the size of data storage and speed of computers: this will continue to be greater and faster in the future. Since the 1970s the importance of continuous auditing to identify exceptions and variables has grown not just in independent auditing but across most operating systems. Advances in technology have contributed significantly in this growth, contributing to the speed of monitoring, the accuracy of data and quality of products and services.

Today, almost without exception, the volume and type of data which can be examined in an audit is enormous, and this will continue to grow. Advances in technology storage across long and complex supply chain data bases, in and across complex structured organisations, make the sampling and examination of data in any audit time frame a difficult task – a task requiring much human wisdom and often luck in sampling and examining the right data to seek the right evidence to file and the right conclusions to make.

In 1993 I was given a chess computer with sixty-four different skill levels as a retirement gift. A programmed decision maker, strategically thinking and challenging each of my moves – a programmed system which is still difficult to beat at even the lowest of levels! This is an early example of what is today an industry of artificial intelligent computers and robots, changing the way we all communicate and learn in all education, business, sports and pastimes. This is the way all auditing must go in the 21st century. Forensic auditing has been a pioneer in the use of technology to analyse, sample and diagnose financial data in investigations into possible criminal offences, such as fraud, bribery and corruption. There are many reasons for this, but two stand out – the speed of analysis increases significantly, and there is less chance of human error in the process of the investigation. Both benefits are very important for auditing today and tomorrow – the volume of data available to analyse is great in most audits. Both reasons can have a significant impact on its quality and the audit findings and results.

Alongside the use of artificial intelligence in the audit of financial data, there have been many technology advances in software to analyse and mine databases during many organisation production and service operations, both to improve efficiency and quality. These advances will continue and grow into more artificial intelligence systems and even more sophisticated robots capable of accurate decision-making using existing and new algorithms. Research organisations are already moving in these directions at a fast pace: many accounting/auditing firms are recognising this must be the way forward for both financial accounting and its audit. There is also evidence of this in the learning programmes and professional qualifications for all auditors, and visions and missions of their professional institutions. But has this been enough, and is it yet in all auditing practices?

Data mining, analysis and diagnosis, and the seeking of evidence, is a significant part of every organisation and its employment, financial, production, service and marketing strategies. Each is supported by many developed theories of constraints, compliance, variations and statistical reporting. Today's and tomorrow's technology advances will create more innovations in selection techniques and will change the way each is managed. Each will always be a significant part of every independent audit. Each has its own science and theories.

All auditors must see themselves as scientists in the use of these tools when examining the ever-increasing volumes of data available in their compliance inspections of organisations and functions for economic, environmental or social objectives. Recently the UK Financial Reporting Council (2017 p. 15),[17] in its discussion on developments in financial auditing, observes audit firms investing more in data analytic tools and describing in their tenders 'a greater use of data analytics in the audit process to improve audit quality and bring more insights to management'. This investment can only increase and such tools be used to innovate in all auditing practices, leading to the creation of robotic auditing techniques speeding up data mining, analysis and diagnosis in every audit. This is a must for the 21st century. In its review of this investment,[18] it uses a definition of the International Auditing and Assurance Standards Board (IAASB) Data Analytics Working Group (DAWG) in 2016, based largely on 'a definition used in an American Institute of Certified Public Accountants (AICPA) publication titled *Audit Analytics and Continuous Audit, Looking toward the Future*':

> Data Analytics when used to obtain evidence in a financial statement is the science and art of discovering and analysing patterns, deviations and inconsistencies and extracting other useful information in the data underlying or related to the subject matter of an audit through analysis, modelling and visualisation for the purpose of planning and performing the audit.

Today and tomorrow, all auditors must be scientists in their mining, analysis and diagnosis of data.

6.6 Chapter Review

In this chapter I see auditing as a science and auditors as scientists. It is a science with theories and principles developed mainly over the 20th century to today. It is a science which is continuous in the pursuit of Good and Best practices in auditing in a complex world with increasing assurance reporting responsibilities at board, executive and operations levels across global supply chains; responsibilities for economic, environmental and social objectives in every audit, taking into consideration the ethics in auditing conduct and the ethical conduct of those being audited.

6.7 Creative Audit Thinking Activities

Activity 22   Creative Principia for Cutting-Edge Auditing

In 1998 Professor Andrew Chambers and I developed principia for leading-edge internal auditing.[19] I developed and improved these ten years later into principia for cutting-edge internal auditing[20] and the environment in which it provides assurance. These principia came from many years of theory and practice in auditing, including teaching and research. Compare and contrast your own auditing against our principia for internal auditing. Improve on these for your own creative and innovative auditing. Consider and study the scientific principles and research underlying the principia and improve them.

Cutting-Edge Internal Auditing Principia 2008

1 World-class status for internal auditing requires a vision for its professionalism, quality and standards that meets the needs of all its customers, at all levels in an organisation and those outside the organisation.

2 All internal audit teams should strive for a world-class status in their engagements and be appropriately rewarded when this is achieved.

3 Internal auditing is developing as a spectrum of unrestricted traditional, new and cutting-edge activities across all organisations of all sizes, in all sectors.

4 Good governance is fundamental for all management practices, in all parts of an organisation, at all levels and across all its supply chains and operating relationships: this includes the principles of integrity, openness and accountability in all transactions.

5 Governance should be established as a framework of directing and controlling to encourage good performance and discourage Evil in the achievement of economic, social and environmental objectives.

6 Internal auditors should be trained and experienced to be able to promote themselves as experts in the practices and coordination of governance, risk management and control processes.

7 Internal auditing performance should always be measured against the status and state of governance in an organisation.

8 Internal auditing should encourage and contribute to the self-assessment of governance, risk management and control processes by all employees at all levels in an organisation: this contribution can be by teaching the principles on which these are based.

9 Internal auditing should fight all types of crime at all levels in an organisation at all levels, across all relationships with its stakeholders and the public.

10   The primary role of internal auditing is to assist board performance in the achievement of the organisation's vision and objectives, within a well-governed, regulated and legitimate environment.

11   A total commitment to quality principles, practices and customer delight in an internal audit activity is essential for its success, if not survival.

12   Knowledge and experience of benchmarking are essential for internal auditing in the management of its performance, in the auditing/ review processes in all its engagements, and the assurance/consulting services it provides.

13   The focus of internal audit benchmarking should always be on the needs of its customers and stakeholders of the organisations it serves.

14   Benchmarking should never be a 'one-off' activity. It is a continuous process for improvement.

15   A commitment to continuous improvement in all the services provided by internal auditing is essential if the needs of all its customers and suppliers are to be satisfied now and in the future.

16   Creative thinking in internal auditing is essential and should be encouraged by experiment and development to support continuous improvement in all its resources and practices.

17   Internal auditing should use its engagements to evaluate the creative thinking and processes in all the operations it reviews.

18   It is essential for internal auditing to ask the right questions of the past, present, future and 'beyond the horizon', to the right people and from a good knowledge and understanding of governance, risk management and control process principles and practices.

19   Internal auditing has a responsibility to contribute to the processes of assessing reputation risks and advising at all levels in their organisations on how reputation can be managed and enhanced through good corporate responsibility practices.

20   Success of internal auditing lies in how its professional best practices are researched, developed and promoted in its organisation market place.

21   Understanding its customer's governance, risk management and control process needs is key to how internal auditing should be sold throughout the audit process.

22   Use superlatives to reinforce internal audit staff and promote their services.

23   Internal auditing must attract and encourage knowledgeable and talented people to be internal auditors and to be members of the internal audit team.

24   Internal auditors must manage their knowledge well, for their own continuous development and success of the teams in which they participate.

25   Knowledge in internal auditing needs to be maintained, developed and managed continuously, as a means to an end and not an end in itself.

Activity 23   Creative and Innovative Professionalism

In 2004, I wrote and had published a short opinion on the theories of professionalism in internal auditing and how these have underpinned its development of auditing practices and continue to do so. This same article can be applied to all auditing. Research and consider the 'core principles and values of quality' mentioned in the article and creatively think how these influence your own auditing and how they can be used to innovate in its practices.

Celebrate Internal Audit Professionalism[21]

Internal auditing is moving into an era of increased regulation, and this indeed is cause for celebration. Higher standards – both self-imposed and mandated by external regulators – are helping to elevate the status of our profession and enabling practitioners to gain a more influential role in their organisations. One of the most recent examples of regulatory activity comes from the New York Stock Exchange, which now requires all of its listed companies to have an internal audit function. But this requirement and others like it fall short in one key area – specifying a standard of professionalism. Despite what we celebrate today, internal auditors still need to promote and establish the regulation of internal audit professionalism.

How should the internal audit profession be regulated? Achieving professionalism is like achieving quality. The process requires management leadership, standards for the manner in which services are provided, measurement of achievement, input from customers, and a total commitment to excellence by all involved. But above all, professionalism – like quality – hinges on adherence to a set of core principles and values. All other aspects of professionalism stem from this commitment.

Specifically, the set of principles to which a profession adheres is typically defined in its code of ethics. For internal auditors, The Institute of Internal Auditors (IIA) has established its own code that covers principles and rules governing integrity, objectivity, confidentiality, and competency. That code should be understood by all internal auditors and explained to those who rely on the profession's services. Questions all internal auditors should ask themselves are – "Does my professional conduct meet the requirements of The IIA code?" and "Does The IIA code match or improve the ethical cultures required by my organization, regulators, governments and other professional bodies?" Knowing the answers to these questions is key to measuring their own professionalism, and the conduct they should expect to see in others. But compliance with a set of principles at a given point in time is only part of the picture. Professionalism also requires commitment to continuous improvement.

Quality assurance and continuous improvement are fundamental to achieving high levels of quality in all products and services, and programs aimed at achieving this result typically require both internal and external assessments. The same applies to internal audit professionalism – implementation of principles and standards needs to be monitored on an ongoing basis to ensure adequate performance. Yet how many internal audit activities have such a program up and running? How many report the results of such programs to their management and board of directors? Research shows that many fall short in this area.

Professionalism is essential to the achievement of high standards in internal auditing. Like quality, it is not a destination but a road that should be followed — one that calls for a customer-focused vision and requires passion and commitment to continuous improvement. Although hazards may exist along the way, these can be overcome with integrity, objectivity, confidentiality, and competency. Internal auditors should certainly take the opportunity to celebrate advances made by the profession thus far, but we should not let this progress serve as an excuse to become complacent.

Activity 24   Think Creatively About Ethics and Values

Research by Maitland (2015)[22] into values used and promoted by the 100 FTSE companies in the United Kingdom revealed the following as among the top core values (all discussed in the chapters in my book):

Integrity	Teamwork	Care
Respect	Honesty	Customer-focus
Innovation	Trust	Passion
Safety	Responsibility	Listening
Transparency	Collaboration	Striving
Excellence	Accountability	

The following other values were only mentioned once. Consider how each of these values applies to your auditing and to those you audit. Select ten of these for your organisation and creatively think how they could lead to innovation in your audit processes and organisation.

Values that appeared once

Forward thinking	Pragmatism	Prudence
Science-led	Risk	Commercial-focus
Open-mindedness	Ingenuity	Velocity
Protection	Agility	Urgency
Exploration	Conviction	Nimbleness
Inspiration	Difference	Confidentiality
Consistency	Creativity	Security
Autonomy	Ability	Equality
Curiosity	Compliance	Effectiveness

Restlessness	Responsiveness	Probity
Relentlessness	Freshness	Enthusiasm
Perseverance	Ethical behaviour	Forthrightness
Excitement	Availability	Evidence-based
Empowerment	Motivation	Recognition
Accuracy	Bravery	Kindness
Pioneering	Imagination	Spiritedness
Expertise	Decency	Dignity
Client-centric	Achievement	Commitment
Dependability	Valuing our people	Progress
Connectedness	Boundarylessness	

Notes

1 *Principles of Auditing* (1914 p. 1), F.R.M. De Paula, Sir Isaac Pitman and Sons Ltd., London, England.
2 *Nicomacean Ethics* (bk1, 1094a 1 – 3), Atistotle384 – 322 BC.
3 *Science Desk Reference* (1995), Patricia Barnes-Swarney, New York Public Library, The Stonesong Press Inc., US.
4 *Principles of Auditing* (1914 pp. 1 and 20), F.R.M. De Paula, Sir Isaac Pitman and Sons Ltd., London, England.
5 *The Philosophy of Auditing* (1961), R.K. Mautz and H.K. Sharaf, American Accounting Association, Florida, US.
6 *Philosophy and Principles of Auditing* (1988), David Flint, Macmillan Education Ltd., Basingstoke, England.
7 *Internal Control – Integrated Framework* (1992), Committee of Sponsoring Organisations of the Treadway Commission (COSO), New York, US.
8 *Thought Leadership in ERM: Demystifying Sustainability* (2013), Committee of Sponsoring Organisations of the Treadway Commission, New York, US.
9 *Internal Control – Integrated Framework* (2013), Committee of Sponsoring Organisations of the Treadway Commission (COSO), New York, US.
10 *Internal Control – Integrated Framework* (2013), Committee of Sponsoring Organisations of the Treadway Commission (COSO), New York, US.
11 *Code of Ethics and Conduct* (2011), Association of Certified and Chartered Accountants, London, England.
12 *Strategic Plan 2011–16*, International Organisation of Supreme Audit Institutes (INTOSAI), Vienna, Austria.
13 *Code of Conduct* (2012), National Audit Office, London, England.
14 *Code of Conduct* (2012), European Court of Auditors, Brussels, Belgium.
15 *Code of Ethics – Revised* (2009), The Institute of Internal Auditors Inc., Orlando, US.
16 Chartered Institute of Internal Auditors. www.iia.org.uk, accessed 12 March 2016.
17 *Developments in Audit February 2017 Update* (2017 p. 15), Financial Reporting Council (FRC), London, England.
18 *Audit Quality Thematic Review – The Use of Data Analytics in the Audit of Financial Statements* (2017 p. 6), Financial Reporting Council (FRC), London, England.
19 *Leading Edge Internal Auditing* (1998), Jeffrey Ridley and Andrew Chambers, ICSA Publishing, London, England.
20 *Cutting Edge Internal Auditing* (2008), Jeffrey Ridley, John Wiley and Sons Ltd., Chichester, England.
21 *Celebrate Internal Audit Professionalism* (2004), Jeffrey Ridley, published in Internal Auditor, The Institute of Internal Auditors, Orlando, US.
22 *The Values Most Valued by UK PLC* (2015 pp. 6 and 14), Maitland, London, England.

7 Auditors Are Futurists

A person who studies the future in order to help people understand, anticipate, prepare for and gain advantage from coming changes[1]

In this chapter I see all auditors and all auditing as not just an evaluation of the past, present and immediate future, but a consideration of what might happen beyond the horizon and into the future. Some may see auditing conclusions formed by auditors only from their past and present experiences and evidence from their present audit findings. I see it as a responsibility for all auditors to go beyond their immediate conclusions and recommendations and to be visionary:

to foresee with insight a wider and deeper understanding of future scenarios – scenarios in which situations may, can or should happen if an organisation or function is to continue to be successful in an economic, effective, efficient sustainable world. Predicting scenarios of future events that may, could or should happen is the art and skill of the futurist. All auditors have opportunities to be futurists and to create the auditing techniques that future scenarios will need.

7.1 Futurists Are Auditors

The Association of Professional Futurists[2] in its website describes the professional futurist as:

> a person who studies the future in order to help people understand, anticipate, prepare for and gain advantage from coming changes. It is not the goal of a futurist to predict what will happen in the future. The futurist uses foresight to describe what *could* happen in the future and, in some cases, what *should* happen in the future. . . . A professional futurist uses formal methods to develop descriptions of possible futures. The output of a futures study may include the driving forces, assumptions, evidence or indicators of the futures. A futurist is more likely to say how or why a future could appear rather than to say what the future will be.

Bell (1997)[3] in his introduction discusses a concern that futurists have about 'the nature of the good society and the standards of evaluation by which it is defined and judged'. He sees 'a major goal of futurists as human betterment'. His discussions are around judging preferable futures. He concludes with questions on what human values ought to be changed and includes many of the possible changes foreseen then that are just as important, if not more so, today, including:

> the recent rapid growth of the earth's population, the increase in the scale and intensity of human interactions and interdependence to encompass the globe, and threats to the life-sustaining capacities of the Earth from human behavior.

His focus on the importance of the values that drive human betterment is seen today in all corporate governance principles and values, promoted by many organisations across the world in their visions and mission statements. Values seen as right for the future, not just by futurists, but also auditors at national and international levels and by many associations of professions and nations at global level.

The future is what we all make it to be, individually and collectively. Futurists think about the possibilities of what might happen in the future – what can and should be shaped by inspirational visions and actions in the present to influence the future. Such visions require intellectual activities which maintain the values people cherish today and contribute to the growth of knowledge from the past to present and into the future – visions that paint a vivid picture of a better scenario. Visions can be created by all disciplines to empower change in their futures for the better.

Futurism can be considered as an art and science: an art in its use of personal skills, experience and knowledge; a science in its use of established theories and principles to form judgements on what might, could or should happen in particular circumstances and scenarios. Its tools are all those an academic would use in research methodology, both qualitative and quantitative, to establish evidence, develop findings and make recommendations for actions and policy changes, at individual, organisation, group, national and internal levels.

My first introduction to futurism was in the early 1950s when I came across the term 'mind power' in a book given to me by my parents at the start of my life's adventures – *Wisdom of the Ages* (1936) by Mark Gilbert[4] – 'An assembly of two hundred everyday subjects by four hundred great Thinkers of thirty nations extending over five thousand years.' Futurism is not mentioned, though many of the quotations in the book influenced visions of what might and should be at their time, and still do today. On future, it contains three quotations from the 18th and 19th centuries relevant in every audit:

The Future is purchased by the present.

—Samuel Johnson (1709–1784)

It is vain to be always looking toward the future and never acting toward it.
—Christian Nestell Boyes (1820–1904)

Look not mournfully into the past – it comes not back again; wisely improve the present – it is thine; go forth to meet the shadowy future without fear, and with a manly heart.
—Henry Wadsworth Longfellow (1807–1882)

At the end of Gilbert's book, under the title 'X-Y-Z', three statements caught my imagination then and have inspired my creative thinking as an auditor ever since. I believe these statements apply to all futurists today:

Mind Power rightly developed and applied to proper ends can produce anything whatever in the life and circumstances of anyone.

We can become whatever we aspire to become, but the growth must come from Within.

The Great Law of Cause and Effect operates everywhere.

The first two are personal to the individual and drive vision-making in people, professions, organisations, governments and international associations. Vision-making has been discussed in earlier chapters and is an essential skill for all futurists. The third is a universal law that states for every cause there is an effect and likewise for every effect there is a cause. Too often this law is not studied and applied in the development of visions and their pursuit, with unforeseen and sometimes unfortunate results occurring. In auditing, this law is too often neglected in audit findings, resulting in the wrong change or lack of it for particular circumstances and scenarios. Too often the effect is addressed only and not the cause or causes.

7.2 Future of Internal Auditing – 1975

In 1975, when I was elected president of the then United Kingdom Chapter of Internal Auditors representing professional internal auditing in the United Kingdom (now the Chartered Institute of Internal Auditors), I wrote and published my election speech as a futurist, looking into the future for internal auditing with the following address. It is an address which could be spoken and published again today with little change for the future of internal auditing, if not all auditing:

The Future Is Ours[5]

One of the main purposes of any professional institute is to provide for all members a professional identity with high standards of conduct and common objectives. The Institute of Internal Auditors with its Statement of Responsibilities and Code of Ethics provides these. In the past, Chapters in the United Kingdom have developed this identity in their regions, with close ties with each other and the Institute headquarters. Indeed, the history of each Chapter is a record of which we can all be very proud.

We live in times of high economic risk and important social and business decisions. Every day we are reminded at work, in newspapers and by television of the opportunities that can be taken to develop ourselves and the profession we have chosen. The apparent insoluble problems of the present economic situation; the controversial discussions caused by exposure drafts and new accounting practices; involvement in the European Community; a new awareness of social responsibilities; higher health and safety standards; the now clearly recognised need for more efficient manpower planning and training; the urgency of energy saving; the complexity of advanced computer technology are all changes that management cannot ignore, and neither can we as internal auditors. To be successful we must be sensitive to the problems of each day. All can have an impact on our professional activities far beyond the changes we may foresee at the present time.

A strong professional identity needs the support of members who are committed to its development. One of the major obstacles we have to overcome in our development is the temporary nature of many of our members' commitment to internal auditing as a career. I believe there is evidence that this is changing. There are now an increasing number of internal auditors who see a career development in internal auditing, either over a period or returning to internal audit after seeking experience in other areas. This is evidence of our growing strength as a Professional Institute and can be attributed to the:

- increased reporting by internal auditors to higher levels of management;
- increasing numbers of organisations using modern internal auditing;
- encouragement given for disciplines other than accountancy to take positions in internal audit;

- increased use of the internal auditor as a consultant because of his [and certainly now her] experiences and knowledge of control techniques; and,
- increased use of internal auditors as teachers, participating in management training schemes.

All these developments are evidence of the growing importance of modern internal auditing in all types of organisations and the work of Institute members during past years. I personally believe that if we are to be truly professional we need to continue to encourage more dedication to internal audit as a career. Such a change in attitude could be one of the significant developments we will see in our profession during the next decade.

'Progress through Sharing' is our slogan of integrity, trust and help, which from its beginning[6] has represented the attitude of the Institute to a future of growth, a future of service to members and a future of strength. As a profession in the United Kingdom we have grown tall in our first 25 years. Our integrity and professional standards are high and we are respected by management for the service we offer. We have not stopped growing by our merger[7] but are on the threshold of a new period of development and growth. It is now our responsibility to see the opportunities that surround us are not lost.

7.3 Future of Internal Auditing in the 21st Century

In 2000 I was invited to write an article on the internal auditor for the 21st century.[8] For this I used as an acronym the key word CONTROL, each letter representing an imperative for internal auditing, and the whole word representing the overriding theme of 'control' for internal auditing roles in the this century. The acronym and each of the words it represents spoke for themselves at that time, and still do today for all auditing. Together, they forecast many opportunities and challenges for all auditing in the 21st century to be creative and innovative. Test your own services against each. Create a definition for each that is appropriate for your organisation and the customers you serve Research the implications of your definitions. As a start, consider the following suggestions for your definitions:

A New Internal Auditor for a New Century[9]

The IIA launched earlier this year its new definition of internal auditing for the 21st century's professional internal auditor.

Internal auditing is an independent, objective, assurance and consulting activity designed to add value and improve an organisation's operations. It helps an organisation accomplish its objectives by bringing

a systematic, disciplined approach to evaluate and improve effectiveness of risk management, control, and governance processes.[10]

It should lead and guide all internal auditors and their customers into a new
internal auditing service. A service that requires new knowledge, skills, objectives and planning. Although a new definition, the service image it contains
has been growing in many organisations across the world over a long period.

Internal auditors must be experts in how organisations are controlled.
This requires a study of control concepts, the primary objectives of control
(see The IIA general standard 300/1983) and the characteristics of control
(see the COSO report/1992, cited by the ICAEW Turner Internal Control
Consultative Draft/1999 in its risk-based approach to control). Current
requirements for reporting on control continue to mix the terms 'control'
and 'internal control'. Recent studies are no exception. In 1983 The IIA
considered 'control' and 'internal control' to be synonymous (Guideline
300.06.3). In the 21st century we should stop referring to 'internal control'
and its implied 'within the organisation' restriction. Management's control
responsibilities span all an organisation's supply chains. This includes
many relationships with others (owners, partners, alliances, contractors,
suppliers, customers, regulators, inspectors, communities etc.). Consider
your own organisation's supply chains and many external control requirements. These should all be subject to review and report by management,
and independent appraisal. The new IIA definition of internal auditing
refers to 'control'. Let us hope the revised IIA professional standards will
drop the use of 'internal', and others will follow. Design 'control' not 'internal control' into all your internal auditing. Encourage your board, management and accountants to do likewise for their control responsibilities.

Earlier this year I was invited to participate in an internal audit conference at a leading building society. My theme was 'Internal Auditing in
2005'. For this I used as an acronym the key word CONTROL. Each letter
representing an imperative for the new internal auditor of the 21st century. The whole word representing the overriding feature for all internal
auditing roles – Auditor, Consultant and Teacher. The acronym and each
of the words it represents speak for themselves. Together they offer many
opportunities and challenges for the new internal auditing service of the
21st century. Test your own services against each. Create a definition
for each that is appropriate for your organisation and the customers you
serve. Research the implications of your definitions and redefine each
year. As a start consider the following suggestions for your definitions:

Competition

For all auditing (and assurance) services it will increase. Study the
marketing of services by all professional firms – not just auditing!

Learn from their 'selling' skills. Market your internal auditing services as a business. Improve your auditing market share. The IIA's 199411 recommended response to outsourcing requires internal auditing to be proactive, innovative, focused, motivated, and ' . . . with information systems integrated and designed to support auditing and management processes.' In a competitive market place you also need to be a quality champion. Self-assess the value of your quality initiatives and measure your customers' satisfaction.

Objectives

Have a clear sense of internal auditing purpose and values that everyone understands. Create commitment to an exciting vision of the internal auditing services you believe your customers will need in five years time. Make sure your entire current internal auditing objectives link into this vision, your organisation's objectives, and span all your organisation's supply chains – suppliers, processes and customers.

New Business

Keep up to date with research into internal auditing practices and use this knowledge to experiment, develop and market your future services (also products). Products are the most under-developed part of internal auditing services. Focusing on products requires you to address specifications, processes and packaging. It also draws your attention to by-products, often resulting in new business. Plan for growth. Particularly focus on your organisation's strategies and contribute to their development and implementation. This is the most neglected part of internal auditing.

Technology

Up to date technology will be the key to all internal auditing best practices in the future. Use information technology as a means to improve your knowledge management. Internal auditing knowledge spans all organisation operations at all levels. Organize and manage this knowledge properly and it will lead you to your organisation's most significant risks. Sell your information technology and knowledge management skills as part of the internal auditing services you provide.

Regulation

New inspectors and regulators are being established by government and industries across all sectors. Some are being merged with stronger teeth. Some have established guidance for governance, control and internal auditing. Others will follow. Understand the authority responsibilities and activities of inspectors and regulators in your own sector, and that of your suppliers and customers. Use this knowledge in the planning and quality of your internal auditing services.

Outstanding

Do not just be 'best' or 'excellent', be 'outstanding'. Recognise achievements and celebrate. In your organisation openly reinforce outstanding internal auditing by appropriate rewards, at individual and team levels. Be recognised by your management and peers as leading the development of professional internal auditing services. Build this commitment into your internal auditing vision and objectives. Benchmark your leading edge practices with others and published research.

Learning

Be part of the new learning age.[12] Your working environment must be a learning environment. Carry out a continuous skills audit of your knowledge and abilities. Identify your strengths and weaknesses. Plan to improve both. Master a critical understanding of the concepts and principles needed to understand how organisations should be managed and controlled today and tomorrow. This is essential for all the roles you provide as an internal auditor.

Standards

Search for relevant and appropriate external standards and codes of conduct for all the operations you audit. Test against these standards and codes. Publicise your own standards and codes. Benchmark the services you provide with relevant international standards – professional, accounting, auditing, quality, environmental, training, data, technology etc. Use the results to add power and value to your services and your reporting to management and at board level.

Finally, as you start the new century as a new internal auditor focus on the ethics of your service. Remember always that 'Members and CIAs shall continually strive for improvements in their proficiency, and in the effectiveness and quality of the services they provide.'13 Good striving (and luck). Enjoy your part of the 21st century.

The art and science of futurism can also be seen in scenarios in both my previous books and much of my past research. I wrote the following vision in 1998 in the preface of my part of *Leading Edge Internal Auditing*, co-authored with Professor Andrew Chambers. It has stood the test of time and formed the scenario of much of the professional development of all auditing since. It still has creative thinking for the future:

> More recently, values from internal auditing have been attracting attention from regulators, non-executive directors in listed and private companies, governing members of many public sector and voluntary organisations, and even the public. This attention arises from an increasing focus on governance and codes of conduct issues by all types of organisation, not only in the UK but worldwide. This focus is not new. There has always been concern over how organisations are managed and controlled. Concern not only by management and internal auditing, but also by many outside regulators – all with an interest in good management practices, meeting legal requirements, and success. Even survival.
>
> What is new is that many of these outside regulators are now starting to influence the development of internal auditing practices. Over the next few years this influence will change the way many internal auditing units now operate. Competition amongst audit providers is now a key issue in many organisations and this will spread across sectors as audit committees continue to grow in number and experience. This competition will also change many of the current practices by internal auditors and increase the use of technology in their audit work.

7.4 Future of All Auditing in the 21st Century

My book, *Cutting Edge Internal Auditing* (2008) was based on six directions for auditing – **INSPIRE: EXPLORE: IMAGINE: IMPROVE: INNOVATE: CREATE** – displayed on its cover by a signpost pointing to the future. Each sign pointed to actions by internal auditors to arrive at the cutting edge of their profession; each had an association then and now with the development of visions and professional futurism. In each chapter of that book I created cutting-edge visions for future scenarios of internal auditing, collectively discussing these in the final chapter: *The Future of Internal Auditing is Yours* – see Figure 7.1. These visions can apply to all auditing. Many can be seen today as forecast future scenarios in auditing practices across the world. All should be seen in future auditing during the 21st century.

Looking now into the future of auditing in the 21st century, I foresee many changes in each of the steps in the Ten Step Audit Process described earlier in this book. These changes will take place because the scenarios of governance will improve in and around organisations of all sizes across the world. Some of these improvements will be because of new and revised laws and directives, both national and global; some by regulation, some by pressure groups of stakeholders; some by advances in technology; some by disasters in and outside

To be seen as a professional service adding significant value with our high quality, independent and objective services.

We provide a service seen by all our customers and stakeholders as world-class.

We wear a variety of independent and objective hats to meet all our customers' needs.

We aim to add best value to good governance.

Our services include a fight against all types of crime.

Our independence, resources and professional practices assist board performance.

Our quality delights all our customers.

To continue to be the best supplier of professional auditing services.

We are committed to continuously improve.

We have no boundaries in our thinking.

We understand your business needs and ask the right questions to help you achieve these.

We add value to the organisation's good reputation.

We promote our professional values at all times.

Knowledge is our moist important asset – we manage it well.

Figure 7.1 Visions for all auditors

Source: Cutting Edge Internal Auditing (2008), J. Ridley

organisations, both fraud and environmental; some by needs for greater transparency; some by distrust; some by war and rebellion; many by politicians and political manifestos influencing economic, environmental and social needs and aspirations of civic societies.

For auditing, I see these governance improvements already influencing changes in all auditing practices, as advertised by auditing firms and functions, and required by their regulators. The roles of all auditors should be creating a better future for all the organisations they serve. This is not an easy role for any auditor, and may not always be achievable for a variety of reasons. But it should be the vision for every auditor.

Consider the following thoughts on what I believe will change future scenarios in and around organisations and the creative thinking and innovation needed to walk these paths in your future audit processes:

- More cooperation, coordination and collaboration across all those who are providing independent assurance services to an organisation.
- All auditors will consider the results of self-assurance actions across an organisation and at all levels in their evaluations of governance, risk and control.

- Audit committees becoming more like supervisory boards as they assume monitoring activities across the implementation and establishment of best practice governance principles in their organisations and being seen as servants of all an organisation's stakeholders.
- All auditors will be encouraged/required to report their findings to the public as well as to their clients and clients' stakeholders.
- Technology will continue to provide opportunities for easier and quicker analysis of data during the course of an audit, increasing the penetration of all audit processes.
- Use of artificial intelligence to carry out the routine work of auditors will grow. This already exists in some forensic auditing and other professional services. Its growth is needed and will increase in all auditing through creative thinking and innovation.
- Governance by organisations will be across all their supply chains. This already takes place with contracts and codes of conduct, but will expand to include all good governance principles. In future this will form a greater part of every audit, both within internal supply chains and external.
- Developments and requirements in integrated accounting and reporting of sustainability issues will become an essential part of the transparency of reporting in every organisation.
- Pressures will grow at international and national levels for more responsibility to be taken by leaders in organisations for their actions, with more liabilities, penalties and punishments when they are not.

I have no problems in the reader adding their own thoughts on future auditing needs and possible changes to this list – please do so, but do not delete any. The signs are that they are all happening now and will grow in significance and importance for all auditors.

7.5 Today's Futuristic Visions of Auditing by Others

Today, professions for auditors are looking beyond the horizon as they address the needs of their members and their members' clients in a rapidly changing world, growing smaller in time travel every year. In the United Kingdom both the Institute of Chartered Accountants in England and Wales (ICAEW) and Association of Chartered and Certified Accountants (ACCA) have future-focused programmes for auditing. The ICAEW with its AuditFutures[14] thought-leadership initiatives is exploring and pioneering audit thinking and behaviour for the future. Its aim is to create inspiration in audit to drive innovation and best practice for today and in the future:

> The aim of AuditFutures is to construct a holistic view and an innovative approach to rethinking the profession and to create opportunities for dialogue and for collaborative solutions to emerge. We are building a movement for a wider behaviour change and we are developing innovation projects for systemic effect.

Research by the United Kingdom Royal Society of Arts[15] on behalf of Audit-Futures places emphasis on the auditor as a 'public servant working in the public interest'.

> An elusive and messy concept, the public interest cannot be seized simply through regulations and tests. It can only be realised in ongoing dialogue. Audit can become exemplary in this regard. Instead of an audit report being a trust-producing *product*, the audit process should become a trust-producing *practice* in which the auditor uses his or her position as a trusted intermediary to broker evidence based learning across all dimensions of the organisation and its stakeholders, and bring into consideration all aspects of the organisation's value – economic, social and environmental. From being a service consisting almost exclusively of external investigation by a warranted professional, modern technology will allow auditing to become more co-productive, with the auditor's role expanding to include that of an expert convener willing to share the tools of enquiry. The auditor as convener will need new skills, and will need to work in a more agile and interdisciplinary environment. Technical rigour will need to be maintained through training and professional support, but qualities like empathy, imagination and moral reasoning should be an increasingly important part of the training and support package. The auditor of the future will be a multidisciplinary team member, operating within and between companies as the market takes on the form of flexible platforms and innovative start-ups.

The introduction to this research paper recognises issues and scenarios faced by auditors in the 21st century are also faced by other professions (referencing into a paper on professionalism, defining its roles in a 21st-century scenario, published by the Chartered Insurance Institute.[16] This paper is well worth a visit by all professional auditors):

> The struggle is unusually public, but the issues it faces are shared by many other traditional professions, whose value is challenged by our inexorable move into a demanding, global, data-rich and trust-poor world. We believe that the decisions made by the audit profession in the coming years could prove influential in shaping the future value of professionalism. We hope that this report will serve to encourage greater collaboration and debate across all the professions.

The Federation of European Accountants (FEE) (2016)[17] has its own thoughts on actions auditors should take in the future to meet the challenges and take the opportunities that will be there 'in an ever-changing environment':

> Many challenges lie ahead for the audit profession, but so do plenty of opportunities to further evolve and better serve new markets' needs. FEE is committed to supporting constant adaption of the profession to an ever

rapidly changing environment, while continuously promoting the fundamental principles of integrity objectivity, independence, professionalism, competence and confidentiality that makes our profession stand out. Our charter to society of seeking to uphold the public interest remains embedded in our day to day activities. Ultimately, we all have the same end game: improving quality in both corporate reporting and assurance to make the products we provide to the market place the best that we can possibly achieve.

These fundamental principles sum up well the character all auditors will need to meet the future challenges and take the opportunitures researched by their professions. All auditors will need to be futurists in their preparation of the profesionalism and competency needed for that future.

7.6 Chapter Review

In this chapter I have compared the role of auditors to futurists in their role of considering future scenarios in governance, risk management and control during their time travelling through the Ten Step Audit Process in organisations across the world – a world which will be subject to rapid changes during the 21st century in technology, trade, economics, populations and the civic societies in which they live, work and play. In every audit, the future will always be more important than the past and present.

7.7 Creative Audit Thinking Activities

Activity 25　Be Creative in Your Future Intelligence Gathering

Futurologists exist in every organisation, either in name or in a future-thinking role. The setting of direction through strategic thinking, assessment of risks, seeking of opportunities and receiving of assurances involves considering possible future scenarios and how risks can be mitigated and opportunities taken. Kubitscheck (2014)[18] discusses how working beyond functional boundaries to gain collective risk intelligence at board level is essential for the foreseeing board and its corporate governance and sustainability responsibilities. Consider some of her thoughts on this below. Be creative in evaluating collective future intelligence gathering at board level in your organisation. Does your board receive the future intelligence from assurance advisers in her list? This will open doors for innovation in the auditing of intelligence gathering for risk assessment and opportunities for the betterment of both your organisation and society.

Seeking Collective Future Intelligence at Board Level

The board agenda is not decreasing and neither are board packs. The introduction of electronic board packs for a more sustainable solution to *save the trees* as well as the administrative burden is not a coincidence. With increased regulation in corporate governance, board agendas are largely influenced by mandatory items such as statutory and regulatory developments and related reporting. The agenda of the board sub-committees, such as the audit committee, risk committee, remuneration committee and nomination committees, are of course by their specific areas of focus and terms of reference.

Information that constitutes assurance on the sound operation of the relevant system of risk management and control is typically embedded in the board packs in various guises; they can be also embedded on an ad hoc basis when requested by the board or its sub-committees or as part of an agreed plan as determined by the function area such as compliance, health and safety or internal audit. In addition to the reporting of financial and strategic performance of the organisation, some typical examples of standing reports of a compliance nature, which board may receive from various assurance providers include:

Anti-financial crime, including the Money Laundering Reporting Officer's report
Bribery Act compliance report
Customer complaints analysis
Report of external auditor independence and provision of non-audit services
Fund and investment management auditor's report
Health and safety report
Information security and Data Protection Act compliance report
Litigation report
Health checks on key outsourcing arrangements
Management letters from external auditors
Audit report of quality standards such as International Organization for Standardization
Sarbanes-Oxley Act sections 302 and 404 certifications
Sustainability and corporate social responsibility report
Annual report of whistle-blowing and Public Interest Disclosure Act

Additionally, the board and its relevant sub-committees may receive functional reports from its risk, compliance, finance and internal audit functions that cover similar areas of interests. The list of reports and papers that constitute assurance to the board is clearly long. It is easy to see how directors and management could have different understandings of the residual risks and issues pertaining to the same subject *[including the future]*.

Activity 26   Future Scenarios for the Creative and Innovative Audit Committee

Creatively think about the governance codes of practice your audit committee will be required to monitor in twenty years' time. What do you foresee are the changes there will be to current codes of governance by 2026? Start your thinking process by reading the Report of the Committee on the Financial Aspects of Corporate Governance (Cadbury Report: 1992) discussion on audit committees and current guidance by the UK Financial Reporting Council. Then consider the following extract from an article I wrote in 2002 foreseeing a future scenario for audit committees. What innovative changes must you make to meet the assurance requirements your audit committee will need and give in 2026 to your board and your organisation's stakeholders?

What Was the Point of Cadbury – Today and Tomorrow?[19]

Even though good levels of control are now more frequently required and reported by regulators, boards, management and audit, there are still too many control weaknesses that encourage abuse, nationally and internationally. Today's media includes too many stories of bad governance in too many organisations – public, private and voluntary – and will continue to do so. Research shows there is still some way to go for all organisations to fully comply with governance codes and their audit committees to monitor all governance practices.

Does your audit committee today:

*   *Link corporate governance codes of practice to social and environmental practices in their organisation?*
*   *Link corporate governance codes of practice to the quality of their organisation's products and services and economic performance?*
*   *Monitor governance practices at board level?*
*   *Monitor control across all their organisation's supply chains and associated business partners, not just internally within their organisation?*
*   *Report on its monitoring activities in your organisation's published annual reports?*

Activity 27   Creativity and Innovation Differentiates Assurance Providers

Chambers (2015)[20] debates the present and future opportunities internal auditors have to 'endeavour to differentiate themselves' from other assurance providers. In foreseeing their future scenarios, he suggests internal auditors must include public interest in their reporting roles. He lists 'important challenges' for all chief audit executives to address in development of their services to the board, management, and organisation's stakeholders. Consider this list as an auditor and the innovations needed to address some, if not all, of these in your audit role, be it internal or external auditor, or other provider of assurance to the board.

Important Challenges for the Chief Audit Executive (CAE)

1 Share the responsibility of avoiding excessively risky and unethical business practices by the entity.
2 Attend as of right ExCo meetings, though not as a member, with a status equivalent to ExCo members.
3 Attend and participate in board and board committee meetings when issues are discussed where the CAE should have a contribution to make.
4 Set out to contribute significantly to the principal assurances that the board needs.
5 Audit governance, culture, all critical risks (including strategic risk and the risk management process), key corporate events, significant infrastructure changes and customer outcomes.
6 Achieve higher standards than those set out in the global internal auditing *Standards*.
7 While reporting to management and the board on the results of audit work, report administratively and professionally exclusively to the board.
8 Move into the future by developing significant reporting lines to external stakeholders.
9 Negotiate with the board the authority to make external disclosures in the public interest when appropriate.
10 Re-designate yourself from being 'CAE' to avoid implying executive responsibility as a member of the first or second lines of defence.

Notes

1 Downloaded from the Association of Professional Futurists website, www.associationof-professionalfuturists.org, accessed 12 February 2016.
2 See Note 1.
3 *Foundation of Futures Studies* (1997), Wendell Bell, Transaction Publishers, New Brunswick, US.
4 *Wisdom of the Ages* (1948), Mark Gilbert, The Saint Catherine Press Ltd., London, England.
5 This paper was written and presented by me in 1975 as my presidential address, on the integration of the five separate United Kingdom Chapters of The Institute of Internal

Auditors into the one United Kingdom Chapter. It was then published in the Chapter Audit Newsletter in the same year.

6 This was Raymond E. Noonan's presidential theme when 13th international president of The IIA in 1953. In May 1955 it was formally adopted as the institute's theme and added to its corporate seal.

7 At the time of the merger the IIA membership in the United Kingdom was 1,000.

8 *A New Internal Auditor for a New Century* (2000), In Internal Auditing and Business Risk, Institute of Internal Auditors – UK and Ireland, London, England.

9 Published in *Internal Auditing & Business Risk* (January 2000), IIA-UK and Ireland.

10 Approved by The IIA Inc. Board (1999).

11 *Perspective on Outsourcing Internal Auditing* – A professional briefing for chief executives, 1994, The IIA.

12 *The Learning Age: A Renaissance for a New Britain*, Department for Education and Employment, 1998.

13 *The IIA Code of Ethics*, first published in 1968 and latest revised version at Appendix J.

14 AuditFutures is a thought-leadership programme of ICAEW, run in partnership with the Finance Innovation Lab. www.AuditFutuires.org.

15 *Enlightening Professions? A Vision for Audit and a Better Society* (2014 p. 7), Institute of Chartered Accountants in England and Wales, London, England.

16 *Professionalism for the 21st Century – Revisited* (2011), The Chartered Insurance Institute, London, England.

17 *Pursuing a Strategy Debate – The Future of Audit and Assurance*: Discussion paper (2016 p. 10), Federation of European Accountants, Brussels, Belgium.

18 *Integrated Assurance – Risk Governance Beyond Boundaries* (2014 p. 85), Vicky Kubitscheck, Gower Publishing Limited, Farnham, England.

19 *What Was the Point of Cadbury – What Should Be the Point Tomorrow?* (2002), Internal Auditing and Business Risk, Institute of Internal Auditors UK and Ireland, London, England.

20 *Recalibrating Internal Audit* (2015), Chambers A.D., Internal Auditing, 30 (5) (September–October pp. 28–34), Thomson Reuters.

Part III

Assurance

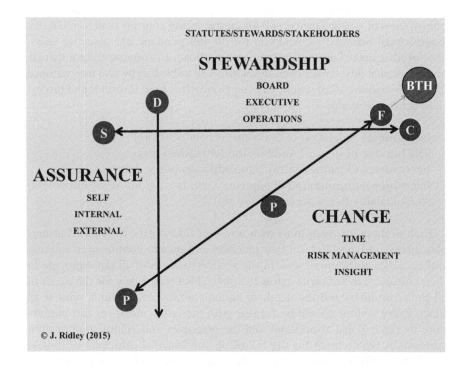

STATUTES/STEWARDS/STAKEHOLDERS

STEWARDSHIP

BOARD
EXECUTIVE
OPERATIONS

BTH

D

S

F

C

ASSURANCE

SELF
INTERNAL
EXTERNAL

P

CHANGE

TIME
RISK MANAGEMENT
INSIGHT

P

© J. Ridley (2015)

Ultimately, we all have the same end game: improving quality in both corporate reporting and assurance.[1]

The concept of assurance in today's organisations across the world goes back in history to the military hierarchy of command and control adopted by management to supervise subordinates and seek confirmation that commands are being complied with at all times for the benefit of the organisation and its owners. As organisations and their operations have developed to satisfy today's complex legal requirements, structures, significant resources and wide scope of needs from a variety of stakeholders, so have the needs of boards and management for more and better assurances to ensure their style of direction and control is operating in accordance with the law and best interests of the organisation and its objectives, not forgetting also all its stakeholders. Those assurances have multiplied over recent years to a 'collection' of tasks and professional services, each often providing assurances at different times and with separate remits, quality standards and often with little coordination, collaboration or cooperation with each other. In today and tomorrow's economic, environmental and social worlds, this is not good governance, risk management or control.

My framework shows a line of Assurance pointing down, representing the need for all assurances to go deep into an organisation's operations to satisfy the assurance needs of both the Stewardship and Change lines, representing the responsibilities at Board, Executive and Operations levels. It is a key responsibility of the board to ensure it gains appropriate assurances to determine the effectiveness of its governance, risk management and controls at all levels. Today, International Standards of Auditing for the independent and objective assurance of all aspects of operations – accounting, finance, economy, environmental, social, sustainability – have been developed and published by five international global associations, all of whom have representatives from institutes and professions across the world:

International Federation of Accountants (www.ifac.org)
The Institute of Internal Auditors Inc. (www.theiia.org)
International Organization for Standardization (www.iso.org)
International Organization of Supreme Audit Institutions (www.intosai.org)
Accountability (www.accountability.org)

Each of these standards in its own way, over many years, has created principles, advice and guidance on best practices and quality control over auditing and assurance, to promote trust in the services auditors of all types provide to their customers in countries across the globe. That trust is key for the needs of all audit customers and the depth of assurances they are provided with at all times. Every auditor should be familiar with the work, initiatives and innovations by these global associations and the principles underpinning all of their standards. A requirement for the following 'fundamental principles of professional ethics when conducting an audit'[2] can be seen in all auditing standards:

Integrity
Objectivity
Professional competence and due care
Confidentiality
Professional behavior.

These principles are underpinned by other requirements concerning auditor competence; independence in the public interest; professional judgement; professional scepticism; significant appropriate audit evidence, audit risk and, conduct of an audit; requirements for all assurance services. Each can have a significant impact on the depth of assurance being provided by every auditor and how it is communicated and followed up.

A recent discussion paper from the Federation of European Accounts (2016),[3] developed from its conference on reporting and assurance in 2014, and from which the chapter epigraph is taken, highlights the importance all auditors should apply to their reporting and assurance roles. Respondents and attendees at the conference emphasised the following actions, all offering opportunities for creative audit thinking and innovations:

- Engagement with stakeholders needs to be enhanced. Auditor communication was one of the key areas where the profession had recently demonstrated its ability to adapt and engage with its stakeholders. Further initiatives should be explored, such as responding to stakeholders' needs on new types of assurance, and among others, over non-financial information.
- Harnessing the benefits of technology and in particular ongoing innovations in IT was identified as one of the key challenges ahead. Understanding the capabilities that technology offers, and the skillset development required to harness these capabilities, was acknowledged as a key strategic objective.
- The way the future generation of auditors is educated and trained may need to be adapted to reflect a changing environment. The audit profession needs to have the courage to question itself and to propose changes in response to both the evolving needs of stakeholders and to an increasingly innovative business environment.

Many organisations of all sizes, across all sectors and countries have established audit and risk committees at board level to coordinate and monitor all internal and external assurances, providing reports to the board on their quality and findings. Such coordination does not always take place. A joint statement by the European Confederation of Institutes of Internal Auditors (ECIIA) and the Federation of European Risk Management Associations (FERMA) (2014),[4] commented on this in the financial services sector after the recent global financial crisis highlighted criticism on assurances and risk management in that sector:

> Criticism was also raised in respect of assurance functions that failed to communicate appropriate information to the board and executive management and did not help protect the organisation, by assessing all significant risks and the effects of the changing risk environment and by challenging the executive management to improve the effectiveness of governance, risk management and internal controls. Complex and inconsistent reporting made it difficult for the board and executive management to provide effective risk oversight. Finally the lack of harmonisation between the different assurance functions was perceived to have led to confusion at the board level. Primary weaknesses identified were differences in risk language and terminology, in methodologies and in the assessment of similar processes or departments.

I believe this conclusion could also apply in many organisations outside the financial sector. Mapping and coordinating assurances at board level is still in its infancy in all sectors. Audit and risk committees still have a lot of work to do to make this happen. Yet it is critical for stewardship, change and assurance responsibilities in every organisation.

Assurance mapping at board level is now a must in every organisation requiring a thorough understanding of all the assurances required at board, executive and operational levels. It is a two-way process between and sometimes across each of the levels. Consider whistleblowing and complaints policies, for instance. These require operational communications to cross over the executive level with negative or positive assurances being monitored at board level. Other assurances, such as self and supervisory, lie in and between each level. UK HM Treasury (2012)[5] published its own guidance on assurance mapping for the public sector, seeing the benefits as:

> 1.10 There are significant benefits to improved co-ordination of assurance. Fundamental to these is the provision of streamlined and synchronised information on organisational performance and the management of associated risks, helping the organisation to operate efficiently and effectively and to report to parliament accurately, meaningfully and without misleading.
>
> 1.11 More specifically, an effective assurance framework:
>
> - provides timely and reliable information on the effectiveness of the management of major strategic risks and significant control issues;
> - facilitates escalation of risk and control issues requiring visibility and attention by senior management, by providing a cohesive and comprehensive view of assurance across the risk environment;
> - provides an opportunity to identify gaps in assurance needs that are vital to the organisation, and to plug them (including using internal audit) in a timely, efficient and effective manner;
> - can be used to raise organisational understanding of its risk profile, and strengthen accountability and clarity of ownership of controls and assurance thereon, avoiding duplication or overlap;
> - provides critical supporting evidence for the production of the Governance Statement;
> - can clarify, rationalise and consolidate multiple assurance inputs, providing greater oversight of assurance activities for the Board/Audit & Risk Assurance Committee in line with the risk appetite; and
> - facilitates better use of assurance skills and resources.

All auditors have a key role to play in assisting audit and risk committees to establish assurance maps in the organisations in which they provide services. Audit and risk committees have a key responsibility in making this happen to ensure their own terms of reference are complied with and reported on at board level. The role of audit and risk committees has developed over the past twenty years with guidance from regulators, internal and external auditing professions and firms. The UK Financial Reporting Council (FRC) (2012)[6] sees company management as responsible for managing risk and establishing and monitoring internal control, providing assurance of this to the board. It sees that the audit committee should receive appropriate reports that these responsibilities are being carried out: 'the audit committee should receive reports from management on the effectiveness of the systems they have established and the conclusions of any testing carried out by internal and external auditors'. This guidance places responsibility on these committees to monitor the effectiveness of all assurances reported to the board. That effectiveness requires a mapping of all assurances to ensure these are coordinated and timely.

The UK Government Treasury promotes the use of assurance frameworks and mapping to 'give sufficient continuous and reliable assurance on organisational stewardship and the management of the major risks to organisational success and delivery of improved, cost effective public services'. This promotion can be seen in many of the government regulators, standards and guidance. Assurance mapping at a Registered Housing Provider I currently advise has produced the map at Figure C.1 to start its process of coordinating all the assurance received to and from its audit committee and identifying the stakeholders it has to assure for the services it is providing. This is an innovative start: it will

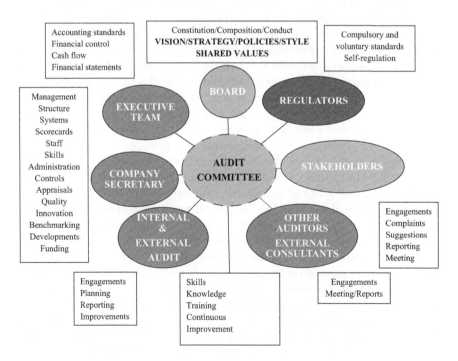

Figure C.1 Assurance map – Lincs Rural Housing Association (www.lrha.co.uk)

develop in time and be a measure for the coordination of assurance providers and its compliance with laws, regulations, standards, its selected code of governance and achievement of its objectives.

Each assurance and its relationships with others needs to be addressed during the financial year leading to a final report by the audit committee chairman to the LRHA board and its stakeholders in its operating report and at its AGM.

During my six years at this social housing provider I have seen many changes in the laws and regulations it needs to comply with, its selected code of governance and many other standards, as well as board membership, staff and stakeholders. During this period the same can probably be said of change in almost every, if not all, organisations across the world. Change never stops. It can be slow and quick but it is continuous. The skill every board needs is to forecast its effect and mitigate the risks it brings, seeking assurances from appropriate sources. Assurance mapping improves the quality and quantity of those assurances.

The role of internal auditors is now seen in many organisations as key to evaluating the adequacy, quality and depth of assurances the audit and risk committees have received in the past, are receiving and will receive in future years. This evaluation must also consider how independent and objective is each assurance; how and when it is communicated; what level of co-ordination there is; how each assurance provider co-operates with the others and all the self-assurance activities within an organisation. This is becoming more important and critical as economic, environmental and social reporting to an organisation's stakeholders through financial and non-financial sustainability external reporting merge. Today it is happening and will continue to be important for all an organisation's stakeholders. The IIA (2016)[7] recognises the strong links arising from assurance activities between the second and third lines of defence – see again Figure 4.1 – providing new guidance on this to maintain the independence and objectivity attributes of internal audit in an organisation's assurance practices. There is also a growing relationship between the third line of defence and external audit and a growing interest by regulatory bodies in the second, third and external audit lines of assurance defence.

Highlights at the end of the 2013 International Conference on Internal Auditing, held in Orlando, Florida, was the announcement by Richard Chambers, President and CEO of IIA Global, of his appointment to represent The Institute of Internal Auditors Inc. on the International Integrated Reporting Council (IIRC).[8] In its first publication, the IIRC (2013)[9] saw internal auditing as a mechanism to enhance the reliability of information as an integral part of internal control. Internal auditors in their planning and engagements, over many years, have focused on the component 'information' in the 1992 COSO Integrated Control Framework.[10] In future they will need to widen their view on information in the integrated reporting proposed by the IIRC: its focus on integrated reporting starts with strategy and leads the reader through what has happened, is happening and will happen and the influence of each on an organisation's direction, in the short, medium and long term. This includes the status of its governance, risk management and control practices in its economic, social and environmental issues and impacts. It opens up a new world of sustainability assurance and its reporting for all auditors. The IIRC task of implementing integrated reporting is not going to be easy. It will need monitoring by those who seek to give assurances at board and executive levels. This should become part of every audit charter, planning, engagement and consulting service.

Global reporting on sustainability is influenced by a mixture of law, regulation, guidance and philanthropy at national and international levels. Not all organisations today are reporting on their sustainable strategies and practices. Not all organisations state how their reported sustainability practices are independently assured. Not all organisations use the same definition of sustainability. The United Nations Global Compact (UNGC),[11] in its 2010 published research paper, defined sustainability as encompassing 'environmental, social and corporate governance issues, as embodied in the United Nations Global Compact's Ten Principles . . . covering areas of human rights, labour, the environment and anti-corruption'. All its member nations signed up to this principle and importance of sustainability in all their affairs. But do all organisations? Does your organisation?

> The IIA Inc. and many of its National Institutes and Chapters/Clubs worldwide have been addressing sustainability issues for some time. Social and environmental objectives can be interpreted in many parts of The IIA's first and subsequently published Standards. Guidance notes have been published around the world by many of its associates Institutes. The IIA's joint venture[12] with Auditing Roundtable Inc. since 1997 developed and promoted standards and certifications for environmental, health and safety auditing. Its latest global practice guide[13] for management and its members states – 'Internal auditors should maintain the skills and knowledge necessary to understand and evaluate the governance, risks, and controls of CSR [corporate social responsibility] strategies.'

Underlying many of the themes and messages at the 2013 Institute International Conference in Orlando was 'integrated auditing'. Delegates, general speakers and workshop leaders were all invited to experience 'One World, One Profession, One Destination' – that world being its global presence; that profession being the maturity of today and tomorrow's internal auditing; that destination being added value to organisations and sustainability of our planet. There are many interpretations of the term 'integrated auditing' and the assurances it gives. Integrated auditing embraces economic, social and environmental issues; technology impacts; compliance with governance and regulatory requirements; and, fraud prevention. (Note the similarity to the UNGC definition of sustainability). Such audits require different staffing with inputs from outside the internal audit function, multiple audit techniques; increased use of external resources; project management skills; and creativity and innovation in the audit process

Today, there is a world of sustainability opening up many opportunities for all auditors to provide new depths of assurance and recommendations at board, executive and operations levels: assurances into social, environmental and sustainability issues; assurances from which increased collaboration, cooperation and co-ordination among all auditors using integrated auditing innovations can bring stronger convictions and confidence. That world is not new. It has been there with us for centuries yet little recognised in the past in governance, risk management and control assessments. Today all auditors must recognise these issues in their audit processes and assurance services. I wrote and published the following article in 2000 on the importance of this assurance. Today the sources referenced could be easily updated and should be by all those providing assurance services. Written for internal auditors, it applies to all auditing and all auditors:

Social Responsibility – A Challenge for Organisations and Internal Auditing[14]

This article discusses the importance of social responsibility for organisations and internal auditing. It starts with John Humbler's social audit of the 1970s and introduces some of the current developments in social and ethical accounting, auditing and reporting. It shows how social responsibility is now being integrated into economic and environmental performance measures: provides evidence that social responsibility is now an important part of the principles of good corporate governance, requiring both internal and external auditing: and, challenges internal auditors to take a more proactive role in how social responsibility is being managed and audited. The discussion is based on a presentation by the author at an International Internal Auditing Summer School, organised by Management Audit LLP in London, during August 2000.

MANAGEMENT OF SOCIAL RESPONSIBILITY

Writing on the social responsibility audit in the 1970s John Humble[15] viewed the challenge of social responsibility at that time as ' . . . one of the critical and difficult management tasks is balancing these objectives at any time, taking into consideration the changing requirements of stockholders, employees, customers and society generally . . .' He goes on to define social responsibility as one of the key areas of the business ' . . . typically concerned with the external environment problems of pollution, community and consumer relations, and the internal environment problems of working conditions, minority groups, education and training.' His definition of the social responsibility audit and analysis of its scope spanned both the external and internal environments of an organisation – see Figure C.2.

In many organisations key areas of social responsibility are now measured against new external standard initiatives, such as quality, environmental and best practice awards. Developing international standards also offer accreditation and auditing processes for quality and environmental management. Many of the requirements in these standards address social responsibility issues. The European Foundation for Quality Management (EFQM)

It asks the right questions about:

1 SOCIAL RESPONSIBILITY: STEWARDSHIP

- Is the business so organised that it makes the most effective and balanced use of its financial, physical and human resources?
- Is there a full understanding within the business that long-term profitability, earned within the context of progressive social policies, is essential for all stakeholders ... including Society at large?

2 SOCIAL RESPONSIBILITY: POLICY & ORGANIZATION

- Does the board/general management team recognise the need to look systematically at Social Responsibility as part of the planning process?
- What problems/pressures/felt needs exist which would appear to make further studies worthwhile?
- Which of the existing company policies are relevant to this field? When were they last reviewed and their inter-relationship examined in the light of changed circumstance?
- Recognising that virtually every department/function is involved, is there, however, a single person/small group at Corporate level with the responsibility for a continuing overall review of developments?
- If you have a public relations department, is it fully involved in the development and communication of social policies?

It includes:

Internal environment
Physical environment
Working conditions
Minority groups
Organisation structure and management style
Communications
Industrial relations
Education and training
External environment
Social responsibilities and new opportunities
Community relations
Consumer relations
Pollution
Packaging
Investment relations
Shareholder relations

Figure C.2 John Humble's social responsibility audit

Source: Social Responsibility Audit (1973), John Humble, Foundation for Business Responsibility, London, England.

Excellence Model[16] is based on eight fundamental concepts, one of which is Public Responsibility. This concept states that the 'long-term interest of the organisation and its people are best served by adopting an ethical approach and exceeding the expectations and regulations of the community at large'. It requires that societal expectations are measured and actioned.

All organisations should review their conduct towards social responsibility issues on a regular basis and as part of their risk management. The questions in Appendix C provide a start. The results from such assessments will always require actions for control, monitoring and improvement. Many organisations now report on social responsibility in audited annual statements, published with their annual reports or separately. This trend will increase. What is important is that these reports are related to all other objectives in the organisation, with clear links showing how the adoption of a high standard of social responsibility is contributing to all other achievements.

SOCIAL RESPONSIBILITY AND CORPORATE GOVERNANCE

The 1990s has seen an increasing focus on social responsibility, reporting and auditing, reflected in a growing number of governance principles. Most governance guidelines include references to social responsibility as an important part of risk management and control, across organisation supply chains.

The OECD (2000)[17] *Guidelines for Multinational Enterprises* set out the policies multinationals should adopt in the countries in which they operate. The first guideline establishes a commitment to contribute to economic, social and environmental progress with a view to aching sustainable development. This is followed by other social and economic guidelines, including 'Support and uphold good corporate governance principles and develop and apply good corporate governance practices.' All the guidelines encourage application across multinational supply chains as well as the operations they manage. The OECD also recognises that 'many enterprises have developed internal programmes, guidance and management systems that underpin their commitment to good corporate citizenship, good practices and good business and employee conduct'.

Also, the Global Reporting Initiative (GRI)[18] published international guidelines[19] for the reporting and verification of sustainability: 'Since its inception in 1997, the GRI has worked to design and build acceptance of a common framework for reporting on the linked aspects of sustainability – economic, environmental and social.' This is a powerful and far-reaching initiative, creating principles that will encourage and drive debate on many governance and control issues related to sustainability. Both as separate elements standing alone, but more and more as the elements are integrated in the practice, verification and reporting of sustainability.

The GRI guidelines examine much that has been achieved already in the reporting of sustainability, albeit that this varies across organisations and sectors across the world. The GRI hopes that the principles in its guidelines will encourage development and integration of improved economic, environmental and social performance in future sustainability

Economic	Social	Environmental
Profit	Quality of management	Energy
Intangible assets	Health and Safety	Materials
Investments	Wages and benefits	Water
Wages and benefits	Non-discrimination	Emissions, effluents and waste
Labour productivity	Training and education	Transport
Taxes	Child labour	Suppliers
Community development	Forced labour	Products and services
Suppliers	Freedom of association	Land use/bio-diversity
Products and services	Human rights	Compliance
	Indigenous rights	
	Security	
	Suppliers	
	Products and services	

Figure C.3 Key global reporting initiative performance indicators

Source: Sustainability Reporting Guidelines on Economic, Environmental and Social Performance, Global Reporting Initiative (2000)

reporting. Figure C.3 shows the key GRI performance indicators for sustainability reporting. Compare these with Humble's scope of a social responsibility audit in Figure C.2.

On the independent verification of sustainability reports the GRI recognises that the ' . . . quality, usefulness, and credibility . . . can be enhanced in several ways', one of which is the 'internal auditing of systems and procedures for measuring, recording and reporting performance data'. No mention is made of a possible role for internal auditing in advising or teaching organisations how to report on sustainability. Nor is the alignment of governance with the elements of sustainability explored in any great detail. These are clearly aspects that will evolve across sectors, as best practices develop, influencing and being influenced by government and regulatory requirements.

Today, there is a focus on culture and behaviour at board, executive and operational levels in every organisation. This has always been the case in organisations for the achievement of objectives at every level, mostly for the good but sometimes seen for the bad. For auditors, an assessment of culture has always been a part of every audit – an assessment not just for financial behaviour but also for efficiency, effectiveness and economy in the achievement of and organisation's vision, mission and its values. Since the banking crisis in 2009, the financial sectors across the world have been addressing how this can be avoided in the future for the achievement of good governance. The audit and assurance of culture has taken a higher profile across the auditing professions. A recent UK Financial Reporting Council Observation Report[20] on culture at board level is opened by Sir Winifred Bischoff in his foreword, emphasising the importance of good governance for an organisation's culture:

> Strong governance underpins a healthy culture, and boards should demonstrate good practice in the boardroom and promote good governance throughout the business. The company as a whole must demonstrate openness and accountability, and should engage constructively with shareholders and wider stakeholders about culture.

All auditing and the assurances given should address, not just the culture of an organisation but also the behaviour of everyone involved with achievement of the organisation's vision and mission. Table C.1 compares the FRC discussion paper on culture with Table B.1, reinforcing the word/terms already selected by

Table C.1 FRC (2016) compared with Table B.1

	Industry	Finance	Charity	Health	Profess	EFMD	INTOSAI	Global	COSO	Global	FRC
Part I											
Stewardship											
Accountability	Y	Y	Y	Y	Y	Y	Y	Y	Y	Y	Y
Behaviour	Y	Y	Y	Y	Y	Y	Y	Y	Y	Y	Y
Beliefs	Y	Y	Y	Y	Y	Y	Y	Y	Y	Y	Y
Care	Y	Y	Y	Y	Y	Y	Y	Y	Y	Y	Y
Compliance	Y	Y	Y	Y	Y	Y	Y	Y	Y	Y	Y
Culture	Y	Y	Y	Y	Y	Y	Y	Y	Y	Y	Y
Customer	Y	Y	Y	Y	Y	Y	Y	Y	Y	Y	Y
Duty	Y	Y	Y	Y	Y	Y	Y	Y	Y	Y	Y
Ethics	Y	Y	Y	Y	Y	Y	Y	Y	Y	Y	Y
Governance	Y	Y	Y	Y	Y	Y	Y	Y	Y	Y	Y
Law	Y	Y	Y	Y	Y	Y	Y	Y	Y	Y	Y
Leadership	Y	Y	Y	Y	Y	Y	Y	Y	Y	Y	Y
Principles	Y	Y	Y	Y	Y	Y	Y	Y	Y	Y	Y
Responsibilities	Y	Y	Y	Y	Y	Y	Y	Y	Y	Y	Y
Stakeholder	Y	Y	Y	Y	Y	Y	Y	Y	Y	Y	Y
Stewardship	Y	Y	Y	Y	Y	Y	Y	Y	Y	Y	Y
Supplier	Y	Y	Y	Y	Y	Y	Y	Y	Y	Y	Y
Sustainability	Y	Y	Y	Y	Y	Y	Y	Y	Y	Y	Y
Transparent	Y	Y	Y	Y	Y	Y	Y	Y	Y	Y	Y
Trust	Y	Y	Y	Y	Y	Y	Y	Y	Y	Y	Y
Values	Y	Y	Y	Y	Y	Y	Y	Y	Y	Y	Y
Chapter 2											
Leadership											
Collaboration	Y	Y	Y	Y	Y	Y	Y	Y	Y	Y	Y
Partnership	Y	Y	Y	Y	Y	Y	Y	Y	Y	Y	Y
Manage	Y	Y	Y	Y	Y	Y	Y	Y	Y	Y	Y
Chapter 3											
Diplomat											
Represent	Y	Y	Y	Y	Y	Y	Y	Y	Y	Y	Y
State	Y	Y	Y	Y	Y	Y	Y	Y	Y	Y	Y
Brand	Y	Y	Y	Y	Y	Y	Y	Y	Y	Y	Y
Chapter 4											
Gatekeepers											

Table C.1 (Continued)

	Industry	Finance	Charity	Health	Profess	EFMD	INTOSAI	Global	COSO	Global	FRC
Defend	Y	Y	Y	Y	Y	Y	Y	Y	Y	Y	Y
Protect	Y	Y	Y	Y	Y	Y	Y	Y	Y	Y	Y
Monitor	Y	Y	Y	Y	Y	Y	Y	Y	Y	Y	Y
Part II **Change**											
Change	Y	Y	Y	Y	Y	Y	Y	Y	Y	Y	Y
Risk	Y	Y	Y	Y	Y	Y	Y	Y	Y	Y	Y
Future	Y	Y	Y	Y	Y	Y	Y	Y	Y	Y	Y
Part III **Assurance**											
Assurance	Y	Y	Y	Y	Y	Y	Y	Y	Y	Y	Y
Audit	Y	Y	Y	Y	Y	Y	Y	Y	Y	Y	Y
Quality	Y	Y	Y	Y	Y	Y	Y	Y	Y	Y	Y

me to encourage creativity and innovation in organisations and all auditing. By adding ASSURANCE and AUDIT QUALITY it also shows how these important messages are reflected in each of the previous statements. Corporate governance, risk management and control all reflect these word/terms in the messages they give to everyone at all levels in an organisation through all changes.

Creative Audit Thinking Activities

Activity 28   Creative and Innovative Integrated Assurance

Integrated reporting of financial and non-financial information is now an important part of accountability by boards to all their stakeholders, whether formally through published statements, or through intranet and internet statements. More than ever before auditors are being required to provide assurances on the information being given to all stakeholders. Consider the statement below by the International Integrated Reporting Council. What innovative integrated assurance practices can you introduce in your auditing to provide the assurances your board needs today and in the future for its integrated reporting.

Integrated Reporting <IR> Aims[21]

- Improve the quality of information available to providers of financial capital to enable a more efficient and productive allocation of capital.
- Promote a more cohesive and efficient approach to corporate reporting that draws on different reporting strands and communicates the

full range of factors that materially affect the ability of an organisation to create value over time.

- Enhance accountability and stewardship for the broad base of capitals (financial, manufactured, intellectual, human, social and relationship, and natural) and promote understanding of their interdependencies.
- Support integrated thinking, decision-making and actions that focus on the creation of value over the short, medium and long term.

<IR> is consistent with numerous developments in corporate reporting taking place within national jurisdictions across the world. It is intended that the International <IR> Framework, which provides principles-based guidance for companies and other organisations wishing to prepare an integrated report, will accelerate these individual initiatives and provide impetus to greater innovation in corporate reporting globally to unlock the benefits of <IR>, including the increased efficiency of the reporting process itself.

Activity 29   Audit Committees Will Always Need Creative and Innovative Auditors

Consider the extract below from the FERMA and ECIIA (2014) at Reference 3:[22]

The Audit Committee assists the board in fulfilling its responsibilities in corporate governance by:

- having a good understanding of the company's structure, controls and types of transactions as well as the business model and its associated risks.
- maintaining a free and open communication with the external auditors, internal auditors, the second line of defence and the management of the company.
- having the power and authority to investigate any matter based on full access to the records, the company's operations and people.

Quality of Information

A principle challenge facing audit committees is the quality of the information they receive. Views were mixed on whether the information currently provided was fit for purpose. For example, most UK interviewees were satisfied on this score, but all interviewees agreed that an audit committee is only as good as the information at its disposal.

There is an imperative that audit committees undertake all reasonable steps to ensure they have access to the 'right' information, in an appropriate form and on a timely basis. This encompasses formal reports and presentations, but also informal discussions with management and professional development activities for audit committee members.

The ways in which interviewees deal with this challenge include:

- effective involvement in the selection of key reports, from external and internal audit and the chief financial officer in particular.
- effective questioning of reports and information both during and outside of audit committee meetings.
- free and open discussion in meetings.
- the use of pre-meetings to identify issues for discussion and sometimes to deal with routine matters.
- effective communication with auditors and executives, including access to management below the senior executive team.
- developing committee members' understanding of the business, for example through site visits.

Activity 30   Innovate Assurance Through Control Risk Self-Assessment

Control Risk Self-Assessment (CRSA) as an innovative facilitation technique has been with us for at least forty years. Created in the 1980s, it is still used today in many organisations to discuss the risks of achieving objectives and how these can be mitigated and controlled. The CRSA Forum in the United Kingdom was one innovation from this technique, which still meets today (www.crsa.com). I used this technique myself as an internal auditor in the 1990s, facilitating and collaborating with managers to improve risk assessment processes and the management and mitigation of risk by controls. There can be few auditors who have not heard of and/or used this technique as a service to management or as part of their risk-based auditing and assurance. Consider the following three messages in the conclusions in my chapter in *Control Self-Assessment* (1999),[23] a collection of edited chapters by leading CRSA practitioners. Create changes in your next risk-based internal auditing engagement with innovations based on these messages.

Quality, Governance and Conduct Are Important Control Drivers Conclusions

Control objectives for quality, governance and conduct will continue to integrate and have an impact on all risks. Links between the control frameworks for each will be needed to reduce and avoid most risks. Those that assess risk in any organisation will need to build reviews of these links into their review process. Auditors will need to ensure that their audits cover the control objectives for quality, governance and conduct across the total supply chain, including suppliers and customers.

Ridley and Chambers (1998) addressed quality, governance and conduct as they impact both control objectives and internal auditing. They developed *Principia* for leading-edge internal auditing, which include the following:

- The financial, social, quality and environmental aspects of control are international issues, across all supply chains.
- Control embraces all aspects of governance, including ethics, equality, honesty, caring and sustaining.

The growing interest in risk management across all types and sizes of organisations, led by consultants and internal auditors, is fuelled by new (assurance) demands from managers and regulators for position statements on internal control. These new demands are encouraging a wider view of control, linked to all organisation objectives and associated risks. The three messages from my chapter are:

- quality, governance and conduct objectives strengthen each other and the control frameworks established for their achievement.
- quality, governance and conduct should be considered during all control and risk assessments.
- auditors, managers, audit committees and governing bodies should consider the importance of integrating all control frameworks in the organisations they serve.

Notes

1 *Pursuing a Strategic Debate – The Future of Audit and Assurance*, Discussion Paper (2016 p. 10), Federation of European Accountants (FEE), Brussels, Belgium.
2 *Internal Standard on Auditing 200 – Overall Objectives of the Independent Auditor and Conduct of an Audit in Accordance with the International Standards on Auditing* (2009 p. 84), International Federation of Accountants, New York, US.
3 *Pursuing a Strategy Debate – The Future of Audit and Assurance*, Discussion Paper (2016 p. 3), Federation of European Accountants, Brussels, Belgium.

4 *Guidance for Boards and Audit & Risk Committees* (2014 pp. 5 and 8), Federation of European Risk Management Associations (FERMA) and European Confederation of Institutes of Internal Auditors (ECIIA), Brussels, Belgium.
5 *Assurance Frameworks* (2012 pp. 4–5 and 12), H.M. Treasury, London, England.
6 *Guidance on Audit Committees* (2012), Financial Reporting Council (FRC), London, England.
7 *Practice Guide – Internal Audit and the Second Line of Defence* (2016), The Institute of Internal Auditors Inc., Orlando, US.
8 The International Integrated Reporting Council (IIRC) is a global coalition of regulators, investors, companies, standard setters, the accounting profession and non-governmental organisations. Together, this coalition shares the view that communication about value creation should be the next step in the evolution of corporate reporting. Further information about the IIRC can be found on its website www.theiirc.org.
9 *The International <IR> Framework* (2013), International Integrated Reporting Council, London, England.
10 This developed into the COSO Enterprise Risk Management Model. More recently COSO published a paper to demystify sustainability risk – *Integrating the Triple Bottom Line into an Enterprise Risk Management Program* (2013), which uses the term sustainability . . . synonymously with corporate social responsibility, corporate citizenship, stewardship and corporate responsibility.
11 *A New Era of Sustainability* (2010), United Nations Global Compact, New York, US.
12 The Board of Environmental, Health and Safety Auditing Certificates (BEAC) vision is to be the recognised global leader in EH&S auditor certification based on its researched and developed standards.
13 *Practice Guide – Evaluating Corporate Social Responsibility/Sustainable Development* (2010), The Institute of Internal Auditors Inc., Orlando, US.
14 Published in *Internal Control* Issue 35 (October 2000), ABG Professional Information, London, England. Reproduced in Tottel's *Corporate Governance Handbook* (3rd Edition 2005 p. 1046), Tottel Publishing, Haywards Heath, England.
15 *Social Responsibility Audit* (1973), John Humble, Foundation for Business Responsibilities, London, England.
16 *The EFQM Excellence Model* (1999), European Foundation for Quality Management, Belgium. www.efqm.org.
17 *Guidelines for Multinational Enterprises* (2000), Organisation for Economic Co-operation and Development, Paris, France. www.oecd.org.
18 *Sustainability Reporting Guidelines on Economic, Environmental and Social Performance* (2000), Global Reporting Initiative, United Nations, US. www.globalreporting.org.
19 *Sustainability Reporting Guidelines on Economic, Environmental and Social Performance* (2000), Global Reporting Initiative, United Nations, US. www.globalreporting.org.
20 *Corporate Culture and the Role of Boards – Report of Observations* (2016 p. 2), Financial Reporting Council, London, England.
21 *The International <IR> Framework* (2013 p. 5), International Integrated Reporting Council, London, England.
22 *Guidance for Boards and Audit & Risk Committees* (2014 pp. 5 and 8), Federation of European Risk Management Associations (FERMA) and European Confederation of Institutes of Internal Auditors (ECIIA), Brussels, Belgium.
23 *Control Self-Assessment: For Risk Management and Other Applications* (1999 pp. 61–78), Chapter by J. Ridley, edited by Keith Wade and Andy Wynne, John Wiley and Sons, Chichester, England.

8   Auditors Are Sceptics

Auditors should be independent, sceptical and challenging.[1]

In this chapter I discuss the importance of all auditors asking the right questions, at the right time, to the right people, at the right locations across all levels in an organisation and when necessary across the globe – at the same time questioning the answers. The art of asking the right questions and questioning the answers is the only way to penetrate deeply into an organisation's governance, risk management and control at board, executive and operations levels. Questioning, and questioning the answers, are key skills for every auditor.

8.1 Auditors Must Be Sceptics

Professional scepticism in auditing has received much publicity of late, particularly concerning the role of the auditor of financial statements and responsibilities of members of audit committees. It has always applied to all auditors in the evaluation of their audit evidence, conditions that may indicate lack of good governance, risk management, control, error, deception or fraud – even situations needing more or different audit procedures. In 2010 the Auditing Practices Board (APB) of the UK Financial Reporting Council stimulated discussion and consultation on the importance of professional scepticism in financial statement auditing, publishing guidance on this in the form of International Standards on Auditing (ISA) 200.[2] This standard addresses professional judgement as essential for evaluating 'sufficiency and appropriateness' and reliability of audit evidence, ranking alongside this the importance of professional scepticism in the auditing of all financial statements. It requires 'that the auditor exercise professional judgment and maintain professional scepticism throughout the planning and performance of the audit'. This was followed by the UK Financial Reporting Council (FRC) (2011)[3] debated proposition that all company external auditors should be sceptics when auditing financial institutions and other sectors: 'The application of an appropriate degree of professional scepticism is a critical skill for all auditors.'

Alongside both professional judgement and scepticism must always be ranked the International Ethical Standards Board for Accountants (IESBA) Code of Ethics quoted in IIAASB (2013):[4] the 'fundamental principles of professional ethics relevant to the auditor when conducting an audit of financial statements' are – Integrity; Objectivity; Professional Competence and Due Care; Confidentiality; and Professional Behaviour. These fundamental principles of auditing have been researched, taught and promoted since the 19th century for all financial auditing and adopted in all forms of independent auditing standards across the globe. De Paula (1914)[5] wrote on professional judgement and scepticism as:

> The extent to which an auditor may rely safely upon internal checks and omit to check the whole of the detail entries, depends entirely upon the whole of the circumstances of the particular case, and this question must be decided by each auditor for himself. In this direction he requires considerable skill, experience, and judgment, and the efficiency of his audit will depend largely upon the skill with which he deals with this question.

He included in his principles of auditing all the IESBA fundamental principles, except Objectivity (he referred to Integrity as Honesty, and Behaviour as Conduct). In the ICAEW Audit and Assurance Faculty journal *Audit & Beyond* for February 2016, Simon Kettlewell[6] advises all auditors to find and demonstrate their inner sceptic in all parts of an audit engagement – 'it's not enough to be sceptical, you have to demonstrate it in practice' – reminding them 'Scepticism is intrinsically linked to the ethical concepts of objectivity and independence; two terms that every auditor should be familiar with'. Kettlewell refers to the 'lack of professional scepticism' in audit quality seen as a failing by some of the country members of the International Forum of Independent Audit Regulators (IFIAR) (www.ifiar.org), established in 2006 with the key objective of improving 'audit quality globally'. Its current work plan[7] is a document all auditors should read and consider, not just in the services they provide to audit financial statements but for all assurance services.

In 2009 I wrote and published the following opinion on objectivity in internal auditing for The Institute of Internal Auditors Inc. (IIA) professional journal. The same messages on quality in internal auditing apply to all auditing.

The Value of Objectivity[8]

The ability to remain independent and objective is key to effective practice across all internal audit processes and reporting. But while independence receives considerable attention in professional research and other literature, the importance of objectivity is often overlooked. Audit objectivity is essential to the quality and reliability of audit work, and to the auditor's credibility in the organisation. In fact, audit practitioners should view objectivity as even more important than independence. In most cases, audit independence can be readily evaluated and measured – it is usually visible in the audit function's charter and through its reporting lines to the top of the organisation. Moreover, impairments of independence can be recognised, noted, and often corrected by appropriate persuasion and delegation. By contrast, audit objectivity can be difficult to measure accurately, as it comprises individual judgment and a personal mind-set that is not always transparent. Objectivity can also be impaired easily, whether knowingly or unknowingly, and these impairments are often difficult to correct. Scientists have long recognised the necessity of objectivity in research processes, defining it as an ability to analyse and report facts accurately and with integrity. Moreover, it is an essential attribute in virtually every profession, akin to ethical behaviour. Maintaining objectivity requires an unbiased analysis of all pertinent facts during the audit process, enabling an honest belief in the work product. In fact, any weakness in the auditor's 'systematic and disciplined approach to evaluate and improve', as described in The IIA's definition of the profession, will impair his or her objectivity. Objectivity factors prominently into The IIA's Code of Ethics [see Appendix J] as a rule of conduct for all internal auditors. It should be emphasized in audit charters and training efforts, and it should be reflected in the quality of services auditors provide. Audit leaders should test their staff members' understanding of objectivity and measure the results against the objectivity principle and rule in the Code of Ethics. The important link between objectivity and the quality of audit work should also not be overlooked. Objectivity should never stand alone from the other attributes of professional internal auditing. Instead it should be connected to every aspect of the services provided, including risk-based planning, consulting services, engagement processes, objectives setting, audit program development, testing, reporting, and follow-up. Objectivity is constantly under threat from conflicts of interest, poor-quality audit work, lack of confidence, strong adversaries, and sometimes the culture in which internal auditors work. It requires courage of conviction based on well-researched knowledge, experience, wisdom, and sound judgment. It is an essential part of the value added in all professional internal auditing.

Like all researchers, evidence for conclusions formed by the auditor comes from two main sources – secondary and primary. Secondary evidence comes from data and information created by others in the form of procedures, documents, records, statements, reports and observations. Primary evidence comes from the auditor's own creation, either from secondary data or from data originated by the auditor. In both cases, secondary and primary, the auditor should always evaluate the results objectively with some scepticism as to whether it is reliable and form conclusions accordingly. My belief has always been that if there is any doubt to carry out further audit procedures and, if necessary, qualify the final conclusions in the audit report. In the past I have even used the term 'not susceptible to audit' when evidence could not be relied on.

The Auditing Practices Board (APB) (2010)[9] advises on the importance of professional scepticism by the individual auditor, engagement team and firm. It is essential advice for every auditor, management of an auditing team and firm, recommending the issue by every firm of a policy statement on its importance, covering such issues as:

• adequate planning;
• proper assignment of personnel to the engagement team;
• the application of professional scepticism; and
• supervision and review of the audit work performed.

In further guidance the UK Financial Reporting Council (FRC) (2012)[10] considers the philosophical origins of scientism and 'how it later influenced scepticism in the scientific method that began to flourish in the 17th Century'. If, like me, you believe auditing is a science with principles, this reinforces the importance all auditors should place on the preceding advice. Does your audit function have a professional scientism policy to guide the 'questioning mind' for all its auditors and the hierarchy of their management?

8.2 Sceptical Auditors Must Ask the Right Questions

Asking the right questions is often like shooting an arrow into the air. Like archery, with skill, the aim to the target can be improved. Asking such questions is sometimes like shooting an arrow into the air, not knowing whether it is addressed to the right person, if it is the right question, or the right direction. Asking the right questions is not always an easy skill for all auditors to acquire.

Lawrence Sawyer (1973)[11] approached the skill of questioning as one of the six forms of auditing:

Observing
Questioning
Analysing
Verifying
Investigating
Evaluating.

He saw the first five 'as part of the measurement process. The last – evaluation – gives meaning to the information that the auditor has gathered'. Questioning is a measurement to determine what other form(s) of fieldwork should be undertaken. The most important part of fieldwork and probably most difficult to get right – the first time. Sawyer saw this as 'the most pervasive technique of the auditor':

> Oral questions are usually the most common, yet probably the most dif-
> ficult to pose. Obtaining information orally can be raised to the level of
> an art. To get to the truth and to do so without upsetting the auditee is
> sometimes not an easy task. If the auditee detects an inquisitional tone or
> perceives a cross-questioning attitude.

Oral questioning is one part of other forms of fieldwork, a measurement pro-cess, and an art, which can be changed by tone. Tact can have an important part to play. How questions are asked and the answers considered is important for the auditor seeking depth in the assurances being given at the end of an audit. The Institute of Internal Auditors Inc.,[12] in its News Sheet 'Tone at the Top' in early 2015, referred to this as tactful scepticism. Another style of more formal ques-tioning can be through written questionnaires, either as a guide for the auditor to ask orally, or as a communication for the auditee to answer. For many years, the questions auditors should ask were listed clearly in questionnaires printed in auditing textbooks. In some organisations these were further developed into questionnaire manuals, both general and specific for departments and operations.

Many auditors have been trained in their careers to use such questionnaires and questionnaire manuals. I was one of them. Yet, even with all the questionnaires I have used, there has never been one that was complete and did not need some questions changed and others added. Sawyer saw the development of a question-naire essential at the preliminary survey stage of every audit: 'but let haste not interfere with the orderly listing of questions; for without a methodical guide, the conversation will ramble, the manager's time will be wasted [if not also the audi-tor's], and the first impression the manager receives will be one of disorganisation.'

A useful start to development of any questionnaire is the drawing of flowcharts – 'a combination of science and art'. Flowcharting is an excellent creative process, developed by questioning. It can be informal, or formal using standardised templates and instructions. Flowcharts take time to produce and deserve a place in all working paper files. They are evidence of an understanding of the operations being audited. My early audit training through De Paula's guidance taught me that 'Flowcharts probably represent the most satisfactory method of recording systems, consistent with a disciplined approach to systems audits.' They also lead to developing the right questions.

Modern auditing has been built on questioning the three 'E's of **EFFICIENCY, EFFECTIVENESS, ECONOMY** as targets, developed as objectives into audit planning; reviewed and tested during audit work; reported on and followed up. Last century Value for Money (VFM) auditing adopted these same 'E's in the public sector and still requires this today. All auditing in the public sector in the United Kingdom and I believe across the world has a VFM element in its reviews and evaluations. Even in all the other sectors, VFM auditing has a place both in financial and operational auditing.

Today more 'E's can be added. Consider now adding **ETHICS, ENVIRONMENTAL EMPOWERMENT, ENLIGHTENMENT** and **EQUALITY** issues. They all require important questions that can reveal significant control strengths and weaknesses. Each impacts governance, risk management and the control environment: ethics as an important influence in an organisation's culture; environmental because of its impact on sustainability of the planet; empowerment as part of process reengineering and quality management; enlightenment through technology and a growing pursuit of knowledge and innovation, by both organisations and the people they employ; and equality as a significant social issue.

These eight 'E's make many question 'boxes' spanning the four phases of time (past, present future and beyond the horizon), questions for each audit objective – see Figure 8.1.

How? What? Why? When? Where? Who?			
Covering Eight Themes and Spanning Time			
6 Questions × 8 Themes × 4 Times = 192 Questions			
	PAST	PRESENT	FUTURE	BEYOND THE HORIZON
EFFICIENCY	?	?	?	?
ECONOMY	?	?	?	?
EFFECTIVENESS	?	?	?	?
ETHICS	?	?	?	?
ENVIRONMENTAL	?	?	?	?
EMPOWERMENT	?	?	?	?
ENLIGHTENMENT	?	?	?	?
EQUALITY	?	?	?	?

Figure 8.1 Structure for six sceptical questions spanning time

Source: J. Ridley (2016)

More than ever before, it is important now and in the future that all auditors ask the right questions to the right people, at the right time and over time during the audit processes. The right questions will always be the key to the quality and effectiveness of auditing. So will the right listening and questioning of the answers!

8.3 All Audit Committees Must Be Sceptical, Too

All committees at board level have a responsibility to ensure board members have assurances they need to achieve their objectives. Audit committees have particular responsibility to ensure the quality of all the assurances board members receive concerning their governance, risk management and control responsibilities – assurances not just from auditors but from executives and all those who report at its meetings. This requires scepticism and challenging in committee level discussions, ensuring all reporting to it are sceptic in the services they are providing. This scientism should underpin also its questioning and evaluation of the quality of communications it receives.

In 2013 the Federation of European Accountants (FEE), the Institute of Chartered Accountants in Australia (ICAA) and the Centre for Audit Quality (CAQ)[13] cosponsored a series of three roundtable discussions in Brussels, Hong Kong and New York City with the objective to share 'a common goal of strengthening audit committee practice'. Each roundtable discussed audit committee membership and recognised the 'benefit of an audit committee composed of members with diverse experience and expertise . . . to enhance the objectivity and scepticism of committee members'.

The responsibility of an audit committee to promote a sceptic role in its organisation is also reflected in the guidance by the APB discussed earlier: 'In this role, the APB believes that Audit Committees should seek to foster appropriate professional scepticism in the external audit.' The APB guidance goes on to expect the audit committee to challenge auditors and executive with appropriate scepticism on their understanding of the business and its environment, expecting a 'fresh perspective' to the making of their risk assessments and requiring rationale for the audit conclusions, recommendations and follow-up actions. It sees this guidance as an aid to auditor scepticism, contributing to improve the audit committee role and its reporting to the board and externally.

The UK Financial Reporting Council (FRC) (2015)[14] published a practice aid that all audit committees should adopt in assessing the quality, professional scepticism and judgement of their external auditors (guidance which should be applied to all assurance services providing a service to the board): 'Adherence to high professional and ethical principles supports a mindset and culture that enables the auditor's judgments to be made without being affected by conflicts of interest.' Its aid focuses on the importance of the auditor's skill, character and 'depth of knowledge' together with the right quality of control over their work, 'setting a tone that emphasises the need to apply professional scepticism'.

In summary, this practice aid sees the evaluation of audit quality entailing four key elements:

Mindset and culture
Skills, character and knowledge
Quality control
Judgement.

These are discussed in my book as keys to creativity and innovation in all auditing. Quality control and its management will be discussed in a later chapter in Part IV.

8.4 Chapter Review

In this chapter I see all auditors as sceptics in each of the steps in the Ten Step Audit Process – questioning and objectively questioning the answers they receive. Scepticism is essential if the assurances they give penetrate deep into the organisations being audited. This scepticism applies also to audit committee members when monitoring the assurances they receive from auditors and the actions being taken by the executive and operations levels on audit recommendations and follow-up actions.

8.5 Creative Audit Thinking Activities

Activity 31   Be Creative in Your Art of Questioning

The following is a summary of my introduction to *Leading Edge Internal Auditing* (1998) and appeared as a case study in my book *Cutting Edge Internal Auditing* (2008). Consider it in the light of this chapter's discussion on the sceptic auditor and your own auditing processes. Look for its links into the themes of professional judgement and scepticism and their importance in the quality of all audit work. Ask yourself the following questions:

1   Do your auditing engagements include questions on the use of technology today and in the future?
2   What evidence do you have of how well management is managing today and will in the future?
3   Is the professionalism of your judgement and scepticism sufficient to evaluate the answers you receive to these questions?
4   What other questions should you be asking?

When Asking Questions, Be Modern and Confident[15]

An understanding of modern management responsibilities is fundamental to the asking of all questions during an internal audit engagement. Internal auditing practices will always require an understanding and application of the science of management as it is today and will be tomorrow, including all its principles of planning, assessing, doing and verifying. This importance of management principles and standards is in all aspects of auditing. The best internal auditors ask managers the best management questions.

All auditors should be aware of current thinking and good practice concerning management and managing. This means knowing about how businesses are established, work, grow with success and survive. This rule applies across all sectors and in very organisation, regardless of size. Most organisations have their own specific sector or industry issues, but all have common management and managing issues.

Auditors also need to understand the challenges and impacts of technology on management and organisations. These challenges and impacts are rarely only internal. They span across organisations and their supply chains at national and international levels. Technology embraces the use of all applied sciences and technical methods in an industry and its sector. Information systems and communications are an important area using technology, but there are many other areas. Technology is also fundamental to control in all operations and their success. It is much more than the present day use of computers to process information. In many textbooks and research projects it is now given a much wider definition covering the present and future use of technology in information systems, telecommunications, office and operational automation. IT can be defined as '. . . the combination of computers, telecommunications and information resources in an organisation and its sector to achieve objectives.'

As well as knowledge and skills, auditors need to be imaginative and confident when asking questions. Many of the situations and control issues that face auditors require ability to think, both laterally and with certainty that their views are correct. In developing audit recommendations there can be many influences that might persuade internal auditors to change their views, reducing the quality of their service to the organisation. Questions must be asked with confidence.

Current developments in the market places for auditing and management are:

- *appointment of new non-executive board members and new auditing committees;*
- *management interest in internal control frameworks, public statements on governance and compliance with externally imposed codes of conduct;*
- *management interest in risk assessment and risk management;*
- *recognition of the importance of strong supply chains within and across organisations;*
- *new organisation alliances, associations and joint ventures;*
- *use of consultants to facilitate organisation change and improvement;*

- *use of technology to process and store increased information with speed, flexibility and accuracy;*
- *increased auditing and regulatory activities;*
- *new global market places.*

Some of these developments have been evolving internationally for many years, others are new and recent. All are stimulating new and cutting edge auditing questions. It is important all auditors understand and recognise the impact they should have on the questions they ask.

Activity 32   Be Innovative in Your Sceptical Audit Process

Consider each of the steps in the Ten Step Audit Process developed in this book, and for each step, ask the question in the European Commission Green Paper Consultation on Audit Policy (2010) – Q.6: *Should the professional scepticism be reinforced? How should this be achieved?* As a start, consider the following response to this question by the UK Department of Business, Innovation and Skills in 2010.[16] Be creative in your answer to Q.6.

UK Government Response to the European Commission's Green Paper on Audit (2010) Answer to Q.6

Professional scepticism is key to maximising the usefulness of audit, and is an issue for auditors worldwide. In the US, research has shown that the failure to demonstrate an appropriate level of scepticism was a deficiency found in 60 per cent of the cases where the SEC brought fraud related actions against auditors. The UK's Audit Inspection Unit in their 2009/10 Annual Report[17] reported that audit firms are not always applying sufficient professional scepticism in relation to key audit judgements. This has prompted UK regulators to examine this issue carefully.

Activity 33   Scepticism and Courage Are Creative Auditing

Consider the following statement on scepticism and courage in auditing and assurance, made by Lord Jonathan Hill, EU Commissioner Financial, in the Federation of European Accountants[18] publication on the future of audit and assurance in 2016. What innovative changes can you make in your organisation and the practices of auditing and assurance to ensure auditors always have and maintain the FEE values and are encouraged and prepared to 'speak truth unto power'?

Speak Truth unto Power

To build trust, we need the values that I read about on the FEE website: the values of integrity, objectivity, independence, professionalism, competence and confidentiality. To which I might add that auditors need a good dose of scepticism and courage: they need to be prepared to speak truth unto power. These are qualities which need to come from within the profession, attitudes of mind, standards of conduct which reflect a determination to do the right thing, not simply to comply with a legal requirement.

Notes

1 *Audit Quality – Practice Aid for Audit Committees* (2015 p. 7), Financial Reporting Council, London, England.
2 *ISA 200: Professional Scepticism – Establishing a Common Understanding and Reaffirming Its Central Role in Delivering audit Quality* (2012 pp. 14, 16, and 73–74), Auditing Practices Board, Financial Reporting Council, London, England.
3 *Auditor Scepticism – Raising the Bar – Feedback Paper* (2011 p. 1), Financial Reporting Council, London.
4 *A Framework for Audit and Assurance – Consultation Paper* (2013 p. 30), International Auditing and Assurance Standards Board, New York, US.
5 *Principles of Auditing* (1914), F.R.M. De Paula, Sir John Isaacs and Sons Ltd., London, England.
6 *Find Your Inner Sceptic* (2016 pp. 10–11), Simon Kettlewell, Audit and Beyond Journal of the Audit and Assurance Faculty, Institute of Chartered Accountants in England and Wales, London, England.
7 *Work Plan 2015–17* (2015), International Forum of Independent Audit Regulators (IFIAR), Amsterdam, Netherlands.
8 *Value of Objectivity* (2009 p. 72), Jeffrey Ridley, Internal Auditor – October, The Institute of Internal Auditors Inc., Orlando, US.
9 *Isa 200: Professional Scepticism – Establishing a Common Understanding and Reaffirming Its Central Role in Delivering Audit Quality* (2012 p. 18), Auditing Practices Board, Financial Reporting Council, London, England.
10 *Professional Scepticism – Establishing a Common Understanding and Reaffirming Its Central Role in Delivering Audit Quality* (2012 p. 4), Financial Reporting Council, London, England.
11 *The Practice of Modern Internal Auditing* (5th Edition 1973 p. 283), Lawrence B. Sawyer, The Institute of Internal Auditors Inc., Orlando, US.
12 *The Tactful Sceptic* (2015 p. 1), Tone at the Top January-February, The Institute of Internal Auditors Inc., Orlando, US.
13 *Global Observations on the Role of the Audit Committee* (2013 p. 3), Federation of European Accountants, Brussels, Belgium.
14 *Audit Quality – Practice Aid for Audit Committees* (2015 p. 7), Financial Reporting Council, London, England.
15 *When Asking Questions Be Modern and Confident* (2008), Cutting Edge Internal Auditing (p. 295), John Wiley and Sons Ltd., Chichester, England.
16 *UK Government Response to the European Commission's Green Paper on Audit* (2010 pp. 4–5), Department of Business Innovation and Skills, London, England.
17 *Audit Inspection Unit Annual Report* (2009–10), Financial Reporting Council, London, England.
18 *Pursuing a Strategic Debate – The Future of Audit and Assurance*, Discussion Paper (2016 p. 5), Federation of European Accountants (FEE), Brussels, Belgium.

9   Auditors Are Lawyers

Be consistent with the rule of law and support effective supervision and enforcement.[1]

In this chapter I see auditors as lawyers in all the steps of the audit process. The rule of law and how it is practiced and regulated is the foundation for all control and good corporate governance. All auditors are part of the process of law and regulation in their organisations and in the organisations in which they provide their services. Auditors have an important role to play in the fight against crime in every organisation.

9.1   Compliance With Laws and Regulation

Governance, compliance with the law and regulation has always been essential for any organisation or collection of organisations to be 'efficient' and 'effective', whether established by the organisation through its own values, principles, standards and rules, or established externally by responsible contract, law and regulation. This is not new. It has been a fact of survival for organisations since first they came into being through families, tribes, regiments, nations, federations and other forms of unification and association. Today, the world is full of organisations of different sizes, structures and strategies; private, public and charitable; some quite small, some the size of nations in wealth, and many global in operation.

There can be few, if any, organisations not governed by laws and subject to monitoring and supervision internally and externally at local, national and international levels. There can be few organisations not subject to supervision by collective and representative associations, or by many stakeholders – internal and external. There can be few organisations where their members and employees are also not subject to supervision by a higher authority and regulation. Failure to be committed to and assured of responsible governance and compliance with laws and regulations has resulted for many organisations in disaster.

There can be no debate in the United Kingdom on the corporate governance and legal responsibilities of directors of companies – or legal responsibilities of any other members of governing bodies – without recognising the general duties of directors in the UK Companies Act 2006[2] Section 172 (discussed in Part I Stewardship) – see Figure 9.1 – including detail in the following

---

A director of a company must act in the way he considers, in good faith, would be most likely to promote the success of the company for the benefit of its members as a whole, and in doing so have regard (amongst other matters) to:

(a) the likely consequences of any decision in the long term,
(b) the interests of the company's employees,
(c) the need to foster the company's business relationships with suppliers, customers and others,
(d) the impact of the company's operations on the community and the environment,
(e) the desirability of the company maintaining a reputation for high standards of business conduct, and
(f) the need to act fairly as between members of the company.
(g) where or to the extent that the purposes of the company consist of or include purposes other than the benefit of its members, subsection (1) has effect as if the reference to promoting the success of the company for the benefit of its members were to achieving those purposes.
(h) the duty imposed by this section has effect subject to any enactment or rule of law requiring directors, in certain circumstances, to consider or act in the interests of creditors of the company.

Figure 9.1 General duties of directors

Source: United Kingdom Companies Act 2006: Chapter 2: 172

sections: 173 Duty to exercise independent judgment; 174 Duty to exercise reasonable care, skill and diligence; 175 Duty to avoid conflicts of interest; 176 Duty not to accept benefits from third parties; 177 Duty to declare interest in proposed transaction or arrangement. These general duties are based on 'certain common law rules and equitable principles as they apply in relation to directors'. Those 'equitable principles' clearly have, as their foundation, the corporate governance principles of accountability, openness and integrity discussed as the principles of corporate governance by Cadbury (1992) and underpinning all other codes of governance published ever since across the globe.

It is also not difficult to see in the legal requirements in the Companies Act 2006, and many similar Acts in the United Kingdom and across the globe, the components in my corporate governance framework – **STEWARDSHIP**, **CHANGE**, **ASSURANCE** and **EXCELLENCE** – with their underlying theories and values of life. These links between the law and principles of corporate governance and my framework clearly demonstrate all auditors must understand the legal requirements of the organisations they audit and those that apply to their audit processes, even at times seeing themselves as lawyers and being seen as such.

9.2 Lawyers Are Auditors

Lawyers have a significant responsibility in the practice of good governance when they advise on law and regulation in every organisation. In advising in their capacity as legal experts, they comply with their own professional codes of practice, whether internally as employees of an organisation or externally as consultants. In many organisations lawyers are at board level, either as directors or as company secretaries, with both secretarial and legal responsibilities to ensure decisions at board level and throughout an organisation comply with all relevant laws and regulations. Lawyers have a duty to serve a number of different stakeholders in the services they provide. Duty to their clients is clearly set out by the Council of Bars and Law Societies of Europe (CCBE) (2013)[3] in its core principles and code of conduct for their profession. The core principles on which the code is based are shown in Figure 9.2.

The CCBE describes the functions of a lawyer as follows:

> In a society founded on respect for the rule of law the lawyer fulfils a special role. The lawyer's duties do not begin and end with the faithful performance of what he or she is instructed to do so far as the law permits. A lawyer must serve the interests of justice as well as those whose rights and liberties he or she is trusted to assert and defend and it is the lawyer's duty not only to plead the client's cause but to be the client's adviser. Respect for the lawyer's professional function is an essential condition for the rule of law and democracy in society.

It is not difficult to see the spirit of the core principles and code of conduct in the codes of conduct established for auditors and many of the steps in the

1   The independence of the lawyer, and the freedom of the lawyer to pursue the client's case.
2   The right and duty of the lawyer to keep clients' matters confidential and to respect professional secrecy.
3   Avoidance of conflicts of interest, whether between different clients or between the client and the lawyer.
4   The dignity and honour of the legal profession, and the integrity and good repute of the individual lawyer.
5   Loyalty to the client.
6   Fair treatment of clients in relation to fees.
7   The lawyer's professional competence.
8   Respect towards professional colleagues.
9   Respect for the rule of law and the fair administration of justice.
10 The self-regulation of the legal profession.

Figure 9.2 Core principles of the European legal profession

Source: Charter of Core Principles of the European Legal Profession and Code of Conduct for European Lawyers (2013 p. 5), The Council of Bars and Law Societies of Europe (CCBE), Brussels, Belgium.

creative and innovative audit process in the lawyer's independent and objective daily routine of questioning, seeking of evidence and advising.

In its 2014 Annual Report,[4] the retiring CCBE president ends his foreword and executive summary with the following:

I believe that the legal profession should remain at the forefront of innovation and change, in order to carry its principles into the 21st century. This year I launched a discussion on the future of the profession within the unique forum that is the CCBE, exploring avenues for the conditions under which we work, and the challenges we will have to face. This exercise is especially important for young lawyers: their practice will be profoundly different from ours as the world changes. How should we handle new technologies and increased globalisation? What can be done to ensure that the legal profession remains relevant? I hope that you, dear colleagues and concerned citizens, will join this debate and carry it forward wherever you go, for the benefit of justice, fairness and the rule of law.

His profound statement of today's challenges for the legal profession will require much auditing by all lawyers in the future. Such a statement could well have been written by the auditing profession for all auditors.

Loughrey (2011)[5] has written an excellent book on the relationships between corporate lawyers and corporate governance, introducing this with the following: 'In the United Kingdom there has been little recognition that corporate lawyers have any role to play in corporate governance.' Compare this situation with the United States following the Enron collapse and Sarbanes-Oxley Act 2002, which led to 'imposed obligations on lawyers to report managerial mis- conduct up the line within the company' and to provide corporate governance advice at board level. Loughrey discusses the corporate governance role of cor- porate lawyers, many of whom in companies are also the company secretary, a role now recognised with very important corporate governance responsibilities. The Institute of Chartered Secretaries and Administrators (ICSA)[6] describes the duties of company secretaries as follows:

> Chartered Secretaries are high-ranking professionals with a diverse set of skills unique amongst many professions. Trained in corporate law, finance, governance and corporate secretarial practice, Chartered Secretaries are the focal point for independent advice about the conduct of business, governance and compliance. They can also offer legal and accounting advice and manage the development of strategy and corporate planning.

The law and corporate governance are clearly linked at board level and at all levels in every organisation. As early as the Treadway Commission (1987)[7] in the United States, there was a recognition that lawyers and many other profes- sional and technical groups had advisory roles in the financial reporting process, with a strong influence on the 'tone set by the top management of corpora- tions'. (Culture and behaviour in corporate governance are now seen in today's corporate governance codes and developments as key to the achievement of good corporate governance practice.)[8]

Legal, Financial, and Other Advisors

The professional and technical skills of several other groups within the business and professional community enable them to work closely with key participants in the financial reporting process. Among these groups are law- yers, investment bankers, financial analysts, business advisors, and those in charge of systems for securing company assets. Whether they operate from inside or outside the public company, these advisors are uniquely situated to influence the tone set by the top management of corporations. Through the advice and opinions they extend to top management or the board of direc- tors, these advisors can affect the outcome of the financial reporting process.

However lawyers see themselves in corporate governance across the globe, compliance with laws and regulations is an essential requirement in the corpo- rate governance framework and good governance practice. An exercise I was involved with recently was to review the number of laws an organisation I am associated with needs to comply with as a part of the services it provides to its customers on a daily and annual basis. The list had been prepared by a forum of company secretaries in the sector the organisation is in. This review covered all its operations from the board to the actions by its staff and the contracts it has across all its supply chains. The forum identified eighty-six such laws, and this was without considering the legally established regulations associated with the laws or the codes of practice and standards related to the organisation's provision of services, or European Directives and international laws. Such a similar list applies today for all organisations across the globe. Yet, to 'comply or explain' with such a list in the context of its supporting regulations, codes and standards is a must for good corporate governance practice.

9.3 Auditors Are Lawyers

It has always been important to me in my auditing that an awareness of the laws and regulations relating to an audit engagement is an essential part of its planning and establishing its scope. This awareness at times must lead and has led me to a general understanding of what is required by the laws, and in some cases the detail. Such an understanding can take an auditor into advice from lawyers, both inside the organisation being audited and outside to independent advice. This process of legal understanding can influence many of the steps in the Ten Step Audit Process, even creating an auditor into being perceived as a lawyer. McIntosh (2016)[9] recently discussed in his article on internal audit and company secretary collaboration, interviews with heads of internal audit who are recognising such collaborations exists in their audit processes:

> Company secretaries and internal audit usually meet both formally and informally, to discuss issues and share ideas. Internal audit can elicit a company secretary's opinion on areas of concern in the organisation, which can then inform the audit plan. The view of the company secretary is especially valuable as they often have a broad skillset, incorporating corporate law, finance, governance, strategy and corporate secretarial practice, and have the ear of the chair, CEO and non-executive directors.

The Institute of Internal Auditors (IIA),[10] in its *International Standards for the Practice of Internal Auditing*, requires internal auditors to evaluate risk exposures relating 'Compliance with laws, regulations, policies, procedures, and contracts'. Similar requirements apply to other auditors in their different roles. In my book, *Cutting Edge Internal Auditing*, one of the chapters is titled 'Auditors Must Fight Crime'. To do so, auditors must understand the law as it relates to their profession and the organisations in which they provide their services. This does not mean they have to be lawyers (but they could be!), but it does mean that they must be aware of the requirements of the law as it relates to responsible governance, risk management and control in their engagements with the board, executive and operations.

9.4 Audit Committees Must Be Lawyers, Too

There are now a number of guidance statements for audit committees and their role in corporate governance. The Treadway Commission (1987), mentioned earlier, recommended the following role for counsel in audit committee discussions. Such attendance placed the advisory role of the lawyer alongside that of the auditor:

> *Company Counsel.* The [audit] committee should meet regularly with the company's general counsel, and outside counsel when appropriate, to discuss legal matters that may have a significant impact on the company's financial statements. In a number of companies the general counsel and/or outside counsel attend meetings.

In 1999, in the United States, the Blue Ribbon Committee[11] studied audit committee effectiveness recommending a charter, stating the audit committee should have specific powers to review 'the programs and policies of the Company designed to ensure compliance with applicable laws and regulations and monitoring the results of these compliance efforts'. Since that date, other guidance has been published across the globe with similar legal compliance responsibilities. Loughrey, referred to earlier, also recognises and discusses a need for lawyers in the United Kingdom to have access to audit committees and the same Sarbanes-Oxley Act ethical and legal reporting responsibilities 'up the line' as those in the United States.

The Institute of Chartered Secretaries and Administrators (ICSA 2013),[12] in its latest guidance for the terms of reference for audit committees in private companies, recommends the committee should 'give due consideration to laws and regulations, the provisions of the Code and the requirements of the UK Listing Authority's Listing, Prospectus and Disclosure and Transparency Rules and any other applicable rules, as appropriate'. Such a requirement should influence both the membership of the committee and the resources it needs to fulfil its legal responsibilities. In the United Kingdom, HM Treasury (2013),[13] in its guidance for all audit committee members in the public sector, requires an understanding 'of any relevant legislation or other rules governing the organisation'. Today, there is every reason why audit committees in all sectors should both review and monitor compliance with the laws and regulations – and even to be seen as lawyers and require their assurance monitors and advisors to be seen as such as well, particularly so if their charters require responsibilities to review and monitor corporate governance, but definitely so for all laws and regulations surrounding financial reporting and auditing.

In the following article I published in 2000, I wrote on the effectiveness of audit committees at that time. All the guidance in that article is as relevant today to audit committees, and all of its recommendations are either included in today's guidance for audit committees or still under discussion. In the article I used the opportunity to emphasise the importance of audit committees, recognising their responsibilities to address legal issues concerning their responsibilities, to monitor not just financial reporting but also governance, risk management and controls. This latter responsibility is still not seen today in many audit committee terms of reference.

How Effective Is Your Audit Committee?[14]

In 1996[15] I wrote on six essential characteristics that exist in the best audit committees – see Figure 9.3.

---

1   Independence
2   Rotation of membership
3   Unrestricted responsibility
4   Monitoring of all control
5   Provides advice only
6   Reports results of its work to full board and externally

Figure 9.3 Six steps to success for all audit committees

Source: J. Ridley (1996)

I recommended that these should be measured by governing bodies and audit committees in all organisations. Since then, the worldwide focus on good governance has emphasised and reinforced the importance of such measures. There have also been a number of important national and international studies with recommendations for audit committee practices. Both government and regulators across all sectors now encourage the establishment and development of audit committees at board and governing body levels. Today, such committees are seen by many worldwide as an essential part of good governance in all types of organisation, large and small. Their influence on control and conduct will continue to increase.

What measures and benchmarks are being used by audit committees to evaluate their performance? How do audit committee members measure their effectiveness? Do they have any measures? These are important questions that all stakeholders should ask. There is little evidence to show that audit committees self-assess their own performance, or even if this is required by their boards. A 1993[16] study by The Institute of Internal Auditor's Research Foundation covered organisation of the audit committee, its training and resources, meetings, activities and working relationships with internal auditors, management and external auditors. It reported 'Survey results indicated that 88 percent of 'state-of-the-art' audit committees have conducted self-assessments of performance by comparing their own activities to those recommended by commissions. . .'

The IIA study includes an audit committee self-assessment guide with recommendations for its use and review by the full board. At that time the guide included recognised best practices for audit committees across the world. Such an approach to measuring the effectiveness of an audit committee has not been bettered. Self-assessment measures are now characteristic of good governance and good practices in many organisations. Risk management, control, quality, training, health and safety and other management programmes all use self-assessment techniques. Yet, despite the popularity of this type of measure with management, there is little evidence to show today that many boards or audit committees in the UK have implemented regular performance self-assessment processes. In 1996 I summed up my six steps to success for audit committees with the statement:

> An audit committee's membership should be **independent of executive authority** at board level and **rotate (membership and chair)**, with **unrestricted responsibility** to **review the monitoring of all control activities**, the impact of change on control, **offer advice** and **report results of its work to the full board and externally**.

Each of the six highlighted characteristics in this statement is capable of being self-assessed by all audit committee members and measured by their boards or governing bodies. Over the past four years each has increased in its importance to good governance. That importance will continue to grow well into the future. The learning curves of audit committee members, increasing publicity over weak governance and the influence of regulators (and perhaps some stakeholders?) will make this happen!

The framework of audit committee organisation and oversight responsibilities at Figure 9.4 shows key characteristics and responsibilities for an audit committee's activities.

ORGANISATION		OVERSIGHT	
1	Independence	1	Financial Reporting
2	Membership	2	Financial Statements
3	Knowledge	3	Risks
4	Experience	4	Controls
5	Meetings	5	Legal/Regulatory/Tax
6	Reporting	6	Auditing
		7	Additional Resources

Figure 9.4 Framework of audit committee responsibilities 1995

Source: J. Ridley (1996)

This framework can be used to question audit committee members on their organisation and oversight responsibilities. It is based on my own experience, research and research published by others. More recently, that research by others has been mainly in North America.[17] However, since 1996, the following three important guides for measuring audit committee performance have been published from studies in the UK:

1   In 1997,[18] The ICAEW Audit Faculty published Audit Committees – A Framework for Assessment. This framework provides an excellent set of benchmarks, with many emerging best practices. Although ' . . . deliberately not prescriptive. . .' and recommending 'experimentation rather than imposition', it provides detailed and far-seeing recommendations for boards and audit committees, from a practical experience in both large and small plcs and other entities. How many regulators, boards or audit committee members have studied this framework and benchmarked their practices with its recommendations? How many managers, internal auditors and external auditors have used its recommendations to evaluate their audit committee working practices? How many stakeholders have used this framework to question boards on their audit committee effectiveness?

2   In 1998,[19] the UK Auditing Practices Board (APB) published 'Audit Briefing Paper – Communication between external auditors and audit committees'. This paper focuses on the nature and matters to be communicated by external auditors and related auditing standards – from appointment, audit planning, through all financial statement and annual report auditing, to findings and actions by management. References are also made to accounting policy/legal changes, associated risk management, reviews of corporate governance/internal control and working relationships with internal audit. How many audit committee members have studied this paper?

3   Also in 1998,[20] the Institute of Chartered Secretaries and Administrators (ICSA) published a guide for those working in and with audit committees 'Best Practice Guides – Terms of reference: Audit Committee'. This guide focuses on the audit committee's constitution, remit and authority. One important recommendation on audit committee reporting has still to receive the action it deserves – 'We do believe, however, that the Audit Committee should compile a brief report for shareholders which we have suggested be included in the company's annual report although it could equally be produced as a separate statement.' Not surprisingly, there is little evidence to date of such reports across all sectors. This will change.

Results from a questionnaire I used at a recent conference I attended produced responses confirming the importance of the framework's content.

However, there was little positive response to my question concerning the use of formal self-assessment processes for measuring performance of the audit committee. Only three of the twenty-five delegates responding to the questionnaire stated that their audit committee members had used such a measure. At workshops during the conference other delegates, who did not respond to the questionnaire, confirmed a conclusion that formal self-assessment by audit committees is not a common practice.

There are many questions all audit committee members should ask in an assessment of their organisation and oversight responsibilities. Using the above framework they could start with the following:

ORGANISATION

1   Have they any executive or other responsibilities and relationships that could weaken the independence of their oversight responsibilities?
2   Is their membership and the chair rotated regularly to bring new thinking into their reviews?
3   Have they sufficient knowledge for all the control, audit and governance issues they are required to oversee?
4   Is their experience of the business plans and operations sufficient?
5   Do they meet the right people regularly and at the right time, to consider both planning and results?
6   Is the reporting of audit committee responsibilities and oversight results known to all stakeholders?

OVERSIGHT

7   Do they review all financial reporting throughout the year – both accounting and related operating information?
8   Do they review both the preparation and content of all financial statements published externally?
9   Do they review the adequacy of risk assessment by the board, management and auditors?
10   Do they review the control environment and impact of change, across the organisation and all its supply chains, not just within the organisation?
11   Do they consider legal/regulatory/tax issues when reviewing management's responsibilities for good governance?
12   Do they require the coordination of all auditing and inspection at the planning, audit, reporting and follow-up stages?
13   Have they the opportunity to call on additional resources to carry out their responsibilities?

Every audit committee member should independently consider the importance and implications of each of the questions in the framework and report their understanding of the best practices and levels of implementation at committee level. Such discussion should be facilitated by external advisers to ensure the best benchmarks are selected for measurement. Benchmarks are available from the studies mentioned above and, in some sectors, statements by regulators. A formal consideration of the self-assessment and its facilitation should be reviewed by the full board. Action for improvement and decisions for future performance measures should be taken.

All stakeholders should be interested in the performance of audit committees. Only when all audit committees take seriously the importance of benchmarking themselves against worldwide best practices and compliance with laws and regulations will their contribution to good governance be at its best.

9.5 Chapter Review

In this chapter I have discussed the importance of auditors always understanding the laws and regulations governing their organisations operations and their own audit processes Demonstrating this understanding through their audit questions, creative thinking and innovation, even to being seen at times as lawyers. Compliance with the rule of law and its effective supervision and enforcement is an essential part of all governance practices in every organisation.

9.6 Creative Audit Thinking Activities

Activity 34   Create Innovative Legal Collaboration at Board Level

Auditors need to think like lawyers and at times be perceived as lawyers. Thinking like a lawyer can create changes, even new steps, in the audit process. Start your creative audit thinking like a lawyer by considering the following introduction to Alisdair McIntosh's *Natural Allies* article referred to earlier and collaborating with your company secretary.

Become a Trusted Board Adviser

Company secretaries have long had a strategic position at the heart of an organisation. With considerable influence over governance operations, company secretaries can impact strategy and decision-making, as well as the way an organisation is controlled. Similarly, the internal audit function has grown into a more strategic role, with those in this position advising boards on a number of risk and governance matters. Company secretaries and heads of internal audits have become trusted board advisers, and open communication with directors is required in order to support them effectively. This has naturally pushed both functions to collaborate.

Activity 35   Use Laws and Regulations in Your Audits to Create Trust

Consider the following statement on trust and audit and the interviewee's comment, taken from *Enlightening Professions*.[21] How can you innovate in the use of laws and regulations to create trust in your audit process?

Trust and Audit

Trust is what auditors sell. They review the accuracy, adequacy or propriety of other people's work. Financial statement audits are prepared for the owners of a company and presented publically to provide assurance to the market and the wider public. Public service audits are presented to governing bodies and, in some cases, directly to parliament. It is the independent scepticism of the auditor that allows shareholders and the public to be confident that they are being given a true and fair account of the organisation in question. The auditor's signature pledges his or her reputational capital so that the audited body's public statements can be trusted.

> We want to be seen to be professionals and trusted counsel as lawyers might be, upholding the integrity of systems of governance and control and providing assurance that people can trust – assurance that underpins a fair and efficient economy and society.
>
> Interviewee

Activity 36   Be a Lawyer at Your Audit Committee

Consider the extracted quote at the beginning of this chapter from the OECD *Principles of Corporate Governance* (2015). Use the full quote below from its Principle 1 to innovate new discussions on the principles of corporate governance at your audit committee meetings and with the chairman of your board.

Ensuring the Basis for an Effective Corporate Governance Framework

The corporate governance framework should promote transparent and fair markets, and the efficient allocation of resources. It should **be consistent with the rule of law and support effective supervision and enforcement.**

Notes

1 *G20/OECD Principles of Corporate Governance* (2015 p. 13), Organisation for Economic Co-operation and Development, Paris, France. www.oecd.org.
2 *Companies Act 2006*, Her Majesty's Parliament, London, England.
3 *Charter of Core Principles of the European Legal Profession and Code of Conduct for European Lawyers* (2013 pp. 5 and 13), The Council of Bars and Law Societies of Europe (CCBE), Brussels, Belgium.
4 *Annual Report* (2014 p. 13), Council of Bars and Law Societies of Europe, Brussels, Belgium.
5 *Corporate Lawyers and Corporate Governance* (2011), Joan Loughrey, Cambridge University Press, Cambridge, England.
6 *Add Some Colour into Your Career – A Guide to Becoming a Chartered Secretary*. Institute of Chartered Secretaries and Administrators, London, England. www.icsa.org.uk, accessed March 2016.
7 *Report of the National Commission on Fraudulent Financial Reporting* (1987 pp. 7 and 183), National Commission on Fraudulent Financial Reporting, US.
8 *Developments in Corporate Governance and Stewardship* (2014), Financial Reporting Council, London, England.
9 *Natural Allies* (2016), Alisdair McIntosh, Governance and Compliance (March–April), Journal of the Chartered Institute of Secretaries and Administrators, London, England.
10 *International Standards for the Professional Practice of Internal Auditing* (2012), The Institute of Internal Auditors Inc., Orlando, US.
11 *Blue Ribbon Committee on Improving the Effectiveness of Corporate Audit Committees* (1999 p. 66), New York Stock Exchange, New York, US.
12 *Terms of Reference – Audit Committee* (2013 p. 14), Institute of Chartered Secretaries and Administrators, London, England.
13 *Audit and Risk Assurance Committee Handbook* (2013 p. 39), HM Treasury, London, England.
14 *How Effective Is Your Audit Committee* (2000 p. 30), Published in Internal Auditing and Business Risk December, The IIA-UK and Ireland, London, England.
15 *Six Steps to Success – Does Your Audit Committee Add up?* Article by J. Ridley, Internal Auditing (May 1996), The IIA-UK and Ireland, London.
16 *Improving Audit Committee Performance: What Works Best* (1993), A research paper by Price Waterhouse, The IIA, USA.
17 *Committee Report of the Blue Ribbon Committee on Improving the Effectiveness of Corporate Audit Committees* (1999), New York Stock Exchange and National Association of Securities, US.
18 *Audit Committees: A Framework for Assessment* (1997), The ICAEW – Audit Faculty, London, England.
19 *Communication Between External Auditors and Audit Committees* (1998), Audit Briefing Paper, The Auditing Practices Board, London, England.
20 *Terms of Reference: Audit Committee: Best Practice Guide* (1998), The Institute of Chartered Secretaries and Administrators, London, England.
21 *Enlightening Professions? A Vision for Audit and a Better Society* (2014 p. 12), Institute of Chartered Accountants in England and Wales (ICAEW), London, England.

10 Auditors Are Quality Managers

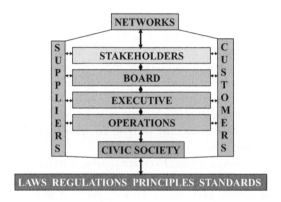

The primary focus of quality management is to meet customer requirements and to strive to exceed customer expectations.[1]

In this chapter I see all auditors as quality managers in the environments in which they provide assurances and quality in their audit processes – not just in the audit itself but also the impact this should have on the quality of audit findings, how these are communicated and actions taken by each level of an organisation to achieve total quality in their products and services. The achievement of quality in an audit and organisation is achieved by total commitment to the principles underlying quality management. For auditors, that commitment requires a passion to be best in all the steps of the Ten Step Audit Process. Quality is required by laws, regulations, principles, standards and stakeholder engagements across all organisations, their supply chains and networks. It is essential for a good reputation and the reputation of all auditors. It always has to be managed.

10.1 Quality Management Creates Trust

Quality achievement is a contributor to trust and improvement. Control over quality has been developing over the past fifty years, across all sectors and nations in the form of policies, awards, standards, guidance and codes of practices.

The Chartered Quality Institute (CQI)[2] in the United Kingdom explains the importance of this movement as follows:

> The quality movement holds the potential to be the fulcrum on which the world is transformed into a better place. Leaders need to have desire, persistence and energy, but the quality movement is the only way to build truly customer focused and capable organisations. From the most trivial technique to the most profound principle, the quality concept is universal:
>
> - The quality tools can be applied to every process across the organisation, from sales to delivery, from development to accounting, from manufacturing to teaching
> - Improving processes improves results, nothing else does this
> - System thinking enables leaders to optimise their whole system – for the customer, for safety, for the environment, for the owners. Compromise will always be needed, but no other approach brings the scientific method to bear in generating theories and providing the evidence to validate them
> - The quality movement is, at its heart, an honest movement. The philosophy demands involving people who know about the process being worked on, as the tools only work in an open environment where data is made visible and is not distorted
> - Leading ones organisation to create capability to serve its customers, and reducing its impact on the environment, is an activity amongst the most noble of human endeavours. Those who lead and participate in such efforts find fulfilment in the work and in the achievement. This is not just hype; it is the reason that the quality movement has so many enthusiasts who have learned about its potential over many years.

Future quality developments need to focus upon the motivations of leaders, and on ways to get alongside those who will need to change, not to confront them and threaten them. It demands that practitioners develop a broad skill set in:

- understanding their system
- learning how to learn and describe their world accurately
- involving and motivating those who are in the system
- getting the processes on target with minimum variation in the cause of innovating and optimising the whole system.

These are all very good reasons for all auditors to be seen as managers of quality in all their audit processes now and in the future. The CQI description of quality as a movement has strong links and support from the growth of organisation corporate governance and sustainability codes across the world. Its Competency Framework[3] for quality professionals demonstrates the importance of quality in governance, assurance and improvement, creating innovation as an essential contributor to good corporate governance in every organisation – see

Figure 10.1. Each of the components of its Framework can be seen in all the chapters in my book.

Underpinning the management of quality in all types of services and products is a series of laws and regulations requiring compliance, supported by developed quality policies, principles, standards and schemes to encourage and motivate best practices and achieve high quality and protect customers. Total Quality Management (TQM) is one such policy, created when quality schemes are established by a 'total commitment' to quality in all strategies, structures and systems by everyone involved. Over past decades, quality consultants across the world have created exciting quality principles, motivating many organisations to adopt TQM policies and practices, with significant benefits not just for the organisation, but also for their customers, suppliers and employees. These consultants, together with other quality networks and professional institutes, have over many decades surrounded organisations and supply chains with a wealth of knowledge and experience on quality management and its benefits – and they still do.

In the 1980s I researched and developed the following five key principles of quality management which I included in *Leading Edge Internal Auditing* (1998)[4] and repeated without any change in a chapter I subsequently wrote for *Best Practice Approaches to Internal Auditing* (2011).[5] These principles guided me in both the managing of my own auditing and the auditing of quality management by others.

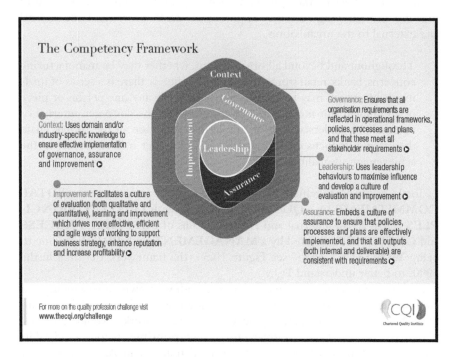

Figure 10.1 The Chartered Quality Institute (CQI) Competency Framework

Source: © The Chartered Quality Institute 2016

1   customer focus
2   management leadership
3   teamwork
4   measurement
5   total commitment to continuous improvement.

Compare the detail of my five principles of quality management – see Figure 10.2 – with the following set of seven principles now published by the International Organization for Standardization (ISO) (2015) – quoted from at the beginning of this chapter. These principles reinforce mine of the 1980s, and are essential for every audit engagement:

1   customer focus
2   leadership
3   engagement of people
4   process approach
5   improvement for every audit engagement
6   evidence-based decision making
7   relationship management.

At the time of my book, *Cutting Edge Internal Auditing*, Oakland (1989),[6] in his book *Total Quality Management*, described quality as a continuous chain of meeting and satisfying customer requirements across processes, both internal and external to the organisation:

> Throughout and beyond all organisations, whether they be manufacturing concerns, banks, retail stores, universities, or hotels, there is a series of quality chains which may be broken at any point by any one person or piece of equipment not meeting the requirements of the customer, internal or external. An understanding of this simple definition of the supply chain theory and its focus on the supplier and customer is fundamental to the achievement of quality.

Total Quality Management (TQM) was seen by me at that time as a **TOTAL COMMITMENT** to a **QUALITY POLICY** with **QUALITY PRINCIPLES** across all the internal and external chains of **SUPPLIER**, **PROCESS** and **CUSTOMER**, directed by a **MANAGEMENT** with **PRIDE** leading to being **WORLD CLASS** – see Figure 10.3 – the framework I created in the 1990s to better understand TQM.

How does this TQM framework compare with your own understanding and commitment to TQM and creativity and innovation to achieve a high standard of quality in your own auditing process? In the Framework I would add today '**Creative**' under Quality, '**Governance**', '**Responsible**' before Leadership, '**Sustainable Goals**' with its United Nations definition and '**Assurance**' under Management, and '**Innovation**' after Continuous Improvement. Sustainability is not mentioned in the ISO Quality Management Principles, but I believe can

1 Customer focus

- All customers are different, their satisfaction is paramount
- Focus on both internal and external customers, primary and secondary
- View all customers as partners in your supply chains
- Understand all your customers' needs
- Aim for customer delight at all times, not just satisfaction
- Do not ignore customer complaints.

2 Management leadership

- Organise for quality
- Establish a clear and motivating vision understood by everyone
- Identify your key success factors and build these into a clear mission statement
- Provide the right structures, methods and resources for quality achievement
- Communicate well at all levels, both in clarity and timeliness
- Give high visibility to your quality policy.

3 Teamwork

- Recognise and encourage the power of teams
- Develop teams across the whole supply chain, internal and external
- Interlock all teams at operation, function and cross function levels
- Reinforce and reward teams for success
- Teach teams to focus on your vision and mission statements
- Delegate responsibility to teams to take action.

4 Measurement

- If it cannot be measured, it cannot be improved
- Measure by statistics – do not inspect
- Establish measures in all processes, across all supply chains, with high visibility
- Relate all measures to your vision and mission statements
- Focus measures on customers, both internal and external
- Take prompt corrective action on all measurements.

5 Total commitment to continuous improvement

- Look for problems, develop solutions and train
- Create a learning organisation with a constant commitment to improve
- Encourage a constant and continuous search for excellence
- Be creative – look for paradigm shifts
- Benchmark – internally and externally
- Verify the success of change.

Figure 10.2 Quality principles

Source: J. Ridley (1990)

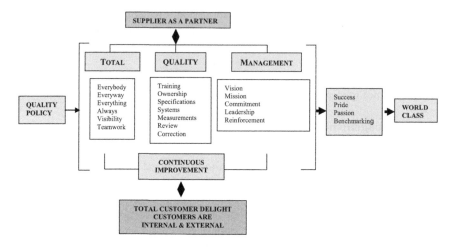

Figure 10.3 TQM framework – total commitment across the supply chain

Source: Leading Edge Internal Auditing, J. Ridley (1998)

be implied under Relationships by '**Long Term**' and '**Sustain**'. In view of the now ISO 2015 Quality Principles discussed above, I would add '**All Stakeholders**' in the Supplier box and '**Analysis and Evaluation**' under Quality, moving '**Correction**' to that box. Otherwise I believe the latest quality principles are included. See these changes in bold in Figure 10.4. Can you make or add others?

10.2 Who Are the Customers of Auditors?

Customer focus, satisfaction if not also delight, are still the most important drivers of quality perception across all supply chains – both internal and external – and is essential for all of the quality principles. But who are the customers of auditors? This question has generated and is still generating considerable debate. I believe answers lie in the both the frameworks discussed above and in the framework at the beginning of this chapter.

There can be little doubt in the minds of most if not all auditors that their primary customers in an audit engagement are those in the line of reporting the results of their auditing, whether these customers are the ones who contract and pay for their the services or not. For most of the 20th century, this was a factual statement, but still with some philosophical debate – the client was the customer. De Paula saw this in his discussion of the external audit of a company and the client as the shareholder:

> The directors have the right to decide whether the auditor's report shall be attached to the published Balance Sheet or not, but the intention of the Section appears to be that the report should be looked upon as a confidential

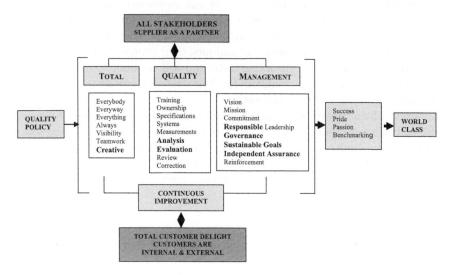

Figure 10.4 TQM framework – total commitment across the supply chain – updated

Source: J. Ridley (2016)

one from the auditor to the shareholders, and, therefore, the better course is to make it a separate document, which is not published broadcast, as the Balance Sheet often is. The report referred to on the Balance Sheet has to be read at the shareholders' meeting, is open to inspection, and any shareholder is entitled to demand a copy, so that there is no risk of the information contained in the report being held back from the shareholders. There is no doubt that, if the report is not published with the Balance Sheet, the auditor is given a much freer hand, as he may have no hesitation in reporting fully to the shareholders any matters which, in his opinion, should be made clear to them. On the other hand, if the report is published with the Balance Sheet, and thus reaches the hands of the general public, the creditors, customers and competitors of the business; should the auditor have to report adversely upon any matters, the credit of the concern might be – seriously affected. Therefore, the report should be made accessible to shareholders only, so that the auditor may be in no way hampered by these other considerations.

In every audit of whatever type in an organisation, there can be a wide range of parties interested in and even involved in the quality of its results. Parties at all levels in an organisation and across its supply chains – both internal and external to an organisation: parties who have financial, professional and regulatory interests – mandatory or optional. Are any or all of these parties today, customers an auditor should seek to satisfy, if not delight? In today's corporate governance standards and codes of practice, can the standard of quality in any audit be considered to have only the interest of one customer? Can confidentiality clauses in an auditor's code of conduct and contract be binding on the results of an audit, which can affect so many different stakeholders in and around an organisation? These are questions all auditors, their professional institutes and regulators of organisations are asking today and will continue to debate during the 21st century, as auditing standards for their services continue to develop and improve, creatively and with innovation.

Supply chain theory opens up a new dimension on the question of who is the auditor's customer. In 1995 I wrote the following short article, suggesting this question should be widened to bring into the debate the auditor as a customer as well as being the supplier. The quality implications of this suggestion still apply today, in the corporate governance environment in most organisations, possibly even more so.

You Are My Customer – You Are Also My Supplier[7]

Understanding the supply chain is an important part of performing any internal audit. Supply chains link all activities and relationships in the transformation of materials and information into a product and service: they are a complex web of control activities, internal, external to the organisation and mixtures of both. They have many owners. They can be the whole organisation or the smallest part of a process. They are dynamic, ever changing and snap at the weak points, causing many failures.

Most, if not all supply chain theories separate supplier from customer. This is a mistake. Recognising the supplier as a customer and the customer as a supplier can have a significant impact on product and service development. Developing the right specifications for both supplier and customer interfaces are the key to quality. Recognising that these should be developed at the same time with the same person is fundamental to high quality achievement.

Most internal auditors will recognise the persons they audit as either primary or secondary customers. Primary if they are the first priority and have direct control over whether internal audit stays in business: secondary, if they are receiving an internal auditing product or service and have only an indirect control over whether internal audit stays in business. Primary can be the audit committee and senior management: secondary can be operating management and the workforce being audited.

How many internal auditors see their primary and secondary customers also as suppliers? Yet, they provide time, information, materials and sometimes processes which can add significant value to internal auditing performance. Recognising this contribution as a supply switches the internal auditor's mind set into a different quality relationship with the auditee. It is now the turn of the internal auditor to set the quality specifications, establish a contract and measure cost, delivery and reliability. It is now the internal auditor's role as the customer to be delighted or dissatisfied.

10.3 Auditors Are Quality Managers

The quality of audit work has been a focus of attention by professional institutes, the law, regulators, standards and audit customers for a very long time. In the early part of the 20th century, this focus was more on the quality and qualifications of the auditor rather than the audit process itself. De Paula (1914)[8] in his principles of auditing, discussed in previous chapters, focused more on the qualification of the individual auditor – see Figure 10.5. The attributes of external financial auditors (men and women) described by De Paula still apply today and can be seen woven into quality management of the audit processes for all auditors and required by their professions and regulators, and by their customers.

The following is an extract from an article I wrote on quality schemes and had published in 2001, which though addressed to internal auditors at that time did and still does apply to all auditors today. Many of the references need updating. I leave that for the reader to do, a task which will never end during the 21st century:

An auditor requires a considerable legal knowledge and must be complete master of the principles of auditing in all its bearings. In addition to his scientific knowledge, he must:

– be above all things a man of affairs, and possess tact and character;
– not be easily led and influenced by others, but knowing what his duty is, he must be able to do it in spite of direct or indirect pressure. He may find himself in positions when his duty to his client is opposed to his own interests, and in such circumstances he must have the courage to carry out his duty faithfully, regardless of the effects it may have upon himself. In the long run, the reputation he will thus gain for absolute integrity will prove of far greater value to him than any temporary loss in the first case;
– be painstaking and he must be endowed with considerable perseverance, for much of the work is of a somewhat mechanical nature, but it is essential that the whole should be thoroughly and carefully done;
– never pass any item unless he understands its nature and is absolutely satisfied that it is in order; if he is not, he must make intelligent and exhaustive enquiries until he has ascertained the exact state of affairs. One of the greatest dangers is to pass entries which are not completely understood, because the auditor is fearful of displaying ignorance by asking questions. If he cannot ascertain for himself, he should, without fail, ask for the necessary information, for should he affect to possess knowledge which, in fact, he does not, he inevitably will make mistakes that will be far more damaging to his reputation than would be the case if he asked for information upon, for instance, technical details of which he has not had previous experience;
– be practical, and if asked for professional advice, must appreciate the practical requirements and circumstances of the business, and thus avoid making recommendations which, though perhaps theoretically perfect, are entirely unfitted to the circumstances of the particular business.

Figure 10.5 Qualifications of the auditor

Source: *Principles of Auditing* (1914 pp. 20–2), F.R.M De Paula. Sir Isaac Pitman & Sons Ltd. London, England.

Quality Schemes and Best Value in the 21st Century[9]

CHALLENGES OF QUALITY

There can be few suppliers and customers that do not recognise the importance of quality. It challenges all products and services. The use of quality schemes to meet these challenges is evident in most countries. Quality schemes change strategies, structures, processes and people, Governments and managing bodies in all sectors have learnt to lead, develop and monitor them, often for survival. The challenges of doing so have been difficult for many. The consequences of not doing so have been disastrous for many.

Every day, internal auditors meet these same challenges and recognise the same consequences in their own work and the work of others. A successful internal auditing role as ' . . . an independent, objective, assurance and consulting activity, designed to add value and improve an organisation's operations.'[10] requires all internal auditors to understand how quality schemes contribute to success. Their knowledge and experience of control is a good starting point.

Consider all the elements in the now well-used COSO[11] integrated control model – Control Environment, Risk Assessment, Control Activities, Monitoring, Information and Communication discussed in previous chapters. The descriptions of each of these elements – see Figure 10.6 – have direct links to all quality principles. Look for these elements in your own and your organisation's quality schemes. Require them in all your suppliers' quality schemes. Integrated they can meet all the challenges of achieving quality in everything you do.

PRINCIPLES OF QUALITY

The 1980s and 1990s saw a worldwide increase in the teaching and implementation of quality schemes. Most of these programmes focused on economics and customer satisfaction, with controlled processes, feedback mechanisms and appropriate measures. Most motivated those involved with the need for continuous improvement. All required total commitment. Many evolved from existing quality control and assurance functions. Many were new, established because of regulatory, competitive or cost pressures.

During this period 'quality objectives' in business and public sector organisations moved into all levels of direction and management decision-making. Strategic plans embraced the need for quality and customer satisfaction, if not delight. Directors of Quality appeared on many boards. The results could be seen in a growth of quality cultures and quality system standards, fuelled by many governments and consultants. Competitive

CONTROL ENVIRONMENT

Tone	Discipline and structure
Ethic	Competence
Philosophy	Style
Organisation and methods	People development
Attention and direction by board	

RISK ASSESSMENT

How to achieve consistently all objectives linked at different levels
Identification and analysis of all relevant risks – internal and external
Consider change

CONTROL ACTIVITIES

Policies and procedures	Verifications
Reconciliations	Reviews
Security	Segregation of duties

INFORMATION AND COMMUNICATION

Information capture, storage and issue in an appropriate timeframe
Information flows up, down and across the organisation
Clarity
Communication with external parties (stakeholders)

MONITORING

Supervision and management
Compliance
Independent reviews

Figure 10.6 Components of the COSO Integrated Control Model

Source: Internal Control – Integrated Framework (1992)

national and international quality awards were created to stimulate the development of these cultures. These awards still attract many organisations to quality self-assessment programmes and external quality audits.

DEVELOPMENT OF QUALITY SCHEMES

Research in the 1990s showed that there were different levels of quality commitment in organisations, usually recognised by the types of schemes used. Quality assurance was and still is the basic level, characterised by agreed specifications, supervision, inspection and rectification. Next came ad hoc quality improvement projects, using staff in motivated teams with performance targets focused on customer satisfaction. Then came TQM systems satisfying the quality principles already mentioned. At the same time international quality standards (ISO 9000) were developed and promoted. These require external registration of quality systems to international quality requirements and a quality manual with operating procedures. All subject to independent internal and external quality audit. After TQM and ISO 9000 came national and international quality awards by external assessment, e.g. Business Excellence Model, Quality Charters, Investors in People, ISO 9000, etc. These awards have developed with a wider stakeholder focus on results and impacts on society as a whole. All these quality levels do not stand in isolation from each other. They can all be linked, even integrated, under an umbrella of quality schemes. That they are not in many organisations weakens their impact, on both the organisation and its stakeholders.

QUALITY SCHEMES AND ISO 9000

There have been many debates over the years as to whether a quality system registered to ISO 9000 is TQM. Those that agree that it is, usually base their opinion on the detailed requirements of ISO 9000 and its supporting guidelines (9004–1: 1994). These guidelines do not form part of the registration process. However, they are advisory for the development of a quality system and clearly written in a TQM context. They require quality systems to meet and satisfy both customer and organisation needs and expectations:

a) The customer's needs and expectations

For the customer, there is a need for confidence in the ability of the organisation to deliver the desired quality as well as the consistent maintenance of that quality.

b) The organisation's needs and interests

For the organisation, there is a business need to attain and to maintain the desired quality at an optimum cost; the fulfilment of this aspect is related to the planned and efficient utilisation of the technological, human and material resources available to the organisation.

Those that do not agree usually base their opinion on the detailed documentation required for registration of a quality system and the compliance nature of quality auditing. Many also believe that there is not sufficient focus on customer satisfaction and continuous improvement in ISO 9000, even though both are referred to in the guidelines. This debate is reflected in the current revisions to ISO 9000:1994, which will consolidate the family of ISO 9000 standards into four primary standards (9000, 9001, 9004 and 10011 (Guideline for auditing quality systems)). The 1998 introduction to the final draft of ISO 9000:2000 gives 'customer needs' as the main force driving the revision. It also introduces a revised guideline ISO 9004:2000, developed to be consistent with the new ISO 9001:2000.

There is evidence that ISO 9000 has been used by organisations to achieve other awards leading to marks of excellence, e.g. Business Excellence Model, Investor in People award, charters, supplier awards, productivity awards, training awards, etc. This wide variety of relationships was recognised by the British Standards Institute in its 1996 annual report:

> Our (ISO 9000) clients have enjoyed considerable success in the UK Quality Awards, the Wales Quality Awards, the European Quality Awards and the Construction Industry Awards.

QUALITY SCHEMES AND BEST VALUE

The UK government recently introduced Best Value Review (BVR) concept for local government defined[12] . . . as a duty to deliver services to clear standards (covering both cost and quality) by the most economic, efficient and effective means available.' From this year, all local authorities must have a Best Value Performance Plan (BVPP) that includes a programme of BVR's, applying the government's four best value principles (4Cs) of:

> *CHALLENGE   why, how and by whom a service is being given.*
> *COMPARISON   with the performance of others across a range of relevant indicators, taking into account the views of both service-users and potential suppliers.*
> *CONSULTATION   with local tax-payers, service users, partners and the wider business community in setting new performance targets.*
> *COMPETITION   fair and open wherever practicable as a means of securing efficient and effective services.*

Its guidance on Best Value published in 2000[13] recognises that quality schemes " . . . will not in themselves guarantee Best Value. However, if used properly they can provide considerable help in achieving Best Value . . .". The guide references into a number of schemes in support of Best Value:

> Business Excellence Model[14]
> Investors in People[15]
> Charter Mark[16]
> ISO 9000[17]
> Local Government Improvement Plan[18]

In 1999,[19] the UK government established a task force to consider how these quality tools can be used and linked together to help the public sector meet its challenges ahead. It is not difficult to identify theoretical relationships between each of the schemes and Best Value. Developing

Business Excellence Model	ISO 9000	Charter Mark	Investors in People
ENABLERS			
Leadership	X	X	X
Policy and Strategy	XX	XX	XX
People Management	X	XX	XXX
Resources	XX	XX	X
Processes	XXX	X	X
RESULT S			
Customer Satisfaction	XX	XXX	X
People Satisfaction	X	X	XXX
Impact on Society			
Business Results	XX	XX	XX

XXX critical impact XX secondary impact X indirect impact

Figure 10.7 How business excellence model criteria match other quality systems

Source: A Guide to Quality Schemes for the Public Sector (2000), Cabinet Office, London, England.

these relationships in practice has been more difficult. Too often they are driven with uncoordinated quality strategies. Both these studies only covered the public sector but the results have some important messages for organisations across all sectors. Not least, that quality and best value need to be managed with coordinated strategies, if each is to support the other. Figure 10.7[20] shows how the task force matched its chosen quality tools. (It should be noted here that the Business Excellence Model and ISO 9000 have been revised since this table was prepared.)

QUALITY SCHEMES AND GOOD GOVERNANCE

The 1996, research by Bain and Band[21] into governance, demonstrates some recognition of quality and governance integration:

> We hold the view that corporate governance is very much about adding value. Companies and other enterprises with a professional and positive attitude to governance are stronger and have a greater record of achievement. In fact, some company directors . . . suggest that there is an important direct relationship between a country's corporate governance system and its economic success.

In 1998, these links were explored by me[22] with little success:

> There is ample evidence in developed theory and principles that quality is associated with competition, performance and profitability; yet there is little evidence that control and governance has been a focus in any of this research.

At that time only a few researchers had linked control and governance into achieving quality in products and services. In practice, few organisations were reporting these links and there are still few today. Yet, as already demonstrated earlier, control is an essential part of all quality schemes and governance can be related to many of the principles driving quality. Why is it that too few organisations see quality and governance as bedfellows? This is a question that all should ask in every organisation.

More recent publications have started to link governance to effectiveness. Sir Adrian Cadbury, in his foreword to A Strategic Approach to Corporate Governance,[23] states:

> The essential point is that good governance is an aid to effectiveness. It is not there to shackle enterprise, but to harness it in the achievement of its goals.

International organisations, such as the Commonwealth Association for Corporate Governance (CACG)[24] and Organisation for Economic Cooperation and Development (OECD)[25] recognise the synergy between governance and economics. Both the CCAG and OECD have published international principles that link economic objectives and long-term success with good governance. Although it may take some time, these principles will revolutionise the way business and government is conducted in many countries across the world.

QUALITY CHALLENGES FOR INTERNAL AUDITING

In 1978, The IIA standards for the professional practice of internal auditing recognised the importance of quality assurance. These professional guidelines recommend four steps to achieving quality in internal auditing work – due professional care, supervision, internal reviews and external reviews. This is still part of the standards. However, most research shows that many internal auditing functions do not have formal quality assurance programmes. Contrast this with the recently revised UK Auditing Practices Board – Quality Control for Audit Work,[26] which establishes basic principles for quality in external auditing. This statement balances the quality drivers of ownership, control responsibilities, policies, procedures and monitoring, in a framework of quality requirements for all external auditing functions. Non-compliance with this statement can have serious consequences for external auditors.

In 1992, both The IIA Inc., USA and IIA-UK & Ireland published statements on internal auditing and TQM. The IIA Inc.[27] promoted internal auditors as 'agents of change':

> In this role, (internal) auditors can actively participate in helping management achieve their (quality) objectives and still maintain independence and objectivity

Interviews with a number of North American organisations had shown that TQM was used to improve internal auditing processes as well as a means of contributing to improving control environments, risk assessment, control activities and monitoring. Internal auditing benefits from involvement in TQM were seen to come from improved training, teamwork, measurement techniques and benchmarking.

The IIA-UK started its Professional Briefing Notes series in 1992 with a definition of TQM[28] and an exploration of the following options for internal auditors to explore:

1   The internal audit appraisal of departmental TQM activities.
2   The relationship between 'internal audit' and 'quality audit'.
3   The extent to which heads of internal audit may seek to gain ISO 9000 registration for their audit departments.

In the 1990s, some internal auditing functions registered to ISO 9000. This required all their processes to comply with the standard's quality requirements. The IIA-UK & Ireland published an example of such a registration in 1993.[29] This internal auditing interest in ISO 9000 continues today,

Research into internal auditing registrations30 prior to 1993 identified the reasons listed in Figure 10.8. Not all had the same reasons. In most, the initial intentions were not to seek improvements in professional practices but to document current practices more clearly and uniformly. However, addressing ISO 9000 quality requirements focused attention on the structure needed to achieve and maintain a quality organisation and system. This changed responsibilities for quality at all levels. The continuous cycle of monitoring and correction, driven by the quality system and its required internal auditing, also encouraged staff to be innovative in new and better methods – sometimes with paradigm shifts!

Reasons for registration to ISO 9000

♦ **Procedural**

– need to update procedures
– need to improve procedures
– need to motivate internal auditing staff to comply with procedures
– need for more uniform procedures

♦ **Strategic**

– requirement by organisation to pursue ISO 9000
– requirement by organisation to demonstrate quality in services provided

♦ **Organisational**

– need to change structure of global/national service
– need to improve supervision
– improve team building

♦ **Marketing**

– part of programme to market test the internal auditing service in competition with other bids
– part of a programme to market internal auditing services within the organisation

---

Figure 10.8 Internal audit reasons for registering to ISO 9000

Source: International Quality Standards: Implications for Internal Auditing (1996)

The same research showed the benefits from registration as listed at Figure 10.9. These were mainly in the quality vision and mission, which required management leadership, teamwork and good communication, to mould existing internal auditing practices into compliance with ISO 9000 quality requirements. Changes also required training and a writing or rewriting of audit procedures.

Whatever the options internal auditing follow to achieve quality, it is clear that the challenge of quality schemes cannot be left out of audit planning and risk assessment. Today and tomorrow's drive for quality and best value across all organisations requires all internal auditors to add the following to the IIA-UK & Ireland's 1992 list of options:

1 Provide advice on all quality scheme/Best Value planning and implementation.
2 Link all quality schemes and Best Value Reviews to all risk assessments.
3 Relate quality and Best Value policies to the implementation, monitoring and reporting of good governance practices

---

Benefits from registration to ISO 9000
♦ **Quality policy**

Like The IIA standards, ISO 9000 requires a declaration of quality purpose. For ISO 9000 this is the publication of a quality policy. Each of the internal auditing functions had incorporated such a statement in its charter.

♦ **Standard of conduct**

The IIA standards require internal auditors to take due professional care in their audit work. Compliance to ISO 9000 quality requirements promoted diligence in audit work and established an environment, which embraced many of the principles in The IIA Code of Ethics.

♦ **Documentation**

The IIA standards require written policies and procedures for all audit work. Such evidence was reinforced by the ISO 9000 quality requirements for controlled documentation and records.

♦ **Quality assurance**

The IIA standards require evidence of supervision and quality assurance in all of all audit work. The ISO 9000 quality assurance and quality audits requirements provided a framework for the supervision and management of all internal auditing practices.

Figure 10.9 Internal audit benefits from registering to ISO 9000

Source: International Quality Standards: Implications for Internal Auditing (1996)

The schemes in this article are repeated in a publication by the Scottish Executive (2005)[31] – Promoting Excellence in Scotland – A Guide to Quality Schemes and the Delivery of Public Services. In this publication the importance of innovation, audit, assurance change and excellence in the achievement of quality appear frequently.

The ISO 9000 (2015)[32] discussed earlier sees the benefits from this quality standard now towards aspect of the requirements of good governance:

What benefits does the new version bring?

The new version of the standard brings the user a number of benefits. For example, ISO 9001:2015:

• puts greater emphasis on leadership engagement
• helps address organisational risks and opportunities in a structured manner
• uses simplified language and a common structure and terms, which are particularly helpful to organisations using multiple management systems, such as those for the environment, health and safety, or business continuity
• addresses supply chain management more effectively
• is more user-friendly for service and knowledge-based organisations.

In addition to these updates, BS ISO 26000:2010[33] on social responsibility and BSI 13500:2013[34] on effective governance and importance in achieving quality should be considered by all auditors as new sources to my article on the management of quality schemes and best value.

My TQM Framework is also key to the achievement of quality in all auditing as well as in all organisations. In 2008 the UK Financial Reporting Council (FRC)[35] created its own Audit Quality Framework following a consultation period. This Framework has been designed to support communication of audit quality to all interested parties promoting the following key drivers of audit quality:

Culture within an audit firm
Skills and personal qualities of audit partners and staff
Effectiveness of the audit process
Reliability and usefulness of audit reporting
Factors outside the control of auditors affecting audit quality.

Each of these drivers is supported by a checklist of indicators demonstrating a high quality standard. The FRC hopes that the Framework will assist audit committees, all stakeholders and regulators to evaluate the actions taken by audit firms 'to ensure that high quality audits are performed, whether in the UK or overseas'. This Framework and its drivers and indicators are being used today to evaluate the quality of external audits and could be used for the evaluation of other types of audit, both by the auditors and those they audit. In its 2015 review of Annual Transparency Reporting by audit firms, the FRC[36] gives recognition to the use of its Quality Framework by audit firms in preparing their reports.

The quality of all audit work has always been of importance and still is, both to those who carry out the work and are responsible for its results, and those who receive the results and rely on its quality. All auditors are managers of the quality of their work, and those who manage that work have an important responsibility to make certain that its quality is of the highest standard. There can be no exception to this rule. All auditors are quality managers over the assurances they provide to those whom they audit and those stakeholders in the audit who rely on its results. This rule is endorsed by both professional auditing codes of conduct, and all auditing standards auditors are required to comply with in the course of an audit. It is also usually binding in contracts and charters for audit work agreed to by executive management, audit committees and governing bodies of organisations. If not, it should be!

As early as the beginning of the 20th century, it was recognised by those developing the science of auditing that trust in the quality of its services needed to be supported by continuous 'additions and improvements' [creativity and innovation!] in the management of the audit process and by those who carried out the audits. De Paula (1914) discussed this as follows:

the efficiency of the audit will depend, not upon the skill and competency of the principals, but upon the skill and competency of the member of the staff in charge of the particular audit. There is one objection to this mode of procedure, and that is, that the clerks in charge may lose a sense of responsibility, and carry out the work in an automatic manner. It should be impressed upon them, therefore, that the programme set out is the basis upon which the audit is to be conducted, and that they must use their intelligence when carrying out the same, and they should be encouraged to recommend additions and improvements in the scheme, for it is most important, as time goes on, that the scheme should be kept constantly up to date, as otherwise serious flaws may develop. For this reason, it is important that the principals should reconsider the programme from time to time.

10.4 Audit Committees Are Quality Managers, Too

The past thirty years have seen growth both in the number and scope of audit committees in organisations of all sizes and sectors nationally and internationally across the globe. One of the functions of an audit committee is to monitor the quality of audit work in an organisation and from outside the organisation by internal and external auditors, regulators and other compliance inspectors. The Treadway Commission Report (1987)[37] made recommendations on the form and scope of audit committees in the US. It contains the term 'audit quality' on thirty-two occasions – audit quality is not therefore a new concern! Since then guidance and advice on audit committee form and scope has spread around the world in all sectors of industry – private, public and charitable.

FRC (2012)[38] in its recommendations on the form and scope of audit committees in the United Kingdom advises the committee to evaluate the quality of external audit work and the transparent reporting of this:

> The audit committee should annually assess, and report to the board on, the qualification, expertise and resources, and independence of the external auditors and the effectiveness of the audit process, with a recommendation on whether to propose to the shareholders that the external auditor be reappointed.

In the same guidance it recommends for internal audit when it is established: 'The audit committee should monitor and review the effectiveness of the company's internal audit function' – by implication including its quality management processes. The same guidance exists (or should exist) across the globe in other national statements on audit committee effectiveness.

The second half of the 20th century and so far this century have seen professions for auditors, those that have developed auditing standards, including the International Organization for Standardization, governments and regulators publishing guidance and requirements on the quality of auditing processes, reporting and attributes required of auditors. Recently the FRC,[39] in its roles of audit standard setting and monitoring the quality of auditing and its reporting, recognised a need for more innovative reporting by auditors of financial statements to a wider audience following the 2008 financial crisis:

> The aftermath of the Financial Crisis of 2008 significantly increased the intensity of the focus on the effectiveness of company stewardship and the

adequacy of the communications to the market made by both Audit Committees and auditors.

The FRC[40] embarked on further consultations and evidence gathering. In early 2011, arising from feedback to its consultation paper, the FRC concluded that more still needs 'to be done to demonstrate that auditors are achieving the fundamental purpose of an audit'.

The Institute of Internal Auditors Inc.[41] has international auditing standards and guidance on the quality of internal audit work, requiring formal auditing processes, continuous improvement, peer and external quality assessment: 'The chief audit executive must develop and maintain a quality assurance and improvement program that covers all aspects of the internal audit activity.' Its standards are structured 'between Attribute and Performance Standards'. The Performance Standards 'describe the nature of internal auditing and provide quality criteria against which the performance of these services can be measured'. All audit committees need to ensure the ISO 2015 Quality Management Principles apply, are in all the auditing standards and monitoring and promotion of the quality of auditing of financial statements, and reporting by all auditors.

Recent developments in assurance frameworks/mapping and the creation of assurance defence models have extended audit and risk committee responsibilities for evaluating the quality of independent auditing they receive to cover all types of auditing in an organisation. In the United Kingdom such framework/mapping is a key part of its public sector governance.[42] Quality guidance is also provided by most of the major professional accounting/auditing firms. All this guidance should be a requirement by all audit committees in their monitoring of audit and risks an their organisations.

10.5 Chapter Review

In this chapter I discuss Total Quality Management as essential for satisfying, if not delighting, audit customers, and for all auditors to have a passion for a high standard of quality in their professional auditing services. Everyone being audited and interested in the results should see the auditor as a quality manager with a quality policy based on recognised quality principles. All auditing must measure its performance on a continuous basis, seeking at all times continuous improvement by creative thinking and innovation. Quality is a defence in the achievement of good governance. It should also be seen as an attack on bad governance.

10.6 Creative Audit Thinking Activities

Activity 37 Create a Total Quality Management Framework

This chapter has discussed the principles for quality achievement for products and services, developed over many years by quality practitioners, consultants and academics. It has introduced you to my own developed Total Quality Management Framework and the United Kingdom Financial Reporting Council (FRC) Audit Quality Framework. Now read the following article I published in 1990 for quality in internal auditing and develop your own TQM Framework for your audit processes.

Audit Opportunities in the TQM Environment Can Lead to World–Class Auditing[43]

The TQM concept requires all SUPPLIER and OPERATING PROCESS relationships to create excellent products and services that satisfy all customers' needs. Developing supplier partnerships and knowing customer needs become paramount in the quality environment of team-building and continuous improvement, which develop between groups within the organisation and between other organisations. Identifying the 'customer' is not that easy, particularly in large and international organisations.

In TQM everyone is involved, in every way, in everything they do-the involvement is TOTAL, all management and all staff. The internal supplier and customer become just as important as the external supplier and customer. It is the excellence of these working relationships and all the processes that guarantees the high quality of the product or service and satisfies the customer. Reliance is not placed on quality checks after the service has been completed or product made. The TQM environment develops teams and monitoring activities that are always 'customer' orientated. THE CUSTOMER BECOMES PARAMOUNT.

Many organisations already provide internal TQM training and all internal audit managers should take advantage of this for themselves and their staff. If your organisation does not do so in whatever sector-then ask why. Do not wait for your organisation to adopt TQM, seek the training and use the knowledge gained in the scope of all your audits. What are some of the gains to be achieved?

Recognition of the SUPPLIER-PROCESS-CUSTOMER CHAIN for the audit process drives the audit programme into the heart of business activity and highlights the key controls needed for business success.

Establishing who are the customer and CUSTOMER NEEDS helps focus audit tests into the most important areas and issues.

The concept of AUDITOR/AUDITEE teamwork during the audit process is achieved and participative auditing becomes a reality.

AUDIT RESULTS and RECOMMENDATIONS concentrate on prevention rather than detection, looking to the control of quality in the future, rather than the past.

QUALITY ASSURANCE requirements to meet IIA Standards take on a wider meaning, linking the quality aims of the internal audit department into those of the organisation.

Emphasis on CONTINUOUS IMPROVEMENT in the TQM environment encourages internal audit staff 'to continually seek improvements in the audit process.

TQM requires QUALITY MEASURES in all processes, to monitor quality and highlight non-conformance with standards.

The audit process becomes a QUALITY SYSTEM, which can lead to recognition under the national accreditation standard BS5750 (ISO9000).

QUALITY SUCCESSES are more easily recognised and rewarded at team and individual levels.

TOTAL QUALITY MANAGEMENT in an organisation (even if only in the Internal Audit Department) requires the total commitment of management. However, it is not a journey's end, just the beginning. It is the start of a road that requires a continuing quality commitment by everyone, every day, in every way, in everything. The enthusiasm a commitment to quality generates can lead to the highest accolades of excellence and the achievement of WORLD CLASS status.

Activity 38   Delight Your Customers with Creativity and Innovation

Download the brochure *ISO 9000:2015 Quality Management Principles*[44] from the International Organization for Standardization (ISO) website (www.iso.org) and consider how its quality principles – rationale and benefits – can create innovation in your audit process and delight your customers. Should your auditing be registered to ISO 9000:2015?

ISO 9000:2015 Quality Management Principles

The seven quality management principles are:

QMP 1 Customer focus
QMP 2 Leadership
QMP 3 Engagement of people
QMP 4 Process approach
QMP 5 Improvement
QMP 6 Evidence-based decision making
QMP 7 Relationship management

Activity 39   Creative and Innovative Reporting

Study the creative and innovative online PriceWaterhouseCoopers Annual Report 2015[45] at www.pricewaterhousereport.co.uk/our-year-in-review.

Will this be the future for all annual reporting? Will this be the future for all audit reporting? In particular, download and read the PWC 2015[46] reporting of its transparency in accordance with the EU Transparency Directive – see the introduction by Chairman Ian Powell below. This is followed by a vision of the future – a vision of the future for all assurances and the quality of all auditing. Consider this vision in the light of quality management in your own auditing and reporting. How does it compare?

Building Trust through Assurance

Our assurance business is at the core of our firm. Throughout our 165-year history we have always recognised the importance of building trust and confidence in business. Reporting, audit and assurance have been a critical part of the journey.

In this report we showcase the steps we continue to take to enhance the quality of our assurance services through investment in our people, technologies and processes.

This year, we have produced a digital annual report, a first for our firm and a reflection of trends in the delivery of information to make it accessible and usable. Ensuring that we respond to a changing world is also a theme that continues through this Transparency Report, as we share how our assurance business is adapting to a developing regulatory environment and technological disruption.

Fundamentally, our business is guided by a clear purpose, to build trust in society and to solve important problems. This purpose comes to life through our people working with thousands of organisations delivering assurance where it is needed most.

A Vision of the Future

Imagine a world where society has trust in business. All capital providers are empowered to make decisions about business through access to information they can trust – it's always available on Wiki-style platforms where everyone can contribute to a picture of performance. Financial audits are powered by artificially intelligent machines; assurance is also available over all aspects of risk, qualitative as well as quantitative. Assurance professionals have become trusted curators of business information, offering shareholders and other stakeholders a route through the data maelstrom.

Notes

1 *Quality Management Principles* (2015 Principle 1), International Organization of Standardization, Geneva, Switzerland.
2 *Quality in Its Total Business Concept* – accessed from the Chartered Quality Institute's website www.cqi.org, accessed 22 June 2016.
3 *The New Quality Profession Challenge* (2014 p. 18), Chartered Quality Institute, London, England.

4   *Leading Edge Internal Auditing* (1998 p. 113), J. Ridley and A.D. Chambers, ICSA Publishing Ltd., London, England.

5   *Best-Practice Approaches to Internal Auditing* (2011 pp. 77–78), Contribution by J. Ridley, Bloomsbury Information Ltd., London, England.

6   *Total Quality Management* (1989), Oakland, John S., Butterworth-Heinemann, Oxford, England [Now published as *Total Quality Management and Operational Excellence* (4th Edition 2014), Routledge, London, England].

7   *You Are My Customer – You Are Also My Supplier,* Jeffrey Ridley, Internal Auditing (October 1995), IIA-UK and Ireland, London, England.

8   *Principles of Auditing* (1914 pp. 13, 20–22 and 132–133), F.R.M. De Paula, Sir Isaac Pitman and Sons Ltd., London, England.

9   *Quality Schemes and Best Value in the 21st Century – Challenges for Many Organisations and Internal Auditing, Internal Control,* Issue 38 (February 2001), ABG professional information, part of the CCH group, Institute of Chartered Accountants in England and Wales, London, England.

10 *New Definition of Internal Auditing* (1999), The IIA.

11 *Internal Control – Integrated Framework* (1992), Committee of Sponsoring Organisations of the Treadway Commission, New York, US.

12 *Modernising Government White Paper (Cm 4310)* (1999), Cabinet Office Website: www.cabinet-office.gov.uk/moderngov/1999/whitepaper/index.htm

13 *Guide to Quality Schemes and Best Value* (2000), Department of the Environment, Transport and the Regions, London, England. Websites: www.detr.gov.uk and Its Improvement and Development Agency – www.idea.gov.uk.

14 *Business Excellence Model, The British Quality Foundation,* www.quality-foundation.co.uk
     EFQM Excellence Model, European Foundation for Quality Management. www.efqm.org.

15 Investors in People – UK, London, 020 7467 1900.

16 Charter Mark. www.servicefirst.gov.uk.

17 British Standards Institute. www.bsi.org.uk.

18 Local Government Improvement Programme, The Improvement and Development Agency, London. E-mail: Igip@idea.gov.uk.

19 *A Guide to Quality Schemes for the Public Sector* (2000), Cabinet Office, London, England.

20 *A Guide to Quality Schemes for the Public Sector* (2000), Cabinet Office, London, England.

21 *Winning Ways Through Corporate Governance* (1996), Bain and Band, Macmillan Business, London, England.

22 *Leading Edge Internal Auditing* (1998), Ridley and Chambers, ICSA Publishing Ltd., London, England.

23 *A Strategic Approach to Corporate Governance* (1999), Adrian Davies, Gower, Farnham, England.

24 *Commonwealth Association for Corporate Governance.* www.cbc.to/governance/finalver/cacg.htm.

25 *Organisation for Economic Cooperation and Development.* www.oecd.org/daf/governnance/principles.htm

26 *Statement of Auditing Standards 240 – Quality Control for Audit Work* (2000), Auditing Practices Board, London, England.

27 *Internal Auditing in a Total Quality Environment – A Reference Manual* (1992), Elaine McIntosh, The Institute of Internal Auditors Inc., Orlando, US.

28 *Total Quality Management: The Implications for Internal Audit Departments, PBN One* (1992), The Institute of Internal Auditors Inc., Orlando, US.

29 *A Quality System Manual for Internal Auditing* (1993), Jeffrey Ridley, The Institute of Internal Auditors UK and Ireland, London, England.

30 *International Quality Standards: Implications for Internal Auditing* (1996), Ridley and Stephens, The Institute of Internal Auditors Inc., Orlando, US.

31 *Promoting Excellence in Scotland – A Guide to Quality Schemes and the Delivery of Public Services* (2005), Scottish Executive, Edinburgh, Scotland.

32 *Moving from ISO9001:2008 to ISDO9001:2015* (2015), International Organization for Standardization, Geneva, Switzerland.
33 *International Standard Guidance on Social Responsibility* (ISO 26000:2010), International Organization for Standardization (ISO), Geneva, Switzerland.
34 *Code of Practice for Delivering Effective Governance of Organisations* (BS 13500:2013), British Standards Institution (BSI), London, England.
35 *The Audit Quality Framework* (2008), Financial Reporting Council, London, England.
36 *Transparency Reporting by Auditors of Public Interest Entities: Review of Mandatory Reports* (2015), Financial Reporting Council, London, England.
37 Report of the National Commission on Fraudulent Financial Reporting (1987), US.
38 *Guidance on Audit Committees* (2012 pp. 7 and 11), Financial Reporting Council (FRC), London, England.
39 *Extended Audit Reports – A Review of Experience in the First Year* (2015 p. 7), Financial Reporting Council (FRC), London, England.
40 *Effective Company Stewardship – Enhancing Corporate Reporting and Audit* (2011), Financial Reporting Council, London, England.
41 *International Standards for the Professional Practice of Internal Auditing (Standards)* (2012/1300), The Institute of Internal Auditors Inc., Orlando, US.
42 *Assurance Frameworks* (2012), H.M. Treasury, London, England.
43 *Audit Opportunities in the TQM Environment can lead to World-Class Auditing* (1990), Internal Auditing Journal, Chartered Institute of Internal Auditors, London, England.
44 *Quality Management Principles* (2015 Introduction), International Organization for Standardization, Geneva, Switzerland.
45 *Annual Report* (2015), PricewaterhouseCoopers LLP, London, England.
46 *Building Trust Through Assurance Transparency Report* (2015), PricewaterhouseCoopers LLP. London, England.

Part IV

Excellence

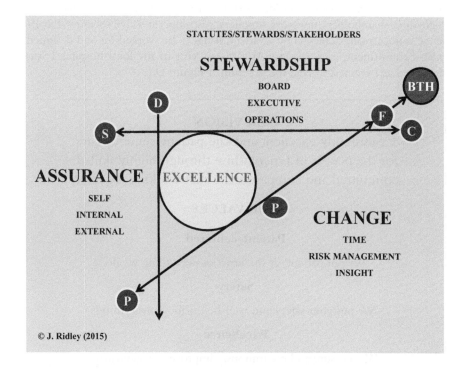

© J. Ridley (2015)

Excellence requires purposeful development of those involved and not just some short term superficial adjustments.[1]

Excellence in governance, like the achievement of quality in products and services, is a road, not a destination. You do not arrive at Excellence in a product or services or in the processes by which they are created by accident – its achievement should always start with a capital **E**. That creation has to be managed and governed at all levels in an organisation. That governance starts with an organisation's aims and objectives and the culture and values it adopts and promotes. It depends on good management and a motivation by everyone involved being the best. It requires continuous improvement by everyone at all levels, creativity and innovation in everything an organisation does, every day and in every way. It is an achievement at all levels – board, executive and operations. It is an essential part of Stewardship, Change and Assurance, influencing the underlying theories and values chosen at the top of the organisation and practiced at every level. Excellence is an important achievement for each of the components in my Governance Framework. Today its achievement must include addressing all the United Nation's Sustainability Goals in Appendix H.

All auditors should be searching for and achieving Excellence in the assurance products and services they provide to organisations across all levels – board, executive and operations. Today, there are signs that this search by auditors is interesting many more stakeholders external to an organisation: governments, regulators, shareholders, investors, suppliers, customers and civil societies. Excellence is not usually achieved by accident. It has to be worked for and designed with commitment, even passion. At a recent visit to my local hospital, I was delighted as I entered to read the greeting at Figure D.1.

OUR VISION

Consistently excellent and safe patient-centered care
for the people of Lincolnshire through highly skilled,
committed and compassionate staff working together.

OUR VALUES

Patient-centered

We put patients at the heart of everything we do

Safety

We put your safety and well-being above everything

Excellence

We measure and continuously improve our standards,
striving for excellence at all times

Compassionate

We offer you the compassion we would want for a loved one

Respect

We show respect for you and for each other

BEYOND GOOD

Figure D.1 Our vision of excellence

Source: Seen by author at Lincoln County Hospital, Lincolnshire England – December 2015

Compare the messages in this greeting of care, teamwork, skills, quality, safety, excellence, values and assurance in your own audit services. Are they similar? They should be! How better are yours? Note how the greeting touches on values expressed in both strategic and operational aspects of the hospital's delivery of services. Excellence is a value and with other values should appear as a commitment in strategic thinking, operational policies and procedures and measured assurances for all products and services.

For over twenty-five years, the European Foundation for Quality Management (EFQM)[2] has developed and promoted its Excellence Model and Fundamental Concepts of Excellence 'for achieving sustainable Excellence' (discussed in Chapter 2 – see Figure 2.1) as a way of people understanding 'the cause and effect relationships between what their organisation does (the Enablers) and the Results it achieves'. The model is promoted as 'non-descriptive and can be applied to any organisation, regardless of size, sector or maturity'. Established in 1988 EFQM is a forum of business leaders across Europe 'committed to helping organisations drive performance improvement through the EFQM Excellence Model'. Its model and concepts have empowered many organisations across all sectors over many years to develop a culture of Excellence through Leadership, People, Strategy, Partnerships and Resources as the Enablers to achieve Excellence in their People Results, Customer Results, Society Results and Business Results, through Learning, Creativity and Innovation of all of their resources within the overall organisation. Its Model requires an organisation to focus on Excellence using many management tools. In its explanation for what is Excellence the EFQM define this as ' . . . *doing your best'*.

At its simplest level EFQM sees its Excellence Model as ' . . . *a cause and effect diagram.'* EFQM's references to supporting management tools to achieve Excellence can be added to by many other such tools. All three of the interactive components in my Governance Framework – **STEWARDSHIP, CHANGE** and **ASSURANCE** need to achieve **EXCELLENCE** in how they are managed and governed. All auditors have the opportunities to achieve Excellence in the services they provide. They also have the opportunity if not duty to contribute to the achievement of Excellence by others in the organisations in which they work.

There are strong links between Total Quality Management and the achievement of Excellence. Each requires total commitment, if not a passion, to achieve. Both are a perception by a customer. Both are promoted by organisations to market themselves and their products and services. Quality is recognised by most regulators as essential in the organisations they regulate but Excellence less so. Yet both require the same framework of **Strategies, Structures, Systems, Skills, Style, Staff and Shared Values** created by Peters and Waterman (1982)[3] in their search for Excellence: this 1980s McKinsey 7S's Framework for Excellence is an integrated model for measuring Excellence in an organisation. The model has stood the test of time well and is still relevant today, if not more so. Used by many organisations across the world to support strategies for Excellence. Each component links into and supports the others. At the centre are the values shared by everyone in an organisation. It is essential for each component in the measuring process to be seen to be better than best in any benchmarking with competitors or standards. Tom Peters's authorship of books on Excellence since 1982 has had and still does have international fame. Readers should explore his website (www.tompeters.com) for the history of this Excellence model, in particular his book *Little Big Things: 163 Ways to Pursue Excellence,*[4] and his video thoughts on strategic listening – a must for every auditor.

Underlying the concept of Excellence is a commitment to quality in all the services and products an organisation requires from its suppliers and provides for its customers. That commitment is both internal within the organisation's supply chains and in all its external supply chains. Each of the 7S's of the McKinsey Framework should be seen to be influencing, driving and measuring the Quality and Excellence aims. Try this exercise for yourself in your own organisation. Review evidence of each of the 7S's in your organisation's latest annual report and the frequency in which my framework components **STEWARDSHIP, CHANGE, ASSURANCE** and **EXCELLENCE** appear. See how the 7S's appear in Table C.1. They are all there. They should all be evaluated in every audit engagement.

At random I have selected one annual report of a retail company and one of an audit firm and carried out a content analysis of the terms discussed, including one other term for each which has a similar meaning – see Figure D.2 for the results. The importance is in the use of all of the 7S's demonstrating the value of the McKinsey 7S's Framework today, and the use of my Corporate Governance Framework components – **STEWARDSHIP: CHANGE: ASSURANCE: EXCELLENCE**.

	Retail	Audit*
Strategy (direction)	46	51
Structure (organisation)	55	56
Systems (process)	85	113
Staff (people)	35	85
Skills (talent)	22	12
Style (culture)	7	20
Shared values (beliefs)	29	24
Stewardship (trust)	58	30
Change (improve)	317	39
Assurance (audit)	28	628
Excellence (quality)	24	274

Figure D.2 Content analysis of Excellence in two 2015 annual reports

Source: J. Ridley

Note: *includes Transparency Report 2015

Quality in auditing is taught through examination processes and required by auditing professions and firms as a requirement in all the services they provide. Regulators of auditing require quality to be part of audit and its evaluation by those who audit and those who receive the services. The UK Financial Reporting Council (FRC) (2008)[5] framework for quality already discussed in Chapter 10 is an excellent understanding of the quality management and control requirements across the audit process. This Framework is complementary to existing regulations and guidelines promoting the following key drivers of audit quality:

- the culture within an audit firm;
- the skills and personal qualities of audit partners and staff;
- the effectiveness of the audit process;
- the reliability and usefulness of audit reporting; and
- factors outside the control of auditors affecting audit quality.

For each of the first four drivers, controls and measures must be established to determine the perceptions of the quality and measures, which often require both internal and independent monitoring: quality perceptions are by both the provider of the audit and those being audited and receiving the audit findings and report. Factors outside the control of the auditor are those associated with the organisation/function being audited in respect of its attitudes to governance, risk management control and audit itself. Discussed under culture is 'Creates a climate where achieving high quality is valued, invested in and rewarded.' Essential for quality and for 'high quality' – read Excellence.

In most quality programmes, 'Excellence' is not mentioned as an aim. It is a term used more often in the competitive marketing of a product or service, and in some cultures is not used at all. Whatever the preferences between quality, high quality and Excellence, the goal is to create a perception in the minds of the customer of a passion for value, values and perfection in what is being received throughout the process of its creation.

At a recent annual dinner of professional internal auditors I attended in the Guildhall in London, at the reception desk was displayed a statement by the Chartered Institute of Internal Auditors concerning its passion – 'Passionate about promoting and developing internal auditors'. Excellence is about that total commitment to a passion to achieve a standard that is seen as best in the market place. How often do we hear, read or see passion associated with Excellence in auditing? In Figure D.2, 'Passion' is used by the Retail Company (3 times) and 'Commitment' by both (Retail 8 times; Audit 8 times): 'Total Commitment' is not used by the Retail Company but is used once by the Audit Firm. Make what you will of this, but do content analyse your own organisation's annual reports for these terms and those in Figure D.2.

I leave readers to interpret their own meanings for the term Passion. I interpret Passion as an enthusiasm to be the best in a competitive environment. To be best auditor I need to inspire, explore, imagine, improve, innovate and create.

To be all of these things, I need to continuously research, benchmark and be a runner. These are the road signs and milestones for all auditors.

I wrote and published the following article in 2008 for internal auditors in the public sector after speaking at their annual conference of heads of internal audit. It contains messages which will always apply to all auditors in their passion for Excellence. The 'theories on quality achievement' discussed in the article are based on my quality principles in Figure 10.2 in the previous chapter. The messages in this article apply to all auditors. They still should encourage creativity and innovation in auditing.

The Road to Quality and Excellence Takes You to the Cutting Edge[6]

Delegates attending the Annual Audit Conference this year should now be on the road to Excellence in the internal auditing services they are providing in their organisation. That is if they were not already travelling this road before the conference. What all roads to Excellence must have is a vision that inspires and creates a well managed and measured plan of actions at team and individual levels: focused on customers and improvement. Excellence is a continuous exploration into best practices using imagination, innovation and benchmarking skills. It will always lead to the cutting edge of internal auditing professionalism.

In my article on internal audit and quality, published in Audit Viewpoint in 2003 I discussed theories on quality achievement. Fundamental guidance for all that travel the Excellence road. These theories were not new then and have not dated. They have always served me well. They can be seen in all quality management programmes and awards today. They are:

1 The road to quality and Excellence always starts with a vision led by MANAGEMENT.
2 That vision for quality and Excellence should be focused on CUSTOMER needs.
3 Achievement of quality and Excellence in the eyes of the customer requires TEAMWORK across the organisation.
4 Teams need to MEASURE the risks and performance of quality and Excellence in their products and services always linked to their vision.
5 Organisations, people, processes, products and services need to CONTINUOUSLY IMPROVE if they are to be excellent.

They are an essential part of any commitment to Excellence. They do not stand alone. Each integrates with the others. What has changed since 2003 is how each is now being applied today.

1   Leadership in organisations adopting quality and Excellence has to be at all levels, by every employee. All lead if they are committed to the organisation's vision. Vision statements are used by many organisations to create and promote its direction and governance policies for all stakeholders. Strategic planning requires key missions, risk assessments and control to ensure the vision's achievement and opportunities for improvement are not lost. Quality and Excellence initiatives, such as the Balanced Scorecard[7] and Business Excellence[8] Models provide strategic and operational frameworks for implementing the right structures, methods and resources for this achievement. Self-assessment of these frameworks by all leaders is an essential part of their Excellence.

2   Customers are now not just receivers of a product or service, but in many organisations seen as partners. Customer focus is not just supported by customer feedback: it is a strategic tool in most organisations, whether public, private or voluntary. A tool that collects and analyses data about customer needs and satisfaction, using this to understand the customer and tailor products and services to satisfy those needs. This requires the information technology that is available today in every organisation. It should have a significant influence on strategic planning. It can be used for customers in any supply chain, whether internal or external to the organisation. The aim should be not just to satisfy customers, but to anticipate their needs and delight them with Excellence.

3   Teamwork. The best quality teams are those that are inter-functional, using resources and skills across the organisation and not just within a function, and empowered to take action. They should have clear terms of reference and the resources to carry these out. Quality cultures require this. For many years researchers have analysed behaviours between teams and their customers, recommending a participative teamwork approach, involving the customer and focused on customer needs and satisfaction. Teams should not stand alone but interlock with other teams in the organisation. Their aim should always be Excellence.

4   Measures. All measures must flow from an organisation's vision, through its missions to the actions being taken at operating levels. Measures alone are not sufficient. Their results should drive correction, action and improvement. They should also be transparent so that all those involved and interested in the results can be aware of these. They should be timely so that corrective action can be taken quickly. Too often measures are reported late. Timely, accurate, reliable measures that make things happen are those that achieve Excellence.

5   Continuous Improvement. Today and tomorrow, the increasing speed of change must be part of every organisation's strategic planning. Change not just for change sake, but also to meet global

competition in almost every product and service supplied in every sector. Continuous improvement in every organisation should start with innovation as a strategy and policy, implemented through drive and encouragement at all levels. There is ample evidence of this across the globe, in all sectors and professional bodies. To be at its best, continuous improvement needs each of the previous four quality principles practiced successfully, if it is to delight customers and meet the needs of those who provide products and services. It must have feedback from customers; drive by leadership through learning and a continuous search for Excellence; integrated teams of suppliers and customers; and, timely verification and analysis of results. It needs to continuously delight customers in the short and long term. That delight will mark out the best and claim Excellence.

The road to Excellence is always about continuous benchmarking to seek best practices for your skills, services and organisation. It can be internal in an organisation or external. It can be part of other review programmes or a programme on its own. Benchmarking should be formal with a developed scale of extremes such as 'awful' and 'superior'. Using such a scale an interesting model can be developed as a measure. Consider using the following scale:

Awful
Poor
Adequate
Good
Excellent
Superior.

All travellers along the Excellence road will have their personal definitions for these: or their own similar, terms, and be able to apply them in benchmarking. Placing awful before poor classes it as the extreme: a situation rarely encountered, but unfortunately is, too frequently. Placing superior after excellent demonstrates there can be situations when even Excellence is not sufficient to beat competition: an organisation's performance has to be better than any other, it has to be superior. In all operations there will be different interpretations and perceptions for each level of performance, but there will always be levels. Seeking consensus for levels and their definitions can be an interesting exercise in the management of internal audit and internal audit engagements, if not also for all management. The cutting edge internal auditor will be the one that can master the art of benchmarking to measure not just Excellence, but superiority.

Start benchmarking with your code of practice for internal auditing in local government.[9] Its compliance checklist should be a white line in the centre of your road to Excellence. The aims in that code include being innovative and challenging and:

Forward looking – knowing where the organisation wishes to be and aware of the national agenda and its impact.

That national agenda now includes a recent government White Paper[10] on innovation in all sectors: emphasising the importance of innovation learning across all sectors and in all professions. For the public sector it states:

The Government can drive innovation in public services through the way it allocates resources and structures incentives. Major forces such as attitudes to risk, budgeting, audit, performance measurement and recruitment must be aligned to support innovation. Together and with effective leadership, these will progressively overcome existing cultural and incentive barriers. Those responsible for public service delivery must also learn the lessons of open innovation and adopt innovative solutions from the private and third sectors.

An important message for all those travelling the road to Excellence in internal auditing.

Next, compare the behavioural, technical and management skills you have as an individual and in your team, with the matrix in your good practice guide to skills and competencies.[11] All travellers down any road need to be properly equipped if their explorations are to reach their vision. Even more so if their aim is to be superior.

On either side of the road to Excellence and in front there will always be economic, social and environmental risks and opportunities: their importance needs to be continuously assessed, managed and controlled. All can have an impact on an organisation's Excellence – its reputation and implementation of good governance practices. This is clearly recognised in the 2007 local government corporate governance framework[12] (based on the six core principles recommended by Sir Alan Langlands[13] in 2004) and introduced by:

Good governance leads to good management, good performance, good stewardship of public money, good public engagement and ultimately, good outcomes for citizens and service users. Good governance enables an authority to pursue its vision effectively as well as underpinning that vision with mechanisms for control and management of risk. All authorities should aim to meet the standards of the best and governance arrangements should not only be sound but also be seen to be sound.

Messages in this framework are important aspirations for all internal auditing:

- Engaging stakeholders and making accountability real
- Performing effectively in clearly defined functions and roles
- Promoting values for the whole organisation and demonstrating good governance through behaviour
- Developing the capacity and capability of the governing body to be effective
- Taking informed, transparent decisions and managing risk
- Focusing on the organisation's purpose and on outcomes for citizens and users.

Risk management has always been an important tool for analysing and evaluating risks and opportunities for all travellers along the road to Excellence. COSO[14] also recognises this in its enterprise risk management model (ERM):

Enterprise risk management helps ensure effective reporting and compliance with laws and regulations, and helps avoid damage to the entity's reputation and associated consequences. In sum, enterprise risk management helps an entity get to where it wants to go and avoid pitfalls and surprises along the way.

Travellers have to be much more aware of the societal and environmental issues organisations face today. That awareness is recognised at government and local government levels by government departments and in the CIPFA[15] sustainability framework for the public services – a practical guide to measuring and reporting sustainability performance. Sustainability as a vision is influencing many decisions in all organisations today and will continue to do so. It cannot be overlooked as internal auditing travels its road to Excellence. Use this framework as you follow the practical steps in helping your organisations to manage risk along their roads to Excellence. These are well set out in your guide[16] for risk based auditing.

The following internal auditing attributes have grown in importance and value in all local government organisations today. All can be seen on the road to Excellence. All are at the cutting edge of internal auditing practices. Keep looking for these as you explore and travel your own roads to Excellence, always anticipating the risks and opportunities that lie ahead and around your:

Achieving World-Class status
Wearing many hats
Knowing how to govern well
Fighting crime
Assisting those that manage at all levels
Commitment to total quality
Benchmarking for best practices
Continuously Improving
Being Creative
Asking the right questions
Contributing to good reputations
Promoting the best professional internal auditing services
Managing knowledge well.

These are all explored in my book[17] using the following signposts:

INSPIRE
EXPLORE
IMAGINE
IMPROVE
INNOVATE
CREATE.

All pointing to a cutting edge future horizon along your road to Excellence, with a white line as a 'highway' code of practice and surrounding fields of economic, social and environmental risks and opportunities.
All requiring a vision; leadership at all levels; a focus on customers; measures that correct; interlocking teamwork; and, continuous improvement.

Achievement of Excellence, like beauty is in the eye of the beholder. Whatever auditors think of the services they are providing, it is the receiver of that service that sees and measures the quality and Excellence of the service, be it at the beginning, during or end of the service being provided. Excellence is not a one-off measure. It is a continuous measure throughout the service, sometimes there long after the service has been provided. We know this from all the services we receive ourselves, at work, at home, in our travels and in society itself. We constantly measure the services we receive and what others provide. And so it is with auditing. Today, we are reminded of this in many different ways through the use of 'customer surveys' by organisations keen to receive their customers' views on the products and services they have bought or are buying. These take many forms from immediate responses to telephone requests and form filling questionnaires. Even some auditors now do this – but I suspect not yet all.

When I introduced customer survey questionnaires in my audit department in the 1980s, these were given to the customer at the end of the audit with a request to be completed and returned to the department. They were then analysed, concerns responded to and feedback given to the customer and board. After a while we decided to give the questionnaires out at the beginning of the audit engagement with some explanation as to what our customers should expect from an Excellent audit. This had a more positive response from our customers and at the same time reinforced with the auditors the Excellence standard in the service they were expected to provide. Today, the providing of a questionnaire at the beginning of a service is more common. Some are sceptical about the use and benefit of such questionnaires. My view is if they only provide a reminder to the giver and receiver of a service of the standard of Excellence required by an auditor's profession and charter, they are a useful prompt to achieve Excellence.

In each of the parts and chapters in my book I have touched on and referenced into the Excellence, Improvement and Innovation by many organisations and other authors. In Table D.1 I show how in each of the publications in Table C.1 these word/terms can be found underlying the messages they send out to the world. In today and tomorrow's global market place of governments, professions, economic activity, developments and civic societies, Excellence', 'Improvement' and 'Innovation' will always be key to the success of any activity. Each is created by research, benchmarking and running in every activity. Each will have to be in auditing if it is to provide the services its customers want and need in the 21st century.

In 2016 the UK Government published a Green Paper on corporate governance reform for consultation and in August 2017[18] published its views on how corporate governance should be changed in the future 'Putting in place higher expectations for all our largest companies, and in particular for our leading, premium listed companies, should also encourage the development and uptake of good practice in the wider business community.' Without exception all the words/terms in Table D.1 are in the Government's recommendations, including innovation 'Our best companies . . . invest in their workforce's skills, and are a source of creativity and innovation, knowing that this is the way to succeed in the long term.' A significant endorsement of this TABLE, the publications it represents and creative thinking and innovation in all auditing.

Table D.1 Excellence – Improvement – Innovation in Table C.1

	Industry	Finance	Charity	Health	Profess	EFMD	INTOSAI	Global	COSO	Global	FRC
Part I											
Stewardship											
Accountability	Y	Y	Y	Y	Y	Y	Y	Y	Y	Y	Y
Behaviour	Y	Y	Y	Y	Y	Y	Y	Y	Y	Y	Y
Beliefs	Y	Y	Y	Y	Y	Y	Y	Y	Y	Y	Y
Care	Y	Y	Y	Y	Y	Y	Y	Y	Y	Y	Y
Compliance	Y	Y	Y	Y	Y	Y	Y	Y	Y	Y	Y
Culture	Y	Y	Y	Y	Y	Y	Y	Y	Y	Y	Y
Customer	Y	Y	Y	Y	Y	Y	Y	Y	Y	Y	Y
Duty	Y	Y	Y	Y	Y	Y	Y	Y	Y	Y	Y
Ethics	Y	Y	Y	Y	Y	Y	Y	Y	Y	Y	Y
Governance	Y	Y	Y	Y	Y	Y	Y	Y	Y	Y	Y
Law	Y	Y	Y	Y	Y	Y	Y	Y	Y	Y	Y
Leadership	Y	Y	Y	Y	Y	Y	Y	Y	Y	Y	Y
Principles	Y	Y	Y	Y	Y	Y	Y	Y	Y	Y	Y
Responsibilities	Y	Y	Y	Y	Y	Y	Y	Y	Y	Y	Y
Stakeholder	Y	Y	Y	Y	Y	Y	Y	Y	Y	Y	Y
Stewardship	Y	Y	Y	Y	Y	Y	Y	Y	Y	Y	Y
Supplier	Y	Y	Y	Y	Y	Y	Y	Y	Y	Y	Y
Sustainability	Y	Y	Y	Y	Y	Y	Y	Y	Y	Y	Y
Transparent	Y	Y	Y	Y	Y	Y	Y	Y	Y	Y	Y
Trust	Y	Y	Y	Y	Y	Y	Y	Y	Y	Y	Y
Values	Y	Y	Y	Y	Y	Y	Y	Y	Y	Y	Y
Chapter 2											
Leadership											
Collaboration	Y	Y	Y	Y	Y	Y	Y	Y	Y	Y	Y
Partnership	Y	Y	Y	Y	Y	Y	Y	Y	Y	Y	Y
Manage	Y	Y	Y	Y	Y	Y	Y	Y	Y	Y	Y
Chapter 3											
Diplomat											
Represent	Y	Y	Y	Y	Y	Y	Y	Y	Y	Y	Y
State	Y	Y	Y	Y	Y	Y	Y	Y	Y	Y	Y
Brand	Y	Y	Y	Y	Y	Y	Y	Y	Y	Y	Y
Chapter 4											
Gatekeepers											
Defend	Y	Y	Y	Y	Y	Y	Y	Y	Y	Y	Y
Protect	Y	Y	Y	Y	Y	Y	Y	Y	Y	Y	Y
Monitor	Y	Y	Y	Y	Y	Y	Y	Y	Y	Y	Y
Part II											
Change											
Change	Y	Y	Y	Y	Y	Y	Y	Y	Y	Y	Y
Risk	Y	Y	Y	Y	Y	Y	Y	Y	Y	Y	Y
Future	Y	Y	Y	Y	Y	Y	Y	Y	Y	Y	Y
Part III											
Assurance											
Assurance	Y	Y	Y	Y	Y	Y	Y	Y	Y	Y	Y
Audit	Y	Y	Y	Y	Y	Y	Y	Y	Y	Y	Y
Quality	Y	Y	Y	Y	Y	Y	Y	Y	Y	Y	Y
Part IV											
Excellence											
Excellence	Y	Y	Y	Y	Y	Y	Y	Y	Y	Y	Y
Improvement	Y	Y	Y	Y	Y	Y	Y	Y	Y	Y	Y
Innovation	Y	Y	Y	Y	Y	Y	Y	Y	Y	Y	Y

Creative Audit Thinking Activities

Activity 40   Create Innovation from Butterflies

The *butterfly effect* is a principle used frequently in fiction, but also seen as a main principle in chaos theory. It is described by mathematician Edward Lorenz as a small effect in one part of the world that can, through time, make a significant difference in another part of the world – metaphorically stated, the flutter of a butterfly wing in one country may in time create a cyclone in another. Steps in an audit trail can also have butterfly effects. Whether the step is at the beginning, during, end or after, there can, in time, be significant global effects across the world, in both the output and outcome of the audit. Consider the following experience of mine in 2015. Do the EXCELLENT Strategies, Structures, Systems, Skills, Styles, Staff and Shared Values it contains apply along your audit trails? In today's global political and market place, can your creative audit thinking activities and innovation make differences across the world, for those you audit and their stakeholders?

The Butterfly Effect

Make a World of Difference along Your Audit Trails

On a visit to London in 2015 I travelled with my granddaughters Lucy and Daisy, both talented musicians. We were in London to see and listen to an open-air big screen performance of *Don Giovanni* in Trafalgar Square – the well-known opera with music by Wolfgang Amadeus Mozart and Italian libretto by Lorenzo Da Ponte, based on the legends of Don Juan. Did Mozart realise when it was first performed in 1787, the effects his composition would have throughout the world and across time – its butterfly effect? Not just in its performance and future performances, but the effects it would have on musicians, conductors, theatres, performers, stage hands and audiences in so many countries across the world over time and in today's global environment? Its music and libretto also required and still does depend upon supporting talents from inventors of instruments and audio technicians in many countries. Like all music, an opera represents an achievement of creative thinking and innovation by not just its composer but by many supporting talents. All operas require many **EXCELLENT Strategies, Structures, Systems, Skills, Styles, Staff and Shared Values** to achieve their peak in performance. When I commented to Lucy and Daisy that we did not have the best position to view the screen they replied as a musician would – to listen to the music was sufficient. Interestingly both audio and audit have a common derivative from the Latin verb to listen. Do we as auditors always listen enough in our auditing and in a creative and innovative way?

We also visited the View From The Shard, the tallest viewing platform in London – another peak in performance. The Shard is also the tallest building in Western Europe, six times the height of Nelson's Column in Trafalgar Square. The trails of its **EXCELLENT Strategies, Structures, Systems, Skills, Styles, Staff and Shared Values** over a period of fifteen years came from imaginative contributions by many from many countries. Built on an irregular site alongside the London Bridge Quarter it shines with environmental and social friendly features. Not just in its construction but also with how it is and will be operated and managed. It is a monument to creative thinking and innovation. Its future impact on the London skyline will go beyond England to all corners of the world – it will have a butterfly effect.

It was a hot day and I bought a bottle of One Water.[19] In size, compared with the Shard it was a small dot. Yet, that bottle and the water it contained had travelled a similar trail to the Shard of **EXCELLENT Strategies, Structures, Systems, Skills, Styles, Staff and Shared Values**. Equally it shone with environmental and social friendly features. The steps in its water trail had started in Wales and reached me in a bottle made of recycled material and containing a strong message of Chaos Theory and its butterfly effect:

> According to Chaos Theory the tiny flutter of a butterfly's wing can cause a cyclone on the other side of the world. It's how we think about our work at One, because 100 per cent of our profit funds life-changing water projects in the world's harshest regions.

Three creative and innovative butterfly effects in one day – each with **EXCELLENT** economic. environmental and social impacts across the world. There were certainly others that had an effect on our travels that day. There will always be many more for me, Lucy and Daisy. Look for these in your creative and innovative auditing.

Activity 41 Create Excellence From Innovative Measures

Study the creative thinking and innovative Ten Step Audit Process in Figure 1.5 repeated below. Consider the McKinsey 7S's Framework requirements discussed in Part IV for the Ten Step Audit Process. What innovative measures can you develop for your own audit processes to achieve Excellence?

Innovative Measures for the Ten Step Audit Process: Creative Thinking and Innovation in the Ten Step Audit Process

1   Create the audit vision and strategy to **MOTIVATE** excellence, quality and add value and improvement in the **EXPERTISE** and **SKILLS** needed in all auditing processes.
2   Plan each audit engagement over a period of time.
3   Seek insight into operations being audited – their theory and best practices, through **ASSOCIATION: QUESTIONING: OBSERVING: NETWORKING**.
4   Assess risks involved by the operations being audited and the audit.
5   Establish scope and objectives for the audit engagement.
6   Develop a risk-based audit programme and identify controls.
7   Select techniques/methodology and **EXPERIMENT** to search for appropriate evidence.
8   Objectively evaluate audit outputs, consider outcomes and agree findings.
9   Communicate audit findings to those accountable.
10   Follow-up and consider actions taken by the organisation.

Activity 42   Create Excellence From Competent Teamwork

Consider the following statement on Competent Teamwork from EFMD (2005) *Globally Responsible Leadership – A Call for Engagement*.[20] Compare this with how you define competent teamwork in your auditing to achieve Excellence in the products and services you are providing.

Statement 1

The core of corporate action is creativity. Observe successful companies over the medium or longer term, and you will notice one thing that they share: pulled by daring leadership, many have adapted, renewed and/or transformed themselves, proving their capacity to act creatively. Creativity is a concrete blend of human commitments and qualitative realities. These can include a clearly stated and widely shared vision; the willingness to take risks and face up to uncertainty; listening and learning; the weaving of strong relationship networks; the patient build-up of diversified approaches; the productive management of tensions and efforts; **the recruitment and shaping of competent teams and leadership at**

all levels. Instruction or training may enhance creativity, but only in a highly supportive environment that encourages individual initiative, trial and error, risk taking and learning from both positive and negative experiences. Given that many of the most creative impulses arise from distress, ambiguity and uncertainty, the challenge of enabling such thresholds in a learning and development environment is not to be underestimated.

Notes

1 *Globally Responsible Leadership – A Call for Engagement* (2005 p. 37), European Foundation for Management Development (EFMD), Brussels, Belgium.
2 *EFQM Open Doors Day*. efqm.org, accessed 11 January 2016 and 15 April 2016.
3 *In Search of Excellence* (1982), Tom Peters and Robert H. Waterman Jr.
4 *Little Big Things: 163 Ways to Pursue Excellence* (2010), Tom Peters, Harper Business, New York, US.
5 *The Audit Quality Framework* (2008), Financial Reporting Council, London, England.
6 *The Road to Quality and Excellence Takes You to the Cutting Edge* (2008). Audit Viewpoint Issue 85, Chartered Institute of Public Finance and Accountancy, London, England.
7 *A Balanced Scorecard Framework for Internal Auditing Departments* (2002), Mark L. Frigo, The IIA Research Foundation, Orlando, US. www.theiia.org
8 *Business Excellence Model* (1999), European Foundation for Quality Management (EFQM). www.efqm.org
9 *Code of Practice for Internal Audit in Local Government in the United Kingdom* (2006), The Chartered Institute of Public Finance and Accountancy, London, England. www.cipfa.org
10 *Innovation Nation* (March 2008) Department for Innovation, Universities and Skills (Presented to Parliament by the Secretary of State for Innovation, Universities and Skills, the Chancellor of the Exchequer and the Secretary of State for Business Enterprise and Regulatory Reform by Command of Her Majesty), Cm 7345. www.dius.gov.uk
11 *The Excellent Internal Auditor: A Good Practice Guide to Skills and Competencies* (2006), The Chartered Institute of Public Finance and Accountancy, London, England.
12 *Going Forward with Good Governance* (2007), Office for Public Management Ltd www.opm.co.uk and The Chartered Institute of Public Finance and Accountancy, London, England.
13 *The Good Governance Standard for Public Services* (2004), The Independent Commission for Corporate Governance in Public Services, Office for Public Management Ltd www.opm.co.uk and The Chartered Institute of Public Finance and Accountancy, London, England.
14 *Enterprise Risk Management – Integrated Framework Executive Summary* (2004) Committee of Sponsoring Organizations of the Treadway Commission, USA. www.coso.org
15 *Sustainability in the Public Sector* (2005), The Chartered Institute of Public Finance and Accountancy, London, England.
16 *It's a Risky Business: Risk Based Auditing* (2005), The Chartered Institute of Public Finance and Accountancy, London, England.
17 *Cutting Edge Internal Auditing* (2008), Jeffrey Ridley, John Wiley and Sons, Chichester, England.
18 *Corporate Governance Reform* (2017 pp. 1, 5), Department for Business, Energy & Industrial Strategy, London, England.
19 One, a registered Charity in the United Kingdom, is a certified 'Carbon Neutral' company. www.onedifference.org
20 *Globally Responsible Leadership – a Call for Engagement* (2005 p. 19), European Foundation for Management Development (EFMD), Brussels, Belgium.

11 Auditors Are Researchers

Mind Power rightly developed and applied to proper ends can produce anything whatever in the life and circumstances of anyone.[1]

In this chapter I discuss the role of auditors as researchers. All auditors research and create knowledge that will change auditing practices recommend change in the principles and practices of governance, risk management and control; changing policies and procedures in their organisations, not only to create knowledge but inspire Change by innovation in the Stewardship of the organisations they audit. As important as the passion for and marketing of its independent and objective reviews, duty of care and scepticism, is a passion to research. Researchers are motivated in what they see, hear, examine and evaluate into the outputs and outcomes of their findings, conclusions and recommendations – so should all auditors.

11.1 Researchers Are Auditors

In Chapter 7 I reference an Excellent book on knowledge – *Wisdom of the Ages* – from which the chapter epigraph is taken:

> My first introduction to futurism was in the early 1950s when I came across the term 'Mind Power' in a book given to me by my parents at the start of my life's adventures – *Wisdom of the Ages* (1936) by Mark Gilbert[2] – '*An assembly of two hundred everyday subjects by four hundred great Thinkers of thirty nations extending over five thousand years*'. Futurism is not mentioned, though many of the quotations in the book influenced visions of what might and should be at their time, and still do today.

Although not stated in the book, it was written after considerable research by the author and all the authors of the quotations in the book. In all that research, the author and his selected authors were acting as auditors – creating from enquiring minds and a search of knowledge new understandings and guidance for their futures and the futures of others.

There are now many researched publications on auditing containing creative thinking and innovative ideas for the future of auditing. This has not always been so. Such publications were few before the mid-20th century. What there was, mostly related to financial auditing – its principles and practices and study material for professional accounting and auditing qualifications. In the latter half of the last century and today, there are many publications on all types of auditing by many authors with Excellent guidance for their auditing practices, updating their standards and syllabi of professional auditing qualifications. This research will continue to grow this century, fuelled by auditors, their research, other researchers, professions and regulators. All the signs for this to happen are there today across the world. From this research and its guidance for practice, innovations will change future auditing practices and its reporting.

In 2007 my colleague and friend, Professor D'Silva, and I researched innovative practices in internal auditing in the United Kingdom, presenting a paper at the Fifth European Academic Conference, University of Pisa, Italy.[3] One of the conclusions of that research suggested more attention should be paid to the expansion of internal auditing services and skills through innovation:

> The pattern that tends to emerge from the research in relation to current U.K. Internal Audit innovation is one that suggests higher attention in terms of innovation is being paid to quality and efficiency with less attention being devoted to the expansion of services and the boosting of staff skills and performance. If so, there is a professional tension here, as much of the professional literature suggests that, for most professions, it is in the expansion of services and boosting of staff skills and performance that innovative resources and practices are most needed.

In 2012 we again researched innovation in internal auditing presenting a paper at the 10th European Academic Conference on Internal Audit and Corporate

Governance at the University of Verona, Italy. Our research abstract at the start of the research (our plan and strategy) read as follows. Although focused on internal auditing, its theme and the following research could apply to all auditing with only some changes to the references and sources:

Creativity and Innovation: Keys to a Successful Future for Internal Auditing[4]

ABSTRACT

Research context, motivation and objectives

It is often alleged that the continued pursuance and success of many activities is closely tied in with the ability of that activity to be undertaken and performed in increasingly creative and innovative ways. Accordingly, the purpose of this research is to provide a reflective analysis of past, current and future issues, in terms of creativity and innovation by considering appropriate theory (the theoretical research) and then evaluating this by reference to an Internal Audit department – using that department as the case unit (the empirical research).

RESEARCH DESIGN/METHODOLOGY/APPROACH

Consistent with the dual objectives of the research, two forms of research design and methods are employed within it. The theoretical research is undertaken by completing a review and evaluative analysis of relevant (primarily theoretical and-or professional) literature – particularly of theoretical creativity and innovation models that have been advanced. Inter alia, within an internal auditing context, these theoretical models draw on issues such as motivations, goals and categories of innovation. The empirical research is completed by undertaking a Case Study analysis (primarily through interviews and document consideration) within a particular case, so as to determine how well the previously identified theory resonates within the case unit and to then draw evaluating inferences. Within the relevant case unit, the research attempts to reveal how creativity and innovation adds status and value to internal auditing – particularly in relation to its current and future roles and practices. The case unit is an internal audit activity operating in a social housing and care services group. Its 2011 Group income was circa £40 million and in that year it employed circa 1,000 staff. Its internal audit department has evolved over recent years into operating in a Continuous Improvement and Risk Management Unit reporting to a board member and with an independent line to a Group Board Corporate Governance Committee. Against that back drop, it was judged to be an appropriate case for study in relation to the empirical objectives of the research.

FINDINGS/LIMITATIONS

Our research enables two types of findings. The first is offered in terms of the general utility and effectiveness of key theories of creativity and innovation within the context of the quality and continuous improvement of internal audit services in the Group, while relating these to an increase in value in terms of its contribution to good governance, risk management and control. The second set of findings is an evaluation of the resonance of key theories of innovation and creativity within the internal audit department of the relevant case unit. As is the case for all case studies, the findings of the present case are limited and non – generalisable. However, such findings may well be indicative of institutions in other sectors and sizes of internal audit departments, both in the United Kingdom and globally because of the nature of its compliance to international professional standards.

ORIGINALITY/VALUE

The importance of creativity and innovation in professional internal auditing has always been strongly driven by its global professional body The Institute of Internal Auditors Inc.[5] In part, this has been influenced by increased and changing demands of corporate boards and senior management as well as the imagination of its ambitious members. Concurrently, there has been some encouragement from internal audit management and other stakeholders who take an accountability and interest perspective in the added value of internal auditing services. This is evidenced from related research and compliance with the continuous improvement of its "International Professional Practices Framework" of standards and guidance. Prior research into innovation in internal auditing has been mainly in large internal audit activities. However, our research recognises that the majority of internal auditing activities are small with limited resources and therefore deliberately focuses its research into creativity and innovation processes with that level of size and activity.

PAPER TYPE

As indicated, the research is both theoretical and empirical. The theoretical research determines how creativity and innovation are being promoted in organisations and internal audit activities – at both strategic and operational levels. The empirical research seeks to do the same through an examination of (but) one internal auditing department and the environment within which that service is provided.

KEYWORDS

Continuous improvement, creativity, innovation, internal auditing, quality.

The final paper presented at the conference and published in its proceedings is at Appendix K. Although not researched and evaluated as an audit process, the creative thinking and innovative steps of the Ten Step Audit Process at Figure 1.5 in Chapter 1 can be seen in its research methodology with the exception of the important follow-up step – look for the other steps in the final research paper. Also, note the metaphors Leadership, Time Traveller, Researcher, Quality Manager and Benchmarker used in this book are referred to in the paper; the other metaphors used for auditors are not, though all are implied in parts of the discussion.

At a recent research master class, I was asked to give a talk on my research into this book and was followed by two other talks given by my research colleagues, one on the planning and development of research and the other on organisation structures and empowerment of staff. In each of these talks, innovation and its importance in today's world was touched on by me and the other professors.

My own talk opened reflecting on the values and beliefs currently seen in cultures across the world communicated by many organisations to their stakeholders across all sectors on an annual, if not in some cases on a daily basis through websites displaying vision and mission statements, codes of conduct and compliance with governance codes and standards. I also discussed the importance all researchers attach to collecting pebbles of knowledge during their careers – seeking to turn these into gems in future research activities and encourage others to do so. My own collection of pebbles includes the gems below, each of which is becoming more valuable for my own future research, auditing, leadership at all levels, regulars and governments across the world:.

The links between CORPORATE GOVERNANCE, QUALITY PER-
    FORMANCE and SUSTAINABILITY
The links between RESPONSIBLE LEADERSHIP and VALUES
The links between CREATIVE THINKING and INNOVATION
The links between AUDITING CONSULTING and ASSURANCE

Knowledge needed to create the theories and principles that have formed the practices in these links has been growing over many centuries, but even more so in the 20th and now 21st century. The availability and speed and explosion of that knowledge and its spread across then planet are now unstoppable. The result is an inevitable growth in creative thinking and innovations in all practices, including auditing. At least one of these links, if not each, should be considered in every research into Stewardship, Change, Assurance and Excellence whatever its aim(s) and objectives.

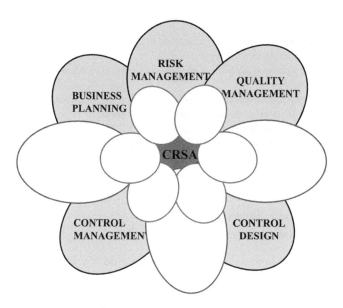

Figure 11.1 Control self-assessment 'Daisy'

Source: J. Ridley (2016) (Adapted from Figure 1.1 in *Control Self Assessment for Risk Management and Other Practical Applications* (1999), Chapter by Keith Wade, Edited by Keith Wade and Andy Wynne, John Wiley and Sons, Chichester, England

I used in my talk the 'Daisy' in Figure 11.1 adapted from the book *Control Self-Assessment: For Risk Management (1999)* (see Creative Thinking Activity 30 in Part III). The petals with names appeared in the original 'Daisy'. I added more to represent changes to assurance risk and control issues since 1999, many discussed in this book. I leave the reader to fill in the other petal. For a start consider *Responsible Leadership: Innovation: Governance: Security: Sustainability: Values.* By adding more 'petals' to the daisy, aim for each to inspire new creative thinking and innovation in the approach to your next audit.

Professor Kenneth D'Silva[6] followed my talk with a discussion on the role of theory within governance research, its nature and significance within empirical research and design. His explanations of qualitative and quantitative research can be seen in many auditing practices and should be understood by all auditors – see Figure 11.2. An understanding of each of the terms in his classification can open new and innovative doors in the design of auditing techniques.

Included in Professor D'Silva's talk was guidance to students and academic staff on the importance of forms of theory linkage, from new theory, its enhancement and testing, leading to the creation of theoretical models from the results of gathering data and its analysis. Analysis of quantitative and qualitative data and the links between each is key to the success of every audit and basic requirement in the Ten Step Audit Process: leading to research (and audit) reporting of findings, practical suggestions, policy contributions and good

- • **Interpretivist** (emerging ex observations and consistent with **inductive** logic and thinking) – exploratory linkage
- • Seeks the existence (or not) of **phenomena** by using **evolving** research methods in the design
- • Other terms include revolutionist, phenomenological, humanistic and **qualitative**
- • **Positivist** (emerging ex and consistent with **deductive** logic and thinking – empiricism) – confirmatory linkage
- • Seeks **causality** by using '**scientific**' (predetermined and/or semi-fixed) methods
- • Other terms include scientific, objectivist, experimentalist traditionalist and **quantitative**.

Figure 11.2 Key research classifications

Source: Professor Kenneth D'Silva (2016)

practice; leading to 'better outcomes – better world – values' for the function and organisation and civil societies.

Professor D'Silva's research design ingredients are an essential part of the design of an audit engagement and should be understood by every auditor, starting with its aim(s) and leading into:

- • research objective(s)
- • theoretical 'linkage'
- • appropriate research method(s)
- • appropriate relevant data (evidence)
- • appropriate analytical approach supported by suitable tools and techniques
- • limitations and assumptions
- • ethical implications
- • all above captured within a research plan (proposal).

Note the similarities with the steps 1–6 in my Ten Step Audit Process – preparation of an audit assignment – planning appropriate resources, insight, establish objectives and development of audit programme. Continuous innovation and how this will be motivated and researched will be key to the successful completion of each of these steps through the 21st century. These same steps are used by researchers all over the world, in organisations and universities to develop creative thinking and innovate in their findings.

At the same research master class, Professor Paul Moxey discussed his presentation at a recent Control Risk Self Assessment (CRSA) Forum (www.crsa-forum.com), a presentation based on Frederick Laloux's (2014) research on reinventing the organisation from how it has developed over the centuries to a new 'way of life' with more empowerment, trust and public interest:

> All wisdom traditions posit the profound truth that there are two fundamental ways to live life: from fear and scarcity or from trust and

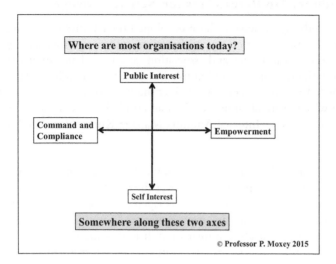

Figure 11.3 Where are most organisations today?

Source: Professor Paul Moxey (2015)

abundance. In Evolutionary-Teal, we cross the chasm and learn to decrease our need to control people and events. We come to believe that even if something unexpected happens or if we make mistakes, things will turn out all right, and when they don't, life will have given us an opportunity to learn and grow.

The results of Professor Moxey's research showed that most organisations today are in a self-interest, control and compliance mode – see Figure 11.3. This gave the forum an opportunity to discuss this status and the effects of changes in organisations to greater empower people and interest not just primary stakeholders but a wider public in an organisation's operations and results. The effect of such a change will need innovative changes to the auditing and assurances being provided by auditors at all levels in their organisations and externally. In some organisations and in the auditing professions, this is happening today.

It has been shown in some research control and compliance in an organisation can reduce motivation for continuous improvement, quality, creativity and innovation at all levels. Today's researched global and national motivations and requirements for sustainability strategies and reporting are clearly designed for more public interest in and by organisation decision-making: this is now evidenced by the United Nations global research and work promoting sustainability targets over the past twenty years and its recently developed Sustainability Goals addressed to all organisations across the world – see Appendix H – and their reporting and assurance requirements. Not only have these goals required considerable global research, but now and in the future their achievement will have to be audited and improvements made by the same researchers.

11.2 Auditors Are Researchers for New Knowledge

All of the auditing professions have developed their professional standards and guidance on research, often in collaboration with each other and often with other professional institutes and associations at national and international levels, often with governments and non-government organisations. Research into new knowledge and its management is at the heart of all professional development. So why not in all audit work? In an article I wrote in 2012 following a visit to Dubai ('Wise Internal Auditors Manage Knowledge Well'), I referred to this:

> Those that study and advise on knowledge management in organisations have written well on this subject over the past ten years. Both as a product of learning and as an important management tool to motivate and stimulate innovation. Knowledge management is a means of developing, capturing and communicating information. It is also about wisdom – searching information to improve strategic thinking and decision-making processes. Most good knowledge management processes now use electronic methods to ensure all information available is being used to best advantage for the organisation and its staff. Gates (1999)[7] discusses the value of an electronic library of knowledge in all organisations ' . . . *to gather and organize information, disseminate the information to people who need it, and constantly refine the information through analysis and collaboration.'* His simplified definition of knowledge management is ' . . . *nothing more than managing information flow.'* But is management of information flow enough and can it ever be simplified? In most organisations management of information flow is one of the most difficult tasks. Too often disorganised and not always used wisely.

In the course of writing this book, I have tried to manage knowledge well from researching auditing and innovation extensively, both in the past over many years as academic and writer. Before that, over many years as an auditor, I researched knowledge in a long list of strategies, structures, systems, skills, staff, skills and shared values at board, executive and operation levels, associated with an equally long list of audit engagements over the same many years across all sectors in the United Kingdom and internationally. As an auditor, I believe auditing is all about research, and a search for new knowledge and its management – a search which in cross-functional teams, seeking insights into how an organisation or part of an organisation operates, locally, nationally and internationally to achieve its objectives economically, efficiently and effectively in an environmental and ethically friendly way.

Each of the components of my corporate governance framework of **STEWARDSHIP, CHANGE, ASSURANCE** and **EXCELLENCE** is based on theories and developed concepts to create principles of management and good corporate governance. These principles all have an influence on creativity and innovation. Today there are many researchers, auditors and practitioners across the world researching all the components in my framework. New theories will emerge in the future with new principles and codes of practice. It is essential there is participation by auditors in this research and they contribute to both its output and outcomes. They have a wealth of knowledge to contribute.

The same theories and an earlier version of the framework were included and discussed throughout my book *Cutting Edge Internal Auditing* (2008) (referenced in this book) and its seventy case studies contributed by authors across the world. These themes and their underpinning theories will generate new knowledge and continue to influence all auditing and its practices throughout the 21st century, impacting the quality of their work, as perceived by auditors and all those they audit. They will be the driving force for creative thinking and innovation by many auditors – hopefully all! They will also be the concern of all regulators, governments and professional associations and the standard setters for all auditing practices. The researched case studies included in *Cutting Edge Internal Auditing* listed in Figure 11.4, and the new knowledge messages

---

World-Class Internal Auditing in the United Nations
Key Attributes, Strategies and Actions for World-Class Internal Auditing
Internal Audit Consulting provides Cutting Edge Opportunities
Internal Auditors as Facilitators of Risk Management
Internal Audit and Ethics
Corporate Governance and Internal Audit
The Stop Light Model
Key Questions for an Audit Committee
A Unique Approach for External Quality Assessment
Internal Auditors Too can be Quality Champions
Use a Delphi Study to develop Best Practice Internal Auditing
Continuous Improvement in Internal Auditing is a Must not a Luxury
Implementing Teamwork for Continuous Improvement – The Drive Model
Innovative Practices in Today's Internal Auditing
Performance Measurement and Innovation in Internal Auditing
Creative Problem Solving for Internal Auditors
Succeeding Through Innovation
Creativity, Innovation and Change
Why Study Creativity – Here are Twelve Solid Reasons
An Internal Auditing Contribution to Good Reputation
Risk and Control Issues for Health, Safety and the Environment
Reputational Risk the Challenge for Internal Audit
Auditing Sustainable Development
Meeting New Demands
There are no more Internal Audit Experts only *Communities Of Practices* Experts
Internal Auditing is Re-branding Itself
Opportunities for Strategic Innovation – Examination Question
Issues that will Impact Internal Auditing in the 21st Century

---

Figure 11.4 Examples of case studies in *Cutting Edge Internal Auditing* (2008) relevant to *Creative Thinking and Innovation* for all auditing

Source: *Cutting Edge Internal Auditing* (2008)

each title contains, will influence future creative thinking and innovation in the future of all auditing practices.

The same theories can be seen in all the following twelve metaphors I have given to every auditor in this book. I invite you to add more from your own auditing experiences:

Responsible Leader	Scientist	Quality Manager
Ambassador	Futurist	Researcher
Gatekeeper	Sceptic	Bench Marker
Time Traveller	Lawyer	Runner

In 2006 I supervised an academic lecturer in his successful PhD research into internal auditing communities of practice. At the time, Ronald Lackland directed a very successful postgraduate programme in auditing and risk management at Birmingham City University, which was a forerunner of a similar postgraduate programme still offered today to both national and international students. He produced a case study for my book *Cutting Edge Internal Auditing*. Its themes of teamwork, partnerships and learning in the search for and creation of knowledge are very relevant today and tomorrow for all auditors, not just in their audit teams but across their supply chains, from supplier to customer. Its messages are based on his research and appropriate to this chapter and every audit engagement. In his research he quotes from my own research with Professor Andrew Chambers in the 1990s:

> Ridley and Chambers also identified the following emerging best and successful internal auditing practices promulgated by The IIA as new and 'leading edge' activities that can be embraced and incorporated within communities of practices:
>
> • developing a partnering role with audit clients and utilising integrated auditing (Participative Auditing; Total Quality Management and Control Self-Assessment Techniques),
> • educating management and the board of directors on their internal control, governance and risk management responsibilities (COSO and CoCo Control Frameworks; Enterprise Risk Management),
> • utilising self-directed, integrated work teams (Participative Auditing; Control Self- Assessment Techniques),
> • external quality assurance reviews of internal auditing practices (Best Practice Benchmarking; Professional Practice Framework),
> • emphasising TQM principles and applying them aggressively (Total Quality Management; Best Practice Benchmarking and Balanced Scorecard Framework),
> • utilising computer-assisted techniques (Continuous Auditing and Information Technology Assurance),

- audits of environment, health and safety (Corporate Social Responsibility Framework; and Best Practice Benchmarking),
- developing a formal risk assessment system involving management (COSO and CoCo Control Frameworks; Enterprise Risk Management; Best Practice Benchmarking and Balanced Scorecard Framework),
- empowering staff to experiment with a variety of approaches in developing innovative solutions to problems (Control Self-Assessment Techniques; Best Practice Benchmarking and Balanced Scorecard Framework),
- providing internal consulting services, such as focusing on problem solving rather than problem finding (Total Quality Management; Best Practice Benchmarking and Balanced Scorecard Framework).

Furthermore, Ridley and Chambers stated that, 'all of these trends are encouraging internal auditing experimentation and development of leading edge practices'. Thus, an internal audit function establishing communities of practices fulfils a number of functions with respect to the creation, accumulation, and diffusion of intellectual capital.

Furthermore, an internal audit function constructing communities of practices inside and outside the function creates a knowledge universe, which will help develop its own intellectual capital and add value to the organisation's intellectual capital. Such communities of practice will indeed produce 'cutting edge' results. More importantly, the internal audit function can retain and maintain such intellectual capital in 'living ways,' for instance, audit report repositories that all internal auditors can access and share information, via Internet and Intranet.

An internal audit function establishing communities of practices with members from across the organisations it serves, can share the intellectual capital of the entire organisation, and assist senior management in keeping the organisation in a sustainable advantageous 'cutting edge' position. This in turn will prevent the internal audit function from becoming conservative by nature; obstructing creativity and innovation, and; demotivating the spirit of entrepreneurship or even stifling organisational learning. To this end, collective human capital in an internal audit function with structural and relational capital is the most ideal situation; however, it requires more than just internal auditors learning from each other. Collective learning outcomes require that internal auditors develop a shared understanding and awareness about the learning process and the new intellectual capital that is developed as a result of this as depicted in Figure 11.5.

11.3 Researching Auditors Seek Continuous Improvement

Continuous improvement is key to the achievement of Excellence in every activity. This concept can be seen in every walk of life, every occupation, every profession, from birth onwards. In research the researcher, like an auditor, is seeking fact, opinion and evidence to achieve objectives, which include ideas

Shared Human Capital Domain:

• the Common Body of Knowledge for Internal Auditing (CBOK).
• common Ground (shared discourse reflecting the Standards/Code of Ethics of internal auditing).
• sense of Common Identity (The Professional Practice Framework; Due Diligence; Maintaining auditor's 'Independence' to be 'Objective'.
• shared (learning) Interdependent Knowledge (independent expertise of audit engagements in assurance, consulting and facilitation is fostered as well-tacit knowledge transferred into explicit knowledge into collective knowledge.

Shared Structural Capital Domain:

• vision, Values and Strategies.
• charter, Manual and Reports.
• IT Working Systems.
• internal Processes.
• information Systems Networks.
• culture (shared ways of engaging in audit procedures).
• retain Knowledge in 'living ways' (audit report repositories for IAF staff members).

Shared Relational Capital Domain:

• training, Coaching, Facilitating, Educating, Consulting.
• client – Auditor Relationships (participating auditing).
• communicating Audit Report Findings/Recommendations (Audit Committee, Management, Clients internally and externally, all Stakeholders).
• flexibility 'real-time continuous auditing' (rapid flow of information). (importance of boundaries/peripheries and crossing internally and externally).

Collective Learning Externalization:

• experiences (explicit).
• communication with all Stakeholders, internally and externally.
• collective 'Reflective Practice' in problem solving for future engagements 'best practices' (forward thinking).
• management Training Ground (training and development of IAF's staff).

Collective Learning Outcomes

• knowledge reports/documents on collective learning processes and history of audits and events.
• IAF achieved collective objectives and goals for itself and the organisation.
• a collective innovative and creative outcome achieved.
• poblem-solving techniques with a clear collective outcome established, recorded and documented.
• a collective atmosphere of entrepreneurship exist (teamwork, commitment and development of meaning and purpose for the IAF and the organisation).
• intellectual Capital strengthen and 'adding value' to the IAF, the organisation, stakeholders, and society-at-large IAF's organisational status enhanced.

Figure 11.5 Internal audit function characteristics

Source: Ronald Lackland (2007)

and explanations of what should be expected (in research called hypotheses, in auditing called best practices) and proving this for others to interpret and change direction and behaviour. Too often behaviour is the cause and changing is missing in the action. In 1994 I wrote and published the following short article on this theme – it is still true today for all researchers and auditors:

If You Have a Good Audit Recommendation – Look for a Better One[8]

The concept of continuous improvement is a process-oriented team approach to continually providing the best product and service. It applies to both the quality of audit work and the recommendations included in the final report. Findings arising from the performance of audit work should be discussed with appropriate levels of management during the course of an audit and problem-solving methods used to seek the best recommendations.

All of the discussions arising from the audit work should be team driven, involving everyone participating in the audit, including those responsible for the controls being reviewed. The internal auditor should ensure that all findings and recommendations are based on a full and clear understanding of the following:

- What standards, measures and expectations are in the audit conclusions?
- The clear evidence of what exists.
- The reasons for the difference between expected and actual conditions.
- The risks being taken.

This methodical approach to the process of establishing the cause and effect underlying audit conclusions ensures a continuous improvement in the development of audit recommendations. Remember, audit recommendations are best when:

- They can be clearly linked to agreed desirable results.
- They correct the cause of a problem and not just the effect.
- They are accepted by management and implemented.

As mentioned earlier, continuous improvement should not be an accidental process but part of a programme linked into an organisation's vision and strategic objectives. This applies to all parts of an organisation, including its internal audit activity, and all its operations. At times such improvement may only be slow and evolutionary. At other times it will involve reengineering complete operations with paradigm shifts at strategic and operating levels. Such improvement can hurt.

Today, in the climate and significance of achieving Excellent corporate governance, risk management and control in every type of organisation across the world, 'correct the cause' should take every researching auditor into evaluating policy making and policies at board level – a place where every auditor has a right to be if they are auditing corporate governance, risk management and control. The 'best recommendations' by researchers and auditors contribute to the continuous improvement of policies, policies in both the methods of research and auditing and policies relevant to the research and audit objectives.

11.4 Chapter Review

In this chapter I have compared the role of academic researchers with the role auditors practice for the organisations in which they provide assurance services. Both researchers and auditors step along similar paths in their searches for new knowledge and Excellence in the methodologies they use theories and principles to examine and evaluate practices. They walk pathways which involve communities, networks and partnerships to seek understandings of existing knowledge before forming conclusions and recommendations to create new knowledge to improve future policies and practices.

11.5 Creative Audit Thinking Activities

Activity 43 Create Innovative Perceptions for Excellent Auditing

Consider the following research by Dr. Rainer Lenz, published in his article 'The Open Auditor' (2015)[9] and in Table 11.1. Try developing similar research in your organisation, comparing the perceptions all auditors have of their roles and the perceptions of auditing by the people being audited. Draw conclusions from the metaphors – both negative and positive – seek catch-lines from the perceptions by both auditors and their clients. What negative and positive benefits of using metaphors for auditing in your organisation do you see? How can you use both to create change and innovation?

The Open Auditors

The literature on Internal Audit effectiveness indicates a significant disconnect between the "demand-side perspective", – that is, the stakeholder's expectations and perceptions – and the "supply-side perspective" – that is, self-assessments by internal auditors. Self-perception and external perception differ greatly, which can be attributed both in part to hubris on the part of internal auditors, and to a lack of understanding from management regarding the service Internal Audit actually provides. Narrowing this expectation gap increases the effectiveness of the Audit, as customers measure the perceived benefit in relation to the expected benefit. Within organisations,

Van Peursem (2004 and 2005)[10] regarded the role of Audit as enigmatic, meandering between the roles of watchdog and consultant. She reflects on the nature of the internal auditor's role confusion, and alerts to the dangers of a "jack-of-all-trades" image of internal auditors . . . To find more out about the self-perception of internal auditors, I asked them: "If you were asked to write down a catch-line to sum up your role as internal auditor in your organisation, what would it be?" I posted that question in LinkedIn, in the official global group of The Institute of Internal Auditors (IIA) and obtained 141 comments within 6 months, between March 17 and September 17, 2010. All self-images received are clustered into five groups acknowledging that "metaphors create insights. But they also distort. They have strengths. But they also have limitations. In creating ways of seeing they tend to create ways of not seeing" (Morgan 2006).[11] Thus, the clustering is normative.

Some metaphors and self-images sow the seeds for non-acceptance of Audit, and contribute to its marginalisation within organisations . . . Five clusters of self-images are distinguished – see Table 11.1. Negative self-images – as put by internal auditors themselves – like "An auditor is a watch dog and not a blood hound" may create distance and form the basis of non-acceptance (1. Police). Overly modest self-perceptions like "I am the one you want me to be" (2. Servant) and the use of self-evident and empty words like "Increase stakeholder value" (3. Consultant) can lead to marginalisation in the eyes of the Audit stakeholder. Overly ambitious claims like "We are doctors" (4. Doctor) or "A modern-day hero . . ." provide the basis for disappointment as Audit then risks over- promising and under-delivering. Eventually, there are also original and helpful self-images (5. Change Agent) that point to positive characteristics and differences; helping to create a unique and sustainable identity, and supporting Audit's pursuit to become more effective.

Table 11.1 The Open Auditor (2015)

	(1) Police	*(2) Servant*	*(3) Consultant*	*(4) Doctor*	*(5) Change Agent*
Negative image		Lack of identity, downgrading, too modest	Self-evident, empty words	Over-ambitious (superman), arrogant, not respectful	Making a difference, creating a unique and sustainable identity
	Everyone else has bad intentions; negative starting point; attack modus; too much focus on status; making people afraid of you	Profiling yourself as an assistant serving someone else	"Consulting talk", high level words, strong focus on independence and objectivity which is hard (impossible) to achieve	Pretending to be the expert in a lot of things, things that you can never realize on your own, assuming that you take the decisions yourself	Focus on strengthening things (which assumes that there may also be good things), asking questions instead of pretending

Table 11.1 (Continued)

(1) Police	(2) Servant	(3) Consultant	(4) Doctor	(5) Change Agent
				to be the expert upfront, modesty, inspire people to change
Basis for non-acceptance, distance	Basis for marginalisation	Basis for marginalisation	Basis for disappointment	Basis for LA effectiveness
"An auditor is a watchdog not a bloodhound"; "We tell the executives what is right/wrong operationally"; "Spies for Board and Management".	"I am the one you want me to be";"I am your friend …";"On your side …"; "… to assist management …".	"Increase stakeholder value"; "Support the company in achieving its goals and objectives"; "Think things through"; "My purpose is to increase our company's values"; "Independent internal consultant".	"We are doctors"; "I am the guardian of the company's profits"; "A modern-day hero, helping save companies, governments and economies".	"Fresh perspective"; "Inspire decision making"; "Focus on root cause"; "Treating the business with respect";"Is sowing the seeds of control improvements".

Source: Dr. Rainer Lenz – The Open Auditor (2015)

Activity 44   Culture Research by Auditors Can Create Better Behaviour

Following its report on culture and the role of internal audit in 2014[12] the Chartered Institute of Internal Auditors has published further guidance on the audit of culture and importance of research by the auditors in their preparation for an audit – *Auditing Culture* (2014).[13] In this guidance reference is made to a special report on culture for internal auditing by Thomson Reuters Accelus (2014),[14] which also recommends internal auditors 'Build in some time for research, not only of internal policies and processes but also of external material from regulators, experts and best practice.' Supporting these reports, The Institute of Internal Auditors (2016)[15] has published its own guidance on assessing culture in organisations with the following statement:

> Internal audit cannot effectively assess culture without a profound and deep understanding of the organisation's values and expected

behaviours coupled with a thorough appreciation of how they influence the organisation's priorities in relation to good governance, risk
management, and control.

Consider how all your audits need to include research into an understanding of culture in your organisation and audit function and how this
understanding can be achieved by collaboration with others.

Create a New Approach to Auditing Culture

Start with your organisation and function's vision and values statements.
Each of these should have an influence on all of the steps in your audit
process. Research **HOW** these statements were created, by **WHOM** and
WHEN. Have they changed recently? **WHAT** has changed and **WHY**?
WHERE can these statements be seen at all three levels in your organisation and across all external supply chains – both your organisation's and
your own culture statements? Analyse the results of your research. Create
a new audit approach in your engagements for achieving this analysis. You
will always find both cultural strengths and weaknesses. Benchmark your
results across your organisation and externally. Consider the influence of
your analysis and research on your organisation's governance, risk management and control in every audit engagement today and in the future.

Activity 45   Creative Research Drives Collaboration and Innovation

In its report *Enlightening Professions?*[16] discussed in earlier chapters, the
Institute of Chartered Accountants in England and Wales forecasts a 'vision
for audit and a better society'. That vision draws on research 'a literature
review, a call out for evidence through the RSA Fellowship, semi-struc-
tured interviews and a variety of contributions from people inside and
outside of the audit profession who became aware of the project'. Consider its following views on collaboration in your next audit and how this
could increase creativity and innovation in your Ten Step Audit Process.

Audit Leaders and Innovators Must Collaborate

Audit leaders and innovators now have the technological tools to push
collaboration in ambitious new directions, up to and including crowd-
sourced Open Audit, for example. But the technology should be in

service of a public interest vision, rather than simply a tool for efficiency. Audit works best by engaging widely. In order to take charge of
its own destiny, the audit profession will need to reach out and collaborate, not fragment into small specialisms. It needs to learn from existing
developments that can provide valuable lessons and models to adapt.

Notes

1 *Wisdom of the Ages* (1936 2nd Edition 1948), The St. Catherine's Press Ltd., London, England.
2 *Wisdom of the Ages* (1948), Mark Gilbert, The Saint Catherine Press Ltd., London, England.
3 *Innovative Practices in Today's Internal Auditing* (2007), Jeffrey Ridley and Dr. Kenneth D'Silva, The Fifth European Academic Conference, University of Pisa, Italy.
4 *Creativity and Innovation: Keys to a Successful Future for Auditing* (2012), Professor Jeffrey Ridley and Professor Kenneth D'Silva, Centre for Research in Accounting, Finance and Governance, London South Bank University, England.
5 In its Annual Report 2010 it boldly states, "The IIA has long pioneered inventive approaches to solving the problems facing internal auditors worldwide. This year, we demonstrated how innovation can make the difference between merely discovering the future and actively defining its success."
6 Professor Kenneth D'Silva is Director – Centre for Research in Accounting, Finance and Governance at the London South Bank University, London, England.
7 *Business @ the Speed of Thought – Using a Digital Nervous System* (1999 p. 238), Bill Gates, Penguin Books Ltd., England.
8 *Published in Internal Auditing April* (1994 p. 6), IIA-UK and Ireland.
9 *Internal Auditors as Change Agents: What a Difference a Year Makes!* Lenz, R. (2015), The Open Auditor, Edition 3, September.
10 *Internal Auditors' Role and Authority – New Zealand Evidence* (2004), Van Peursem K., Managerial Auditing Journal, Volume 19 Issue 3, pp. 378–393.
    Conversations with Internal Auditors, The Power of Ambiguity (2005), Van Peursem K, Managerial Auditing Journal, Volume 20 Issue 5, pp. 489–512.
11 *Images of Organisations,* (2006), Morgan, G., Sage Publications Inc.
12 *Culture and the Role of Internal Audit – Looking Below the Surface* (2014), Chartered Institute of Internal Auditors, London, England.
13 *Auditing Culture* (2016 p. 2), Chartered Institute of Internal Auditors, London, England.
14 *Special Report Culture – Tips for Internal Auditors* (2014 p. 10), Thomson Reuters Accelus.
15 *Global Perspectives: Auditing Culture – A Hard Look at the Soft Stuff* (2016 p. 7). The Institute of Internal Auditors Inc., Orlando, US.
16 *Enlightening Professions?* (2014 p. 22), Institute of Chartered Accountants in England and Wales, London, England.

12 Auditors Are Benchmarkers

Shout how best you are in all your auditing market places[1]

In this chapter I discuss benchmarking as an essential management tool in every profession and organisation. Benchmarking is a continuous search for and implementation of best practices and Excellence. It describes the steps in a formal benchmarking process and how these can and should be used by all auditors, leading to creative thinking, continuous improvement, innovation and Excellence in the quality of their audit processes and recommendations for Excellence in corporate governance, risk management and control in the organisations in which they provide services. Excellent auditors are always benchmarkers.

12.1 Benchmarking Is a Management Tool

The introductory cartoon does not fully represent best practice benchmarking. Rarely are there only two participants in a competitive benchmarking process, nor is there only one measure, or one product or service. But it does demonstrate the importance of benchmarking when promoting the quality and class of your product and service. Benchmarking is not a new tool. In the past and on a less formal basis, it has been called 'comparing'. Today it is seen as a formal management tool to identify where improvements should take place to achieve Excellence, and monitor its implementation. It should always be a continuous process in all organisations, their functions and professions.

Oakland (2002)[2] in his concept of world-class performance defines a benchmark as a 'reference or measurement standard used for comparison' and benchmarking as 'the continuous process of identifying, understanding and adapting best practice and processes that will lead to superior performance'. He saw the need for benchmarking to:

Change the perspectives of executives and managers
Compare business practices with those of world-class organisations
Challenge current practices and processes
Create improved goals and practices for the organisation.

Bain and Company (2015) recognise benchmarking as one of the management tools executives need to consider and use 'Whether they are trying to boost revenues, innovate, improve quality, increase efficiencies or plan for the future, executives have searched for tools to help them' – see Appendix L for its description of benchmarking, its methodology and common uses. As you read this chapter, reflect on how this guidance relates to the need for all auditors to continuously benchmark to be Excellent.

The American Productivity and Quality Centre's (APQC) Code of Conduct for Benchmarking[3] (www.apqc.org) has been adopted by the European Foundation for Quality Management (EFQM) as a guide for the legality and ethics of benchmarking between organisations. It contains useful guidance for the formal process of benchmarking and introduces the code with 'Benchmarking – the process of identifying and learning from global best practices – is a powerful tool in the quest for continuous improvement and breakthroughs.'

Formal benchmarking requires a measurement of gaps between what is and what is considered to be better or even best. Such measures used should be carefully thought out. In all benchmarking measures, it is useful to develop a qualitative scale. However, qualitative measures are rarely sufficient in benchmarking. The skill of benchmarking is to develop detailed analytical analysis using quantitative

1   select the features to benchmark.
2   agree what influences there are on your features.
3   use your measures to identify and agree 'current gaps'.
4   analyse your 'current gaps' and improve.
5   continuously follow-up achievement.
6   shout your best practices and products.
7   continuously improve.

Figure 12.1 Seven benchmarking steps

Source: J. Ridley, Cutting Edge Internal Auditing (2008)

measures that will support the qualitative judgements. The best auditor will be the one that can master the art of benchmarking to measure both qualitatively and quantitatively, to achieve not just better, best, Excellence, but superiority.

In the past I have used the seven steps in Figure 12.1 when benchmarking.

'Select', 'features' and 'influences' need further explanation. *Select* is key to the benchmarking process. What is selected should be significant for performance. *Features* are those key features chosen in the process, practice or attribute being benchmarked. These need to be chosen carefully to ensure they are the strongest influences in measuring better and best and Excellence. *Influences* are what will make change happen to what is being benchmarked. Compare the process in Figure 12.1 with the Bain benchmarking methodology in Appendix L. What is added by me is 'Shout your best practices and products'. Benchmarking is not an end in itself. Changes made should be used to promote results to all an operation's stakeholders and influence the strategic thinking for the assurance services being provided.

Benchmarks can be internal and external to the organisation. They can be structures, practices, technology, equipment and people. They can be a mixture of any or all of these. They can be standards, codes of practice, regulations and laws. They can be social, environmental, economic and financial. They are what customers see as being best for them at a given time. Behaviour, innovation, research, development and above all competition create them. They are constantly changing, because competition drives continuous improvement.

There are many examples in sectors, industries, nationally and internationally of good practice and quality models being developed as benchmarks. Benchmarking is used by many organisations to make significant change happen and to meet new challenging objectives. Benchmarking is an exploration into practices within an organisation and those outside the organisation, not always in organisations with similar objectives. It can be an adventure with many surprises: opening up new networks and starting changes that lead to many improvements in performance. MacDonald and Tanner (1998 p. 5)[4] summed this up well in their one-week published teaching of benchmarking, concluding with the following:

This week we have seen that benchmarking requires a strong degree of commitment – from management and from all others involved. It takes time and resources. It needs a disciplined and systematic approach. In short, it is not easy and it is not for the faint-hearted.

But then who has the right to believe that *aiming to be the best* should ever be easy? And, who better to be the best than an auditor. Benchmarking is more than just comparing. It is a continuous management tool with well-established formal processes used by many managers and auditors. It is fundamental in the achievement of quality, Excellence and superiority in all products and services.

12.2 Excellent Auditors Need to Continuously Benchmark

Benchmarking has been a tool of the auditor since the earliest forms of auditing and certainly since the beginning of the 20th century. All of the professions supporting and researching auditing practices have used and are using benchmarking, both nationally and internationally, to develop their auditing standards, education, qualifications, training and guidance. Networks and groups of their members have always benchmarked informally and formally to improve their products and services and will continue to do so in the future. Benchmarking is a methodology in research used by academics to explore principles, concepts and theories, and create new thinking and recommendations on auditing practices. Benchmarking is used by governments and regulators to create laws and regulations over and for auditing services. But is it used by all auditors in their audit processes? It should be, because it is an essential component in quality management, continuous improvement and the achievement of Excellence in auditing.

Sawyer's *Internal Auditing* (2003)[5] discusses benchmarking as a tool to be used 'to enhance all levels of the internal auditing function':

> It can be applied to the basic philosophy of internal auditing's relationship to the organisation; to the organisation of the auditing function; to the planning process, including risk assessment and self-evaluation processes; to field work, including methods of examination and evaluation; to the reporting processes; and, to relationships with external auditors and boards of directors. The important thing is that change be made not just to use new methods, but also to result in substantial improvements in the audit operation.

Regan (2004)[6] defines 'benchmarking' in his dictionary of auditor's language:

> The comparison of data or operations against those of similar organisations. Benchmarking, whether 'quantitative' or 'qualitative', is often performed with the intention of seeking ways to improve an organisation's operations. Auditors also frequently use benchmarking as part of their analytical review procedures. For example, an industry average of payroll cost per employee is a common benchmark to assess the reasonableness of payroll costs in a specific organisation.

Regan's inclusion of benchmarking in analytical review procedures highlights the importance of this process in auditing. The practice of comparing in analytical auditing is rarely referred to as benchmarking, yet the principles are similar – making comparisons, analysing differences, reviewing the reasons and recommending improvements. Whether benchmarking is a one-off informal comparing exercise or a continuous formal analysis of gaps between existing and best practices, it is still a practice all auditors should be expert in their own professional services, and in the operations they audit.

In their *Operational Auditing Handbook*, Chambers and Rand (1997) discuss benchmarking by auditors as a 'comparison of one's own performance in a specific area' with five principal objectives addressing competition, best practices, future issues, customer expectations and quality. In their second edition (2010),[7] they repeat these principal objectives and discuss the achievement of these by auditors. Few could argue with the importance of these principal objectives both in auditing and in organisations being audited. In today's corporate governance climate of laws and codes, I would suggest 'stakeholder expectations' should replace 'customer expectations'. There can be few audits today in which one or more stakeholders, other than customers, are interested in the quality of the audit and its results.

There is now more use of technology in benchmarking practices across and between organisations than ever before. Websites and search engines have grown in their number, size and shape; their design and search facilities have become more user friendly. Access to knowledge and experience on websites has become commonplace in all auditing activities and engagements. Better knowledge management by organisations and all auditors will continue to encourage and improve the use of benchmarking for steps in the audit process. Today, benchmarking as an audit tool appears in most annual surveys of auditing practices.

A commitment to Excellence always requires best practice benchmarking. During my career as an auditor I benchmarked in all my auditing practices, not just as an informal comparison with others but to formally go through a process of establishing gaps between what I was practicing as an auditor and what other auditors were practicing. And not only auditors, but practices at board, executive and operational levels. And not just in my own sector, but across all sectors. And not just in my own country, but across the world. Frigo (1997)[8] recognised this for internal auditors in his research for The Institute of Internal Auditors (IIARF) Research Foundation, and the same advice applies to all auditors: 'Internal auditors have the opportunity to participate in the process of benchmarking and help organisations to identify and innovatively adapt the "best of the best" methods and practices.'

A recent IIARF (2011)[9] study into the importance of 'insight' by internal auditors in their role as assurance providers followed its task force established in 2008 to determine 'what internal audit should deliver to their customers'. The results from this task force recommended a value proposition of Assurance: Insight: Objectivity as key to delivering value to their stakeholders and how this insight should be achieved:

> based on the results of the survey and the interviews, it would appear that many CAEs [Chief Audit Executives] and stakeholders agree that the use of tools, such as data analysis and benchmarking, enables the experienced eye to glean new knowledge about a situation or issue, share that 'insight'

with stakeholders in a meaningful way, and provide the persuasive evidence supporting a positive change recommendation.

The IIARF 'value proposition' applies across all assurance activities – all auditors need to have insight and use the best management tools to achieve this. In the following article I wrote in 2001, I discussed emerging issues for internal auditing, which applied then to all auditors and still do today as issues for benchmarking best practices. Note also the 'insights' in the article at the time it was written. Add your own insights today for your own auditing.

Shout How Best You Are in All Your Internal Auditing Market Places[10]

In 1996 The IIA in its research publications recognised the following emerging best internal auditing practices[11]:

- development of partnering roles with audit clients;
- participating in corporate task forces;
- aligning corporate goals, audit department plans and performance evaluations;
- educating management on their internal control responsibilities;
- carrying out customer satisfaction surveys;
- providing training to audit committee members;
- external quality assurance reviews of internal auditing practices;
- involvement in Total Quality Management practices;
- using computer assisted techniques;
- including audits of environment, health and safety;
- development of formal risk assessment system involving management;
- empowerment of staff to experiment with a variety of approaches in developing innovative solutions;
- providing internal consulting services that focus on problem solving rather than problem finding.

These internal auditing practices have been adopted by many internal auditing functions in a variety of ways. Evidence for this can be found in the promotion of internal auditing by in-house internal auditing functions; the marketing of internal auditing services by professional accounting firms and consultants; the developing syllabi of professional certificates for internal auditors; training programmes provided by The IIA and other institutes; programmes for internal auditing and risk assessment conferences and their speakers' presentations.

Much of this improvement in internal auditing services has been developed through formal benchmarking processes carried out or influenced by The IIA and its worldwide affiliated National Institutes and Chapters. Those working in internal auditing, both in-house and outsourced, have also been shouting their best practices to each other: formal research by The IIA has recommended internal auditing and control best practices: involvement of internal auditors in national commissions and working parties has influenced significant changes in attitudes to governance, control and internal auditing.

Internal benchmarking has involved internal auditors in comparing their practices with those of other services in their organisations. External benchmarking has involved internal auditors looking outside their organisations comparing their practices with all the sources of best practice mentioned in the previous paragraph. Recognising the key external benchmarks is an important part of the process. For all internal auditors it is important that they study and understand the following list of ten past and current external benchmarks:

BENCHMARK 1

1977: The IIA[12] publication of international statements and standards for professional practices in internal auditing, continuously improved with supporting guidelines and revisions. Publication of a revised international definition for professional internal auditing and code of ethics[13] in 1999 has widened the role of internal auditing into risk assessment and consultancy. This has been followed by a consultative document[14] containing revised standards to be introduced in 2002. These statements and standards [since revised and continuously improved as with all auditing standards] will become even more important as more and more audit committees require internal auditors to define their roles and challenge them to meet high standards of professionalism and methodology.

BENCHMARK 2

1982: First development of a common body of knowledge for internal auditors,[15] followed by research reports published by The IIA in 1988,[16] 1992[17] and a new competency framework for internal auditors in 1999.[18] This body of knowledge supports the framework of knowledge on which The IIA professional examinations have been based since the mid-70s. [The IIA's Common Body of Knowledge (CBOK) is administered through The IIA Research Foundation (IIARF), which provides a programme of research for the internal audit profession through initiatives that explore current issues, emerging trends, and future needs – www.theiia.org/goto/CBOK.]

BENCHMARK 3

1987: USA publication of the Treadway[19] report on fraudulent financial reporting, including recommendations on internal auditing and audit committee practices, followed by the COSO[20] integrated internal control framework in 1992. This framework has been used worldwide to assess control levels in organisations of all sizes and in all sectors. It was the first definition of control that required an assessment of risk linked to an organisation's objectives before control activities are established.

BENCHMARK 4

1987: Publication of an international standard for quality management systems and auditing (ISO 9000), based on the UK standard BSI 5750, revised in 1994 and completely re-written in 2000. The following quality principles and requirements on which the re-written standard is based are essential for the assurance of quality in all internal auditing services:

    Customer focused organisation
    Leadership
    Involvement of people
    Process approach
    System approach to management
    Continual improvement
    Factual approach to decision-making
    Mutually beneficial supplier relationship.

BENCHMARK 5

1991: The IIA[21] publication of guidance for the auditing of information technology (updated in 1994). This guidance has not dated. At the time of its publication it was in advance of its time. For some internal auditors it still is.

BENCHMARK 6

1992: UK Cadbury[22] report on corporate governance (reviewed by Hampel[23] in 1998 and followed by the Turnbull[24] report in 1999, introducing risk-based control techniques linked to the COSO recommendations of 1992). These reports all link internal auditing into satisfying the needs of their audit committees and boards. Risk assessment is now firmly placed in internal audit planning and as a service internal auditors can facilitate and add value to in their organisations.

BENCHMARK 7

1996: Publication of an international standard for environmental management systems and auditing (ISO 14001), based on the UK standard BSI 7750. This standard has been well received across the world. It provides internal auditors with a best practice benchmark for the management of all environmental issues. Its auditing practices provide guidance for all environmental audits, whether carried out by internal auditors or environmental auditors.

BENCHMARK 8

1998: The IIA[25] model for improving the internal audit service to the organisation through risk management techniques. This model demonstrates clearly the links between risk assessment for internal audit planning and risk assessment by management for the achievement of their objectives.

BENCHMARK 9

1999: USA Blue Ribbon Committee[26] report on improving the effectiveness of audit committees. This committee's ten recommendations are focused on financial reporting and audit committee oversight processes. This 'next step' in the effectiveness of audit committees in North America will influence many audit committee terms of reference worldwide. It is important that internal auditing keeps up to date with how audit committees are achieving best practice and how this impacts its assurance role.

BENCHMARK 10

1999: UK Institute of Social and Ethical Accountability[27] publication of a foundation standard in social and ethical accounting, auditing and reporting (AA1000), followed by a guidance statement[28] for internal auditors, published by the IIA-UK & Ireland (1999). In recent years social and ethical responsibilities have become increasingly important at board, management and staff levels in all organisations. The involvement of internal auditing as an adviser and assessor in these issues has started in some organisations. Others will follow. This involvement will grow.

These benchmarks have had and will have a significant influence on how internal auditing best practices evolve. Some are just starting to influence internal auditing. Their improvement will continue to have a significant impact on how internal auditing services develop. Each will influence how control and corporate governance is measured and monitored. It is important all internal auditors should be aware of their content and the best practices they promote. Other new benchmarks will follow in the future, improving on past statements and adding new best practices. Benchmarking internal auditing never ends!

Those emerging best internal auditing practices in The RFIIA research in 1996, listed at the beginning of my article, have grown in their importance and value in all auditing services. All mentioned will continue to develop in the immediate future and beyond the horizon. They are all recognised by current research and thinking in all auditing as being significant practices that have spawned numerous cutting-edge activities. There will be more identified by research and practice in the future. Keep benchmarking these best practices in all auditing. Research has already shown these practices are to be found in auditing activities, innovated by auditors, and required/recommended by their professional bodies, regulators and customers.

Whatever else happens there will be more information; it will be created faster; it will require more, wider and deeper knowledge; it will be more freely available. There will also be more change, and this will spur more benchmarking. Bill Gates (1999)[29] starts his introduction to today's digital age with 'Business is going to change more in the next ten years than it has in the last fifty' – for 'business', read all types of auditing across all sectors. Such change will require continuous benchmarking, creativity, innovation and above all imagination by all auditors.

12.3 Excellent Auditors Continuously Benchmark Governance

Benchmarking is an important part of improvements in governance, not just across industry sectors and nations but internationally as well. There are now a number of organisations, nationally and internationally, using benchmarking to promote good governance and responsible practices in organisations, developing models and principles, and promoting Excellent governance measures. Among these in the United Kingdom are industry models developed by government departments, schools, hospitals, Institute of Directors, Business in the Community, Business in the Environment, the Financial Times Corporate Responsibility Index, Good Corporation and CSR Academy. Internationally there are the Organisation for Economic Co-operation and Development, World Bank, International Monetary Fund, Transparency International and PRI – Principles for Responsible Investment. All, and many others, have in common a mission to promote Excellence in governance and responsible practices, using developed benchmark frameworks and models to measure and rank organisations/countries.

Each year there are published analyses, guides, reports, reviews and guidance on all aspects of governance and responsible practices. One such benchmarking on governance practices in the UK FTSE 350 companies, reported by The Grant Thornton Governance Institute (2015),[30] in its FRC's Perspective and Chairman's Foreword, comment on the following:

Compliance and Non-Compliance reporting
Quality of explanations in reporting
New Strategic Reports – contents
New Viability Reports – contents
Corporate Culture and Values reporting.

These are all issues for future auditing of corporate governance practices. Each will create new benchmarks for auditors to use in their audit processes and the services they provide. This guide touches on and reinforces the importance of all of my Benchmarks 1–10 discussed earlier. It also introduces the following new benchmarks all auditors should be developing and using today in their audit of risk management and control in governance practices (the sources in brackets are mine; there are others that can be researched by readers):

- **Culture and Values** (including Conduct and Behaviour) [Institute of Business Ethics – www.ibe.org.uk and Chartered Institute of Internal Auditors – www.iia.org.uk]
- **Key Performance Indicators** (KPIs) and their link to Visions, Missions and Objectives [*The Balanced Scorecard* (1996), Robert S. Kaplan and David P. Norton]
- **Strategic Reporting** [Financial Reporting Council – www.frc.org.uk and International Integrated Reporting Council – www.integratedreporting.org]
- **Board and Board Committee Effectiveness** (including now Remuneration and Nomination) [Financial Reporting Council – www.frc.org.uk]
- **Sustainability beyond short-term** (including Human Rights, Bribery, Anti-corruption) [United Nations – www.sustainabilitydevelopment.un.org]
- **Compliance (including Law and Regulation)** [Financial Reporting Council – www.frc.org.uk]
- **Stakeholder Relationships** [AA1000 Stakeholder Engagement – www.accountability.org]
- **Supply Chain Management** [Bain and Company – www.bain.com]
- **Insight** [Institute of Risk Management – www.theirm.org]
- **Fraud Prevention and Detection** [Fraud Advisory Council – www.fraudadvisorypanel.org]
- **Health and Safety** [Institution of Occupational Safety and Health – www.iosh.co.uk]
- **Electronic Security** [British Computer Society – www.bcs.org]

The Grant Thornton Governance Institute guide ends with the following:

> This year's changes in corporate governance and reporting seek to promote greater transparency about how boards operate, particularly how the balance between short term performance and long term sustainability will be maintained. Our findings show that in many areas companies are still finding their way. However, we are encouraged by the level of debate that recent changes have provoked between boards, investors, auditors and other interested parties. Dialogue between stakeholders is the bedrock of effective governance and we are interested to see whether a consensus emerges over the coming years.

In particular, culture and values are receiving a lot of attention in governance today, though both have been an important contributor to good governance in organisations since time began. In my inauguration address at the University of Lincoln in 2014, mentioned in Part I, I spoke on the importance of the values of life seen in good governance. It is essential today that those values of trust and integrity which we cherish in our own lives are used to benchmark governance practices in all organisations at all levels, in all strategies across all their supply chains.

The PRI – Principles for Responsible Investment[31] has created another United Nations benchmark for investors in the investment industry, which all organisations seeking investment and auditors should benchmark their responsible practices against – see Appendix M. These principles introduce a new responsible practices term, ESG – Environment: Social: Governance – representing all the responsible practices organisations should address in the achievement of their aims. Investment managers signing up to these principles – and there are now many – agree to analyse ESG practices in the organisations in which they invest at the time of investment and throughout the investment's life, seeking disclosures, promoting concern in ESG practices to the organisation and networking the principles across the investment industry. Each of these principles should create opportunities for auditors to recognise gaps and be innovative in their evaluation of ESG practices in every audit engagement.

12.4 Chapter Review

In this chapter I have discussed the role of all auditors as continuous benchmarkers, not just on the road to achieving Excellence in audit work, but also in searching for Excellence in all environment, social and governance practices in the organisations in which they audit. Benchmarking formally as well as informally, seeking gaps to measure and create improvements and innovations. And when Excellence is achieved in their own services or in the organisations in which they work, shouting this to all.

12.5 Creative Audit Thinking Activities

Activity 46   Create a Benchmarking Team to Seek Innovation

A good approach to benchmarking is to establish a team from those with interest and/or responsibility for audit and assurance in an organisation. The team should include at least one or more of the audit and assurance stakeholders. Then take the following seven steps.

Seven Steps to Best Practice Benchmarking

1   Determine the features of the audit unit to be benchmarked. Do not choose too many. No more than five at first.

2   Agree what influences there are on your features. Consider both internal and external influences.

(Before proceeding create a framework to identify what you need to measure. Select the key features the team need to benchmark: these are the most important actions your organisation needs to take be Excellent in your audit and assurance activities. Having agreed the features, identify the internal and external influences that impact how they perform: see these influences as levels, which can and do interact one with the other. Study how these levels impact your organisation's governance, risk management and control. Agree measures for each of your benchmarks. The right measures are important. Test how appropriate they are by trying to link them into your team's vision of Excellence. If the link is not strong, change your measure.)

3   Use your measures to identify and agree 'current gaps' between your practices and benchmarks.

4   Analyse your 'current gaps'. Look for causes why you do not already meet your benchmark's level of service. Consider structure, processes, delegated responsibilities, competencies, resources, etc. Agree what actions need to be taken to achieve best practice; over what time span and how they will be measured – IMPROVE and INNOVATE.

5   Continuously follow-up achievement of your benchmarks. Celebrate success.

6   Shout your best practices and products to all of your customers.

7   Continuously improve all your benchmarks and add others.

Activity 47 Create Excellent Benchmarks for Your Audit Committee

Every auditor should seek answers to the following questions from their board and audit committee. Auditors can help create benchmarks for each from corporate governance guidance and best practices. Start with five of the questions most appropriate for your organisation. Identify 'gaps' and consider how audit can contribute to any improvements needed to achieve audit committee Excellence.

How Effective Is Your Audit Committee?[32]

The following questions all boards should ask of their audit committee in an assessment of its audit and assurance reporting responsibilities.

Organisation

1   Have they any executive or other responsibilities and relationships that could weaken the **independence** of their oversight responsibilities?
2   Are committee **members and the chair rotated** regularly to bring new thinking into their reviews?
3   Have they **sufficient knowledge** for all the risk control, audit and governance issues they are required to oversee?
4   Is their **experience** of the business plans and operations sufficient?
5   Do they **meet the right people** regularly and at the right time, to consider both audit and assurance planning and results?
6   Is their **reporting** of audit committee responsibilities and oversight results known to all stakeholders?

Oversight

7   Do they review **all financial reporting** throughout the year – both accounting and related operating information?
8   Do they review both the preparation and content of **all financial statements** published both internally and externally?
9   Do they review the adequacy of **risk assessment** by the board, management and auditors?
10   Do they review the **control environment** and impact of change, across the organisation and all its supply chains, not just within the organisation?
11   Do they consider **legal/regulatory/tax issues** when reviewing management's responsibilities for good governance?
12   Do they require the **co-ordination of all auditing and inspection** at the planning, audit, reporting and follow-up stages?
13   Have they the opportunity to call on **additional resources** to carry out their responsibilities?
14   Do they consider **social and environmental issues** when addressing risk and control?

Activity 48   Create Goals for Innovation by Benchmarking

In my book *Cutting Edge Internal Auditing*, I referenced into research by Gray and Gray (1996)[33] and their motivations for innovation in internal auditing. I was indebted to them for their insight. Their analysis and understanding of how innovation is encouraged, achieved and monitored in internal auditing has stood the test of time well. I made my own additions and changes to their innovation goals and invited readers to do the same. Consider how I concluded then and benchmark this with what you believe are the goals today and tomorrow for innovation in your own auditing. Analyse any 'current gaps' and search for Excellence.

Goals for Innovation in Auditing

1　Continuous improvement of the quality of auditing services.
2　Achieve best practice by continuously benchmarking.
3　Expansion of services to increase the value-added of auditing.
4　Manage staff knowledge, skills, performance and morale well.
5　Sell auditing as future focused.
6　To reduce the opportunities for all types of crime in an organisation.
7　Increase satisfaction from all customers.
8　Add new skills in the art of questioning.
9　Auditing services as a contribution to the organisation's good reputation.
10　Shout a passion for Excellence across your organisation and to all your stakeholders.

Notes

1　Adopted from my article at note 9.
2　*Total Organisational Excellence – Achieving World-Class Performance* (2002), John S., Oakland, Butterworth-Heinemann, Oxford, England.
3　*Benchmarking Code of Conduct – Guidelines and Ethics for Benchmarkers* (2014 pp. 2–3), American Productivity and Quality Centre (APQC), Houston, US.
4　*Understanding Benchmarking in a week* (2nd Edition 1998 p. 5), John MacDonald and Steve Tanner, Hodder & Stoughton, London, England.
5　*Sawyer's Internal Auditing – The Practice of Modern Internal Auditing* (5th Edition 2003), Lawrence B. Sawyer, Mortimer A. Dittenhofer, James H. Scheiner, The Institute of Internal Auditors, Orlando, US.
6　*Auditor's Dictionary – Terms, Concepts, Processes and Regulations* (2004), David O'Regan, John Wiley and Sons, Hoboken, New Jersey, US.
7　*The Operational Auditing Handbook – Auditing Business and IT Processes* (2nd Edition 2010 p. 24), Professor A. D. Chambers and Graham Rand, John Wiley and Sons Ltd., Chichester, England.
8　*Providing Benchmarking Services for Internal Auditing Clients* (1997 p. VII), Mark I. Frigo, The Institute of Internal Auditors Research Foundation, Orlando, US.
9　*Insight – Delivering Value to Stakeholders* (2011 p. 31), The Institute of Internal Auditors Research Foundation, Orlando, US.
10　*Shout How Best You Are in All Your Internal Auditing Market Places*, Internal Control Journal (September 2001), Jeffrey Ridley, Accountancy Books, London, England.
11　*Leading Edge Internal Auditing* (1998), Jeffrey Ridley and Chambers A.D., ICSA Publishing, London, England.
12　*Standards for the Professional Practice of Internal Auditing* (1977), The Institute of Internal Auditors, Orlando, US.
13　The Institute of Internal Auditors definition of internal auditing (1999): 'Internal auditing is an independent, objective assurance and consulting activity designed to add value

and improve an organisation's operations. It helps an organisation accomplish its objectives by bringing a systematic, disciplined approach to evaluate and improve the effectiveness of risk management, control and governance processes.'

14 *New Standards Bring Professional Practices Framework to Life*, Internal Auditor Journal (February 2001), The Institute of Internal Auditors, Orlando, US.

15 *The Common Body of Knowledge for Internal Auditors*, Gobiel R.E., Internal Auditor Journal (November–December 1982), The Institute of Internal Auditors, Orlando, US.

16 *A Common Body of Professional Knowledge for Internal Auditors (CBOK)* (1985), Barrett M.J. et al., The Institute of Internal Auditors Research Foundation, Orlando, US.

17 *A Common Body of Knowledge for the Practice of Internal Auditing (CBOK)* (1992), Albrecht W.S. et al., The Institute of Internal Auditors Research Foundation, Orlando, US.

18 *Competency Framework for Internal Auditing (CFIA)* (1999), McIntosh Elaine R., The Institute of Internal Auditors Research Foundation, Orlando, US.

19 *Report of the National Commission on Fraudulent Financial Reporting* (1987), Treadway Commission, Sponsored by American Institute of Certified Public Accountants, American Accounting Association, Financial Executives Institute, The Institute of Internal Auditors and National Association of Accountants, American Institute of Certified Public Accountants, New Jersey, US.

20 *Internal Control – Integrated Framework* (1992), Committee of Sponsoring Organisations of Treadway Commission (COSO), American Institute of Certified Public Accountants, New Jersey, US.

21 *Systems Auditability and Control® (SAC)* (1991) – revised (1994), The Institute of Internal Auditors Research Foundation, Orlando, US.

22 *Committee on the Financial Aspects of Corporate Governance* (1992), chaired by Sir Adrian Cadbury, Gee Publishing Limited, London, England.

23 *Committee on Corporate Governance Final Report of the Committee on Corporate Governance* (1998), chaired by Sir Ronald Hampel, Gee Publishing Limited, London, England.

24 *Internal Control – Guidance for Directors on the Combined Code* (1999), Turnbull Report, Institute of Chartered Accountants in England and Wales, London, England.

25 *Risk Management: Changing the Internal Auditor's Paradigm* (1998), George M. Selim and David MacNamee, The Institute of Internal Auditors Research Foundation, Orlando, US.

26 *Improving the Effectiveness of Corporate Audit Committees* (1999), The Blue Ribbon Committee, New York Stock Exchange and National Association of Securities Dealers, New York, US.

27 *Accountability 1000 (AA1000), A Foundation Standard in Social and Ethical Accounting, Auditing and Reporting* (1999), Institute of Social and Ethical Accountability, London, England UK. www.AccounAbility.org.uk.

28 *Ethics and Social Responsibility, Professional Briefing Note Fifteen* (1999), IIA-UK and Ireland.

29 *Business and the Speed of Thought- Using a Digital Nervous System* (1999 p. xiii), Bill Gates with Collins, Hemingway, Time Warner Books Company, New York, US.

30 *Corporate Governance Review: Plotting a New Course to Improved Governance* (2014 pp. 3–4), The Grant Thornton Governance Institute, London, England.

31 *Principles of Responsible Investment: Report on Progress* (2015), United Nations Global Compact, New York, US.

32 Published in *Internal Auditing & Business Risk* (December 2000 p. 30), The IIA-UK and Ireland. Reproduced in *Cutting Edge Internal Auditing* (2008) Jeffrey Ridley, Wiley and Sons.

33 *Enhancing Internal Audit Through Innovative Practices* (1996), Glen L. Gray and Maryann Jacobi Gray, The Institute of Internal Auditors Research Foundation, Orlando, US.

13 Auditors Are Runners

"Will you walk a little faster?" said a whiting to a snail. There's a porpoise close behind us, and he's treading on my tail.

Lewis Carroll (1832–1898) *The Lobster Quadrille*

In this chapter I see all auditors as runners in the race for Excellence. To be runners in the professions they have chosen to race in, they must be inspired to be committed to continuous improvement, passionate about the Excellence of the services they provide and PROACTIVE in all their auditing. All these qualities must be part of the marketing of their services, during their auditing and consulting and in the communication and follow-up of their findings. And not just written communications, but also with all they meet at board, executive and operations levels and with their organisation's stakeholders.

13.1 Running Auditors Are PROACTIVE

In my book *Cutting Edge Internal Auditing* (2008), I discussed the many hats running internal auditors were wearing at that time, often changing these at times

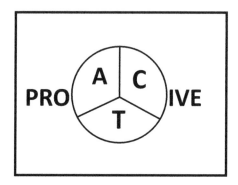

Figure 13.1 The proactive auditor

PROfessional – **A**uditor – **C**onsultant – **T**eacher
Independent – Added **V**alue – **E**thical

Source: J. Ridley (1970)

during the audit process. Those hats could have been applied to all auditors in the services they provide. And, they still can be worn today and into the future. The hat I liked most was the one of the runner wearing the hat with the logo '**ACT**' at the front. This was a hat I expected all my auditors to wear during their auditing. To me '**ACT**' represents how creativity and innovation should be driven in all in auditing and the underlying theories in this book. ACT stands for **A**ssurance: **C**onsulting: **T**eaching. It is also at the centre of **PRO ACT I V E** which every auditor should be to achieve Excellence – **PRO**fessional: Independent: [Added] **V**alue: **E**thical in every step of the Ten Step Audit Process – see Figure 13.1 – is this the Brand you market in your organisation?

I started my internal auditing experiences and learning in General Motors in the mid-1960s, an Excellent learning curve then for modern internal auditing in manufacturing and in all organisations across all sectors. Many years later, I was pleased to see Jacqueline Wagner (2000)[1] (former general auditor at General Motors) see internal auditors 'out in front in their organisations . . . leading our business units from both an overall process and a control perspective and focusing on strategic business objectives'. This concept of internal auditors wearing leader and strategic hats in their organisations and in the profession of internal auditing is essential for any approach to creativity and innovation in the audit process. Wagner saw this and included the following guidance in her article for internal auditors running as agents of change (guidance equally applicable to all auditors):

> From environments of change emerge change agents, those people who make change happen or facilitate change throughout the organisation. They have real jobs, do real work – and driving change is built into how they carry out their duties. Creating change is a skill; but getting things done and moving the business are the change agent's passions. Based on the

following key characteristics I think that internal auditors' most important modern role could be as change agents:

- For change to take hold in an organisation, it must be linked explicitly to real performance goals, and it has to be in the hands of people who understand the business first and change second. Change agents ask what the goals of the organisation are, and they focus on how reaching their own objectives affect the organisation's operation.
- The key to making change happen is to create an environment where people gravitate in the direction you want them to go. The best way to accomplish this is to make people aware of best practices. They'll naturally use a better way if you make one available. Change agents enable change.
- If you're going to get something done, you're going to discomfit people around you. Change agents often interrupt routines, reveal problems, and make more work on the way to making less work.
- A change agent must always be in two places at once: where the organisation is and where it's going. They must be equally comfortable dealing with senior, management and frontline workers because change agents need the support of both groups.
- Once you begin to work as a change agent, you're automatically subject to a higher level of scrutiny and a tougher standard of judgment – from those both above and below you. People watch change agents even more closely than others to make sure that they measure up.

Earlier research sponsored by The IIA into internal auditing working relationships (Mints 1970)[2] analysed internal audit relationships into the following three patterns, all of which inspired me in my own auditing career, the creative thinking in this book, and can still be seen today in the hats worn by all running auditors:

1 Traditional Audit Approach

Compliance
Protection
Inspection.

2 Current Moderate Approach

Constructive
Helpful
Solves problems.

3 Participating Teamwork Approach

Involves auditee
Develops team spirit
Relates audit aims to auditee's goals.

Mints recommended the participative teamwork relationship between auditors and their clients works best for the development of internal auditing as a profession. He did not discard the other two relationships, both of which he believed had their place at times. Since then, there have been many published examples of values perceived from all these roles practiced by auditors, including those of 'change-agent', 'improver', 'facilitator', 'partner', 'team player', 'educator' and 'trainer'. Just look at the vacancy notices for auditors in most of today's professional journals and newspapers. Many require some, if not all, of these roles. Hats worn by the 'educator' and 'trainer' auditor are new for many auditors, yet many wear these even though they may not always be seen as such. Auditors wear these hats in their relationships with boards, audit committees, management and operations staff.

Many years ago I remember seeing a job vacancy notice in the press for a senior auditor, which ended with the exciting statement, 'We are looking for a person who will "hit the ground running".' In other words, a person who will be PROACTIVE, who will know the rules and will have continuously practiced running in an Excellent team. I turned this phrase into the following short article for internal auditors in 2002, but now edited for all auditors:

Walk Faster This Year[3]

An auditing job vacancy notice in the UK press called for applicants that would 'Hit the Ground Running'. The speed of movement impressed me, as I am sure it did the applicants. The notice described the person they were seeking as:

> a dynamic professional who will 'hit the ground running' and play a lead role in control systems evaluations, audit programme development and special reviews. The audit team is seen as having a very positive mission to continually improve the business . . .

Those that recruit audit staff in the job market place frequently use superlatives to attract the best experienced and qualified staff. This enhances the value of audit, not just for the applicants but also for their employing organisations. There are also benefits for the profession of auditing. All marketing of auditing as a profession has an impact on those who work in the profession and those who are served by it. An impact that is often wider than apparent at the time.

Today, the most frequently used superlatives describing auditors in job vacancy notices are RIGOROUS, ASTUTE, SELF STARTER, INNOVATIVE, OUTSTANDING, and LEADER. Widen this list by looking up each in any thesaurus and you have a range of attractive and positive, if not some conflicting, descriptive images of today's successful auditor. A good exercise for all auditing conferences! Try it at your next group meeting and measure the reaction to each image.

But is 'keeping up with management' sufficient for the international or national auditor in the year 2016? I think not. Hitting the ground running may have been ahead of the recruitment game in the past, but now there has to be a commitment by auditors to outpace the runner: to be ahead of management. One of the superlatives that must describe auditors of the future must be IMAGINATIVE. Imagination, not so much in the fanciful sense but in a disciplined and professional approach to future events and needs: essential for the auditing new roles in risk assessment and consultancy. Closely linked to imaginative is INNOVATIVE. This has been used in recent years to describe auditors, particularly those in changing environments. Innovation is key to continuous improvement satisfaction of customer needs. Both imagination and innovation will increase in their importance in the future. Internal auditors without these characteristics will not be running as they hit the ground.

Competitors in the auditing market place will always be seeking to be at leading edge in the services they provide. They have to, to stay in business. They will always be looking for auditors who are walking fast, so that they can provide the right level of professional service with the right people.

Efficiency and effectiveness in auditing are today and tomorrow no longer sufficient attributes by themselves in the quality of work they provide. They both need to be there, but in addition running auditors need to be seen to wearing many, if not all, of the hats mentioned above. What I have not discussed are the *colours* of the hats auditors should wear. Edward de Bono (1985),[4] the 'lateral thinking' management guru who invented the concept of lateral thinking, now entered in the Oxford English Dictionary as 'seeking to solve problems by unorthodox or apparently illogical methods',[5] set out in the 1980s his colours for hats, each with its own style of thinking. These colours have stood the test of time well and are still worn today across the world to guide critical thinking in problem solving. Most auditors wear all De Bono's colours of hats at different times in any engagement, mostly without being aware of the colour they are wearing. There is a challenge here for all running auditors to recognise the importance of De Bono's colours in their audit processes.

13.2 Running Auditors Know the Power of Three

The *power of three* has been associated with success for a very long time. It rules that the brain can see relationships between three things easier and more effectively than other numbers of things. It can be seen in all walks of life, in professionalism, marketing, science, literature and almost all sporting and social activities.

It is based on a theory that success comes from associations of three things. Think of all the powers of three you have encountered in your life from literature titles, through marketing of products and services to work and sport. In corporate governance we have the three principles of accountability, integrity and openness. Runners in a race start with 1, 2, 3, GO and end with first, second and third past the winning line. In the Olympics this would be Gold, Silver and Bronze. This book and my Governance Framework have used the power of three intentionally:

A Governance Framework of THREE lines representing

STEWARDSHIP: CHANGE: ASSURANCE

Each with THREE THEMES

STEWARDSHIP – BOARD: EXECUTIVE: OPERATIONS
CHANGE – TIME: RISK MANAGEMENT: INSIGHT
ASSURANCE – SELF: INTERNAL: EXTERNAL

Each with THREE METAPHORS

STEWARDSHIP – RESPONSIBLE LEADERS: AMBASSADORS: GATEKEEPERS
CHANGE – TIME TRAVELLERS: SCIENTISTS: FUTURISTS
ASSURANCE – SCEPTICS: LAWYERS: QUALITY MANAGERS

Each motivated by the THREE COMMITMENTS for EXCELLENCE to be

RESEARCHERS: BENCHMARKERS: RUNNERS

Look for the power of three in your organisation: use the power of three in your auditing. It can be a powerful tool in each of the steps of the Ten Step Audit Process. The following are just some examples, but create your own to influence how you audit, how you train your auditors and how you sell your audit results to those you audit at each of the three levels of Stewardship in the Governance Framework.

Creative Thinking and Innovation in the Ten Step Audit Process

1 Create the audit vision and strategy to **MOTIVATE** excellence, quality and add value and improvement in the **EXPERTISE** and **SKILLS** needed in all auditing processes.

   POWER OF THREE – Motivate: Expertise: Skills

2 Plan each audit engagement over a period of time.

   POWER OF THREE – Strategic Plan: Annual Plan: Engagement Plan

3   Seek insight into operations being audited – their theory and best practices, through **ASSOCIATION: QUESTIONING: OBSERVING: NETWORKING**

   POWER OF THREE – Knowledge: Understanding: Share

4   Assess risks involved by the operations being audited and the audit

   POWER OF THREE – Likelihood: Impact: Alleviate

5   Establish scope and objectives for the audit engagement.

   POWER OF THREE – Aims: Resources: Time

6   Develop a risk-based audit programme and identify controls.

   POWER OF THREE – Protect: Inspect: Detect

7   Select techniques/methodology and **EXPERIMENT** to search for appropriate evidence.

   POWER OF THREE – Explore: Create: Innovate

8   Objectively evaluate audit outputs, consider outcomes and agree findings.

   POWER OF THREE – Cause: Effect: Correction

9   Communicate audit findings to those accountable.

   POWER OF THREE – Inspire: Imagine: Improve

10   Follow-up and consider actions taken by the organisation.

   POWER OF THREE – Progress: Consider: Finalise

Following the trail of the ten steps in your organisations as a runner with the power of three will lead you into successful results for your audits, success for your organisations and success for your careers inside and outside of audit.

Running auditors do not always have the same energy or aims. There are those who are good at running the short distance and those who are very good at the long distance; those who run for pleasure and those who run to win and the success that can bring. In 1997 I wrote on success as not being the aim – the aim being to improve continuously. What I discussed then applies just as much today to the competitive running auditor and will do tomorrow.

What Is Success?[6]

Success should not be the aim.
The aim should be to improve.
Improvement requires controlled change.
Change is best controlled when it is seen as a continuous process

of selection, education and development opportunities.

Processes should always start with commitment to a vision.

A vision that must be right for the time.

Visions require measured strategies and tactics.

The achievements of strategies and tactics depend on the control of people.

People in the supply chain depend on each other for success.

To succeed as individuals is not enough.

All people in the supply chain need to belong to successful teams.

All people in the supply chain need the reinforcement of successful lives.

The role of all managers is to control.

Control requires an understanding of its objectives.

Each control objective impacts and influences success in people.

It is the way people succeed that controls the successful organisation.

Managers in the Best Organisations Select, Educate and Develop the Best People and Teams

The aim of every organisation should be to improve. This means not only the structure and processes, not only the people that make up the organisation, but also the people who surround the organisation, as part of its supply chains. It also means the community that it serves. Improvement generates success. Improvement does not happen by accident, it has to be controlled as a process of change. Continuous improvement is now a way of life in organisations across the world. It knows no national boundaries. The quality it creates is the way of business and government everywhere. It thrives on benchmarking and the search for best practices. It recognises change as a continuous cycle of selection, education and development.

The cycle of selection, education and development is at the heart of all human activity. It always has been and always will be. Best management of that cycle in others requires an understanding of how the cycle works for you. We all learn, from the day we are born, to the day we die. At first, the selection stage is mainly by others – we are fully controlled. We soon move into our own selection process and from thereon life is a mixture of choices by ourselves, and others. Each and every day, each and every moment we are making and being subjected to a selection process. The choices we make forge our destiny. They create the opportunities and emotions we experience all our lives. They contribute to our failures and successes.

In any organisation, it is management's role to communicate clearly the choices people have and the results expected from those choices. Some may call this control, others opportunity. Perhaps, it is always a mixture of both. Selection is best if it is communicated as opportunity. The art of management is to be a good communicator: to communicate the importance of selection in the minds of people: to help choice.

But selection is not the end. Selection starts the education process. Being taught and teaching oneself are everyday experiences. This activity is often seen as the learning curve. In an organisation it starts the day people are employed and continues until the day of leaving. It is at its best when motivated by a feeling of self-selection. I choose to learn is better than 'you will learn'. The good manager will encourage education self-selection. It drives the best understanding. A search for knowledge through education stimulates innovation.

"How, What, Why, When Where, Who" are the six honest workingmen of Rudyard Kipling's Just So Stories. They are as true today as they always have been. They are fundamental to invention and progress. They are the questions all people should ask as they learn. But education is not the end. Education by itself is not sufficient for success. Education requires development. And, development does not come by accident; it needs to be planned. Planned development is a skill in itself. All tasks require a period of training. For some tasks and people this training is brief: for other tasks and people it is a long and sometimes continuous process. Recognising the time needed for development is an important part of good management, in oneself and in others.

Committing time for development in oneself and others is not always easy. Pressure and stress, even in controlled change can reduce the time available for development. We have all experienced reduction of staff and training costs: what follows can too often be a reduction of time spent on development, both at work and at home. Yet, development is the key to success. It always will be the key to successful change. Good managers recognise this. Those that train recognise this. Professions recognise this. Governments recognise this. Why is it then that development receives such a low priority with some managers and some people? To know the answer to this is the key to success.

But good managers and good people do not stop at development. The cycle of selection, education and development starts all over again. It is a continuous process and because of this needs direction. It needs vision. A vision is a forecast of a future desired state at a point in time, which is attractive to the beholder. All people have visions. Visions change: they need to be appropriate to their time. Not all people use their visions to select, educate and develop themselves or others. Good managers create visions for organisations and, through the cycle of selection, education and development establish commitment for the future state.

Commitment not just by people but also by teams of people. Once the vision is agreed, key strategies and tactics must follow, linked and measured to the required future state. A wish for success is part of everyone's vision, though the measure may be different for each person. Personal visions need to be built into team and group visions. All visions should stretch people and teams to improve. All visions should demand change for the better. All visions should aim for success. The art of good management is to establish and achieve visions by the cycles of selection, education and development of people and teams. Creating the wish to succeed in people makes success happen.

Establishing visions and commitment is not easy. Using measures for each strategy involves all people in the process. That involvement can be made easier and more quickly if managers follow the selection, education and development cycle for everyone participating in the associated supply chains. This means considering people who are employed by suppliers and customers. The good manager helps people in both suppliers and customers to succeed. The good manager builds suppliers and customers into their teams. This means that suppliers and customers must also help their people to select, educate and develop. Good managers recognise this.

But is success by people in an organisation sufficient reward and reinforcement for others to follow? All research and evidence shows that this is not so. People need to be successful in all parts of their lives, or at least feel success. This is a tall order! How can managers help people to succeed in their lives outside the workplace? Such a question is not irrelevant. Many organisations and managers have recognised the importance of opportunities for their people to be successful in activities other than work. Provision of resources and time to select, educate and develop in families, hobbies, sports and pastimes is not new. What is new is the reduction of these facilities in times of change. Yet such reduction takes away opportunities for people to be successful, which is not what an organisation wants. Too often managers are seen to be short sighted in the opportunities they provide for selection, education and development both inside and outside the workplace. Yet the key to their own success lies in such opportunities.

The continuous cycles of selection, education and development in and around any organisation and supply chain, need to be managed. This means they need to be controlled. Many will say that they are controlled in the best organisations. But are they? Linking each of the processes to the primary objectives of control provides managers with a useful framework to test how successful they are. The objectives of control can be analysed as:

- RELIABILITY
- COMPLIANCE
- SECURITY
- ECONOMY
- EFFICIENCY
- EFFECTIVENESS
- ENVIRONMENTAL
- ETHICS
- EQUALITY.

None of the above needs explanation to any manager. They are all part of the decision making process in every organisation, whether by people or the teams they form. Some are more recent as objectives than others. All are changing shape and definition as we move into the 21st century. Without exception each is becoming more demanding: each is becoming a requirement, not only of the organisation, but also of the community, nation and world. Yet few managers approach success in their people through the achievement of each. Any success that does not recognise all these control objectives, fails to make the most of people.

All control activities should require each of the nine objectives to be achieved. Every vision, strategy and tactic in an organisation can be influenced by the quality of performance of each. Penalty for failure to achieve any one can make the difference between success or failure, survival or demise. Good managers realise this and use control objectives to influence the cycles of selection, education and development in the people they manage. Corporate history is full of organisations that ignored these relationships: full of the managers who did not link success in people to the management of control and change.

In the same way that visions and success are a moment in time, so is control. Each requires consideration of past and present when planning the future. The framework for controlling the cycles of selection, education and development takes on a multi-dimensional model. It is a clear understanding by managers of this fundamental law of success and control, which helps most people succeed. Success is the key motivation for change: controlled success breeds successful change.

Success, best, better, good, excellent and delight are the hallmarks of customer satisfaction. Each has an association with success – in organisations, their products, services and the people they employ. We all recognise these associations but few analyse the controls that influence each, or award success the applause it so often deserves. Control is the key to success. Applause should be seen as an accolade, not an embarrassment.

How should performance in people be applauded? Is applause seen by people to be more an embarrassment than a reward? Are managers well trained to recognise success, reinforce its achievement or punish failure? There are clearly mixed good and bad reinforcement and punishment practices within and between all organisations. Few recognise the importance of relating such best practices to the control of selection, education and development. If it were otherwise the number of people succeeding would increase many times. There would be no need for training awards and the focus on helping people to succeed would have a high profile in every organisation. Good reinforcement and punishment administered through the process of change is at the heart of all success.

> *Helping people to succeed through their cycles of selection, education and development is the only future for any organisation. It is also the only future for any community, nation or the world. Linking that help into personal and group visions is essential. Linking that help into the objectives of control in an organisation. ensures success, both for the organisation and the people it employs and serves.*

13.3 Running Auditors Market a Brand of Excellence

All auditors need to be **PROACTIVE** in promoting themselves and their profession as Excellent, not just in their organisations, but also in their communities, nations and globally. That promotion is there in the professional bodies supporting auditing practices. Their visions and missions, bodies of knowledge, qualifications, research and forward planning are runners. It should be there in an organisation in all the assurance mapping, auditing charters, contracts, job descriptions and forward planning. It should be seen not just by management and the board, but by all staff through intranet or other forms of organisation communications. It should be seen by all an organisation's stakeholders outside the organisation. This is still rare in organisations across the private sector but is more common in the public sector.

In research I carried out in 1998 into the marketing of auditing, I referenced Webster (1994)[7] and his market-driven management concept seen in many organisations as a total commitment, involving everyone. This concept relates all internal products and services with a primary focus on both internal and external customer satisfaction and loyalty. Webster integrates the new marketing concept with all phases of corporate strategy, structure and culture, and shows how it should work today. He considers brand equity as a replacement for the older concepts of brand image and brand loyalty. Brand equity recognises the financial value of a brand name. Many internal and external audit providers worldwide have focused on the 'brand image' for their auditing services. For those that face competitive situations in and outside their organisations – and these are many – the importance of customer brand loyalty is important, often for survival! I believe the brand image for all auditors should be ACT as runners, continuously proactive and passionate in the creative and innovative services they provide. That 'brand image' if successful should lead to 'brand equity'.

In my book *Cutting Edge Internal Auditing*, I researched the following definition of 'marketing' from literature.

Selling any product or service requires knowledge of potential markets, and understanding of potential customers' needs and satisfaction. It requires research and development, a strategic plan, code of conduct, objectives, appropriate resources and processes, and a skilled sales force. It promotes orally and visually a clear vision and mission statement for its products and services, to its total organisation and all customers. It motivates everyone involved by perceived high levels of quality, value, continuity and growth. It creates improved and new products and services, at the right prices, for existing and new customers. It continuously monitors results. Establishing and maintaining markets is a continuous learning process.

Readers may have their own definitions of marketing. From the above it is possible to select and rearrange the following twenty key terms as a check list for auditors in their marketing planning:

CLEAR VISION AND MISSION
PRODUCTS AND SERVICES
STRATEGIC PLAN
POTENTIAL MARKETS
OBJECTIVES
EXISTING AND NEW CUSTOMERS.
NEEDS AND SATISFACTION
CONDUCT
APPROPRIATE RESOURCES
APPROPRIATE PROCESSES
SKILLED
PROMOTES ORALLY AND VISUALLY
MOTIVATES EVERYONE INVOLVED
PERCEIVED HIGH LEVELS OF QUALITY
VALUE
CONTINUITY AND GROWTH
CREATES IMPROVED AND NEW PRODUCTS AND SERVICES
THE RIGHT PRICES
CONTINUOUSLY MONITORS RESULTS
CONTINUOUS LEARNING PROCESS.

Auditors need to be committed to their professions if they are to be best, better than best and Excellent. This is much more than studying for and passing professional examinations and being employed as an auditor.

The stimulant for being Excellent should always start in the job advertisement for the auditor, based on a marketed auditing vision and charter, followed by the interview and induction programme. Then, in individual job description, targets, appraisals, continuous development, recognitions and rewards. At each stage there has to be an emphasis on Excellence. But is this always so? In my auditing career I have rarely found the aim of Excellence seen in all of these steps in an auditor's services. In some, yes, but not all. Is the word Excellent in any of these steps in your own auditing employment? Is it in your charter, vision or mission statement?

Marketing now sees the achievement of Excellence in products and services as essential for customer satisfaction – good or very good is not sufficient for long-term success. Social profit today can also be seen in many brands of products and services, some already mentioned in this book. The achievement of many, if not all of the United Nations recently published seventeen Sustainability Goals – see

Appendix H – can be seen in the marketing of many products and services. Note the links for each of these into the 7S's McKinsey Excellence Framework of 1982 and today's principles of corporate governance and quality. The importance of this for all auditors and the marketing of their Excellence cannot be overstated. This is essential for their achievement of quality and innovation when identifying and closing 'gaps' when they are benchmarking each other and with others.

13.4 Running Auditors Must Race Into the Future

Today's professionals, of whatever philosophy, cannot stand still in the face of the speed of change across all aspects of our lives and the influences that can make them richer, longer and in many ways more enjoyable, but at the same time less safe. All professions must react to this speed of change. All professions will have to walk faster and be more proactive in their responses to this speed of change. The auditing profession cannot be an exemption to this. Their codes of conduct, qualification processes and continuing professional development must be proactive if they are to meet the needs of their clients and civil society. For many professions, this walking fast must start in the higher education processes, leading their students to professional membership. Evidence for walking faster in the accountancy profession can be seen in the *Manifesto* published by AuditFutures[8] and in its 2015[9] *Philosophy for Accountancy – Educating Responsible Professionals through Critical Thinking and Ethical Reasoning*. Both these current statements use the term proactive for the auditing and accounting professions. In its *Manifesto*, AuditFutures declares:

> Aligning personal motivation with professional aspiration is important in rethinking the role of professionals in society. We will foster a proactive ethos to motivate and encourage people to take the initiative and show leadership in shaping the future of their profession.

Here are my ten forecasts for what will be 'shaping the future' of auditing. All need to be addressed by running auditors, and all have been discussed in previous chapters:

1 Governments and regulators will take more active interest in the quality and quantity of all independent and objective assurances being provided to a board, requiring motivating standards and codes of conduct for the performance of all auditors.
2 Boards across all sectors will extend the scope of activities of their audit committees to cover all aspects of governance and require more assurances on financial, environmental and social issues. In some countries this scope will become law.
3 Audit committees will take a more **PROACTIVE** role in mapping the assurances required by their boards, how these are all coordinated and how all auditors collaborate, coordinate and cooperate with each other.
4 The status of all auditors will grow by new reporting lines to audit committees and their boards.

5   Internal auditors will be seen by organisations as a part of the senior management team.
6   Auditors will be encouraged to be more creative and innovative in all the roles they have in their organisations.
7   Auditors will report more evaluations and judgements to a wider group of their organisation's stakeholders, including their organisation's regulators.
8   Stakeholders will require and take more interest in the external reporting by audit committees and all auditors.
9   Auditing will be taught in more university business schools and colleges as a separate management and governance science, not just a part of accountancy.
10 Auditors will use innovations in technology to continuously improve their auditing techniques.

There is evidence today these forecasts are happening in many organisations and recognised as essential by some governments, regulators and professional institutes representing auditors. Some will change and others will be added, but how they develop must be seen and will be contributed to by running auditors.

13.5 Chapter Review

In this chapter I have discussed the importance of auditors being runners in the services they provide today and in the future: running to market the Excellence of services they provide to all their stakeholders. Their professions do this and so do most of their employers. By running I mean demonstrating their **A**uditing: **C**onsultancy: **T**eaching in professionalism **(PRO)**, through Independent**(I)**, Added value**(V)** and Ethical**(E)** behaviour – by being **PROACTIVE** in all that they do to delight all their stakeholders.

13.6 Creative Audit Thinking Activities

Activity 49   Creativity and Innovation in Auditing Run With Today's Sustainability Goals

Study Appendix H and use the Sustainability Goals to run in your next audit engagement. Challenge your customers with your knowledge of how they relate to your audit objectives and their objectives – across all their supply chains. Creatively think how this definition can encourage innovation in each of the steps in your audit process. Read the following Preamble from the United Nations Statement on its 2015 Sustainability Goals.

Transforming Our World: The 2030 Agenda for Sustainable Development[10]

This Agenda is a plan of action for people, planet and prosperity. It also seeks to strengthen universal peace in larger freedom. We recognise that

---

eradicating poverty in all its forms and dimensions, including extreme poverty, is the greatest global challenge and an indispensable requirement for sustainable development. All countries and all stakeholders, acting in collaborative partnership, will implement this plan. We are resolved to free the human race from the tyranny of poverty and want and to heal and secure our planet. We are determined to take the bold and transformative steps which are urgently needed to shift the world on to a sustainable and resilient path. As we embark on this collective journey, we pledge that no one will be left behind. This Agenda is a plan of action for people, planet and prosperity. It also seeks to strengthen universal peace in steps which are urgently needed to shift the world on to a sustainable and resilient path. The 17 Sustainable Development Goals and 169 targets which we are announcing today demonstrate the scale and ambition of this new universal Agenda. They seek to build on the Millennium Development Goals and complete what they did not achieve. They seek to realise the human rights of all and to achieve gender equality and the empowerment of all women and girls. They are integrated and indivisible and balance the three dimensions of sustainable development: the economic, social and environmental. The Goals and targets will stimulate action over the next 15 years in areas of critical importance for humanity and the planet.

Activity 50   Create an Innovative Running Brand for Your Auditing

Creating a brand image for products and services is an important part of the motivation for developing these and customer perceptions. We see this every day in all products and services, in the media and in the products and services we use in everyday life. Why not also in auditing? Professional auditing firms do this in many different ways. Do you have a brand image for your auditing? Consider the brand image I developed at Figure 13.1 and used in the 1970s. Reflect on how advanced this was in the perceptions of auditing at that time, even today. Use the leadership attributes in Figure 2.3, repeated below, to create your own brand of auditing. Choose a selection of what is most like your auditing. From these create your own brand image. Then consider how you can use this to run a little faster with innovations.

Attributes of Leadership[11]

Being authentic
Demonstrating integrity

Being rational
Being emotionally intelligent
Being adaptable
Seeing the big picture
Making an impact
Being open to difference
Demonstrating value and purpose
Exercising soft power
Digital fluency
Interacting more closely with employees and customers
Handling intense scrutiny
Making time for reflection
Creating and building strong teams
Being resilient.

Activity 51   Run to Create a Vision for Excellence in Auditing

Use the following components of the vision in Figure D.1 to run pro-
actively with your auditing. Create a new vision for your auditing with
innovation in its mission.

Vision

Consistently excellent
highly skilled,
committed
working together.

Our values

Excellence

We measure and continuously improve our standards,
striving for excellence at all times.

Respect

We show respect for you and for each other.

Notes

1 *Leading the Way* (August 2000), Jacqueline K. Wagner, Internal Auditor, The Institute of Internal Auditors Inc., Orlando, US.
2 *Behavioral Patterns in Internal Audit Relationships* (1972), Dr. F. E. Mints, The Institute of Internal Auditors Inc., Orlando, US.
3 *Walk Faster This Year* (January 2002), Jeffrey Ridley, Internal Auditing and Business Risk, IIA-UK and Ireland, London, England.
4 *Six Thinking Hats*® (1985), Edward de Bono, Penguin Books, Harmondsworth, Middlesex, England.
5 *Guide to the Management Gurus – Shortcuts to the Ideas of Leading Management Thinkers* (1991), Carol Kennedy, Mackays of Chatham plc, Chatham, Kent, England.
6 Published in *Internal Auditing* (April 1997 pp. 22–23), IIA-UK and Ireland. Jeffrey Ridley, and as a case study in *Leading Edge Internal Auditing* (1998 pp. 172–176), Jeffrey Ridley and Andrew Chambers, ICSA Publishing, London, England.
7 *Market-Driven Management – Using the New Marketing Concept to Create a Customer-Oriented Company* (1994), Frederick E. Webster, Jr., John Wiley and Sons, Inc., New York, USA.
8 *Manifesto* published by AuditFutures, London, England. www.AuditFutures.org, accessed December 2016.
9 *Philosophy for Accountancy – Educating Responsible Professionals Through Critical Thinking and Ethical Reasoning* (2015), AuditFutures, Institute of Chartered Accountants in England and Wales, London, England.
10 *Transforming Our World: The 2030 Agenda for Sustainable Development* (2015 p. 3), United Nations, New York, US.
11 Source: *Manchester Square Partners* (2015), Manchester, England.

Epilogue

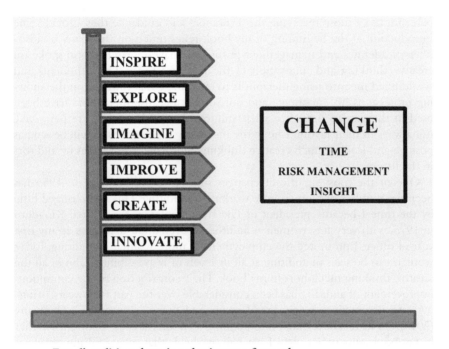

For all auditing there is only six ways forward.

My book has no ending. Inspiration, Exploration, Imagination, Improvement, Innovation and Creativity will always be needed along all audit trails. All will be at every signpost and milestone on the road to Excellence in all auditing. Since the beginning of the 20th century, there has been a continuous auditing road, with many signposts[1] pointing to the directions auditors have taken to meet the assurance needs of past, current and future generations of boards. Today, audit committees, many stakeholders and civil societies across all sectors and nations are travelling that same road. Assurance needs have been influenced by significant and rapid changes in management practices; technologies, laws, regulatory standards and requirements. We live in a shrinking world with instantaneous speeds of communication; global networks of politics; products, services and knowledge; urgent needs to control climates and save the planet; and always the possibilities of bad behaviour, insecurity, fraud and other malpractices. Assurance needs that will require more co-operations, collaborations and co-ordinations between professions, management at all levels in organisations and all stakeholders who have an interest in the Excellence of auditing.

Today, auditors are providing assurances and guidance across all sectors, in all nations and globally. Auditing is an international profession and will continue to grow in numbers, knowledge and techniques. This growth will change auditing principles and practices in the 21st century. These changes will be influenced by their own perceptions of the services they provide and by the perceptions of those receiving the assurances and guidance they provide. The introduction at the beginning of my book relies much on the many philosophers, academics and management gurus who have researched and spoke on creative thinking and innovation in the past and today. Their thoughts and wisdom led me into using metaphors to encourage that thinking in the auditing professions. To encourage and not to start because metaphors have been used in the past to influence what auditors do and how they are perceived, not always in their favour. I hope the metaphors I have chosen will be seen as positive and lead to much creative thinking and many innovations by auditors in the future.

One of the most significant changes since I started auditing in 1953 has been the number of women now working in auditing. This had changed little by the time I became president of The IIA Chapter in the United Kingdom in 1975, with very few women as auditors or even audit managers. In my first year of office, I promoted the employment of more women in auditing. Today, women can be seen in auditing at all its levels of responsibilities and in all the creative thinking metaphors in my book. Their contribution to the continuous improvement of auditing has been considerable over the past forty years, bringing into its practices a new brand image and success. Tomorrow's Company (2014),[2] in its recent research into building a culture, already mentioned earlier in my book, supports a view I have always held, 'that successful innovation is more likely to come from diverse teams compared to homogeneous teams'. Diverse teams in all auditing will be the key to its creativity and innovation in the future.

Auditing will never be simple and easy. It will always be an exploration into the unknown. It will continue to grow in complexity, in development of its own science and creation of principles, standards and technology. Not just in its own policies and search for Excellence in the Assurance, Consulting and Teaching services it provides, but also in the results from its auditing. There will never be an end to the need for Excellent auditing, whether individually or in audit teams and across bridges with its many different stakeholders. That achievement of Excellence by all auditors must embrace the needs of all societies in this century. It already has for some auditors. I have many memories of the results of my auditing having an impact on wider society needs without always recognising this at the time. That recognition must be there for all auditors in their strategies and objectives. One of the metaphors for auditors I did not use in my book was that of being seen as doctors. I recommend to all auditors to study the professional duties of doctors and compare these with their own professional duties. They are very similar and open up many opportunities for creative thinking and innovation.

However creativity and innovation comes about in all auditing in the 21st century, it will be of necessity and needed by all interested in the **EXCELLENCE** of **STEWARDSHIP**, **CHANGE** and **ASSURANCE** in the organisations in which they have a stake and interest. For some auditors as **Scientists** continuous improvement in its principles and practice will be a passion, for others an opportunity to develop their careers outside of auditing, for others just a job, but all must be always **Benchmarkers** and **Runners**, seeking best practice as **Quality Managers**. Their scope of work will grow from being **Researchers** and promoting themselves as **Responsible Leaders, Ambassadors, Gatekeepers** and **Lawyers** in all aspects of governance, risk management and control. Auditors will always need to be **Time Travellers** and **Futurists**, judging economic, environmental and social issues as independent and objective **Sceptics**.

In the previous paragraph I have included all the metaphors for the roles of auditors in my book and the components in my framework for creative thinking and innovation in governance. The best auditors will always be seeing themselves and selling their creativity and innovation in each of the metaphors in the services they are providing, in each of the components – Stewardship, Change and Excellence. Readers are free to create more metaphors for their auditing and to add these to the paragraph. That is what creativity and innovation is all about. Use this paragraph at your next audit training day to start discussion on creating your next innovative audit project.

The creative audit thinking activities I have selected and written for each Chapter, together with my selected Appendices and sources of references in this and century offer opportunities for all auditors to develop new auditing skills and practices for today and the future in each of the steps in my Ten Step Audit Process. This will have to happen if the assurance needs in all today and tomorrow's organisations are to delight across the globe. The word/terms I selected in my tables to create measures for your own understanding of Excellence in auditing and corporate governance, risk management, control and Excellence in those you are auditing. Add to these word/terms for your own organisations and sectors.

Innovative future scenarios for all auditors are being forecast by all their professions. For external auditors, that forecast is in a research report published by the Institute of Chartered Accountants in England and Wales (2014)[3] mentioned in earlier Chapters. Its final paragraph is an imaginative and creative thought for all auditors, which should point the way to many **INSPIRATIONS, EXPLORATIONS, IMAGINATIONS, IMPROVEMENTS,**

INNOVATIONS and **CREATE** the auditing needed for the 21st century and beyond. This is what my book has all been about:

> The spirit of this report is different. It encourages the profession to go beyond Groundhog Day and seize the initiative as the best way of repairing trust, sparking innovation and increasing the economic, social and environmental value it generates. We suggest that it aims high, not just by finding more efficient ways of doing what it does today, but by playing an active role in influencing the development of a society – and within that, an economy – that is better informed by the standards, skills and insights of audit.

This is one scenario for all auditors in the 21st century – there are and will be others from the creativity and innovations of many auditors.

Notes

1 *Cutting Edge Internal Auditing* (2008 cover sheet) Jeffrey Ridley, John Wiley and Sons Ltd., Chichester, England.
2 *Tomorrow's Global Leaders: How to build a culture that enables women to reach the top* (2014 p. 13), Tomorrow's Company, London, England.
3 *Enlightening Professions? A vision for audit and a better society* (2014), Research by Paul Buddery, Steven Frank and Martin Martinoff of the Royal Society of Arts Action and Research Centre, Institute of Chartered Accountants in England and Wales, London, England. [The aim of AuditFutures is to construct a holistic view and an innovative approach to rethinking the profession and to create opportunities for dialogue and for collaborative solutions to emerge.]

Appendices

Appendix A

The Ten Principles of the United Nations

Global Compact Human Rights[1]

Principle 1 Businesses should support and respect the protection of internationally proclaimed human rights; and

Principle 2 make sure that they are not complicit in human rights abuses.

Labour

Principle 3 Businesses should uphold the freedom of association and the effective recognition of the right to collective bargaining;

Principle 4 the elimination of all forms of forced and compulsory labour;

Principle 5 the effective abolition of child labour; and

Principle 6 the elimination of discrimination in respect of employment and occupation.

Environment

Principle 7 Businesses should support a precautionary approach to environmental challenges;

Principle 8 undertake initiatives to promote greater environmental responsibility; and

Principle 9 encourage the development and diffusion of environmentally friendly technologies.

Anti-corruption

Principle 10 Businesses should work against corruption in all its forms, including extortion and bribery.

Note

1 Based on the Universal Declaration of Human Rights (1948), celebrated in a *60th Anniversary Special Edition 1948–2008* (2008), United Nations, New York, US. The first Nine Principles were launched with the establishment of the United Nations Global Compact

organisation in 2000 and the Tenth Principle added by the United Nations in 2004. United Nations Global Compact was a call to companies around the world to align their strategies and operations with universal principles in the areas of human rights, labour, environment, and anti-corruption, and to take action in support of broader UN goals. With more than 8,000 signatories and stakeholders in more than 135 countries, it is the world's largest voluntary corporate responsibility initiative. www.unglobalcompact.org.

Appendix B

Ten Top Tips for Improving Leadership and Capability Management[1]

1) Recognise that good leadership and management matters

Good management is not all about balance sheets and business strategies. Your employees and how they are managed and engaged are crucial to business success. The extent they are aligned to your organisation's purpose and values and are prepared to go the extra mile at work is fundamental to organisation performance. How people are managed on a day to day basis will influence their opinions, behaviours and decisions in the service of your organisation. Managing people is difficult and it is easy to get it wrong, so you need to dedicate time and resources to this.

2) Be a role model: good leadership and management starts at the top

When was the last time you asked your employees 'how are you' or asked for their views? Do you listen to your employees when they ask for help? Do you treat people with consideration, act calmly under pressure and do you act with integrity? You need to be a role model and lead by example if you want to improve your organisation's management and leadership capability.

3) Implement good working practices as a framework for good management and leadership

Good quality leadership and management cannot exist in a vacuum. You need to implement good working practices, such as High Performance Working (HPW), that offer greater autonomy and help to improve the way employees apply themselves in order to embed and enable good management. These practices empower individuals instead of controlling them and therefore increase levels of commitment and organisational performance. They cover a range of practices and an overall approach that includes:

- effective recruiting and resourcing of roles in the organisation
- appropriate skills development and training

- practices to improve the engagement, motivation and morale of the workforce
- ensuring people's skills and motivation can be properly applied through effective organisation and job design.

4) Effective leadership runs through organisations like writing through a stick of rock

Good senior management is only part of the equation for a successful business. First level and middle management are just as important, as they typically make up the majority of a company's total management and they supervise the majority of the work force. It is important to know how to audit for leadership and management capability and how to address skills deficits.

5) Provide training, support and mentoring to new line managers

Do not promote your employees into management positions because of their technical skills and expect them to pick up their management and leadership skills on the job. You would not leave any other skill, in any other job to the lottery of trial and error. Not addressing these training and development needs is asking for trouble and leads to higher levels of absence, conflict and stress in the workplace. Untrained line managers may also mean your organisation ends up in court as a result of things like discrimination, harassment, and constructive dismissal claims. Line management is most employees' first experience of managing people, so it is crucial to provide training, support and mentoring.

6) Be clear about what good management skills and behaviours look like

Managers need to offer clarity, appreciation of employees' effort and contribution, treat their people as individuals and ensure that work is organised efficiently and effectively so that employees feel they are valued, and equipped and supported to do their job. Employees need to feel that they are able to voice their ideas and be listened to, both about how they do their job and in decision-making in their own department, with joint sharing of problems and challenges and a commitment to arrive at joint solutions. The key competencies of a good manager are: reviewing and guiding, feedback, praise and recognition, autonomy and empowerment.

7) Assess your organisations' management capability at individual and organisational level and act upon it

Make sure you know how well individual managers are performing as well as assessing the management capability in your workplace with the help of the available tools (see Tip 8). A wide range of interventions can support better management capability in the workplace. These include 360 degree feedback, blended learning, combination of classroom/e-learning, line management workshops, line management champions, secondments, peer networking, and mentoring.

8) Make the most of the practical tools that are available

Make sure you are aware of the support available. There are a number of organisations that provide free, independent advice and guidance and that have developed tools to assess and support management capability, such as the EFQM Excellence Model.

9) Invest in your workforce, routinely and as part of your business strategy

Do not just fix things when they go wrong. Have a progressive, long-term and sustainable approach to your workforce planning in skills development. Those organisations that continuously invest in people as part of their business strategy tend to also have better managers and higher employee engagement. Schemes such as Investors in People can provide advice on how to align training and skills development to business strategy.

10) Be authentic about good leadership and employee engagement

Important as they are, good systems and practices will not lead automatically to better management and leadership capability. Instead, it is how those practices have been implemented and why that matters. Be clear that you genuinely want to empower people and increase their engagement with your organisation so they can perform to their best.

Note

1 *Leadership & Management in the UK – The Key to Sustainable Growth* (2012 pp. 30–32), Department for Business Innovation and Skills, London, England.

Appendix C

How Good Is Your Culture?[1]

Is your good conduct:

- required by your regulators?
- led from the top – by style and values?
- embedded in all strategies, plans and operations?
- seen in all structures and systems?
- communicated internally to everyone – staff and visitors?
- communicated externally to all stakeholders?
- known across all supply chains?
- included in all review processes?
- independently monitored?

Does your good conduct:

- create/reduce wealth?
- improve/reduce the quality of performance?
- increase/decrease the efficiency and effectiveness of all staff?
- increase/decrease customers' satisfaction?
- improve/lower the organisation's reputation in society?
- increase/decrease competitive edge?
- consider/ignore all stakeholders' needs?
- encourage/discourage good behaviour

Do you have:

- a formal and published code of conduct?
- a procedure for dealing with all irregularities?
- a whistleblowing procedure?
- practical ethics training for all your staff?
- environmental, health and safety policies?
- environmental, social and ethical accounting, auditing and reporting?

Note

1 *Cutting Edge Internal Auditing* (2008 p. 311), Jeffrey Ridley, Wiley and Sons, Chichester, England.

Appendix D
How to Train to Be a Diplomat[1]

[T]he best diplomatic training is all about sharing techniques for diplomats to use in tough situations. Here, in no special order, are skills every diplomat needs to master:

Records of conversation

Diplomacy is all about top people quietly sharing positions and proposals. When they meet, someone has to record what was said in a way that others might use. There is real art to doing this well, capturing key points of agreement and disagreement while conveying the sense of the meeting (plus, perhaps, leaving out especially sensitive things from the main record and recording them separately for a narrow senior distribution).

Speaking notes and public speaking

Sooner or later all diplomats stand up in front of an audience to convey their basic messages. They need to know how to structure a speech or presentation, and how to deliver it convincingly and engagingly. And how to give a witty but gracious after-dinner speech. Good public speaking can be taught. It's like riding a bicycle. Once you know how to do it, you can't not do it.

Steering meetings

All sorts of subtle points of technique can be taught here. Practical aspects include setting out the table to achieve appropriate formality but with just the right intimacy. Plus setting the agenda, reflecting key words, reframing difficult issues, when to speak and when to keep quiet, summing up elegantly, and (last but not least) agreeing robust arrangements to make sure that decisions taken at the meeting are in fact implemented.

Talking to people

Not everyone is naturally confident or socially graceful. Diplomats need to be able to enter a large, noisy room full of senior people they have never met before and strike up useful conversations with as many people as possible. Yes, this can be taught.

Operating above your pay grade

This is important. For many purposes diplomacy is hierarchical and proud of it. But it often happens that younger or less experienced diplomats have to stand in for others much more senior than they are and deliver good results. Can we please be taught how to do that? Yes.

Official entertainment

Official entertainment is all about the thin line between success and embarrassment, if not disaster. Diplomats need to pay meticulous attention to detail and protocol. Most of this is in fact informed by common sense. Yet it is remarkable how things go spectacularly wrong, up to and including the very highest levels. Training that leads with scary real-life examples never fails to help ambitious diplomats avoid making horrible unforced blunders.

Negotiating

Any substantive diplomatic course has to include sharp operational training in negotiating. This should involve some theory (Positions, Interests and Needs), but also powerful case studies and role-plays to help diplomats play with specific subtle techniques. More generally, all diplomats need to grasp that a lot of what they do, even when it seems routine or uninteresting, is all part of deeper, wider negotiations between countries and ideas that go on down the years and decades and centuries. See Russia, **Ukraine** and 'Europe', or **China** and **Japan**, or England v **France** v Scotland, or the Middle East passim.

Mediating

Almost no mainstream diplomatic training includes specific mediation skills. This is madness. Diplomats at all levels from the start of their careers need to be good at listening creatively, and looking out for ways to redefine problems to achieve imaginative solutions that leave everyone more or less happy on different levels simultaneously. Memo to the world's diplomatic academies and institutes: must do better when it comes to mediation training.

Media work

Too many diplomats are wary of the media. They shouldn't be. It's easy to teach the basics of media work and how to share information safely and professionally with media contacts. Pro Tip: confirm with a journalist what is or is not attributable before the conversation starts.

Crisis management

Obvious. Having tough procedures so that when the embassy phones start shrieking the team are ready to drop what they're doing and respond. Then, when an actual crisis erupts, being flexible and disciplined enough to change those procedures on the run.

What's this really all about?

The greatest of all diplomatic skills is judgement. That comes with experience (or not, as the case may be). It's all about perspective. Robin Renwick, one of the UK's finest modern diplomats, likes to quote this insight from an earlier veteran diplomatist: "You need to distinguish what's important from what matters." Or, as a wily Russian diplomat once said to me: "Nothing is linked – but everything is linked."

Note

1 *How to Train Your Diplomat* (2015), Charles Crawford CMG, former UK Ambassador and training expert currently leads the Technique programme of The Ambassadors Partnership LLP. London, England. www.ambassadorllp.com.

Appendix E

The Commonwealth Charter[1]

Signed by Her Majesty Queen Elizabeth II, Head of the Commonwealth, **Commonwealth Day 2013**

1 We the people of the Commonwealth

Recognising that in an era of changing economic circumstances and uncertainty, new trade and economic patterns, unprecedented threats to peace and security, and a surge in popular demands for democracy, human rights and broadened economic opportunities, the potential of and need for the Commonwealth – as a compelling force for good and as an effective network for co-operation and for promoting development – has never been greater.

Recalling that the Commonwealth is a voluntary association of independent and equal sovereign states, each responsible for its own policies, consulting and co-operating in the common interests of our peoples and in the promotion of international understanding and world peace, and influencing international society to the benefit of all through the pursuit of common principles and values, Affirming that the special strength of the Commonwealth lies in the combination of our diversity and our shared inheritance in language, culture and the rule of law; and bound together by shared history and tradition; by respect for all states and peoples; by shared values and principles and by concern for the vulnerable.

Affirming that the Commonwealth way is to seek consensus through consultation and the sharing of experience, especially through practical co-operation, and further affirming that the Commonwealth is uniquely placed to serve as a model and as a catalyst for new forms of friendship and co-operation in the spirit of the Charter of the United Nations, Affirming the role of the Commonwealth as a recognised intergovernmental champion of small states, advocating for their special needs; providing policy advice on political, economic and social development issues; and delivering technical assistance.

Welcoming the valuable contribution of the network of the many intergovernmental, parliamentary, professional and civil society bodies which support the Commonwealth and which subscribe and adhere to its values and principles,

Affirming the validity of and our commitment to the values and principles of the Commonwealth as defined and strengthened over the years including: the Singapore Declaration of Commonwealth Principles, the Harare Commonwealth Declaration, the Langkawi Declaration on the Environment, the Millbrook Action Programme, the Latimer House Principles, the Aberdeen Agenda, the Trinidad and Tobago Affirmation of Commonwealth Values and Principles, the Munyonyo Statement on Respect and Understanding, the Lake Victoria Commonwealth Climate Change Action Plan, the Perth Declaration on Food Security Principles, and the Commonwealth Declaration on Investing in Young People,

Affirming our core Commonwealth principles of consensus and common action, mutual respect, inclusiveness, transparency, accountability, legitimacy, and responsiveness,

Reaffirming the core values and principles of the Commonwealth as declared by this Charter:

I DEMOCRACY

We recognise the inalienable right of individuals to participate in democratic processes, in particular through free and fair elections in shaping the society in which they live. Governments, political parties and civil society are responsible for upholding and promoting democratic culture and practices and are accountable to the public in this regard. Parliaments and representative local governments and other forms of local governance are essential elements in the exercise of democratic governance. We support the role of the Commonwealth Ministerial Action Group to address promptly and effectively all instances of serious or persistent violations of Commonwealth values without any fear or favour.

II HUMAN RIGHTS

We are committed to the Universal Declaration of Human Rights and other relevant human rights covenants and international instruments. We are committed to equality and respect for the protection and promotion of civil, political, economic, social and cultural rights, including the right to development, for all without discrimination on any grounds as the foundations of peaceful, just and stable societies. We note that these rights are universal, indivisible, interdependent and interrelated and cannot be implemented selectively. We are implacably opposed to all forms of discrimination, whether rooted in gender, race, colour, creed, political belief or other grounds.

III INTERNATIONAL PEACE AND SECURITY

We firmly believe that international peace and security, sustainable economic growth and development and the rule of law are essential to the progress and prosperity of all. We are committed to an effective multilateral system based on inclusiveness, equity, justice and international law as the best foundation for achieving consensus and progress on major global challenges including piracy and terrorism. We support international efforts for peace and disarmament at the United Nations and other multilateral institutions. We will contribute to the promotion of international consensus on major global political, economic and social issues. We will be guided by our commitment to the security, development and prosperity of every member state. We reiterate our absolute condemnation of all acts of terrorism in whatever form or wherever they occur or by whomsoever perpetrated, with the consequent tragic loss of human life and severe damage to political, economic and social stability. We reaffirm our commitment to work together as a diverse community of nations, individually, and collectively under the auspices and authority of the United Nations, to take concerted and resolute action to eradicate terrorism.

IV TOLERANCE, RESPECT AND UNDERSTANDING

We emphasise the need to promote tolerance, respect, understanding, moderation and religious freedom which are essential to the development of free and democratic societies, and recall that respect for the dignity of all human beings is critical to promoting peace and prosperity. We accept that diversity and understanding the richness of our multiple identities are fundamental to the Commonwealth's principles and approach.

V FREEDOM OF EXPRESSION

We are committed to peaceful, open dialogue and the free flow of information, including through a free and responsible media, and to enhancing democratic traditions and strengthening democratic processes.

VI SEPARATION OF POWERS

We recognise the importance of maintaining the integrity of the roles of the Legislature, Executive and Judiciary. These are the guarantors in their respective spheres of the rule of law, the promotion and protection of fundamental human rights and adherence to good governance.

VII RULE OF LAW

We believe in the rule of law as an essential protection for the people of the Commonwealth and as an assurance of limited and accountable government. In particular we support an independent, impartial, honest and competent judiciary and recognise that an independent, effective and competent legal system is integral to upholding the rule of law, engendering public confidence and dispensing justice.

VIII GOOD GOVERNANCE

We reiterate our commitment to promote good governance through the rule of law, to ensure transparency and accountability and to root out, both at national and international levels, systemic and systematic corruption.

IX SUSTAINABLE DEVELOPMENT

We recognise that sustainable development can help to eradicate poverty by pursuing inclusive growth whilst preserving and conserving natural ecosystems and promoting social equity. We stress the importance of sustainable economic and social transformation to eliminate poverty and meet the basic needs of the vast majority of the people of the world and reiterate that economic and social progress enhances the sustainability of democracy. We are committed to removing wide disparities and unequal living standards as guided by internationally agreed development goals. We are also committed to building economic resilience and promoting social equity, and we reiterate the value in technical assistance, capacity building and practical cooperation in promoting development. We are committed to an effective, equitable, rules-based multilateral trading system, the freest possible flow of multilateral trade on terms fair and equitable to all, while taking into account the special requirements of small states and developing countries. We also recognise the importance of information and communication technologies as powerful instruments of development; delivering savings, efficiencies and growth in our economies, as well as promoting education, learning and the sharing of culture. We are committed to strengthening its use while enhancing its security, for the purpose of advancing our societies.

X PROTECTING THE ENVIRONMENT

We recognise the importance of the protection and conservation of our natural ecosystems and affirm that sustainable management of the natural environment is the key to sustained human development. We recognise the importance of multilateral cooperation, sustained commitment and collective action, in particular by addressing the adaptation and mitigation challenges of climate change and facilitating the development, diffusion and deployment of affordable environmentally friendly technologies and renewable energy, and the prevention of illicit dumping of toxic and hazardous waste as well as the prevention and mitigation of erosion and desertification.

XI ACCESS TO HEALTH, EDUCATION, FOOD AND SHELTER

We recognise the necessity of access to affordable health care, education, clean drinking water, sanitation and housing for all citizens and emphasise the importance of promoting health and well-being in combating communicable and non-communicable diseases. We recognise the right of everyone to have access to safe, sufficient and nutritious food, consistent with the progressive realisation of the right to adequate food in the context of national food security.

XII GENDER EQUALITY

We recognise that gender equality and women's empowerment are essential components of human development and basic human rights. The advancement of women's rights and the education of girls are critical preconditions for effective and sustainable development.

XIII IMPORTANCE OF YOUNG PEOPLE IN THE COMMONWEALTH

We recognise the positive and active role and contributions of young people in promoting development, peace, democracy and in protecting and promoting other Commonwealth values, such as tolerance and understanding, including respect for other cultures. The future success of the Commonwealth rests with the continued commitment and contributions of young people in promoting and sustaining the Commonwealth and its values and principles, and we commit to investing in and promoting their development, particularly through the creation of opportunities for youth employment and entrepreneurship.

XIV RECOGNITION OF THE NEEDS OF SMALL STATES

We are committed to assisting small and developing states in the Commonwealth, including the particular needs of small island developing states, in tackling their particular economic, energy, climate change and security challenges, and in building their resilience for the future.

XV RECOGNITION OF THE NEEDS OF VULNERABLE STATES

We are committed to collaborating to find ways to provide immediate help to the poorest and most vulnerable including least developed countries, and to develop responses to protect the people most at risk.

XVI THE ROLE OF CIVIL SOCIETY

We recognise the important role that civil society plays in our communities and countries as partners in promoting and supporting Commonwealth values and principles, including the freedom of association and peaceful assembly, and in achieving development goals.

We are committed to ensuring that the Commonwealth is an effective association, responsive to members' needs, and capable of addressing the significant global challenges of the future. We aspire to a Commonwealth that is a strong and respected voice in the world, speaking out on major issues; that strengthens and enlarges its networks; that has a global relevance and profile; and that is devoted to improving the lives of all peoples of the Commonwealth.

Signed by His Excellency Kamalesh Sharma, Commonwealth
Secretary-General, 14 December 2012, on which day
Commonwealth Heads of Government adopted the
Charter of the Commonwealth

Note

1 *The Commonwealth Charter* (2013), Her Majesty's Government, Her Majesty's Stationery Office Ltd., London, England.

Appendix F
Risk Management Checklist[1]

Risk architecture

- statement produced that sets out risk responsibilities and lists the risk-based matters reserved for the Board
- risk management responsibilities allocated to an appropriate management committee
- arrangements are in place to ensure the availability of appropriate competent advice on risks and controls
- risk aware culture exists within the organisation and actions are in hand to enhance the level of risk maturity
- sources of risk assurance for the Board have been identified and validated.

Risk strategy

- risk management policy produced that describes risk appetite, risk culture and philosophy
- key dependencies for success identified, together with the matters that should be avoided
- business objectives validated and the assumptions underpinning those objectives tested
- significant risks faced by the organisation identified, together with the critical controls required
- risk management action plan established that includes the use of key risk indicators, as appropriate
- necessary resources identified and provided to support the risk management activities.

Risk protocols

- appropriate risk management framework identified and adopted, with modifications as appropriate
- suitable and sufficient risk assessments completed and the results recorded in an appropriate manner

- procedures to include risk as part of business decision-making established and implemented
- details of required risk responses recorded, together with arrangements to track risk improvement recommendations
- incident reporting procedures established to facilitate identification of risk trends, together with risk escalation procedures
- business continuity plans and disaster recovery plans established and regularly tested
- arrangements in place to audit the efficiency and effectiveness of the controls in place for significant risks
- arrangements in place for mandatory reporting on risk, including reports on at least the following:

  - risk appetite, tolerance and constraints
  - risk architecture and risk escalation procedures
  - risk aware culture currently in place
  - risk assessment arrangements and protocols
  - significant risks and key risk indicators
  - critical controls and control weaknesses
  - sources of assurance available to the Board.

Note

1 *A Structured Approach to Enterprise Risk Management* (2010 p. 17 Appendix A), Institute of Risk Management (IRM), London, England.

Appendix G

International Integrated Reporting Council

Guiding Principles and Content Elements[1]

The following Guiding Principles underpin the preparation of an integrated report, informing the content of the report and how information is presented:

- **Strategic focus and future orientation**: An integrated report should provide insight into the organisation's strategy, and how it relates to the organisation's ability to create value in the short, medium and long term, and to its use of and effects on the capitals
- **Connectivity of information**: An integrated report should show a holistic picture of the combination, interrelatedness and dependencies between the factors that affect the organisation's ability to create value over time
- **Stakeholder relationships**: An integrated report should provide insight into the nature and quality of the organisation's relationships with its key stakeholders, including how and to what extent the organisation understands, takes into account and responds to their legitimate needs and interests
- **Materiality**: An integrated report should disclose information about matters that substantively affect the organisation's ability to create value over the short, medium and long term
- **Conciseness**: An integrated report should be concise
- **Reliability and completeness**: An integrated report should include all material matters, both positive and negative, in a balanced way and without material error
- **Consistency and comparability**: The information in an integrated report should be presented: (a) on a basis that is consistent over time; and (b) in a way that enables comparison with other organisations to the extent it is material to the organisation's own ability to create value over time.

Content Elements

An integrated report includes eight Content Elements that are fundamentally linked to each other and are not mutually exclusive:

- **Organisational overview and external environment**: What does the organisation do and what are the circumstances under which it operates?
- **Governance**: How does the organisation's governance structure support its ability to create value in the short, medium and long term?
- **Business model**: What is the organisation's business model?
- **Risks and opportunities**: What are the specific risks and opportunities that affect the organisation's ability to create value over the short, medium and long term, and how is the organisation dealing with them?
- **Strategy and resource allocation**: Where does the organisation want to go and how does it intend to get there?
- **Performance**: To what extent has the organisation achieved its strategic objectives for the period and what are its outcomes in terms of effects on the capitals?
- **Outlook**: What challenges and uncertainties is the organisation likely to encounter in pursuing its strategy, and what are the potential implications for its business model and future performance?
- **Basis of presentation**: How does the organisation determine what matters to include in the integrated report and how are such matters quantified or evaluated?

Note

1 *The International <IR> Framework* (2013 p. 5), International Integrated Reporting Council, London, England.

Appendix H

United Nations Sustainability Development Goals[1]

GOAL 1 End poverty in all its forms everywhere.

GOAL 2 End hunger, achieve food security and improved nutrition and promote sustainable agriculture.

GOAL 3 Ensure healthy lives and promote well-being for all at all ages.

GOAL 4 Ensure inclusive and equitable quality education and promote lifelong learning opportunities for all.

GOAL 5 Achieve gender equality and empower all women and girls.

GOAL 6 Ensure availability and sustainable management of water and sanitation for all.

GOAL 7 Ensure access to affordable, reliable, sustainable and modern energy for all.

GOAL 8 Promote sustained, inclusive and sustainable economic growth, full and productive employment and decent work for all.

GOAL 9 Build resilient infrastructure, promote inclusive and sustainable industrialization and foster innovation.

GOAL 10 Reduce inequality within and among countries.

GOAL 11 Make cities and human settlements inclusive, safe, resilient and sustainable.

GOAL 12 Ensure sustainable consumption and production patterns.

GOAL 13 Take urgent action to combat climate change and its impacts.

GOAL 14 Conserve and sustainably use the oceans, seas and marine resources for sustainable development.

GOAL 15 Protect, restore and promote sustainable use of terrestrial ecosystems, sustainably manage forests, combat desertification, and halt and reverse land degradation and halt biodiversity loss.

GOAL 16 Promote peaceful and inclusive societies for sustainable development, provide access to justice for all and build effective, accountable and inclusive institutions at all levels.

GOAL 17 Strengthen the means of implementation and revitalize the global partnership for sustainable development.

Note

1 *Transforming Our World – The 2030 Agenda for Sustainable Development* (2015), Outcome Document from the United Nations Summit 2015, United Nations, New York, US.

Appendix I
COSO Fundamental Concepts of Internal Control – Integrated Framework[1]

Control environment

1　the organisation* demonstrates a commitment to integrity and ethical values.
2　the board of directors demonstrates independence both from management and exercises oversight of the development and performance of internal control.
3　management establishes with board oversight structures, reporting lines and appropriate authorities and responsibilities in the pursuit of objectives.
4　the organisation demonstrates a commitment to attract and retain competent individuals in alignment with objectives.
5　the organisation holds individuals accountable for their internal control responsibilities in the pursuit of objectives.

Risk assessment

6　the organisation specifies objectives with sufficient clarity to enable the identification and assessment of risks relating to objectives.
7　the organisation identifies risks to the achievement of its objectives across the entity and analyses risks as a basis for determining how the risks should be managed.
8　the organisation considers the potential for fraud in assessing risks to the achievement of objectives.
9　the organisation identifies and assesses changes that could significantly impact the system of internal control.

Control activities

10　the organisation selects and develops control activities that contribute to the mitigation of risks to the achievement of objectives to acceptable levels.
11　the organisation selects and develops general control activities over technology to support the achievement of objectives.
12　the organisation deploys control activities through policies that establish what is expected and procedures that put policies into action.

Information and communication

13 the organisation obtains or generates and uses relevant quality information to support the functioning of internal control.
14 the organisation internally communicates information, including objectives and responsibilities for internal control, necessary to support the functioning of internal control.
15 the organisation communicates with external parties regarding matters affecting the functioning of internal control.

Monitoring activities

16 the organisation, selects, develops and performs ongoing and/or separate evaluations to ascertain whether the components of internal control are present and functioning.
17 the organisation evaluates and communicates internal control deficiencies in a timely manner to those parties responsible for taking corrective action, including senior management and the board of directives, as appropriate.

★For purposes of the Framework, the term organisation is used to collectively capture the board, management, and other personnel, as reflected in the definition of internal control.

Note

1 *Internal Control – Integrated Framework* (2013), Committee of Sponsoring Organisations of the Treadway Commission (COSO), New York, US.

Appendix J

The Institute of Internal Auditors Inc.[1]

Code of Ethics

Principles

Internal auditors are expected to apply and uphold the following principles:

1 Integrity

The integrity of internal auditors establishes trust and thus provides the basis for reliance on their judgment.

2 Objectivity

Internal auditors exhibit the highest level of professional objectivity in gathering, evaluating, and communicating information about the activity or process being examined. Internal auditors make a balanced assessment of all the relevant circumstances and are not unduly influenced by their own interests or by others in forming judgments.

3 Confidentiality

Internal auditors respect the value and ownership of information they receive and do not disclose information without appropriate authority unless there is a legal or professional obligation to do so.

4 Competency

Internal auditors apply the knowledge, skills, and experience needed in the performance of internal audit services.

Rules of Conduct

1 Integrity

Internal auditors:

    1.1 Shall perform their work with honesty, diligence, and responsibility.

    1.2 Shall observe the law and make disclosures expected by the law and the profession.

    1.3 Shall not knowingly be a party to any illegal activity, or engage in acts that are discreditable to the profession of internal auditing or to the organization.

    1.4 Shall respect and contribute to the legitimate and ethical objectives of the organization.

2 Objectivity

Internal auditors:

    2.1 Shall not participate in any activity or relationship that may impair or be presumed to impair their unbiased assessment. This participation includes those activities or relationships that may be in conflict with the interests of the organization.

    2.2 Shall not accept anything that may impair or be presumed to impair their professional judgment.

    2.3 Shall disclose all material facts known to them that, if not disclosed, may distort the reporting of activities under review.

3 Confidentiality

Internal auditors:

    3.1 Shall be prudent in the use and protection of information acquired in the course of their duties.

    3.2 Shall not use information for any personal gain or in any manner that would be contrary to the law or detrimental to the legitimate and ethical objectives of the organization.

4 Competency

Internal auditors:

    4.1 Shall engage only in those services for which they have the necessary knowledge, skills, and experience.

    4.2 Shall perform internal audit services in accordance with the *International Standards for the Professional Practice of Internal Auditing*.

    4.3 Shall continually improve their proficiency and the effectiveness and quality of their services.

Note

1 *Code of Ethics – Revised* (2009), The Institute of Internal Auditors Inc., Orlando, US.

Appendix K

Creativity and Innovation

Keys to a Successful Future for Internal Auditing[1]

Research context and methodology

This paper is about the future success of internal auditing. More specifically, while focusing on the theme of **"creativity and innovation"** as an element of **"continuous improvement"** and **"quality"**, the paper provides both theoretical and empirical insights into its creativity and innovation. While the paper is clearly focused on internal auditing, it is helpful to first take regard for its assurance and consulting roles within organisational governance. These roles are seen when one accepts (Pojunis and Steinberg, 2000; Baker and Owsen, 2002) that good internal audit systems contribute to heightened *transparency* (mainly in terms of significant decisions, records and events) while facilitating greater *accountability* (mainly to relevant stakeholders) and so leading to higher levels of *probity* (honesty and integrity) overall – in other words – governance. And, in that sense, the paper is also associated with excellence in governance.

The paper commences with some discussion as to the nature of creativity and innovation generally. It then considers some of the creative and innovation-related pronouncements made by the internal audit profession – mainly by reference to professional statements made by The Institute of Internal Auditors Inc. (in the United States) and those by the Chartered Institute of Internal Auditors in the United Kingdom. It then briefly reviews some prior relevant research literature (particularly Gray and Gray, 1996 and more recently Ridley 2008). We then explore creativity and innovation in the future of internal auditing. Finally, we create a case unit of innovation in a small internal auditing activity today: justifying this choice of size on the basis that the majority of internal auditing activities worldwide are small and therefore the findings will be of particular interest to the most organisations.

Creativity and innovation theory and research

For our paper we use the philosophical meaning of creativity to be the generation of new ideas from wisdom that form cultures and attitudes that lead to change in an organisation – a good example of this is seen in its vision: we define innovation as the process of effecting (positive) change in practices through the use of new (improving) ideas and/or new procedures (Gray and

Gray 1996). Innovation is therefore essentially a creative process that is under-pinned by wisdom. Within management thinking, the nurturing of creativity tends to fall within the ambit of good leadership (a traditional aspect of management) and hence considerations on innovation can be seen through the frame of leadership within change management (IIA, 2004).

When used as a noun, the Oxford English Dictionary defines "cutting edge" as "the latest or most advanced stage or "the forefront" and, when used as an adjective, it is described as "pioneering" and "innovative". Thus the term innovation is synonymous with the term "cutting edge".

What then does "cutting edge" really mean in practical terms? It is a term that has been used to describe various types of activities, from strategies to operations, to product and service outputs. Understandably, it has many synonyms and these include the words – progressive, advanced, forward-looking, radical, even revolutionary (but rarely evolutionary). And, as the following two terms are also used to convey a sense of innovation, it is interesting to note that two other synonyms often encountered in the (academic and professional) literature are the terms "leading edge" and "best practice".

Creativity and innovation always start with a vision – for both without vision has neither proper genesis nor direction. Further, such direction is fostered by the formulation of a stated mission (or set of missions) which may be expressed formally or informally. Regardless, for innovation to become a reality there must be a vision which is initially expressed in mission terms and these must be shared by all concerned. Both visions and missions may be expressed formally in "vision statements" and "mission statements".

The preceding ideas provoke some discussion on the precise nature of "vision" and "mission" and how (in the context of change) the two are inter-linked. Whiteley (1991) describes "vision" as "a vivid picture of an ambitious, desirable state that is connected to the customer and better in some important way than the current state". He contends that a vision has two vital functions. The first is to serve as a source of inspiration. The second is to guide decision-making, so that all parts of an organisation are in alignment and work consist-ently together. Such a shared vision leads to a competitive advantage, with it being an impetus for change and excellence.

In terms of such a "shared vision", Whiteley (1991) argues that when an organi-sation clearly declares what it stands for and its people share that vision, a powerful network is created – an interconnected network of people seeking related goals. Coulson-Thomas (1992) discussed research into vision statements when he wrote on leadership and the management of change. Drawing on an earlier series of three sur-veys of large organisations, he re-confirmed the need for a clear vision to be sustained by senior management commitment in order to bring about successful change.

Additionally, in the same context of successful innovation and/or "change management" Coulson-Thomas (1992) offers the following conclusions and practical suggestions:

•   a clear vision and strategy, supported by top management commitment is of crucial importance in the management of change. If either is lacking, a change programme is likely to be built upon foundations of sand.

- the vision and commitment need to be sustained. This requires an effective board composed of competent directors. Further, all employees need to be equipped to manage change. This often requires a change of attitude, approach and perspective.
- the ability to communicate is an essential management quality. Successful communication and sharing of a vision requires integrity and a relationship of trust.
- a compelling vision both differentiates and transforms. It must be organisationally shared with the purpose of change being communicated so that complete employee involvement and commitment is secured.

Given the importance attributed to creativity and innovation it is no surprise to see that governments throughout the world promote both in many forms of publications and websites. In this context the latest messages from the European Commission[2] and UK government[3] on the importance of innovation in competitive market places are good examples of the importance of such strategies for the growth, even survival, of enterprises, both large and small.

> Innovation provides **real benefits** for us as citizens, consumers, and workers. It speeds up and improves the way we conceive, develop, produce and access new products, industrial processes and services. It is the key not only to **creating more jobs, building a greener society and improving our quality of life**, but also to maintaining our **competitiveness** on the global market." (European Commission – Innovation Union Initiative)
>
> The Coalition Government is putting innovation and research at the heart of its growth agenda. Innovation is essential to competitiveness and higher living standards. Through greater investment and increased collaboration, we will make sure that the UK has a promising future. The Coalition Government is putting innovation and research at the heart of its growth agenda. Innovation is essential to competitiveness and higher living standards. Through greater investment and increased collaboration, we will make sure that the UK has a promising future." (BIS 2001: Foreword)

Ridley (2006)[4] cites Whiteley's new innovation ways, requiring much more organized teamwork (quality circles) and an on-going analysis of each of the following processes:

- learning customers' needs
- keeping up with technology outside the firm
- maintaining basic technical strengths
- discovering new technology that will be useful in products (and services)
- neutralising competitors' basic technical strengths
- keeping the organisation as a whole informed about discoveries.

These ways are still evident in quality programmes, continuous improvement and innovation today.

Oakland (2002) sees vision statements as part of a quality framework. He states that "any organisation needs a vision framework, which includes its guiding philosophy, containing the core values and beliefs and a purpose. These should be combined into a mission, which provides a vivid description of what an organisation would like to achieve. The strategies and plans suggest how it is going to be achieved." In more general terms, Oakland (2002: 16) recommends an organised and systematic approach to innovation and continuous improvement in stating:

> An organisation may identify opportunities for improvement in a number of ways, perhaps through process analysis, benchmarking, or the use of self-assessment against an established framework *[examples could be comparison and compliance with The IIA International Standards and /or ISO 9000 the international standard for quality management]* . . . a distinction needs to be made between those processes which run pretty well – to be subjected to a regime of continuous improvement, and those which are very poor and are in need of a complete re-visioning, re-design or re-engineering activity.

Creativity and innovation drive today's continuous improvement in internal auditing

Since its very foundation the IIA Inc. has been at the forefront of creativity and innovation in internal auditing with its business plans being underpinned and promoted by both vision and mission statements. D'Silva and Ridley (2007)[5] cite the following excerpt as somewhat traditional today, but at the time it was cutting edge thinking - certainly for internal auditing. The IIA Inc.'s *Certificate of Incorporation* (1941) states its objectives and purposes as:

> To cultivate, promote and disseminate knowledge and information concerning internal auditing and subjects related thereto, to establish and maintain high standards of integrity, honour and character among internal auditors; to furnish information regarding internal auditing and the practice and methods thereof to its members, and to other persons interested, and to the general public; to cause the publication of articles, relating to internal auditing and practices and methods thereof; to establish and maintain a library and reading rooms, meeting rooms and social rooms for the use of its members; and to do any and all things which shall be lawful and appropriate in furtherance of any of the purposes . . . expressed (above).

Any research into creativity and innovation in internal auditing must always reflect on the 'words of wisdom' by Lawrence Sawyer. His maxims are still at the cutting-edge of internal auditing today, and will be tomorrow. Recognition of the benefits of innovation within Internal Auditing is not a new phenomenon. More than thirty years ago, Sawyer (1973) contended that innovation plays an important part in the working relationships essential for developing overall Internal Audit strategy, policies, processes, style and the communication of engagement end-results. He further argued that good IA relationships are supported by even better IA resources. In part, this is articulated by him when he recommends the following six personal ingredients for success in Internal Auditing engagements:

1   helpfulness
2   empathy
3   understanding
4   open-mindedness
5   problem-solving
6   attentive listening.

One of his most timeless is:

> Successful internal auditing is constructed on a foundation of technical excellence. But the structure must be firmly buttressed – on the one side by demonstrated acceptance and support at the highest levels in the enterprise; on the other by continued, imaginative service to management.
>
> (1973)[6]

Later, in 1992[7] on creativity he concluded:

> Creativity is not reserved for the arts and sciences. It is needed in our profession as well. But it will never be tapped if we do not develop a divine discontent with what we see and if we fail to search for new ways of solving the problems which we identify or which management present to us. We can offer a new presence to the business community – as creative problem-solving partners to managers at all levels.

There are many exhortations about and for innovation within the internal auditing profession. These are seen in statements made by the profession about (and for) itself and its guidance given to members of the profession 'to continuously improve'. As a simple illustration of the above, one notes comments made by Winters [The IIA Research Foundation President] 2007) in the March 2007 'From the President's Study' Statement, when he states that "staying on the cutting edge of knowledge and understanding our profession is what the IIA Research Foundation is all about', basing his views on words from the foundation's current mission statement i.e. 'to expand knowledge and understanding of internal auditing by providing relevant research and educational products to advance the profession globally', the statement goes on to detail how these objectives are being operationalised. And, more recently from a roundtable of US internal auditors and regulators:[8]

> Current financial circumstances present opportunities for internal auditors to reassess their own audit strategies by stepping back and taking a fresh

look at how the organisation's changing business goals and resulting risks line up with the audit plan. Because the economic outlook is uncertain, CAEs need to be ready to change direction quickly, while keeping an eye on the actions management is taking to cope with today's economy. CAEs are rapidly reprioritizing to identify potential cost savings and efficiencies and devoting more coverage to operational risks. There is a renewed need to provide objective analysis so that those charged with governance and oversight can use the information to improve program performance and operations, reduce costs, and facilitate decision making to oversee or initiate corrective action and contribute to public accountability.

If innovation is crucial in a professional context, it is pertinent to review or consider how innovation and features intrinsic to it (visions and missions) are perceived by the profession itself. Alternatively, is there evidence to suggest that the profession is itself "innovatively" minded? The quotations below suggest good evidence to the positive.

The IIA Inc. today holds its mission statement out to be critical to its activities:

Mission

The mission of The Institute of Internal Auditors is to provide dynamic leadership for the global profession of internal auditing. Activities in support of this mission will include, but will not be limited to:

1   advocating and promoting the value that internal audit professionals add to their organisation.
2   providing comprehensive professional educational/development opportunities; standards and other professional practice guidance; and certification programmes.
3   researching, disseminating, and promoting to practitioners and stakeholders knowledge concerning internal auditing and its appropriate role in control, risk management and governance.
4   educating practitioners and other relevant audiences on **best practices** in IA.
5   bringing Internal Auditors from several countries together to share information and experiences.

This mission statement relates well to The IIA's adopted theme from Raymond Noonan's presidential year in 1953/54 *Progress through sharing*, incorporated in its seal in 1955[9] and aptly creating a vision which continues today. (Fitting appropriately into Whiteley's argument commented on earlier that when an organisation clearly declares what it stands for and its people share this vision is created.)

Gupta and Ray 1995 in their conclusions on the implementation of improvement processes emphasise the related importance of vision and mission statements. They suggest that 'vision and mission statements which lead to a related listing of objectives provide road maps for the implementation of TQM within the internal auditing function'. And, it is the realization of these set objectives that become the expression of innovation.

Dittenhofer 2001 suggests that innovative improvements internal auditing can be classified from three distinct classifications; philosophical, methodological and operational. And, within the *'philosophical'* classification, lie issues relating to 'visions and missions'. He contends that Internal Audit vision statements describe what the IA department 'will do and its contribution to the well being of the organisation'. These statements serve as a means to **enhance** (partly through innovation) the very existence of the IA department, but even more importantly, the service it provides to its beneficiary departments.

In terms of mission statements in Internal Auditing, Dittenhofer (2001:459) sees them emerging from a given *'vision'*. They are a description of how that vision will be accomplished and the activities required to do so. These activities will 'have a specific intent and definable impact in a specific and demonstrable area of (IA) performance'.

In the context of innovation generally and, creating a vision in particular, for the future of Internal Auditing, Ridley and Chambers (1998: 45) describe vision statements in the Internal Audit profession in the following words:

> Imagination needs direction – not in a controlled sense but in a creative sense. It is the art of forming mental images and constructively channelling these into visions for the future. It is not easy to find examples of internal auditing vision statements. Not all internal auditors are committed to the value of vision statements. Yet, in their organisations they are often prominent as management statements or team statements, and always associated with their organisation's products/services. So, why not for Internal Audit? Vision statements now generally aim to promote a vivid picture of an ambitious, desirable state that is connected to the customer and better in some important way than the current state. Vision statements need to be exciting, even emotional. They need a total commitment to succeed. They must be measured and updated as time improves vision. They need to be short and simple.

Gray and Gray 1996 analysed innovation motivation, goals and categories developed in a sample of North American organisations providing the first research focused on innovation in internal auditing. Since that time there have been further developments in internal auditing professional standards and practices mainly in the focus on organisational governance.

Cosmas 1996 researched marketing internal audit to achieve audit customer satisfaction, deducing that at that time this concept in internal auditing was virtually unexplored. Her study, based on experience and much of the thinking at that time of Lawrence Sawyer and Mortimer Dittenhofer,[10] included discussion on performance measurement in internal auditing and the importance of using a systematic approach to continuous improvement to market internal audit services. That systematic approach aligns very well with the concept and discipline of quality management, with its performance measures and commitment to continuously improve.

The link between visions, creativity, innovation and governance has grown since the first framework and its updating in 2008. The European Commission recognised this in 2010 in its published strategy for smart, sustainable and inclusive growth – Europe 2020 requiring a focus and clear goals:

> To achieve transformational change, the Europe 2020 strategy will need more focus, clear goals and transparent benchmarks for assessing progress. This will require a strong governance framework that harnesses the instruments at its disposal to ensure timely and effective implementation.
>
> (p. 25)

Research into governance in small and medium enterprises in the same year by the European Confederation of Directors Associations emphasised the role of the directors to "establish and maintain the company's vision, mission and values" (p. 16). The UK Corporate Governance Code 2010 makes no mention of a vision or mission for good governance though in its linking of governance to performance but does state:

> The purpose of corporate governance is to facilitate effective, entrepreneurial and prudent management that can deliver the long-term success of the company.
>
> (p. 1)

Creativity and innovation will drive continuous improvement in internal auditing in the future

The IIA has set out its clear vision for creativity and innovation in internal auditing in the future. An important pathway for this is emphasised in The IIA Annual report for 2010, celebrating its 70th anniversary:

> The Institute of Internal Auditors, now in the midst of celebrating its rich 70-year history as the leader of the internal audit profession, worked determinedly and successfully throughout 2010 to reassess, enhance and reposition itself to meet its members' rapidly growing and evolving needs. The IIA has long pioneered inventive approaches to solving the problems facing internal auditors worldwide. This year, we demonstrated how innovation can make the difference between merely discovering the future and actually defining its success.

Those needs are aptly expressed by Chambers 2012[11] in his five challenges for internal auditing stated during The IIA Global Council meeting in New Delhi, India in February this year:

Alignment of internal audit work to stakeholder needs
Quality of internal audit work

Risk management
Awareness of change
Status of internal audit profession.

For some time now the IIA[12] has been promoting the 'bridging of gaps' between internal auditors and their clients, building partnerships with management. Bain & Company 2011 in its definition of management tools includes many references to innovation in the tools used today. One such tool, "open innovation" encourages the building of partnerships to create new ideas in the development of products and services. Perhaps this is the next step now for future innovation in internal auditing. The IIA already has created partnerships with a number of key organisations to widen its scope and knowledge: internal audit activities must and will follow this lead with their management and other internal auditing providers and services to harness wider knowledge and experience for the continuous improvement of the services they provide. Only by doing this will the status of internal auditing grow to its potential as a key player in governance, risk management and control in every organisation in which it provides its professional services.

Creativity and innovation in a small internal auditing activity today[13]

Seren Group was formed in 2004, comprising Seren (the parent company), and a group of separately managed companies providing social housing and care services: all Group members are not for profit organisations[14] governed by voluntary boards: all, except Pen yr Enfys, are registered as Industrial and Providence Societies and as Registered Social Landlords, regulated by the Welsh Government and other social and care inspectorates. e.g. Care and Social Services Inspectorates Wales. Seren currently employs 900+ staff providing services and housing developments covering South East Wales, working in partnerships with 13 local government authorities: owning 5,600+ accommodation units in 2011 (with 300 more under development) and providing care and/or support to 4,200+ older people and those with disabilities. Seren's income in 2011 was £39 million, mainly from controlled affordable rents and government grants, with housing developments funded by private providers. Financial viability and governance structure and process arrangements in Seren are assessed and regulated by the Welsh Government through descriptive requirements,[15] which involve annual self-assessment reporting and co-regulation.

Seren prides itself at being part of a group with a full range of expertise, helping people to live the life they want. It promotes its purpose as providing... *housing and support which makes a real difference to people's lives* and values as *openness, respect, fairness, ambition, integrity and responsibility*: these values underlie all its strategies and policies.

Both regulation and the organisation's legal status require annual external financial auditing to appropriate standards. In addition to these assurances the

Seren Group organisations are subject to other internal and external assurances by its staff and other regulators, covering quality, improvement, social and environmental situations. One aspect of Seren's regulation is a recommendation that internal auditing should be in place, complying with appropriate professional standards. Seren established in 2006 an internal audit department reporting to the chief executive and an audit committee, consisting of a manager, senior internal auditor, auditor and a 'best value officer'. Later the emphasis of this group moved to a service of assurance and continuous improvement with a *Continuous Improvement* function title and Head replaced the Audit Manager. Today, the Continuous Improvement function is staffed by a Head of Continuous Improvement, Group Senior Internal Auditor, Internal Auditor, Continuous Improvement Support Officer and Business Improvement Officer, the latter having risk management, performance management, lean working and business planning responsibilities. This function now reports to a Corporate Director at Group Board level and has a reporting line to the Group Corporate Board Governance Committee, with governance, risk management and control monitoring terms of reference: it also has lines of reporting to the Group Chief Executive and Chairman, as well as Chairs in all the group organisations.

The internal audit working link into the Group's continuous improvement and risk management responsibilities is innovative but could be questioned as a weakness in its independence, even though it has opportunities to report at board level. Its independent and objective status is established clearly through an excellent Charter, kept under regular review, approved by the Group Corporate Governance Committee, requiring ... *the internal audit team to meet or exceed the Standards for the Professional Practice of Internal Auditing of The Institute of Internal Auditors*. The status and importance of these standards is emphasized by the Welsh Government adoption of the UK HM Treasury Government Internal Audit Standards for its public sector administration, now based on The IIA standards, and the qualifications and continuing professional development of the head of internal audit (a qualified Chartered Member of the Institute of Internal Auditors). Both the Charter and the status of the internal audit staff are promoted across the Group through an in-house Intranet system.

Although the words creative/ity and innovate/ation do not appear in the Charter, *independent* and *objective* appear once: *improvement* appears 17 times, *professional* 4; *quality* 1. Each of which has creative and innovative connotations.[16] This depictive insight into terms in the Charter show a significant motivation to continuously improve internal audit and to contribute to improvement in the group, but with less focus on quality in its services as measured by itself and its clients and other stakeholders – though its one mention of quality is in its scope to ensure *Quality and continuous improvement are fostered in the organisation's monitoring and control processes* – and this includes itself and its compliance with professional standards.

The mission and scope of work of internal audit is broadly stated at the beginning of its Charter as 'The internal audit function is a management tool for the Seren Group in its drive towards continuous improvement, safeguarding its reputation and sustainability.' Apart from this motivating statement there are other motivations in its internal audit Charter to encourage creativity and innovation in its assurance and consulting services, in particular:

> Opportunities for improving management control, profitability, effective use of resources and the organisation's image may be identified during audits. They will be communicated to the appropriate level of management.
>
> Maintain the links between improvement initiatives and associated reviews and the work of the Business Improvement Officer and the audit work, both of which are instrumental in providing opportunities for performance improvement.
>
> Maintain a professional audit staff with sufficient knowledge, skills, experience, and professional certifications to meet the requirements of this Charter.
>
> Evaluate and assess significant merging/consolidating functions and new or changing services, processes, operations, and control processes coincident with their development, implementation, and/or expansion.
>
> Keep the Group Corporate Governance Committee informed of emerging trends and successful practices in internal auditing.

The Group Senior Internal Auditor recognised in the Gray and Gray/Ridley list of motivations for innovation the following as encouraged by the Charter and the culture of the Seren Group:

> Increasing competition leading to pressures to reduce costs and increase efficiency.
>
> New challenges, such as increasing internal control risks due to staff reductions and restructuring.
>
> Changes in corporate management practices and philosophies, such as Total Quality Management, reengineering, continuous quality improvement, or related approaches.
>
> Importance of organisational governance to meet regulatory and stakeholders' needs.
>
> Recognition that all types of crime in and by an organisation should be fought. Encouragement to think creatively.

And sees the following goals for these reflected in the internal audit programmes, plans and objectives and the internal audit required reporting of its 'significant measurement goals and results to the Group Corporate Governance Committee'.

> Continuous Improvement of the quality of internal auditing services.
> Expansion of services to increase the value-added of internal auditing.
> To reduce the opportunities for all types of crime in an organisation.
> Increase satisfaction from all our customers.

Add new skills in the art of questioning.

Sell internal auditing services as a contribution to the organisation's good reputation.

Finally, in the list of categories of innovation Categories the following were selected with examples of creative and innovative practices:

A   Changes in the way that internal auditors interact with the rest of their enterprises and all those with a stakeholder interest.

The government regulatory focus on financial viability, tenant satisfaction, governance and value of money is included in every internal audit engagement. This has involved internal audit in a consulting role in Seren Group Lean reviews focused on improving customer satisfaction, working with the intervention team to ensure that as part of any improvement scheme the internal control environment is effectively and efficiently maintained.

B   Creation of new audit services and methods.

Internal audit has a focus on continuous improvement in every internal audit engagement, both in the services it provides and the operations in which it is providing assurance and consulting services.

C   Continuously improve knowledge and skills in the teams of staff who carry out internal auditing engagements.

Internal audit staff participate on a regular basis with network groups of internal auditors from other organisations in Wales and England.

Group Senior Internal Auditor has pursued IIA-UK professional qualification and is committed to documented continuing professional development.

D   Continuous improved satisfaction from all our customers.

Auditees are encouraged to express their comments on the internal audit service and results at the end of each audit report and these are fed back to the Group Corporate Governance Committee.

E   Changes in the way internal auditing asks questions.

Internal audit questionnaires are developed for every internal audit engagement as part of the planning process.

F   Contributions to the organisation's good reputation.

Such a contribution is clearly seen in its Charter mission statement – The internal audit function is a management tool for the Seren Group in its drive towards continuous improvement, safeguarding its reputation and sustainability, as well as the scope of its independent professional assurance over Seren's governance, risk management and control.

These Categories selected by the Group Senior Auditor were chosen without sight of and compare very favourably with the five published challenges for professional internal auditing promoted by Richard Chambers, The IIA President and Chief Executive Officer, earlier this year:

Alignment of internal audit work to **stakeholder** needs	**A D E F**
Quality of internal audit work	**A D E F**
Internal audit involvement in and use of **risk management**	**A D E F**
Insight into change in sector and regulation	**A D E F**
Contribution to the **status** of professional internal auditing	**B C**

Conclusions

D'Silva and Ridley at the Fourth European Academic Conference in 2006[17] presented their findings from research into continuous improvement in internal auditing services, concluding then:

> Quality and continuous improvement words and phrases are well represented in The IIA standards and supporting guidelines. Yet, phrases and words such as *'quality circle'*, *'teamwork'*. *'total commitment'*, *'motivation'*, *'innovation'* and *'excellence'* are conspicuous by their absence. Though they do appear in much of the supporting development and practice aids from which the standards have been developed. Raising the profile of such words in the standards and supporting guidelines would be a good start to increasing the importance and effectiveness of continuous improvement in internal audit activities. It would also add value to the contribution it makes to good governance practices.

The evidence from today's theoretical research shows a growth in both the profile and importance of quality, innovation and continuous improvement in internal auditing services since that time, motivated by creative teamwork and a total commitment. Not just in its services but also the focus it now gives to all three words in the strategies and operations it reviews in its governance, risk management and control engagements, at board, function and supply chain levels: engagements, which often contain both assurance and consulting objectives. The challenges and opportunities internal auditors face today and in the future make it imperative that these three words and how they are practiced are measured[18] in their performance and visible, not just to all internal auditors, but also to all their clients, at the planning and reporting stages of every engagement.

The empirical evidence in this research from the selected case unit demonstrates there is a role for internal audit to practice not just in the continuous improvement of its own services, but also in the operations of the organisations in which it works, in particular:

1   opportunities can be taken within organisations and outside organisations for internal auditors to build bridges, share, benchmark and even develop

innovative practices with others. Developing collaborative 'open innovation' teams may be the way forward for all internal audit departments to be creative in their roles and continuous improvement in their practices. Cross functional communities of practice probably exist or can be developed in every organisation: and, externally there are qualifications to be achieved, discussion groups to join, conferences and workshops to attend. Use of the social media today is growing exponentially, creating new opportunities for continuous improvement through innovation.

2   the question of independence and objectivity in today's internal audit engagements has always been recognized as a risk in all internal audit planning and engagements: recognised in its standards, guidance and research reports over many years. It is important that any impairment to its independence and objectivity – whether in its structure, staffing or reporting, are recognised at board level and appropriately managed in its engagements. The independence of internal audit and objectivity of its staff, complying with the international professional standards and code of ethics in all of its services, is a significant power to its elbow and adds value to an organisation's vision, mission, operations and compliance in its regulatory environment.

3   sustainability is included in the case unit's scope of work. The IIA has promoted increasing opportunities[19] for internal auditing to be involved in and contribute to sustainability assurance and consulting engagements in organisations and across supply chains, thus enhancing the reputation of both. In today and tomorrow's environmental and social concerns creating innovative approaches to the issues involved should be a challenge for every internal auditor.

These conclusions impact globally all policy-makers in internal audit departments of whatever size and sector. The importance of creativity and innovation in internal auditing has been demonstrated by The IIA since its inauguration. Not least, by the recent launch of its Audit Executive Centre in 2010 "a portal to a vast array of services designed to provide Chief Audit Executives with everything they need to help them stay empowered, connected, and relevant": designed to "enhance their value to their organisations and stakeholders such as executive management, boards of directors, and audit committees. Every internal audit department needs to continuously address its scope of work, attributes and quality of its performance to improve its empowerment, connections and relevance, through the creation of new and innovative practices.

Bibliography

Bain and Company (2011). *Management Tools – An Executive Guide.* Boston.

Brink, V. (1977). *Foundations for Unlimited Horizons: Institute of Internal Auditors 1941–1976 Appendix C.* Altamonte Springs, FL: Institute of Internal Auditors Inc.

Cosmas, C. E. (1996). *Audit Customer Satisfaction: Marketing Added Value.* Altamonte Springs, FL: The Institute of Internal Auditors Inc.

Coulson-Thomas, C. (1992). Leadership and corporate transformation. *Chartered Institute of Secretaries and Administrators*, Number 2-6 (April).

Department for Business Innovation and Skills (2011). *Innovation and Research Strategy for Growth*. London.

Dittenhofer, M. (2001). Reengineering the internal auditing organisation. *Managerial Auditing Journal, 16*(8): 458–468.

European Commission (2010). *Communication – Europe 2020 – A Strategy for Smart, Sustainable and Inclusive Growth*. Brussels.

Financial Reporting Council (2010). *UK Corporate Governance Code*. London.

Garritte, J.-P. (1998). Building bridges. *Internal Auditor Journal* August: 26–31.

Gray, G. and Gray, M. (1996). *Enhancing Internal Auditing Through Innovative Practices*. Altamonte Springs, FL: Institute of Internal Auditors Research Foundation.

Gupta, P. (1995). *Total Quality Improvement Process and the Internal Audit Function*. Altamonte Springs, FL: Institute of Internal Auditors Research Foundation.

IIA [Institute of Internal Auditors] Inc. (2004). Altamonte Springs, FL: Institute of Internal Auditors. www.theiia.org/index.cfm?doc_id=267 (Accessed on 4 August 2006).

IIA [Institute of Internal Auditors] Inc. (2010). *Annual Reports 2010 and 2012*. Altamonte Springs, FL: Institute of Internal Auditors.

IIA [Institute of Internal Auditors] Inc. (2010). *Responsibility/Sustainable Development*. Altamonte Springs, FL: Institute of Internal Auditors.

IIA [Institute of Internal Auditors] Inc. (2011). *Standards for the Professional Practice of Internal Auditing* Altamonte Springs, FL: Institute of Internal Auditors.

Oakland, J. (2002). *Total Organisational Excellence – Achieving World-Class Performance*. London: Butterworth-Heinemann

Ridley, J. (2008). *Cutting Edge Internal Auditing*. Chichester, UK: John Wiley and Sons.

Ridley, J. and Chambers, A. (1998). *Leading Edge Internal Auditing*. London: ICSA Publishing Ltd.

Ridley, J., D'Silva, K. and Szombathelyi, M. (2011). Sustainability assurance and internal auditing in emerging markets. *Corporate Governance 11*(4): 475–488.

Sawyer, L. (1992). *The Creative Side of Internal Auditing*. Altamonte Springs, FL: IIA Inc.

Sawyer, L. (2003). *The Practice of Modern Internal Auditing: Appraising Operations for Management (1973) (p. 1038)*. Altamonte Springs, FL: IIA Inc.

Stoner, J. and Werner, F. (1995). *Internal Audit and Innovation*. Morristown, NJ: Financial Executives Research Foundation.

Welsh Government (2011). *Regulatory Framework For Housing Associations*. Registered in Wales.

Whiteley, R. (1991). *The Customer Driven Company: Moving from Talk to Action*. London: The Forum Corporation, Business Books Ltd.

Winters, R. (2007). *From the President's Study*. Research Foundation Report – March 2007. Altamonte Springs, FL: Institute of Internal Auditors Research Foundation.

Notes

1 *Creativity and Innovation: Keys to a Successful Future for Auditing* (2012), Professor Jeffrey Ridley and Professor Kenneth D'Silva, Centre for Research in Accounting, Finance and Governance, London South Bank University, England.

2 European Commission website accessed 26 February 2012.

3 Innovation and Research Strategy for Growth, Presented to Parliament by the Secretary of State for Business, Innovation and Skills by Command of Her Majesty, December 2011 (foreword).

4   Extract from *Continuous Improvement in Internal Audit Services*, a joint research paper by Professor Jeffrey Ridley and Professor Dr. Kenneth D'Silva, delivered at Cass Business School, London, England, Fourth European Academic Conference, April 2006.

5   *Innovative Practices in Today's Internal Auditing*, a joint research paper by Professor Jeffrey Ridley and Professor Dr. Kenneth D'Silva, delivered at The Fifth European Academic Conference, University of Pisa, Italy, 2007

6   *The Practice of Modern Internal Auditing* (1973 p. 2), Lawrence B. Sawyer, The IIA Inc.

7   *The Creative Side of Internal Auditing* (1992), Lawrence B. Sawyer.

8   *A World in Economic Crisis: Key Themes for Refocusing Internal Audit Strategy: The IIA GAIN* (2009). These observations were overwhelmingly shared by the 28 CAEs, service providers, and regulators who convened in Washington, DC, by invitation of The Institute of Internal Auditors (IIA) with the goal of gaining insight on the impact of the economy on internal auditing.

9   Cited from *Foundations for Unlimited Horizons* (1977 p. 35), Victor Z. Brink, The IIA.

10   Cosmas frequently refers to *The Practice of Modern Internal Auditing* (1996), Lawrence B. Sawyer and Mortimer A. Dittenhofer, The IIA, Florida. This textbook was first published in 1973 and the latest Fifth Edition published in 2003 contains the following general guidance on implementing quality assurance in internal auditing: 'Create an innovative environment by – allowing for **creativity**; challenging all staff members to question the status quo and suggest improvements; taking every staff suggestion seriously and implementing each when appropriate' (p. 1038). This textbook continues to be recommended reading for candidates sitting the IIA CIA professional examinations.

11   Chambers in The IIA Annual Report 2012 introduces The IIA commitment to innovation with: 'I am proud to say that we made significant progress in 2012. We provided innovative professional development and witnessed the proliferation of a new certification to make internal auditors even more indispensable within their organisations.'

12   *Building Bridges*, J.-P. Garritte (1998), Internal Auditor Journal (August 1998 pp. 26–31). Institute of Internal Auditors Inc., Altamonte Springs, Florida, US.

13   At three separate interviews on 9 March, one at board level, one with the Head of Continuous Improvement and one with the Group Senior Internal Auditor: the Internal Audit Charter, dated February 2012 was reviewed for its motivation of creativity and innovation in internal auditing, the possible categories to which these could be allocated and the goals they are planned to achieve.

14   Charter Housing Association Ltd: Reach (Supported Living) Ltd: Solas-Cymru Ltd.: Fairlake Ltd.: Fairlake Living Ltd. all are Industrial Provident Societies and with the exception of Fairlake Living Ltd are charitable: Pen yr Enfys is a company limited by guarantee and registered charity.

15   The Welsh Government Regulatory Framework For Housing Associations Registered in Wales 2011. (This Regulatory Framework applies to those housing associations registered and regulated by the Welsh Ministers under Part 1 of the Housing Act 1996.) The key features of the Regulatory Framework are:

   Delivery outcomes: Self-assessment: Regulatory Assessment report and publication: Financial viability judgement and publication: Regulatory and enforcement powers. The goal is to provide quality homes and services to tenants and other service users. The different elements of the Regulatory Framework work together to assure this through the information collected by creating a rounded view of an association and an understanding of the experiences of tenants and service users. This allows the findings on self-assessments to be challenged, leading to robust regulatory assessment. One of the requirements of self-assessment is to demonstrate each of the cultures of the organisations in the Group . . . supports the delivery of their purpose and outcomes, innovates, seeks new ideas and evaluates learning from others.

16   D'Silva and Ridley (2007) in their research into innovation in internal auditing asked respondents (41) to comment on a list of selected words used to market their service.

The results then included *creative* (10); *innovative* (20); *independent* (35); *objective* (37); *improvement* (33); *professional* (32); *quality* (29).

17 Continuous improvement in internal audit services, Ridley and D'Silva (2006).

18 The IIA INC *Practice Advisory* Establishing Measures to Support Reviews of Internal Audit Activity Performance identifies 'innovation and capability' as a critical performance category to be measured, routinely analysed and reported: requiring a strategy, which covers training of staff, use of technology and a depth and insight in industry knowledge. Examples of performance measures are provided. This PA is supported by references into other PAs where innovation is a key player in their guidance. Innovation in The IIAs professional examinations and training programmes is seen as a driver to enable internal auditors 'better meet primary stakeholder expectations through process enhancements that focus on organisational changes, expectations. Strategic plans/initiatives and efficiency/effectiveness.'

19 *The IIA INC 2010 Practice Guide* – Evaluating Corporate Social Responsibility/Sustainable Development, also Ridley, D'Silva and Szombathelyi, Sustainability assurance and internal auditing in emerging markets, *Corporate Governance* Volume 11 Number 4 (2011 pp. 475–488).

Appendix L
Benchmarking[1]

Description

Benchmarking improves performance by identifying and applying best demonstrated practices to operations and sales. Managers compare the performance of their products or processes externally with those of competitors and best-in-class companies, and internally with other operations that perform similar activities in their own firms. The objective of Benchmarking is to find examples of superior performance and understand the processes and practices driving that performance. Companies then improve their performance by tailoring and incorporating these best practices into their own operations – not by imitating, but by innovating.

Methodology

Benchmarking involves the following steps:

- select a product, service or process to benchmark
- identify the key performance metrics
- choose companies or internal areas to benchmark
- collect data on performance and practices
- analyse the data and identify opportunities for improvement
- adapt and implement the best practices, setting reasonable goals and ensuring companywide acceptance.

Common Uses

Companies use Benchmarking to:

- **Improve performance**. Benchmarking identifies methods of improving operational efficiency and product design.
- **Understand relative cost position**. Benchmarking reveals a company's relative cost position and identifies opportunities for improvement.

- **Gain strategic advantage**. Benchmarking helps companies focus on capabilities that are critical to building strategic advantage.
- **Increase the rate of organisational learning**. Benchmarking brings new ideas into the company and facilitates experience sharing.

Note

1 *Management Tools – An Executive's Guide* (2015 p. 14), David F. Rigby, Bain and Company Inc., Boston, US.

Appendix M[1]

The Principles for Responsible Investment

As institutional investors, we have a duty to act in the best long-term interests of our beneficiaries. In this fiduciary role, we believe that environmental, social, and corporate governance (ESG) issues can affect the performance of investment portfolios (to varying degrees across companies, sectors, regions, asset classes and through time). We also recognise that applying these Principles may better align investors with broader objectives of society. Therefore, where consistent with our fiduciary responsibilities, we commit to the following:

1 *We will incorporate ESG issues into investment analysis and decision-making processes.*

Possible actions:

- address ESG issues in investment policy statements
- support development of ESG-related tools, metrics, and analyses
- assess the capabilities of internal investment managers to incorporate ESG issues
- assess the capabilities of external investment managers to incorporate ESG issues
- ask investment service providers (such as financial analysts, consultants, brokers, research firms, or rating companies) to integrate ESG factors into evolving research and analysis
- encourage academic and other research on this theme
- advocate ESG training for investment professionals.

2 *We will be active owners and incorporate ESG issues into our ownership policies and practices.*

Possible actions:

- develop and disclose an active ownership policy consistent with the Principles
- exercise voting rights or monitor compliance with voting policy (if outsourced)

- develop an engagement capability (either directly or through outsourcing)
- participate in the development of policy, regulation, and standard setting (such as promoting and protecting shareholder rights)
- file shareholder resolutions consistent with long-term ESG considerations
- engage with companies on ESG issues
- participate in collaborative engagement initiatives
- ask investment managers to undertake and report on ESG-related engagement.

3 We will seek appropriate disclosure on ESG issues by the entities in which we invest.

Possible actions:

- ask for standardised reporting on ESG issues (using tools such as the Global Reporting Initiative)
- ask for ESG issues to be integrated within annual financial reports
- ask for information from companies regarding adoption of/adherence to relevant norms, standards, codes of conduct or international initiatives (such as the UN Global Compact)
- support shareholder initiatives and resolutions promoting ESG disclosure.

4 We will promote acceptance and implementation of the Principles within the investment industry.

Possible actions:

- include Principles-related requirements in requests for proposals (RFPs)
- align investment mandates, monitoring procedures, performance indicators and incentive structures accordingly (for example, ensure investment management processes reflect long-term time horizons when appropriate)
- communicate ESG expectations to investment service providers
- revisit relationships with service providers that fail to meet ESG expectations
- support the development of tools for benchmarking ESG integration
- support regulatory or policy developments that enable implementation of the Principles.

5 We will work together to enhance our effectiveness in implementing the Principles.

Possible actions:

- support/participate in networks and information platforms to share tools, pool resources, and make use of investor reporting as a source of learning
- collectively address relevant emerging issues
- develop or support appropriate collaborative initiatives.

6 We will each report on our activities and progress towards implementing the Principles.

Possible actions:

- disclose how ESG issues are integrated within investment practices
- disclose active ownership activities (voting, engagement, and/or policy dialogue)
- disclose what is required from service providers in relation to the Principles
- communicate with beneficiaries about ESG issues and the Principles
- report on progress and/or achievements relating to the Principles using a 'Comply or Explain' approach
- seek to determine the impact of the Principles
- make use of reporting to raise awareness among a broader group of stakeholders.

The Comply or Explain approach requires signatories to report on how they implement the Principles, or provide an explanation where they do not comply with them. The Principles for Responsible Investment were developed by an international group of institutional investors reflecting the increasing relevance of environmental, social and corporate governance issues to investment practices. The process was convened by the United Nations Secretary-General.

In signing the Principles, we as investors publicly commit to adopt and implement them, where consistent with our fiduciary responsibilities. We also commit to evaluate the effectiveness and improve the content of the Principles over time. We believe this will improve our ability to meet commitments to beneficiaries as well as better align our investment activities with the broader interests of society.

We encourage other investors to adopt the Principles

Note

1 *Principles for Responsible Investment: Report on Progress* (2015 p.2), United Nations Global Compact, New York, US. Accessed www.unpri.org May 2016

Bibliography for the 21st century

By decade from 2000

2000–2009

Accounting for Sustainability Project (2008). *Accounting for Sustainability: Sustainability at Work*. London.

Bolhuis, S. & Simons, R. (2003). Towards a Broader Understanding of Learning. In Kessles, J. & Poell, R. (Eds.). *Human Resource Development: The Organisation of Learning*. Groningen, Netherlands: Samsom.

Cabinet Office (2000). *A Guide to Quality Schemes for the Public Sector*. London: United Kingdom Government.

Coffee, J.C., Jr. (2006). *Gatekeepers – The Professions and Corporate Governance*. Oxford: Oxford University Press.

Department for Education and Skills (2005). *Response to Paul Roberts' Report on Nurturing Creativity in Young People*. London.

Department of the Environment, Transport and the Regions (2000). *Guide to Quality Schemes and Best Value*. London.

Department for Innovation, Universities and Skills (2008). *Innovation Nation*. London.

Department of Trade and Industry (2003). *Competing in the Global Economy – The Innovation Challenge*. London.

European Foundation for Management Development and Global Compact (2005). *Globally Responsible Leadership – A Call for Engagement*. Brussels.

Financial Reporting Council (2000). *Statement of Auditing Standards 240 – Quality Control for Audit Work*. London.

Financial Reporting Council (2008). *The Audit Quality Framework*. London.

Global Reporting Initiative (2002). *Sustainability Reporting Guidelines on Economic, Environmental and Social Performance*. New York.

Godin, S. (2002). *Purple Cow: Transform Your Business by Being Remarkable*. Penguin: New York.

Henry, J. (2001). *Creativity and Perception in Management*. London: Sage Publications and Open University Business School.

Institute of Business Ethics (2005). *Setting the Tone – Ethical Business Leadership: Executive Summary*. London.

Institute of Directors Southern Africa. (2009). *King Code of Governance (KING III)*. Cape Town.

Lackland, R. (2008). There are no more internal audit experts only communities of practices experts. In *Cutting Edge Internal Auditing*. Chichester, UK: John Wiley and Sons Ltd.

Oakland, J. S. (2002). *Total Organisational Excellence – Achieving World-Class Performance.* Oxford: Butterworth-Heinemann.

O'Regan, D. (2004). *Auditor's Dictionary – Terms, Concepts, Processes and Regulations.* Upper Saddle River, NJ, USA: John Wiley and Sons.

Organisation for Economic Co-operation and Development (2000). *Guidelines for Multinational Companies.* Paris.

Organisation for Economic Co-operation and Development (2004). *Principles of Corporate Governance.* Paris.

Osborn, A. F. (2001). *Applied Imagination.* New York: Creative Education Foundation Press.

Pink, D. H. (2005). *A Whole New Mind.* New York: Penguin.

Ridley, J. (2000). *Risk, Change and Control – Challenges and Opportunities for All Auditors.* London: Chartered Institute of Internal Auditors.

Ridley, J. (2000). *Social Responsibility – A Challenge for Organisations and Internal Auditing.* London: Chartered Institute of Internal Auditors.

Ridley, J. (2000). *How Effective Is Your Audit Committee.* London: Chartered Institute of Internal Auditors.

Ridley, J. (2000). *A New Internal Auditor for a New Century.* London: Chartered Institute of Internal Auditors.

Ridley, J. (2000). *Internal Auditors Are Ambassadors in the Commonwealth . . . Across the European Union and Internationally.* London: Chartered Institute of Internal Auditors.

Ridley, J. (2000). *Weak Links in the Supply Chain.* London: Chartered Institute of Internal Auditors.

Ridley, J. (2001). *Quality Schemes and Best Value in the 21st Century.* London: ABG Professional Information, Part of the CCH Group, Institute of Chartered Accountants in England and Wales.

Ridley, J. (2001). *Wise Internal Auditors Manage Knowledge Well.* London: ABG Professional Information, Part of the CCH Group, Institute of Chartered Accountants in England and Wales.

Ridley, J. (2001). *Shout How Best You Are in All Your Internal Auditing Market Places: Internal Control.* London: ABG Professional Information, Part of the CCH Group, Institute of Chartered Accountants in England and Wales.

Ridley, J. (2002). *Walk Faster This Year.* London: Chartered Institute of Internal Auditors.

Ridley, J. (2002). *What Was the Point of Cadbury – Today and Tomorrow?* London: Chartered Institute of Internal Auditors.

Ridley, J. (2004). *Celebrate Internal Audit Professionalism.* London: Chartered Institute of Internal Auditors.

Ridley, J. (2008). *The Road to Quality and Excellence Takes You to the Cutting Edge: Internal Auditing and Business Risk.* London: Chartered Institute of Internal Auditors.

Ridley, J. (2008). *Cutting Edge Internal Auditing.* Chichester, UK: John Wiley and Sons Ltd.

Ridley, J. (2009). *Value of Objectivity.* Internal Auditor. Orlando: The Institute of Internal Auditors Inc.

Roberts, P. (2006). *Nurturing Creativity in Young People.* Department for Culture, Media and Sport, UK Government.

Sawyer, L. B. (2003). *The Practice of Modern Internal Auditing* (5th ed.). Orlando: The Institute of Internal Auditors Inc.

Scottish Executive (2005). *Promoting Excellence in Scotland – A Guide to Quality Schemes and the Delivery of Public Services.* Edinburgh.

The Institute of Internal Auditors Inc. (2009). *International Professional Practices Framework – Practice Advisories.* Orlando.

The Institute of Internal Auditors Inc. (2009). *Code of Ethics – Revised.* Orlando.

Torr, G. (2008). *Managing Creative People.* Chichester, UK: John Wiley and Sons.

Wagner, K. (2000). *Leading the Way: Internal Auditor.* Orlando: The Institute of Internal Auditors Inc.

2010–2016

American Institute of CPAs (AICPA) (2015). *Values and Vision Statement.* Accessed website www.aicpa.org/About/MissionandHistory on 7th August 2015.

American Productivity and Quality Centre (2014). *Benchmarking Code of Conduct – Guidelines and Ethics for Benchmarkers.* Houston.

Ashridge Business School (2012). *Leadership in a Rapidly Changing World – How Business Leaders Are Reframing Success.* Ashridge, UK.

Association of Business Schools (2013). *Innovation and Growth in the Domestic Economy.* London: Booz and Company.

Association of Certified and Chartered Accountants (2011). *Code of Ethics and Conduct: Think Ahead – Annual Report and Accounts (2014–15).* London.

Association of International Accountants (2014). *Annual Report and Accounts.* Newcastle-upon-Tyne, UK.

Bain and Company (2015). *Management Tools – An Executive's Guide.* Boston.

Bloomsbury Information Ltd. (2011). *Internal Auditing Best Practices Approaches to Internal Auditing.* London.

Blowfield, M. (2013). *Business and Sustainability.* Oxford: Oxford University Press.

Buddery, P. Frank, S. and Martinoff, M. (2014). *Enlightening Professions? A Vision for Audit and a Better Society.* London: Institute of Chartered Accountants in England and Wales.

Cass Business School (2011). *Road to Ruin: A Study of Major Risk Events – Their Origins, Impact and Implications.* London: AIRMIC.

Chambers, A.D. (2014). *Chambers' Corporate Governance Handbook, 6th Edition.* Haywards Heath, UK: Bloomsbury Professional.

Chambers, A.D. (2015). *Recalibrating Internal Audit.* Internal Auditing. Thomson Reuters.

Chambers, A.D. and Rand, G. (2010). *The Operational Auditing Handbook, 2nd Edition.* Chichester, UK: John Wiley and Sons Ltd.

Chartered Institute of Internal Auditors (2011). *Professionalism for the 21st Century – Revisited.*

Chartered Institute of Internal Auditors (2014). *Culture and the Role of Internal Audit – Looking Below the Surface.*

Chartered Institute of Internal Auditors (2016). *Auditing Culture.* London.

Chartered Institute of Management (2014). *21st Century Leaders: Building Practice into the Curriculum to Boost the Economy.* London.

City of London Police (2014–15). *Annual Report.* London.

Committee of Sponsoring Organisations of the Treadway Commission (2013). *Thought Leadership in ERM: Demystifying Sustainability.* New York.

Committee of Sponsoring Organisations of the Treadway Commission (2013). *Internal Control – Integrated Framework.* New York.

Committee of Sponsoring Organisations of the Treadway Commission (2013). *Integrating the Triple Bottom Line into an Enterprise Risk Management Program.* New York.

Committee of Sponsoring Organisations of the Treadway Commission (2015). *Internal Control and Governance – Leveraging COSO Across the Three Lines of Defence.* New York.

Committee on Standards in Public (2014). *Life Ethics in Practice: Promoting Ethical Conduct in Public Life (July).* Lord Bew's Foreword addressed to the Prime Minister. London.

Council of Bars and Law Societies of Europe (2013). *Charter of Core Principles of the European Legal Profession and Code of Conduct for European Lawyers*. Brussels.

Council of Bars and Law Societies of Europe (2014). *Annual Report*. Brussels.

Council on Competitiveness (2015). *Making Impact – Annual Report 2014–2015*. Washington, DC.

Crane, A. and Matten, D. (2010). *Business Ethics: Managing Corporate Citizenship and Sustainability in the Age of Globalisation, 3rd Edition*. Oxford: Oxford University Press.

Crawford, C. (2015). *How to Train Your Diplomat*. London: The Ambassadors Partnership LLP.

Department for Business, Energy & Industrial Strategy (2017). *Corporate Governance Reform*. London.

Drake, J. and Turnbull James, K. (2013). Developing a new breed of leaders. *Management Focus* Autumn (35), 16-19. London.

Department for Business Innovation and Skills (2010). *UK Government Response to the European Commission's Green Paper on Audit*. London.

Department for Business Innovation and Skills (2012). *Leadership and Management in the UK – The Key to Sustainable Growth*. London.

Department for Business Innovation and Skills (2013). *Schools in Driving Innovation and Growth in the Domestic Economy*. London.

Dyer, J., Gregsen, H. and Chistenden, C. M. (2011). *The Innovators DNA – Mastering the Five Skills of Disruptive Innovators*. Boston, MA: Harvard Business Review Press.

European Commission (2012). *Action Plan: European Company Law and Corporate Governance – A Modern Legal Framework for More Engaged Shareholders and Sustainable Companies*. Brussels.

European Court of Auditors (2012). *Code of Conduct*. Brussels.

European Foundation for Quality Management (2013). *EFQM Excellence Model*. Brussels.

European Foundation for Quality Management (2014). *25 Years of Excellence* Brussels.

Federation of European Accountants (2009–10). *Audit Inspection Unit Annual Report*. Brussels.

Federation of European Accountants (2012). *The Functioning of Audit Committees – Discussion Paper*. Brussels.

Federation of European Accountants (2013). *Global Observations on the Role of the Audit Committee*. Brussels.

Federation of European Accountants (2016). *Pursuing a Strategy Debate – The Future of Audit and Assurance: Discussion Paper*. Brussels.

Federation of European Risk Management Associations (FERMA) and European Confederation of Institutes of Internal Auditors (2014). *Guidance for Boards and Audit and Risk Committees*. Brussels.

Financial Reporting Council (2010). *The Auditor's Responsibilities Relating to Fraud in an Audit of Financial Statements*. London.

Financial Reporting Council (2011). *Auditor Scepticism: Raising the Bar – Feedback Paper*. London.

Financial Reporting Council (2011). *Effective Company Stewardship – Enhancing Corporate Reporting and Audit*. London.

Financial Reporting Council (2012). *Guidance on Audit Committees*. London.

Financial Reporting Council (2012). *ISA 200: Professional Scepticism – Establishing a Common Understanding and Reaffirming Its Central Role in Delivering Audit Quality*. London.

Financial Reporting Council (2012). *Professional Scepticism – Establishing a Common Understanding and Reaffirming Its Central Role in Delivering Audit Quality*. London.

Financial Reporting Council (2012). *The UK Stewardship Code*. London.

Financial Reporting Council (2013). *Lab Project Report: Reporting of Audit Committees*. London.

Financial Reporting Council (2014). *Developments in Corporate Governance and Stewardship*. London.

Financial Reporting Council (2014). *The UK Corporate Governance Code*. London.

Financial Reporting Council (2015). *Audit Quality – Practice Aid for Audit Committees*. London.

Financial Reporting Council (2015). *Developments in Corporate Governance and Stewardship – Annual Report 2014*. London.

Financial Reporting Council (2015). *Extended Audit Reports – A Review of Experience in the First Year*. London.

Financial Reporting Council (2015). *Transparency Reporting by Auditors of Public Interest Entities: Review of Mandatory Reports*. London.

Financial Reporting Council (2016). *Corporate Culture and the Role of Boards – Report of Observations*. London.

Financial Reporting Council: Institute of Chartered Accountants and Australia: Institute of Chartered Accountants of Scotland (2012). *Walk the Line: Discussions and Insights with Leading Audit Committee Members*. London.

Fraud Advisory Panel (2010). *Fact Sheet – Anti-Fraud Policy Statements*. London.

Goffin, K. Hopkin, P. Szwejczewski, M. and Kutsch, E. (2014). *Roads to Resilience: Building Dynamic Approaches to Risk to Achieve Future Success*. London: Airmic Ltd.

Harden, G. (2011). *How Internal Audit Can Help Against a Company's Fraud Issues*. Contributor in *Internal Auditing Best Practices Approaches to Internal Auditing*. London: Bloomsbury Information Ltd.

Her Majesty's Government (2013). *The Commonwealth Charter*. London: Her Majesty's Stationary Office Ltd.

HM Treasury (2012). *Assurance Frameworks*. London.

HM Treasury (2013). *Audit and Risk Committee Assurance Handbook*. London.

House of Parliament (2013). *Companies Act 2006 (Strategic Report and Director's Report) Regulations*. London.

Institute of Business Ethics and European Confederation of Directors Association (Ecoda). (2013). *A Review of the Ethical Aspects of Corporate Governance Regulation and Guidance in the EU: Occasional Paper authored by Julia Casson*. London.

Institute of Chartered Accountants in England and Wales (2010). *Finance and Management Faculty: Developing a Vision for Your Business*. London.

Institute of Chartered Accountants in England and Wales (2015). *AuditFutures – Philosophy for Accountancy – Educating Responsible Professionals Through Critical Thinking and Ethical Reasoning*. London.

Institute of Chartered Accountants in England and Wales (2015). *Annual Report 2014*. London.

Institute of Chartered Accountants in England and Wales (2016). *Find Your Inner Sceptic, Simon Kettlewell, Audit and Beyond Journal of the Audit and Assurance Faculty*. London.

Institute of Chartered Accountants in England and Wales (2016). *AuditFutures – Manifesto*. London.

Institute of Chartered Secretaries and Administrators (2013). *Terms of Reference – Audit Committee*. Accessed website www.icsa.org.uk in March 2016.

Institute of Chartered Secretaries and Administrators. *Add Some Colour into Your Career – A Guide to Becoming a Chartered Secretary*. www.icsa.org.uk (Accessed March 2016).

Institute of Directors Southern Africa (2016). *King IV on Corporate Governance for South Africa*. Cape Town.

International Auditing and Assurance Standards Board (2013). *A Framework for Audit and Assurance – Consultation Paper*. New York.

International Forum of Independent Audit Regulations (2015). *Work Plan 2015–17*. Amsterdam.

International Integrated Reporting Council (2013). *The International <IR> Framework*. London.

International Organization of Standardization (2010). *International Standard Guidance on Social Responsibility (ISO 26000)*. Geneva.

International Organization of Standardization (2015). *Quality Management Principles*. Geneva.

International Organization of Standardization (2015). *Moving from ISO 9001:2008 to ISDO9001:2015*. Geneva.

International Organization of Supreme Audit Institutions (2010). *Mutual Experience Benefits All – STRATEGIC PLAN 2011–2016*.Vienna.

KPMG International (2010). *United Nations Global Compact, Communication on Progress*. Switzerland.

Kubitscheck, V. (2014). *Integrated Assurance – Risk Governance Beyond Boundaries*. Farnham, England: Gower Publishing Ltd.

Lenz, R. (2015). Effective audit – inspiring change: Audit and Risk. *Journal of Chartered Institute of Internal Auditors*.

Lenz, R. (2015). *Internal Auditors as Change Agents: What a Difference a Year Makes!* The Open Auditor.

Levin, I. (2010). Launching your organisation into an actionable future. In *Developing a Vision for your Business*. Special Report. London: Finance and Management Faculty, The Institute of Chartered Accountants in England and Wales.

London Academy of Diplomacy and University of Stirling (2013). *Pathways to Diplomacy*. London.

Loughrey, J. (2011). *Corporate Lawyers and Corporate Governance*. Cambridge: Cambridge University Press.

Maitland (2015). *The Values Most Valued by UK PLC*. London.

Manchester Square Partners (2015). *Preparing Leaders for the Challenges Ahead: A Guide for Companies and Individuals*. London.

Maslow, A. H. (2013). *A Theory of Human Motivation*. UK: Black Curtain Press.

McIntosh, A. (2016). Natural Allies: Governance and compliance. *Journal of the Chartered Institute of Secretaries and Administrators* (March-April).

National Audit Office (2012). *Code of Conduct*. London.

Oakland, J. S. (2014). *Total Quality Management and Operational Excellence* (4th ed.). London: Routledge.

Organisation for Economic Co-operation and Development (2010). *Innovation Strategy*. Paris.

Organisation for Economic Co-operation and Development (2014). *OECD Guidelines for Multi National Enterprises: Responsible Business Conduct Matters*. Paris.

Organisation for Economic Co-operation and Development (2015). *G20/OECD Principles of Corporate Governance*. Paris.

Organisation for Economic Co-operation and Development (2015). *Innovation Strategy – An Agenda for Policy Action*. Paris.

PricewaterhouseCoopers LLP (2015). *Annual Report*. London.

PricewaterhouseCoopers LLP (2015). *Building Trust Through Assurance Transparency Report*. London.

Ridley, J. (2011). *Best-Practice Approaches to Internal Auditing (2011) Contributing Chapter*. London: Bloomsbury Information Ltd.

Ridley, J. (2015). *Values: Take Your Life Principles to Work (2015) Audit and Risk January 2015 – View from the Top*. London: Chartered Institute of Internal Auditors.

Ridley, J. and D'Silva, K. (2012). *Creativity and Innovation: Keys to a Successful Future for Internal Auditing*. London: London South Bank University.

The Chartered Quality Institute (2014). *The New Quality Profession Challenge*. London.

The Chartered Quality Institute (2016). *Quality in Its Total Business Concept*. London.

The Grant Thorton Governance Institute (2014). *Corporate Governance Review: Plotting a New Course to Improved Governance*. London.

The Institute of Internal Auditors Inc. (2010). *Evaluation of Corporate Social Responsibility/Sustainable Development*. Orlando, US.

The Institute of Internal Auditors Inc. (2010). *Practice Guide – Evaluating Corporate Social Responsibility/Sustainable Development*. Orlando, US.

The Institute of Internal Auditors Inc. (2011). *Insight – Delivering Value to Stakeholders*. Orlando, US.

The Institute of Internal Auditors Inc. (2012). *International Standards for the Professional Practice of Internal Auditing*. Orlando, US.

The Institute of Internal Auditors Inc. (2012). *Practice Guide – Integrated Auditing*. Orlando, US.

The Institute of Internal Auditors Inc. (2014). *Global Strategic Plan 2015–20*. Orlando, US.

The Institute of Internal Auditors Inc. (2015). *Leveraging COSO Across the Three Lines of Defence*. Orlando, US.

The Institute of Internal Auditors Inc. (2015). *The Tactful Sceptic (2015) – Tone at the Top*. Orlando, US.

The Institute of Internal Auditors Inc. (2016). *Global Perspectives: Auditing Culture – A Hard Look at the Soft Stuff*. Orlando, US.

The Institute of Internal Auditors Inc. (2016). *Practice Guide – Internal Audit and the Second Line of Defence*. Orlando, US.

The Institute of Risk Management (2010). *A Structured Approach to Enterprise Risk Management and the Requirements of ISO 31000*. London.

The Stationery Office Ltd. (2013). *The Commonwealth Charter*. London.

Thomson Reuters Accelus (2014). *Special Report Culture – Tips for Internal Auditors*. London.

Tickner, P. (2010). *How to Be a Successful Frauditor – A Practical Guide to Investigating Fraud in the Workplace for Internal Auditors and Managers*. Chichester, UK: John Wiley and Sons.

Tomorrow's Company (2011). *Tomorrow's Stewardship – Why Stewardship Matters*. London.

Tomorrow's Company (2014). *Tomorrow's Global Leaders – How to Build a Culture That Ensures Women Reach the Top*. London.

Tricker, R. I. (2014). *Corporate Governance – Principles, Policies and Practices* (3rd ed.). Oxford: Oxford University Press.

UK National Fraud Authority (2015). *Annual Report 2013–14*. London.

United Nations (2010). *A New Era of Sustainability – Global Compact*. New York.

United Nations (2013). *Citizen Engagement Practices by Supreme Audit Institutions*. New York.

United Nations (2014). *Architects of a Better World: Building the Post-2015 Business Engagement Architecture – Global Compact*. New York.

United Nations (2014). *Sustainable Development Goals – Global Compact*. New York.

United Nations (2015). *LEAD Advancing Sustainability Leadership Through Innovation and Action – Global Compact*. New York.

United Nations (2015). *Principles for Responsible Investment: Report on Progress – Global Compact*. New York.

United Nations (2015). *Transforming Our World – The 2030 Agenda for Sustainable Development (2015), Outcome Document from the United Nations Summit*. New York.

United Nations (2016). *Principles for Responsible Investment – An Investor Initiative in Partnership with UNEP Finance Initiative and the Global Compact*. New York.

Xi Jinping (2014). *The Governance of China – Right Time to Innovate and Make Dreams Come True*. Beijing: Foreign Languages Press Co Ltd.

Index

For Product Safety Concerns and Information please contact our EU
representative GPSR@taylorandfrancis.com Taylor & Francis Verlag GmbH,
Kaufingerstraße 24, 80331 München, Germany

Printed and bound by CPI Group (UK) Ltd, Croydon, CR0 4YY
01/05/2025
01858422-0011